Animals and Nature

Rod Preece

Animals and Nature:
Cultural Myths, Cultural Realities

UBCPress / Vancouver

© UBC Press 1999

Printed in Canada on acid-free paper ∞

ISBN 0-7748-0724-5

Canadian Cataloguing in Publication Data

Preece, Rod, 1939-
  Animals and nature

  Includes bibliographical references and index.
  ISBN 0-7748-0724-5

1. Animals and civilization. 2. Philosophy of nature. 3. Animal welfare – Moral and ethical aspects. I. Title
BD581.P74 1999   I79'.3   C99-910127-7

This book has been published with a grant from the Social Sciences Federation of Canada, using funds provided by the Social Sciences and Humanities Research Council of Canada. Funding was also provided by Wilfrid Laurier University's Office of Research.

UBC Press also gratefully acknowledges the ongoing support to its publishing program from the Canada Council for the Arts, the British Columbia Arts Council, and the Multiculturalism Program of the Department of Canadian Heritage.

UBC Press
University of British Columbia
6344 Memorial Road
Vancouver, BC V6T 1Z2
(604) 822-5959
Fax: 1-800-668-0821
E-mail: info@ubcpress.ubc.ca
www.ubcpress.ubc.ca

For my gaea, Lorna

... how do we let ourselves be moved by pity if not by transporting ourselves outside of ourselves and identifying with the suffering animal, by leaving as it were, our own being to take on its being?

– Jean-Jacques Rousseau, *Emile*, Book IV, 1762

Zweck sein selbst ist jegliches Tier.
Each animal is an end in itself.

– Johann Wolfgang von Goethe, *Athroismos*,
1819

... there is a poetry in wildness, and every alligator basking in the slime is himself an Epic, self contained.

– Putnam Smif in Charles Dickens's *Martin
Chuzzlewit*, 1843

... the presence of Nature in all her awful loveliness.

– George Eliot, *The Lifted Veil*, 1859

Contents

Preface

When we are making comparisons among different types of society – which is the very purpose of this book – the categories employed must be meaningful and commonly understood. This requirement is especially important when the comparisons will be read as evaluations, both where intended and where not.

We all possess more or less vague conceptions of the Occident or the West, the Orient or the East, and the Aboriginal world in our minds, but when we try to be precise we find them as slippery as Lewis Carroll's "slithy toves" from "Jabberwocky" which "gyre and gimble in the wabe." Carroll also says, via Humpty Dumpty in "The Walrus and the Carpenter," "When I use a word ... it means just what I choose it to mean – neither more nor less." In reality, however, convenient as a Humpty-Dumpty world would be, we are not free to stipulate meanings outside the range of customary usage.

If we are to communicate successfully, we must be sure that the listener hears what the speaker intends. And what the speaker intends must conform more or less to what the listener already understands by the concepts employed. Unfortunately, conventional usage is often confusing and inconsistent. Indeed, conventional usage is often shifting. As late as the 1950s, Turkey was thought an integral part of the Orient. From 1883 until the Second World War – and thereafter intermittently – the exotic Orient Express ran from Paris to Islamic Istanbul, which was not only "the gateway to the Orient" but was deemed an essential part of the "mysterious" Orient itself. When such luminaries as Voltaire, Gustave Flaubert, Walter Scott, Edward FitzGerald, and Thomas Mann referred to the East or the Orient, they customarily meant Arabia.

While words like Oriental or Eastern and Occidental or Western may appear initially to indicate geographical location, we can recognize on closer inspection that they have not only geographical but also historical, ideological, economic, and cultural components – sometimes with emotive overtones, as in the ever "enigmatic" and "inscrutable" Orient. Thus, while modern Japan is geographically and historically Oriental, it is increasingly ideologically and economically Occidental, and its culture clings tenaciously to its Shinto and Buddhist past, threatened constantly by the exigencies of its economic reality. Japanese animal experimenters will on occasion meet ceremonially to offer thanks to the animals they have sacrificed in pursuit of their biomedical goals. Secular science synthesizes with Shinto traditions. Whether Japan is truly a part of the Orient depends on the aspects of Orientalism we are seeking.

A convincing case can be made that Islam is in origin and development more a part of Western than Eastern thought. Yet, of course, Bangladesh, Pakistan, and parts of Malaysia profess the Moslem faith and are decidedly parts of the Orient, and decidedly not a part of the West. Their belief systems are even less compatible with Western secularism than with Hindu polytheism. China, which some may view as the quintessential Orient, currently espouses an ideology developed in Europe and proclaimed by its founder to apply only to societies that have undergone a substantial period of capitalist and industrial growth in the Western manner. While the West may appear at first a rather more homogeneous conception, we may have some difficulty in acknowledging, say, Costa Rica or Jamaica as essentially similar to Denmark or the United States.

Because the concepts we employ lack clarity and precision, and may even tend to obfuscation, we may be tempted to abandon them. Yet they are the currency of, and indispensable to, contemporary debate. And they are what this book is about. If inexact, the concepts are nonetheless redolent with meaning.

The term "Aboriginal" is customarily applied to a host of societies from small-scale nomadic foragers through every sort of agro-pastoral society and tribal chiefdoms to expansionist urban state empires such as those of the Maya and the Aztecs. The concept is indeed employed so broadly that we may doubt whether the extremes possess very much in common at all. Certainly, we must be careful constantly to recognize the significant differences among the variety of societies constrained under this conceptual umbrella. But because so many writers today refer generically to Aboriginal societies "at one with nature," it is important to maintain similar terms in response. Moreover, the term is sufficiently meaningful that we know fairly precisely the types of society it excludes. Many anthropologists restrict the use of capitalized Aboriginals to the indigenous population of Australia. However, for the sake of consistency with Oriental and Occidental, with East and West, I have capitalized Aboriginals throughout this book.

Under "Oriental," I have included those societies that have developed along Hindu, Buddhist, Jain, Confucian, Taoist, and Shinto thought paths but also those Islamic and Zoroastrian elements that are geographically contiguous and have at least as much culturally in common with their neighbours as with the Arabic and Middle Eastern roots of their religious belief systems.

I have used the term "Occidental" to apply to societies whose contemporary civilization has arisen out of the conflict between feudal and emergent capitalist forms of societies which took place in Europe from the sixteenth to the nineteenth centuries and which spread to the various European colonies outside Africa and India, such as Australia and the Americas, for example (though the effects were noticeable, far less markedly, in Africa and India, too).

There are no magical solutions to problems of categorical clarity. Attempts to be as precise as possible are necessary if we are to avoid Jabberwocky's "mimsy borogoves," but there are no incontrovertible standards. There are always inconsistencies. The answer lies in constantly bringing to mind the nuanced differences among otherwise similar societies so that the dangers of overgeneralization are minimized. Throughout this book, I will occasionally return to the problem, so that it escapes neither the reader's nor the writer's attention. It would be all too easy, and quite misleading, to take an example from Islamic Bangladesh or from the Imperial Aztecs and use that example to identify Oriental or Aboriginal attitudes in general. But it would be equally misleading to ignore such examples.

The notion of being "at one with nature" may appear as elusive a concept as that of "the Orient" or "Aboriginal." Certainly, it is rarely clear what is meant by those who claim that certain societies are at one with, or in harmony with, nature. As the reader delves further into this book, the potential meanings, and frequent inconsistencies and obscurities in the concept, should become clearer – as will the fact that at least sometimes those who make the claims for harmony are conceptual Humpty Dumpties who make words mean whatever they want them to mean and change the meanings to suit their ideological bent.

I have sometimes capitalized Nature, sometimes left it in lower case. Where it is upper case Nature refers to that usage in which it is sometimes personified as an actor on the world stage, and/or that in which it is offered as a moral standard (usages common among the classical Greeks and Romantics, for example). Where it is lower case it refers to the nature we experience in our everyday lives.

The theme of this book is that the West has been significantly more sympathetic to the natural realm than it has been given credit for. By contrast, the customary depiction of Oriental and Aboriginal concerns for the natural realm, it is argued, has been greatly overdrawn.

To make these points, I shall be praising the West where it is often criticized, and criticizing the Oriental and Aboriginal worlds where they are often praised. It would be most unfortunate if this approach were read to suggest that there is something in principle superior about the West. Any attempt to return to the earlier Western sense of cultural superiority would not only be untenable but a retrograde step when so many commendable advances have been made in recent decades in the diminution of claims for racial and ethnic superiority – which is not to deny there are further significant steps to be taken.

In reality, despite the significant differences implied by religious and ideological myths, far more unites Hadza foragers, Hindu *sadhus,* and Canadian academics than divides them. It is unfortunate that those who decry the West and laud others serve only to create the human divide once more. If we are to recognize a common human dignity, a fundamental shared humanity, we must also recognize a common human being replete with common human warts.

This notion of a human commonality is neither new nor essentially Western, though it is not as popular as it once was. It pervades the traditions of Hinduism, Sufism, and Taoism, as well as the transcendentalism of Friedrich von Schelling and Ralph Waldo Emerson, and the "Divine Idea" of Johann Gottlieb Fichte. It holds that there is a fundamental unity, an essential similarity in all human experience and thought, divergent cultures notwithstanding, which is ultimately of far greater significance than the immediately obvious but potentially deceiving differences. Cultures serve to mask the realities of homogeneity. Such diverse thinkers as Plato, St. Augustine, Immanuel Kant, Henry David Thoreau, Samuel Taylor Coleridge, and the authors of the Indian *Bhagavad Gita*, the Persian *Desatir*, and the Chinese *Tao Te Ching* subscribed to the universalist message; as indeed did the early utilitarians, Thomas Hobbes, Jeremy Bentham, and James Mill, for example, albeit in a now outdated mechanistic manner. Today, the devotees of cultural distinctiveness are in the ascendant, but their inclination hides much from their understanding. Even some of those who write of the "underlying unities in the belief systems and wisdom of the peoples of the world" manage to do the idea a disservice. Thus, T.C. McLuhan, author of *The Way of the Earth: Encounters with Nature in Ancient and Contemporary Thought,*[1] informs us of the cultures of Aboriginal Australia, ancient Japan, early Greece, Africa, the Koki of South America, and Native North America. We are told that "we all have a profound connection to the earth." Yet Western civilization – whether in Australasia, Europe, or North or South America – is left unconnected. Western civilization is excluded from "we all" not by evidence but by default. It is not investigated using the same criteria as the other traditions and found wanting. It is simply not investigated. The absence of the "profound connection" is assumed.

In the Preface (1735) to his translation of Father Jerome Lobo's *Voyage to Abyssinia,* an account of seventeenth-century travels in North Africa, the great lexicographer Dr. Samuel Johnson praised the Jesuit priest for avoiding the contemporary romantic fallacy – a fallacy which has now returned to become our prevailing norm:

> The Portuguese traveller ... has amused his reader with no romantic absurdities or incredible fictions ... He appears, by his modest and unaffected

narrative, to have described things as he saw them, to have copied nature from life, and to have consulted his senses, not his imagination ... The reader will here find no regions cursed with irremediable barrenness, or blessed with spontaneous fecundity; no perpetual gloom, or unceasing sunshine; nor are the nations here described either devoid of all sense of humanity, or consummate in all private and social virtues ... He will discover, which will always be discovered by a diligent and impartial enquirer, that wherever human nature is to be found, there is a mixture of vice and virtue, a contest of passion and reason.[2]

I share Johnson's judgment. In this book, too, the reader will find all peoples mixed in their virtue and vice, their passion and reason. No culture lives in perpetual gloom or unceasing sunshine. It rains on all of us, and occasionally the sun breaks through.

While much is written in this book about Aboriginal and Oriental cultures, there is no attempt to be definitive about those cultures. The book is about the West. Other cultures are examined less to discern something of their essential natures than to provide us with evidence, with comparative data, to help us to elucidate ourselves. Just as Montesquieu's *Lettres persanes* was written to critique French rather than Persian government, and Voltaire's *L'Ingénu*, ostensibly about a Huron, was written to question Western religious doctrines, so too, despite the frequent references to other cultures, the eye here is always cast toward self-understanding.

Each chapter begins with several quotations from different, sometimes disparate, sources. They are not to be read as expressions of my considered opinion but are to be taken as the context of thought which has raised the issues and occasioned the argument of the chapter they introduce.

Acknowledgments

When an author is asked how long it took to write the book in question, the customary witty, and usually accurate, answer is "all my life." But if an author has been as fortunate as I in having associates willing to give unstintingly of their time, reflection, knowledge, experience, and counsel, the appropriate answer is "several lives."

Three colleagues have been especially generous. Without their criticisms, suggestions, advice, and encouragement, this work would have been a quite different book, if, indeed, it had ever become a book at all. Mathias Guenther, a Wilfrid Laurier University anthropologist, read both the first and the final draft. His gentle yet incisive comments led to a significant reordering of my argument and my evidence, and often a rethinking of my tenets. Our working lunches have provided me with constant intellectual sustenance. David Fraser, a University of British Columbia ethologist, read and offered copious, well-reasoned critical commentary on what I had rosily imagined as more than just a second draft. UBC Press employed Stephen R.L. Clark, a University of Liverpool philosopher, as one of the readers of the submitted manuscript. The perspicacity, erudition, and goodwill of his comments allowed me the opportunity to make significant detailed improvements – as well as saving me from at least one intellectual embarrassment. All three wisely encouraged me to omit some tangential material as well as some dubious interpretations. All three have a share in any merit this book may have. Of course, I alone am responsible for its shortcomings – shortcomings that are inevitably furthered by my temerity in delving into and pronouncing on material outside my own immediate realm of expertise. Yet such is unavoidable in a comparative and synthetic work such as this.

My original editor at UBC Press, Laura Macleod, went to inordinate lengths to help me clarify and organize my arguments. She put in far more effort than an author has a right to expect. In sombre times, her commitment to the book carried me through. After she left UBC Press to join

Oxford University Press Canada, her place was ably taken by Randy Schmidt who steered the typescript from peer appraisal to its final form. His professionalism and acumen were a boon.

I am also indebted to Sandra Woolfrey, who helped me think my early meandering notes toward a book; to Ian Duncan, who helped persuade me of the potential for animal welfare science to improve the status of animals, and who provided a needed reference on Descartes; and to Tim Sullivan, Laura Blythe, and Jane Hennig for their thorough bibliographic assistance. I owe something too to my Political Science colleagues at Wilfrid Laurier University for their cheerful tolerance of my idiosyncratic orientations, which are decidedly different from their own.

Sherry Howse not only typed the succeeding versions of the manuscript with her customary skill and goodwill but also offered welcome organizational and content comments – while revelling in deriding my elementary computer skills to anyone willing to lend an ear.

Brie, Blue, and Zach also played a role, none of it helpful, especially Zach, who delighted in chewing pages which contained observations of which he disapproved, and in making Rorschach blots from my inky sentences. He remains convinced, as should we all, that his well-being and that of his fellow non-humans are more important than any intellectual pretentions.

Last, but foremost, my indebtedness to my wife, Lorna Chamberlain, is a joy to record. She sacrificed her time, even when exhausted from her own professional commitments, offered untold insights, scolded benignly, and helped turn scholarly ardour into mutual enjoyment. Above all, she demonstrated that one may share one's identity while maintaining one's individuality.

Rod Preece
Thanksgiving 1998

Introduction:
The Denigration of the West

1   The entire universe and everything in it, animate and inanimate, is His. Let us not covet anything. Let us treat everything around us reverently, as custodians. We have no charter for dominion. All wealth is commonwealth. Let us enjoy but neither hoard nor kill. The humble frog has as much right to live as we.

> – Hindu *Ishopanishad*

2   It is the story of all life that is holy and is good to tell, and of us two-leggeds sharing in it with the four-leggeds and the wings of the air and all green things; for these are children of one mother and their father is one Spirit.

> – Black Elk, Oglala Sioux elder,
> in *Black Elk Speaks*

3   A righteous man regardeth the life of his beast.

> – Proverbs 12:10

4   They themselves are beasts. For that which befalleth the sons of men befalleth beasts ... They all have one breath; so that a man hath no preeminence above a beast: for all is vanity.

> – Ecclesiastes 3:18-9

5   The air is precious to the red man. For all things share the same
     breath – the beast, the trees, the man, they all share the same
     breath ... All things are connected Whatever befalls the earth
     befalls the sons of the earth.

                              – Reported speech of Chief Seattle of the
                                Duwamish, 1854

6   The goal of life is living in harmony with nature.

                              – Zeno of Citium, c. 334-262 BC

7   We can claim no great right over land animals which are nour-
     ished with the same food, inspire the same air, wash in and drink
     the same water that we do ourselves; and when they are slaugh-
     tered they make us ashamed of our work by their terrible cries;
     and then, again, by living amongst us they arrive at some degree
     of familiarity and intimacy with us.

                              – Plutarch, *Symposiacs*, c. AD 100

As the above words from the *Ishopanishad* and the reports of the words of
Black Elk and Chief Seattle (1, 2, 5) suggest, the Oriental and Aboriginal
traditions proclaim a deep respect for nature and its animals. In like vein,
the quotations from the Bible, Zeno, and Plutarch (3, 4, 6, 7) indicate that
an aspect of the earliest Western religious and philosophical traditions also
reflects a recognition of our interdependent role within nature and our
respect for that nature. Indeed, Zeno (6), the founder of the Stoic school,
commends precisely that course we customarily attribute to Aboriginals: a
life lived in harmony with nature, a life respecting nature's necessities.

   Yet if we turn to much of the recent literature on Western, Aboriginal,
and Oriental ecology, we would be hard pressed to find an acknowledgment of it. Chief Seattle of the Duwamish is frequently cited as a primary
representative of the superior Aboriginal orientation to nature – to take but
one of a multitude of instances – in Roderick Frazier Nash's *The Rights of
Nature*.[1] Nowhere have I encountered an acknowledgment that the words
of Chief Seattle (5) bear a striking resemblance to those found in
Ecclesiastes (4). Surely, if the former is to be interpreted as the epitome of
sensitivity to nature, it would be churlish to ignore the import of the latter.
It would indeed beg explanation if we were to portray the Aboriginal tradition – represented by Chief Seattle – as somehow "at one with nature" and

the Judeo-Christian tradition – here represented by the book of Ecclesiastes – as its antithesis. Yet this interpretation is precisely what has occurred.

The almost universal message is that, in contrast with Aboriginal and Oriental identity with nature, the West has set out to dominate nature and manipulate it for solely human ends. For example, in his *An Unnatural Order: Uncovering the Roots of Our Domination of Nature and Each Other,*[2] Jim Mason argues that animal cruelty is a quintessential aspect of Western culture fed by the same source as its racism, sexism, and elitism. For Mason, that source of oppression is the Western form of agriculture. He fails to acknowledge the abundant racism, sexism, and elitism of non-Western societies, including tribal and hunting societies. Indeed, he depicts pre-agricultural societies idyllically as belonging to "A World Alive and Ensouled." We have to wonder why there is no mention of slavery in hunting societies, of the denial of the right of worship to women in some tribal societies, or of the caste system. Where overwhelming evidence requires that we acknowledge what Mason calls "dominionism" in other cultures, he still insists that the West "is the primary culprit" and, where dominionism is present in other cultures, it is "rather less rampant and often diluted."[3] Yet no confirmatory evidence is offered. The prima facie "dominionism" present in the range of activities from animal sacrifice to vaginal mutilation must somehow be accounted for if we are to entertain Mason's hypotheses. The West has much to repent. But we may wonder whether it stands alone, whether its record is worse than that of others, and if not, why it is so depicted.

To take a further example of the dismissal of the Western tradition, we can read in *The Oxford Companion to Philosophy* that in "Western ethics non-human animals were until quite recent times accorded a very low moral status."[4] Other than in the writings of Jeremy Bentham, so we are told, it was not until the 1970s that the rights of animals received recognition. Yet the ideas of Plutarch (7) and Porphyry, followers of Pythagoras, stand out against such a conclusion. So do those of Rousseau and Goethe, cited in the epigraph to this book. A host of thinkers we shall encounter in these pages cry out for recognition. Yet they remain so often ignored. As we shall see, *The Oxford Companion to Philosophy* overestimates the significance of Bentham and underestimates the Western orientation in general.

The origin of this denigration of the Western tradition is customarily ascribed to Lynn White, Jr.'s 1967 article "The Historical Roots of Our Ecologic Crisis."[5] Others, Roderick Frazier Nash,[6] for example, note that the same thesis – the exploitation of nature is endemic to the Judeo-Christian tradition and is not to be found in less "developed" cultures, which truly live at one with nature – can be found in the earlier work of Edward Payson Evans, beginning with an article entitled "Ethical Relations between Man and Beast" in *Popular Science Monthly* for September 1894.[7] Yet, as we shall see in Chapter 1, this denigration of the Western tradition is not new, not even more emphatic, but has been common since the Renaissance, reaching its zenith at the turn of the nineteenth century, and with evident roots in the classical era. Paradoxically, it has existed side by side with a continuous concern within that tradition for the interests of other species. A fourth-century bishop of Constantinople, St. John Chrysostom, proclaimed: "Surely we ought to show [other species] great kindness and gentleness for many reasons, but above all because they are of the same origin as ourselves." Is that not a foretaste of Charles Darwin? Moreover, St. John Chrysostom was more an exemplar than an exception and his works remain required reading in the Russian Orthodox Church through the *Lives of the Martyrs and the Prologues.*

Customarily – in Evans, White, John Passmore's *Man's Responsibility for Nature,* and Peter Singer's *Animal Liberation,*[8] for example – Genesis 1:26 is cited as the beginning of Western oppression of nature in that God gave humankind "dominion over the fish of the sea, and over the fowl of the air, and over the cattle, and over all the earth, and over every creeping thing that creepeth upon the earth." This "dominion" is read as a domination, an oppression, a malversation, and not, as a careful contextual reading would suggest, as a stewardship, a responsibility. Indeed, in the very same chapter (verse 28), humankind is required "to replenish the earth." And if it is a stewardship, is this proclamation of dominion not equivalent to the Hindu denial of the right of dominion?

The Hebrew word *re'du,* which is translated as "dominion," certainly implies overlordship, but the same word is used in the Torah for the governance of slaves where the requirement of just and fair treatment is explicit. And, of course, all domestication of animals, whether it is Occidental sheep-farming, Hindu cow ownership, or Aboriginal rearing of hunting dogs, is a form of slavery. Not only did biblical dominion over animals imply a responsibility toward those animals, but it was a responsibility commonly recognized in the Western experience. "Honourable dominion" is John Brown's gloss in his *Self-Interpreting Bible* of 1776 – and Brown was no radical animal advocate but a staid biblical traditionalist. "Gentle dominion" wrote George Nicholson in his 1801 *On the Primeval Diet of Man.* In his *Seasons* of 1728, former student of divinity James Thomson interpreted our role as "the lord and not the tyrant of the world." Writing in 1802, Joseph Ritson described the "dominion" of Genesis as "for the sake of authority, protection, and the gracious offices of benevolence and humanity."[9] In *Agnes Grey* (1849), Anne Brontë indicated that the doctrine, supplemented by other biblical texts, involves a significant human responsibility toward our fellow "sentient creatures." Of course, we should not exaggerate the respect accorded to non-humans, but neither should we make the Genesis story, or its interpretation in the Western tradition, something which is alien to it.

If the story of Genesis implies a stewardship, does not the biblical proclamation of dominion possess significant similarity to the Hindu denial of dominion in the *Ishopanishad* (1)? There we read that "we have no charter for dominion." We are to act "as custodians." Yet the Hindu custodianship corresponds to the Judeo-Christian stewardship implied by *re'du*. Both require our concern for the interests of non-humans.

Wherever we look in the Western canon, and however different in perspective the authors may be from the customarily cited sources such as St. Francis, Jeremy Bentham, Henry David Thoreau, and Albert Schweitzer, we invariably encounter evidence of animal respect and concern. When, at the age of seven, Charlotte Brontë was asked to name her favourite book, she replied, as we might have expected from a parson's daughter, "The Bible." When asked the next best book, her untutored answer was equally acceptable to her devout but bucolic father. "The book of Nature," was her reply. Emily Brontë expressed her animal affections by taking care of animals in need – apparently at considerable risk to herself. Although Alexander Pope was gored in the throat and trampled by a wild cow, and although he succumbed to a malignant and disfiguring illness through drinking the milk of a tuberculous cow, he not only deemed animals both rational and possessed of souls but was sufficiently humane to query the vivisectionists how "we know that we have a right to kill creatures we are so little above as dogs?" Even Tchaikovsky, whose life was consumed by music and homosexual guilt, found time to write a threnody on the death of a bird, to knock on neighbours' doors to find a home for a needy kitten, and, in general, to display almost as much of a passionate love for nature as for music. Increasingly, customary depictions of the West ignore an important part of the Occidental orientation.

The practice of denigrating the Western tradition and lauding the Aboriginal and Oriental traditions is to be found in the most reputable of writings and in works by non-Westerners and Westerners alike, though far more of the latter. Among the former, we may note the Japanese Hiroyuki Watanabe's depiction of the Eastern "art of living in harmony with nature [which is] the wisdom of life."[10] By contrast, Western cultures view nature as an object set in opposition to humankind. The Indian theosophist G. Naganathan tells us of "the Hindu's reverential approach to every aspect of life." By contrast, he announces that "Judaic monotheism opened for the first time the floodgates to deliberate, wholesale despoliation of Nature ... According to Genesis 1:26-30, God placed the whole of non-human creation at the disposal of humankind."[11] We might wonder why Naganathan chose to ignore not only the requirement to replenish the earth of verse 28 but also the precept of the Talmud: "It is forbidden, according to the law of Torah, to inflict pain upon any living creature, even if it is ownerless." Thus both domesticated and wild animals have certain entitlements. And surely the story of Noah's saving of the animals should be deemed to reflect *something* of their estimation.

Following the lead of such forerunners as Timothy Severin in *Vanishing Primitive Man,* Thomas Berry in *The Dream of the Earth,* and David Maybury-Lewis in *Millennium: Tribal Wisdom and the Modern World,*[12] Peter Knudtson and David Suzuki in their *Wisdom of the Elders* portray Aboriginal attitudes in utopian terms. They employ the Kayapó Indians of the Amazonian heartlands of Brazil as one of their many examples of Aboriginal societies in mystical union with nature. "Deeply embedded within their nature-embracing myths," we are told, "are timeless beliefs that pay homage to ancient reciprocal relationships among animals, plants and human beings." We are informed further that "Kayapó women colour their faces with paint mixed with the bodies of red ants. It is a gesture of respect, perhaps even a prayer, lovingly addressed to the entire kingdom of red ants."[13]

It might strike us as somewhat incongruous that the killing of ants for decorative purposes – or, for that matter, any other purposes – could be described without any apparent qualm as "a gesture of respect" to the ants the Kayapó have killed and others of their species. We are entitled to an explanation of why the killing of ants should have been considered respectful of them. We are entitled to be told how in principle it differs from the Occidental wearing of fur when the proudly adorned tell us how beautiful are these creatures whose coats they are now wearing. We must ask of those who applaud Brazilian Aboriginals for their respectful killing of ants whether their removal of plumage from captured wild birds for decorative purposes is similarly respectful. We must ask what it is in the apparent disregard of the Aboriginals for the interests of the animals that distinguishes them from their Occidental counterparts.

By contrast with the "respect" shown by Aboriginals, we are told by Knudtson and Suzuki that "Western societies ... routinely [employ] ridiculous or demeaning images of animals for human entertainment."[14] Yet we are entitled to wonder whether our comic cartoons with talking animal characters are in principle more "ridiculous" than Native myths in which animals enter into contracts with human beings. Of the seven cartoons in the local newspaper I received today, three depict animal characters. The moral of one is that wild animals, in this case squirrels, belong in the wild and not in captivity. The other two use the animal characters to demonstrate human failings. Larson, in particular, knows how to poke fun without losing respect. In what possible manner could the animal images be deemed "demeaning" in Rudyard Kipling's *The Jungle Book,* Anna Sewell's *Black Beauty,* in the stories of Lobo the wolf, Silverspot the crow, the Springfield Fox, and the Pacing Mustang of Ernest Thompson Seton's *Wild Animals I Have Known?* In film, Lassie, Willy, and Black Velvet are more heroic than ridiculous. In children's stories generally, "good" characters are recognized as such by their benevolent treatment of other species, and "bad" characters by their indifference or malevolence toward them. Thus, for example, in Frances Hodgson Burnett's *The Secret Garden* – a veritable jubilation of nature – the gardener Ben Weatherstaff is initially "sour" and dour, but immediately upon discovering that he has an affection for the robin in the garden, the reader's attitude is swayed from disapproval to grudging admiration. The practice is not restricted to children's literature. In *Shirley,* Charlotte Brontë reports of one of her characters that "we watch him, and see him kind to animals." We are now ready to be told of his service to the poor, his recognition of the worthiness of women, and his abiding interest in justice. Our disgust at Quasimodo first diminishes when we find Victor Hugo describing him raising birds in the towers of *Notre-Dame of Paris.* Indeed, Charles Dickens, Stendhal, William Thackeray, George Sand, and George Eliot used attitudes to animals as bellwethers for judging people's character. In *The Woman in White,* Wilkie Collins provides an enigmatic instance. Count Fosco is a consummate villain who has a mysterious rapport with animals. In the concluding chapters of the novel, the contradiction is resolved. Fosco is a mixture of fine sensibilities and overpowering selfish interests born of impecuniosity and the dangers he faced as a consequence of past political intrigues. So too in film. In the 1941 classic *High Sierra,* our sympathy for the criminal played by Humphrey Bogart is assured by depicting him as kind to dogs.

On television, the Littlest Hobo, Rin-Tin-Tin, and Flipper are scarcely figures of disparagement. And while we should continue to have concern about the treatment of animals in the making of films, and what happens to them after the filming is finished, a reading of *The Beauty of the Beasts*[15] by Ralph Helfer, the doyen of Hollywood's animal trainers, should suffice to convince us that there is at least sometimes a genuine respect. Of course, the response will be made that genuine respect consists in action not words. Disrespectful behaviour may be obscured by misleadingly respectful language. That is undeniably true, but it is a dictum that must be applied every bit as much in the Aboriginal and Oriental worlds as in the West.

There are of course deplorable iniquities in Western treatment of other species, and both I[16] and others have written about them at some length, but that should not blind us to the fact that there is another side to the customary tale – both in the West and elsewhere.

Western science's "reductionist methods" are described by Knudtson and Suzuki, in contrast with "Aboriginal holistic subtleties," as "an ingenious and intellectually potent deceit." "Modern scientists," we are told, "arrogantly set out to engineer the biosphere with only science's sterile blueprints of nature."[17] Because Knudtson and Suzuki are content to quote numerous Western scientists with approval when it suits their purpose – from Einstein to the astrophysicist Stephen Hawking to the neurobiologist Roger Sperry – we have to wonder about the consistency of the representations. After all, Einstein, Hawking, and Sperry employ and vaunt the scientific methods deplored by Knudtson and Suzuki. Prima facie, this finding might suggest to us that ecological sensibilities may be masking a scientific face.

Knudtson and Suzuki are certainly not alone in their depiction of an Aboriginal world at one with nature. They merely repeat with more eloquence than is customary the message that has become the intellectual norm in recent decades. Yet we might wonder whether there is more ideology than accuracy in such descriptions. Are the Aboriginal and Oriental *Weltanschauungen* being employed as yardsticks against which to measure Western failings without much concern for their conformity with behaviour? We are certainly entitled to ask ourselves whether the portrait of an Aboriginal and Oriental identity with nature and the Westerner as its unregenerate exploiter has been overdrawn. Indeed, we must ask whether the image we are now customarily offered is more a caricature than a portrait.

To take an instance at random, we might read in the Balinese Hindu scriptural myth, *Bhima Swarga,* disparaging analogies being drawn between humans and caterpillars, for example, because the latter are capable only of crawling. Cockfighting, which is illegal in much of the Western world, is treated in the *Bhima Swarga* as a normal and acceptable pastime, criticism being levelled only at those who cheat by misapplying the spurs to gain a wagering advantage. Neither the practice of cockfighting itself nor the use of artificial spurs to inflict serious injury, often death, is condemned. There *is* condemnation of those who slaughter animals "without caring about the prescribed ritual" but little concern for the life of the animal itself, for, we are told, "the creature should rightly give up its life for its master."[18] The reputed Balinese Hindu sacredness of nature might be more readily interpreted as a sacredness of ritual. Balinese Hindu practices may be no worse than Western traditions. But they should not be offered as a model for the West to emulate. Nor as a means for chastising Western sinners.

Certainly, we might read in the *Bhima Swarga* of the punishments inflicted on those who "tortured their buffaloes and other animals for the fun of it ... like catching a butterfly and ripping off its wings, to watch its reaction." Likewise, those who hunt wantonly are punished in the afterlife.[19] Nonetheless, it would not be difficult to find similar proscriptions in Western norms. Thus, for example, Alexander Pope writing in the *Guardian* in 1713: "We should find it hard to vindicate the destroying of anything that has life, merely out of wantonness." And in *The Deerslayer* (1841) James Fenimore Cooper's hero insists: "They can't accuse me of killing an animal when there is no occasion for the meat or the skin. I may be a slayer, it's true, but I'm no slaughterer." The statement would not have been made, of course, if wanton killing were not considered reprehensible. One of F. Scott Fitzgerald's infamous brawls occurred when he attempted to stop a cockfight in Cuba in 1939. While Fitzgerald was no bleeding heart, cockfighting exceeded the bounds of legitimacy. Needless harm was proscribed.

Certainly, not all Hindus engage in the practice of cockfighting with equanimity, or even acknowledge its legitimacy. Many are appalled by it. Thus the great explorer and scholar Sir Richard Francis Burton wrote in 1851: "Kukkur-bazi, or cock-fighting, is a common, but not a fashionable, amusement in Sindh [in present-day Pakistan]. The birds are generally fought by Moslems at the Daiva, or drinking houses, on Fridays, as was anciently the practice with our swains on Sundays. [Cockfighting had been outlawed in Britain in 1835.] Formerly, no Hindoo dared to be present, as circumcision would probably have been the result; even in these days they are seldom seen at the cockpit."[20]

Cultural complexity, variability, and inconsistency are as common in the East as the West. It is as problematical to generalize about Oriental belief systems as about Western belief systems. A deep respect for the interests of other species permeates the ideas of the Jains and the Vaishnavas, but it would be a mistake to imagine those ideas truly representative of general practices on the Indian subcontinent. As Gandhi suggested, "The ideal of humanity in the West is perhaps lower, but their practice of it very much more thorough than ours. We rest content with a lofty ideal and are slow or lazy in its practice. We are wrapped in deep darkness, as is evident from our paupers, cattle and other animals."[21] And if the widely praised Indian practices leave as much to be desired as Gandhi insists, then we must thoroughly rethink our attitudes to nature rather than seeking our ideals, our models, in the practices of other cultures.

In his *Sindh Revisited*,[22] Christopher Ondaatje gives us a dramatic and disturbing account of cockfighting practices in present-day Moslem Pakistan. The fights are popular entertainment, much as they are in Central and South America. They are still to be found, though rather less frequently, in Hindu India. Likewise, trained fishing-birds – whose legs are tied to a rod with long pieces of string – are a rather more common sight on the Indus than on the Ganges, but they are still to be found on the latter. On the rare occasions illegal cockfighting practices are discovered in, say, Canada or the United States, the public is rightly appalled and the courts inflict penalties which, if inadequate, indicate at least the recognized criminality of the activity. It would be inappropriate to conclude that, because of the West's greater sensibility in this regard, the West has an overall superior record – fox-hunting, bullfighting, certain circus and rodeo practices, and bear-baiting immediately come to mind. But Eastern practices should entitle us to ponder the legitimacy of the presumptions of superior Eastern attitudes.

We should at the very least be sufficiently sceptical about the uncritical adulation of the Aboriginal and Oriental and the ever critical condemnation of the Westerner so that we demand a more balanced appraisal. We may wonder whether the Western tradition is as one-sided as it is customarily presented to us, whether there are less wholesome aspects of Aboriginal and Oriental thought that we customarily ignore. Does Aboriginal and Oriental behaviour toward the natural realm confirm or deny the nature-loving pronouncements? Is Western bullfighting, pernicious as it is, any worse than Aboriginal animal sacrifice? Is Western sport-hunting any worse than Hindu sport-hunting? It is with these questions in mind that this book has been written.

While I shall, as mentioned in the prefatory note, be casting a more critical eye than is customary on the Aboriginal and Oriental traditions in these pages, I must at the outset offer several significant caveats: even if Oriental and Aboriginal attitudes are in fact less admirable than they are customarily portrayed, we must not lose sight of the fact that the positive attitudes represented in the belief systems of others offer us stimulating ways to imagine what kinds of relationships to nature might be preferable to those currently prevailing in the West. They can become useful metaphors for action within our own cultural context.

And while I shall be pointing to the less salubrious aspects of non-Western attitudes to other species, to those which are almost invariably ignored in the animal rights and ecology literature, we must not forget the admirable principles that are sometimes expounded. For example, the Jain principle of *ahimsa* – non-violence – involves a responsibility to refrain from the infliction of harm to others, including non-humans. While such principles are admirable and deserving of our deepest respect, we must inquire not only whether they are expounded but also to what degree they are practised.

Again, while I shall be attempting to give due, usually unrecognized, emphasis to the positive aspects of the Western tradition, we should not be diverted from the more nefarious roadside zoo practices, the continued, if declining, use of animals for cosmetics research, or the treatment of white veal calves. Nor should we be content with the deplorable experimentation excesses in even the most admirable medical research, the often abominable treatment of food animals in intensive farming, or the grotesque treatment of racing greyhounds. A more realistic emphasis should not assuage our guilt. And if I appear to repeat and stress these points, it is because of the great danger that we might become complacent about our own practices. If we are no more – and no less – sinning than most others, our practices still leave a great deal to be desired and need greatly to be improved.

I have a great deal less to say about Aboriginal and Oriental self-advocacy and condemnation of the West than about those Western intellectuals who have eulogized other cultures in order to disparage their own. Until recently, most non-Western commentators understood the complexity of their own traditions, recognizing the distance between aspiration and reality, as well as the complexities and inconsistencies of the aspirations. In recent years, a few have come to echo the one-sided eulogy and equally one-sided denunciation offered by numerous Western commentators. They have thus in turn offered us an unduly rosy rationalization of their own practices and an unduly jaundiced image of the West. Until the last few years, supposedly Aboriginal self-glorifying pronouncements were little more than the interpretations of the Westerners who reported them. As we shall see in Chapter 1, what we got was sometimes not what was said but what the reporters wished had been said.

The critical non-Western perspective on the West is, of course, readily comprehensible. It must indeed arouse our sympathy. Having suffered centuries of racial abuse, cultural vilification, and, perhaps worse, kindly patronization, revenge is sweet. Yet although the revenge may be psychologically satisfying, and may stimulate our sense that justice is finally being served, it does not aid the understanding. It leads to self-justification rather than truth. Emotion, however justifiable, often blinds.

Among my concerns in this book is to analyze the statements of Western intellectuals who, in the tradition of Karl Marx in his *Theses on Feuerbach*, have complained that earlier "philosophers have only *interpreted* the world in various ways; the point, however, is to *change* it." But if we want to change the world rather than interpret it, we tend to seek primarily that which is conducive to the promotion of the changes envisaged. We ignore the uncomfortable and inconvenient facts. In *Emile*, Rousseau depicted such analysts cogently: "A philosopher loves the Tartars in order to be spared having to love his neighbours."[23] Rousseau's "philosopher" does not depict the Tartars as they are, but as they might conveniently be described in order to offer a model to emulate, a baton with which to cudgel compatriots. It is a practice, as we shall shortly see, with a lengthy history.

And if such an apparently cynical interpretation appears overly cynical, we must ask why it is that so many analysts fail to report the immediately obvious features of societies that stand prima facie in opposition to their hypotheses. We may wonder whether they would have done so if understanding rather than ideology were their goal. Cultural self-flagellation may be good for the guilty soul. But not for comprehension.

The circumspect reader will naturally wonder how representative is the evidence offered in these pages. Is the author guilty of that of which he accuses others? Has the author presented only the evidence that supports his hypotheses? Does his evidence reflect nothing more than a minor aspect of the Western tradition? Has he chosen wilfully to depict an unduly sombre picture of the Oriental and Aboriginal worlds? After all, in drawing on a couple of thousand years of texts, it would be possible to provide a set of quotations to support almost any thesis. I have attempted to address these legitimate potential concerns in several ways. First, I have tried to show that many of the major representatives of the Western canon who are acknowledged contributors to Western culture have also been concerned with animal well-being; and that this aspect of their thought has sometimes been ignored. Second, I have often used the same evidence offered by others and have shown that their interpretation of that evidence is unjustified, that the evidence they offer does not lead to the conclusions they draw. Third, I have provided evidence that the public at large or certain significant segments of it welcomed the animal protection pronouncements of prominent persons or were appalled when animal interests were ignored. Fourth, I have offered evidence that appears to have escaped the attention of others. I have intentionally paid less attention to those usually offered as representatives of positive attitudes to animated nature in the

Western tradition and emphasized the important role of those customarily forgotten or condemned.

The reader may also wonder why it is that many perceptive, diligent, and honourable authors (as well as the ideologists) have looked at the Western tradition and reached different conclusions from those to be found in this book. At least in part it is because we have investigated different sources. The majority of writers sought their evidence predominantly in the history of philosophy. In addition to the philosophers, I have relied heavily on the major figures of Western literature, religion, art, poetry, and music who, I would argue, are at least as relevant as the philosophers, if not more so. Philosophers tend to analyze values; belletrists to advance them and to have more direct influence on the mind of a nation, if for no other reason than that they are more widely read and more readily understood. Voltaire was an exception for he disguised philosophy in the form of novels. Of course, we should not ignore the philosophers – nor have I done so – but we should grant others equal standing.

On reading much of the literature on the history of attitudes to animals and nature, one is struck by the distance said to exist between the Western and other traditions. They are depicted as standing in opposition to each other. By contrast, I find them much more alike than dissimilar. There are differences, of course, but they are far more subtle and nuanced than we are customarily led to believe. Each culture has brought subtle differences to bear on the issue of orientations to nature. There is much of value coming from each. Moreover, there are tensions, contradictions, and complexities within all cultures that are ignored in the idealization of the non-Western and vilification of the Western worlds. In the case of the West, one important aspect of that tension, as we shall encounter, is the conflict between the idea of progress and that of "back to nature." Symbolically, if exaggeratedly, that tension reached its apogee in Jean-Jacques Rousseau who extolled the moral and alimentary virtues of vegetarianism while continuing to consume animal flesh, who argued against the iniquities of hunting while admiring the virtues of the hunter, who praised community while living the life of the solitary, and who wrote books while insisting they were the very cause of society's ills. Throughout much of his writing, he promotes greater gender equality. The final book of *Emile* is a *volte face*. By turns the progressivist and feminist Mary Wollstonecraft was enchanted and repulsed. If Rousseau is a caricature of the contradictions that pervade societies, he is only an exaggeration and not a misrepresentation. If one is to understand any society, one must understand its tensions and its complexities. To attempt to capture the reality of any society in terms of pithy expressions about its "at oneness with nature," or, indeed, of its antipathy to nature, is to be sure to fail to understand its reality.

Animals and Nature

1
Advocacy Scholarship

1   If we shall not be ashamed to confess the truth [the Indians of America] seem to live in that golden world of which old writers speak so much: wherein men lived simply and innocently ... content only to satisfy nature.

> – Peter Martyr, *De Orbe Novo,* c. 1516

2   All things in common nature should produce
Without sweat or endeavour: treason, felony,
Sword, pike, knife, gun, or need of any engine,
Would I not have; but nature should bring forth,
Of its own kind, all foizon, all abundance,
To feed my innocent people.

> – Shakespeare, *The Tempest* 2.1, c. 1610

3   Pygmy people living in the Ituri Forest in the Congo ... are infinitely wise ... [They possess] an intense love for the forest and [a] belief that it is better than the outside world that threatens to destroy it.

> – Colin Turnbull, *The Forest People,* 1961

4   Whatever their differences both liberal capitalism and Marxist socialism committed themselves totally to this vision of industrial progress which more than any other single cause has brought

about the disintegration that is taking place throughout the entire planet.

– Thomas Berry, *The Dream of the Earth*, 1988

5   The Bird has always been a favourite with man ... In the fable of the Greek as in the saga of the Norseman, in the polished odes of the Latin as in the more spontaneous lyrics of the English, it is the image of all that is light, and innocent, and graceful. Especially is it the embodiment of human aspiration; of the desire of the human heart, when oppressed with the burden and the mystery of this unintelligible world, to take to itself wings, and flee away, and be at rest. Poised in the air on equal wings, it is the type of self-reliance and independence. Swooping down-wards with arrowy rush on some doomed prey, it is an emblem of power. Clinging to the part-ner of its little nest, it is the type of love. Carolling in the sunshine it is the symbol of praise ... It is not difficult to understand why between Man and the Birds so close a friendship should exist.

– W.H. Davenport Adams, *The Bird World*, 1878

The fellowship between the human and the natural world described, some-what sententiously perhaps, by Davenport Adams (5) as a significant part of various aspects of the Western cultural tradition is replicated in a host of Western naturalist literature. In general terms, it corresponds fairly closely to the harmony with nature of which so much is written with regard to Aboriginal culture and Oriental philosophy. Are Western writings in the Davenport Adams manner aberrations or are they commonly held sentiments outright contradicted by the realities of the Western world? Or is there an irrational prejudice that refuses to recognize the West's lengthy tradition of deep respect for nature? Perhaps instead the respective respectful claims of the Oriental, Aboriginal, and Occidental worlds are all more aspiration than real-ity. Certainly, as some of the preceding quotations reflect, the condemnation of the West and adulation of others with respect to their attitudes to the natural realm is, and long has been, a commonplace. Whether from the mouth of a sixteenth-century humanist historian (1) or one of the doyens of twentieth-century anthropology (3), a lengthy tradition ascribes a harmony with nature to Aboriginals; and another (4) ascribes its very antithesis to the West.

A perusal of the Western cultural tradition would suggest that the supposed oppression of the natural world requires further investigation. An impartial inquirer is likely to be impressed by the positive sentiments expressed toward other species in the Western literary canon – Milton, Blake, Goethe, Coleridge, Wordsworth, Lamartine, Balzac, Dostoevsky, and Tolstoy are among the more obvious examples. We might wonder why so few appear to have noticed in their comments on Western attitudes toward nature that a significant number of the most renowned pieces of Western music are paeans to nature – Vivaldi's "Four Seasons," Haydn's oratorios, Beethoven's "Pastoral," Brahms's Second Symphony, Mahler's "Titan," and Saint-Saëns's "Carnival of the Animals" are among the more notable. From Titian through Poussin to Cézanne, nature is treated as an object of reverence in visual art. That reverence was not restricted to the brush. Joachim Gasquet wrote of Cézanne that "He loved the animals. He loved the trees. Toward the end, in his need of merciful solitude, an olive tree became his friend." All nature was one.[1]

And if we delve into the Western fairy-tale tradition, we readily find the European counterparts of the Aboriginal myths that are so frequently employed to praise the Aboriginal respect for nature. Thus, for example, in the Scandinavian tradition, we encounter the animal protecting household spirits called *tomtar,* which are "small, gray clad figures, perhaps with red stocking caps (like Christmas elves), who might sometimes be spied in dark corners of stables and haylofts. They were considered a sort of folk conscience, and, as the caretakers of livestock, they offered assurance that life would be conducted in a proper manner on the farm."[2]

Moreover, the *rå* – ruling spirits of the forest, lake, sea, and mountain – often possessed animal characteristics and were deemed the source of luck in human endeavours. Success in life required appropriate respect for both spirits and animals. It would, of course, be unwarranted to suggest that the West has lived in harmony with nature. We encounter more frequently than we would wish the view of the novelist Anthony Trollope. Writing of the joys of the fox hunt, he proclaimed: "In truth I do not care for the stars. I care, I think, only for men and women." We are entitled to be distressed by Ernest Hemingway's and Gertrude Stein's love of bullfights. But it would be misleading to ignore impressive nature-oriented strains in the Western tradition.

Today, we are often told that, unlike ourselves, others – Hindus and Aboriginals, for example – see humans and animals as equal. Thus, the Hindu scholar Ranchor Prine writes of the importance of stressing the "equality of life forms,"[3] a practice he believes is endemic to Hinduism and alien to Western norms. No doubt a good case can be made that there is a greater claim for respect of other species in certain branches of Hinduism than in, say, Christianity or Islam. But to describe such claims as a recognition of the "equality of life forms" is to misrepresent Hinduism. For example, the *Kamasutra* of Vatsayana, written somewhere between the first and sixth century, exhorted women to join men in learning the "art of cock-fighting, quail-fighting and ram-fighting" – scarcely egalitarian (or even considerate) sporting traditions! There is undoubtedly a worthy respect evidenced in Hinduism for other species. For example, the Maharaja of Dewas explained to the novelist E.M. Forster that "men, birds and everything in the universe [are] part of god." But he denied explicitly that this implied equality, for "men had developed further than birds in coming to this realization."[4] Thus the use of animals by humans was permissible. Indeed, so much so that Forster was appalled at animal treatment on the maharaja's estate, especially that of elephants. Few have reached the level of consideration for other species achieved by Mahatma Gandhi – indeed, many Hindu *sadhus* complained he went far too far. Yet even he did not acknowledge the other animals as equals, for he referred to the dangers of descending to the level of "and lower than the beasts."[5] By implication, humans were of a higher order. In fact, the very principle of reincarnation in Hinduism, being reborn in higher and lower forms, confirms it. And in the *Ishopanishad* (Introduction, 1), it is "the humble frog," the lowly frog not the equal frog, that is declared to have its entitlements. Again, even Gandhi found animal use acceptable, for he farmed goats for their milk. Among Hindus, respect and consideration are certainly to be found (along with some disrespect and some abject cruelty), but there is no recognition of an "equality of life forms" if that phrase is to mean anything substantial. Just as the case *for* the non-West is grossly exaggerated, so too is the case *against* the West.

It is in fact not at all uncommon to encounter explicitly egalitarian pronouncements in Western writing. Thus, for example, in *The Love of Cats,* Celia Haddon proclaims, "The love of humans for cats is as strong as the love of humans for other humans. Sometimes stronger. For, despite the gulf between our species, it is a relationship of two equal personalities – if one assumes that human beings are equal to cats, that is. Not all cats do."[6] Of course, one may deride Celia Haddon's pronouncement as sentimental, or insist that in acknowledging "the gulf between our species" she is not being entirely honest in her professed egalitarianism. Perhaps, or perhaps the expression of the egalitarianism is really a reference to some mysterious qualities possessed by cats. The point is that the egalitarian message is not uncommon in Western thought – the poet Percy Shelley's egalitarian vegetarianism in *Queen Mab* is a case in point – and if it really means something other than what it explicitly says, perhaps the same is true of Aboriginal and Oriental egalitarian messages. To understand them, we must look beneath the surface. If we are willing to second guess a Celia Haddon or a Percy Shelley, if we are to be intellectually honest, we must be equally willing to second guess Aboriginal and Oriental thought.

The current clarion call in much naturalist literature is to recapture the essence of "primitive" human culture, to become once more at one with nature. Oriental pantheism is also depicted as a superior alternative to traditional Western attitudes. And Western civilization is depicted as one which, in its concern with "progress," has come to treat nature, including the animal realm, without the respect to which it is entitled, and without which respect civilization is doomed. Whereas Plato and Aristotle, and those who followed them in the Western philosophical tradition, viewed civilization as that which raised the human above demeaning animal nature and proved the source of human fulfilment, the modern ecologist often sees civilization as that which has destroyed natural human sensibilities. The views of the "primitivists" have been repeated so often, so persuasively, and with such emphasis that they have become an intrinsic part of modern intellectual currency. It is my contention, however, that they are myths. They are myths – as are most myths – that contain important kernels of truth but that are ultimately more misleading than instructive.

This is not to suggest that Western civilization cannot learn from other cultures, from other traditions, or that the problems facing us are not gargantuan. It most certainly can and they most certainly are. But it is better that we try to understand those proclaimed alternative traditions for what they were and are rather than to possess some idyllic image of those practices. I doubt that any ecologist would wish to promote the emulation of traditional Oriental practices of killing seals, bear, and deer for their penises, gall bladders, and velvet, respectively, to further aphrodisiac and other dubious ends. We should not overlook the probability that overhunting by Palaeoindians – the so-called Pleistocene Overkill – helped bring about the extirpation in North America of long-nosed and flat-headed peccaries, four-horned pronghorn, giant beaver, Shasta ground sloth, mastodon, mammoth, and perhaps the North American camel.[7] And we ought to be astonished if a Brahminic Hinduism that could create castes of people and treat some as untouchables could also treat other species with a greater respect than certain categories of their fellow humans. Indeed, the fact that the Hindustani word *suar*, pig, is among the most insulting in the language should give us reason to reflect on the status of at least some species on the Indian subcontinent.

The Western tradition, so readily castigated by its opponents, has not been so uncaring as its depiction by detractors would have us believe. For example, M.W. Padmasiri de Silva claims that *"Unlike most Western systems of ethics,* [in Buddhism] the cultivation of socio-moral virtues covers behaviour in relation to all living beings."[8] Yet it should not escape our attention that, in the nineteenth century, a vegetarian movement, anti-vivisection movement, naturalist movement, and animal welfare movement, and, in the twentieth century, an environmental movement and animal rights movement all began, and in most cases have found the greatest response, in Western society. Indeed, Western society's greatest critics are themselves Westerners, and are products of a civilization that has promoted and encouraged intellectual dissent to a far greater degree than any previous society. The fact that Western civilization has treated the criticisms as legitimate has given greater weight to those criticisms than would have been the case in any other contemporary society. The West has certainly not been immersed in the realm of nature; but at least it has been ambivalent.

Robert Louis Stevenson's *Travels with a Donkey in the Cévennes* (1879) provides a telling example of post-Darwinian self-criticism along with an acknowledgment of personal cruelty – there could be no clearer case of self-conscious ambivalence. Stevenson's essay is ostensibly more about the topography of a remote region of southern France than about the wretched Modestine, but, to most readers, it is the treatment of the she-ass that makes the piece memorable. Having purchased the obstinate animal to carry his excessive baggage up and down the hills, Stevenson insists: "It goes against my conscience to lay my hand rudely on a female ... God forbid, thought I, that I should brutalize this innocent creature." Yet brutalize the ass he did when she failed to do his bidding, inflicting injury first with a rod, then a switch, and finally a goad which drew blood – acts whose effects "increased my horror of my cruelty."

At the close of the travels, having heartlessly sold Modestine after "twelve days" in which "we had been fast companions," Stevenson finally felt regret at his loss. The donkey had come to mean more than he had realized. This ambivalence is redolent of a period in which there was a growing recognition, both via Darwin and via Christian evangelism, that other species were entitled to far greater consideration than was customary. Yet it is perhaps surprising that such ambivalence should be in one who otherwise was as devoted to the natural realm as were Thoreau (whom Stevenson admired deeply) and Emerson before him. "You think dogs will not be in heaven? I tell you, they will be there long before any of us," Stevenson opines.[9] On the one hand he reiterates the prevalent antipathy to wolves and gives credence to contemporary myths about them, and on the other proclaims: "There is a special pleasure for some minds in the reflection that we share the impulse [to react to Nature's morning call] with all outdoor creatures in our neighbourhood, that we have escaped out of the Bastille of civilization, and are become, for the time being, a mere kindly animal and a sheep of Nature's flock."[10] To acknowledge civilization as a prison is to announce the oneness of animal creation.

The ambivalence was just as pronounced for Stevenson's wife Fanny Osbourne. She noted in 1890 her loathing and fear of the pigs on their Samoan property. "I love the growing things [vegetation] but the domestic beasts are not to my taste," she complained. She added, however, "I have ... such a guilty feeling toward them, for I know if their murder is not contemplated that at least they will be robbed of their young at my instigation." George Bernard Shaw's putative father harboured and fed an abandoned cat but did nothing to prevent his dog from chasing and killing the foundling. He felt so ashamed of his behaviour that he blamed his lack of success in life on the natural justice of the cat's revenge.

While the ambivalence is clear, even pronounced, in Stevenson, Osbourne, and George Carr Shaw, and with a welcome self-awareness, it is already transcended in the writings of Wordsworth. Thus, for example in "Lines Left upon a Seat in a Yew-Tree":

he who feels contempt
For any living thing, hath faculties
Which he has never used; that thought with him
Is in its infancy. The man whose eye
Is ever on himself, doth look on one
The least of Nature's works, one who might move
The wise man to that scorn which wisdom holds
Unlawful ever. O, be wiser, Thou!
Instructed that true knowledge leads to love,
True dignity abides with him alone
Who, in the silent hour of inward thought,
Can still suspect, and still revere himself,
In lowliness of heart.[11]

A respect far less ambivalent than that of Stevenson even for the demeaned ass may be readily found. Thus Laurence Sterne wrote his *A Sentimental Journey* (1768), so he informed his daughter, "to teach us to love the world and our fellow creatures better than we do." And it was the donkey he chose as his representative of non-human fellow creatures. Indeed, in Sterne's novel the ass was "a friend"[12] whose death was deeply mourned – sufficiently so that Byron chastised Sterne as "a man who can whine over a dead ass while he lets his mother starve."[13] With a similar compassion to Sterne, Samuel Taylor Coleridge addresses the "poor little foal of an oppressed race" culminating in "I hail thee *Brother*" ("To a Young Ass," 1794). Coleridge acknowledges our kinship with one of the least esteemed of our fellow mammals.

There is, of course, also the prejudicial view in the Western tradition that served only to demean the animal image. Thus, in the anonymous poem "New Morality" (reputedly but unverifiably by the Tory politician George Canning) published in *Poetry of the Anti-Jacobin* of 1799, we can read of "all creeping creatures, venomous and low" followed by reference to such radical political adversaries as Tom Paine and William Godwin. "And every beast after [Godwin's] kind." Clearly, a variety of attitudes pervade the Western tradition. Occasionally, we encounter those who are dedicated to nature, often those who are ambivalent about it, and all too frequently, though they are far from a majority, those who are insensitive to it.

While environmental and animal rights criticisms are directed against the predominant tendencies of Western society, they are predicated on inherent but sometimes unpractised values of that society. They are customarily justified by philosophical traditions such as instrumental or intrinsic value theory or transpersonal psychology or Romanticism, which have been developed in Western thought. Western behaviour is as readily criticized through Western philosophical analysis as it is via the borrowing of exoteric critical concepts or the elevation of practices alien to the Western tradition. We must be wary lest in rejecting our failings we also reject our successes.

And we must be equally wary that in proclaiming the virtue of others' successes we do not inherit their failings. As Nietzsche opined, "Be careful lest, in casting out your devils, you cast out the best that is within you."

Rather less than half a century ago, Western civilization in its arrogance often portrayed itself as the apogee of human achievement, as the model for "primitive" and less progressive societies to imitate. In the 1960s, *The Savage Mind* was still acceptable as the title of a highly – and justifiably – reputable academic book, although Thomas Carlyle's "On the Nigger Question" would no longer have been tolerated. For over two centuries after Sir William Petty in 1677 developed (or redeveloped – it was not uncommon before St. Augustine) the thesis that different races were different species,[14] it was commonly believed that "lower" human beings were incapable of achieving the superior norms of "civilized" human beings. That view prevailed among some of the most rigorous of scientists and some of the most popular of philosophers. Indeed, surprisingly, that view pervaded the writings of the doyen of English physiology, Charles Darwin![15] There were certainly a number, however, not least Leibnitz and Voltaire, who were likely to make comparisons that did not reflect well on Western civilization. But such analyses were designed customarily rather more to demonstrate European vices and superstitions than to demonstrate the superiority of Chinese civilization in the manner of Leibnitz, or the "innocence of savages" in the words of Voltaire. Nonetheless, it should not go unnoticed that, in the seventeenth and early eighteenth centuries, travel books lauding the noble savage as superior to the sophisticates of civilization were a commonplace.[16] We learn the same lesson from some of the Jesuit missionaries to Paraguay, Brazil, Canada, and China; and from Antonio Pigafetta, fellow traveller with Magellan, who reported on the Brazilians who went naked, were free from the vices of civilization, and supposedly lived to be 140 years of age.[17] In the nineteenth century, Heinrich Heine, Charles Baudelaire, and George Eliot were among those who wrote of what Paul Verlaine called disparagingly "the refinements of an excessive civilization." This tradition is worthy of investigation if we are to understand the fullness and continuity of Western self-deprecation.

From the very origins of Western civilization, in explicit form from the very earliest writings, there has been an acknowledgment that the benefits of civilization entail considerable cost, that the agonistic psychological characteristics required of civilization are at odds with the harmonious psychological characteristics said to prevail in the state of nature. "Follow nature" was the cry one heard from the Cynics, Stoics, and Epicureans alike – though neither then nor since has it been clear what was meant by "nature." The doctrine can be found in writings as diverse as those of Cicero, Tertullian, and St. Ambrose. And "nature" was more often than not employed to refer to the characteristics of our earliest conditions. The autochthonous human condition was seen as peaceful, compassionate,

egalitarian, and vegetarian; animals and humans lived as one. In civilization the supposed tenderness, kindness, and communitarianism of the
state of nature withered away to be replaced by the audacity, diligence, perseverance, ardour, ambition, and bravery necessary to provide protection
from animal and human predators, and to produce success in the hunt and
in cultivation, and especially in the arts and sciences.

The ideas of the Golden Age, of the competing images of Eden (peaceful
and vegetarian) and Arcadia (hunter-gatherer and carnivorous), pervade
Western thought. The first known written version of the Golden Age story is
to be found in Hesiod's *Works and Days* of the late eighth century BC. There
we are told of the five ages of human history: the age of gold, the age of silver, the age of bronze, the age of heroes, and the age of iron. As the incon-
gruity of "the age of heroes" suggests, this story is a fusion of two earlier oral
myths, reflecting both their longevity and the multiplicity of sources.
Indeed, similar golden age myths are to be found in China, India, Japan,
and Persia, and analogous versions in many Aboriginal societies including
the Bassari of West Africa and the Makritare of the Orinoco.[18] Many societies
seem to have a conception of a perfect, peaceful past, though others, especially among Aboriginals, view the original state as one of chaos, often followed by an arcadia. Many acknowledge that their prevailing cultural
practices are a deviation from their long lost ideals. It is in the West, however, that the tension between "primitivism" and civilization has been most
keenly felt. We find it not only in the sources we will mention in detail but
in Chateaubriand, Herman Melville, Gauguin, and Walt Whitman.
Sometimes, this tension is related directly to life with the animals, as in
Whitman's "I think I could turn and live with the animals, they are so placid
and self-contained."

According to Hesiod, his time was the age of iron, a degraded age of "toil
and misery," an age of "constant distress." It did not take the experience of
an oppressive capitalism and an unhealthy industrialism to persuade critics
that civilization had its drawbacks. In the Golden Age, conditions were purportedly different: "All good things were theirs, and the grain-giving soil
bore its fruits of its own accord in unrestricted plenty, while they at their
leisure harvested their fields in contentment and abundance."[19] In the classical era, Empedocles, Plutarch, and Porphyry were among those who subscribed to the golden age theory.[20] In his first-century *Annals*, Tacitus
described the age as one of "equality," as a "time without a single vicious
impulse, without shame or guilt ... [when] men desired nothing against
morality."[21] The egalitarianism and vegetarianism of the Golden Age were
invariably seen as an implication of living in harmony with the animal
realm. In like manner in contemporaneous Hebrew legend, humanity lived
a period of primal innocence, during which the arts were unknown and
unnecessary, the flesh of animals was not consumed, and humans and animals lived in peace and harmony. It was only later that humans "began to

sin against birds and beasts and reptiles and fish, and to devour one another's flesh and to drink the blood."[22]

In the sixth century, Boethius took up the theme in *The Consolation of Philosophy:*

> O happy was that long lost age
> Content with nature's faithful fruits
> Which knew not slothful luxury.
> They would not eat before due time
> Their meal of acorns quickly found.[23]

In Geoffrey Chaucer's *The Former Age,* a poem he is believed to have written while working on a translation from Boethius's Latin, we find Boethius's points reiterated. Chaucer wrote of an age when there was neither cultivation, nor trade, nor cooking; neither industry, nor war, nor self-indulgence. In the *Tempest,* Shakespeare has Gonzalo (2) offer the popular "back to nature" message as the ideal form of governance. For Gonzalo, civilization implied oppression; and "innocence" included respect for nature by refraining from the killing of animals.

It was following the "discovery" of the Americas that the theme gained immediate political significance. Now the "ideal-type" with which civilization was to be contrasted was not a dubious aspect of an unrecoverable past but the real experience of an identifiable people.

While it was the Spanish missionary Bartolomé de las Casas who represented the interests of the mistreated and maligned American Indians before the Spanish crown, and who described their culture sympathetically in some detail in his writings, it was humanist historians such as Gonzalo Fernández de Oviedo and Peter Martyr (1) who described them in the most fulsome yet unilateral terms, following the initial (and rather less unilateral) idealization of the "noble savage" by Christopher Columbus himself. A part of that nobility involved a respect for animated nature.

In his *De Orbe Novo* ("On the New World"), which went through several editions between 1493 and 1530, Peter Martyr concluded that "these islanders of Hispaniola" are happier even than those of the philosophers' Golden Age, "because they live naked, without weights or measures and, above all without the deadly money, in a true golden age, without slanderous judges or books, satisfied with goods of nature, and without worries for the future." It is the absence of private property that Peter Martyr singles out for special praise: "These natives hold the land in common ... do not know the words 'thine' and 'mine,' seeds of all evil. To such an extent are they satisfied with little, that in their country there is plenty of land and plenty of food for everyone."[24] It did not seem to occur to Martyr that if they did not hold spouses and children in common – which they did not, and which would have appalled him – they must have concepts of "mine" and "thine."

In fact, whether the Natives *really* had concepts of "mine" and "thine" was of little import. Those factors singled out for praise by the likes of Columbus, las Casas, and Martyr were simply the very antithesis of those undesirable characteristics they believed to predominate among their adversaries in their own civilization. The praiseworthy characteristics were those characteristics, indeed, which many Christians claimed to be the essence of primitive Christianity and which, they avowed, should remain its moral core. And these characteristics included a respect for animated nature.

Influenced by the writings of Martyr and Giralome Benzoni,[25] Michel de Montaigne went even further in his idealization of the American Natives and criticism of his compatriots. In his essay "Of Cannibals" (1580), he wrote of the "naturalness so pure and simple" of the Aboriginal peoples, "whose countries never saw one palsied, bleary-eyed, toothless, or bent with age ... [their] whole day is spent in dancing." Without tongue in cheek, Montaigne insists that "what we actually see in these nations surpasses not only all the pictures in which poets have idealized the golden age and all their inventions in imagining a happy state of man, but also the conceptions and very desires of philosophy."[26]

How seriously are we to take such Golden Age representations? Perhaps not too seriously. Montaigne acknowledges both the cannibalism and the broader carnivorousness of the Aboriginals whereas, in the classical Golden Age, a principled animal-respecting vegetarianism was the rule. The purpose of killing and eating fellow humans arose not out of any necessity but, according to Montaigne, was a ritual to seek "ultimate revenge."

In the classical version, humankind gathered the existing abundance of food, which they ate raw. Now, for sustenance, the Natives hunted with bows, killed animals, and cooked. Likewise, in the utopian past, humankind lived at peace both with each other and with other animals. Now, the Natives went to war with their neighbours. Indeed, Montaigne posits "resolution in war" as one of their primary virtues. In the primordial age of gold, humankind was supposedly compassionate. Now, if a soothsayer "fails to prophesy correctly, and if things turn out otherwise than he has predicted, he is cut into a thousand pieces if they catch him."[27] Clearly, the behaviour described does not fit the prior conception of a people which "surpasses ... the golden age ... And the very desires of philosophy." It is Arcadia, not Eden, that is posited.

Why, then, are the Natives so promoted? It is surely not to suggest that they live in reality an utopian existence – after all, Montaigne describes what he sees as their vices as well as their virtues – but to suggest there are certain respects in which their culture is superior to Western civilization, and some respects inferior. The West can learn from them, but not become like them. Certainly, neither Martyr nor Montaigne determined to live the Native life themselves. In fact, having eulogized the perfection of the

Aboriginals, Montaigne tells us incongruously: "I am not sorry that we notice the barbarous horrors of [their] acts, but I am heartily sorry that, judging their faults rightly, we should be so blind to our own."[28] The point then is not to praise the Aboriginals because they are wholly admirable but rather to employ them as a convenient means of criticizing the excesses and injustices of one's own society – its greed, its luxury, and its arrogance. The Aboriginals were being treated unjustly by their Western conquerors and, to demonstrate they are not inferior beings for whom such treatment may be deemed justifiable, their virtues are greatly exaggerated.

Courtesy of the Dean of St. Patrick's, Jonathan Swift, Lemuel Gulliver visited the Brobdingnagians, Lilliputians, Laputans, and Houyhnhnms – peoples with virtues unmatched in Western civilization. Swift created "ideal types" with which to chastise his compatriots. Because he is writing fiction, Swift has the licence to make his characters whatever suits his purpose. Montaigne has no such luxury. Because he is dealing with a real culture, Montaigne faces constraints Swift could readily ignore. Montaigne's purpose is indeed akin to that of Swift, but he has a more difficult time of it. His ideological intent persuades him to exaggerate the virtues of the Natives. His intellectual honesty dissuades him from ignoring their vices. The result is that the evidence and the judgments are at odds. Yet, like Swift, Montaigne has persuaded us that the West is far from as good as its myopic admirers imagine. In addition, he has argued convincingly that the Aboriginals are not the blighted fools some in their naivety have imagined them. It was a case that needed to be made and emphasized. Two centuries later even, a number of the otherwise enlightened had failed to heed the lesson. Thus the democrat Rousseau thought "neither the Negroes nor the Laplanders have the sense of the Europeans"[29] and the feminist Mary Wollstonecraft deemed Natives to inhabit "the night of sensual ignorance."[30]

We would be unwise to imagine the "return to nature" theme, the idea of living in harmony with other species, merely peripheral in Western literature. Two nineteenth-century books carry precisely that title – one by John Frank Newton in the early years of the century, and one by Adolf Just toward its end. Two French fiction versions of the theme were especially popular. Fénelon's *Télémaque* of 1699 immediately went into more than twenty editions. Bernardin de Saint Pierre's *Paul et Virginie* of 1788 was reprinted some 150 times.[31] Perhaps the best known variants on the topic are Daniel Defoe's *Robinson Crusoe* (1719) and Rousseau's *Discourse on the Origin and Foundation of Inequality among Men* (1755). A careful reading of Rousseau will, however, as Arthur O. Lovejoy demonstrated more than seventy years ago,[32] lead us to a recognition that his "primitivism" is not what it appears on the surface. The further reality is that the ambivalence is present throughout the literature; at least it was until the beginnings of the nineteenth century.

Following the argument of both Peter Martyr and Michel de Montaigne that people are happier without books – while, of course, they both continued to read and write them – Rousseau states in the *Discourse on Inequality:* "I venture to affirm that the state of reflection is contrary to nature and that the man who meditates is a depraved animal."[33] In *Emile,* Rousseau denies explicitly the value of book-learning for his eponymous hero. Yet in direct and immediate contradiction of his admonition, he introduces *Robinson Crusoe* as, in Allan Bloom's words, "a kind of Bible of the new science of nature [that] reveal's man's true original condition."[34] In fact, *Robinson Crusoe* tells us almost nothing about the "true original condition," or, indeed, about contemporary Aboriginals – other than of their ritual cannibalism. Defoe describes the Brazilian Natives as "wretched creatures ... the most brutish and barbarous savages."[35] The lessons of *Robinson Crusoe* are not about life in the Aboriginal state of nature but about the life of Robinson Crusoe. In telling us that *Robinson Crusoe* reveals the true state of nature, Rousseau is acknowledging that his concerns are with the errors of civilization, not with Aboriginal life itself. The task is to remain as uncorrupted as possible in civil society.

To be sure, Crusoe tells us he "was reduced to a state of nature," but he had guns, ammunition, tools, clothing, bedding, a tent, pens, ink, paper, compasses, mathematical instruments, and a book or two.[36] Crusoe not only possessed some of the goods of civil society but also had a half a lifetime of experience of civil society, and a bookish education to boot. In Rousseau's view, it was Crusoe's good fortune to be deprived of the needless luxuries and polite excesses of civilization, to be freed from its greed, its competitiveness, and its lack of "authenticity." However much Rousseau and Defoe write of the "state of nature," what they are promoting is in fact civil society without its warts. The Aboriginals are merely a convenient peg on which to hang the argument. Indeed, neither Montaigne, nor Defoe, nor Rousseau had any experience of Aboriginal society. The "state of nature" was an abstract petard on which to hoist their self-satisfied adversaries.

The power of the state of nature argument was certainly felt in general in the Western tradition but in an astonishingly self-contradictory manner. Thus, for example, Dr. Samuel Johnson praised the altruism of the Golden Age in 1750, and in 1753 castigated the uncivilized life of the primitive savage.[37] If we are somewhat surprised to find James Boswell, Johnson's biographer, subscribing to return to nature "primitivism," we are astounded to find him later considering slavery beneficial to the slaves. Equally contradictory was the theme in eighteenth-century fiction. Explaining how she came to write her 1934 book *Primitivism and the Idea of Progress in English Popular Literature of the Eighteenth Century,* Lois Whitney tells us she was casually reading some novels of the period and was "astonished at the curious mixture of ideas [she] met there – theories of the superiority of primitive man" competing with theories of historical progress "all huddled together ... sometimes two antagonistic points of view in the same sentence." She remarks: "The primitivistic ideology bade men look for their model of excellence to the first stage of society before man had been corrupted by civilization, the idea of progress represented a point of view that looked forward to a possible perfection in the future. The primitivistic teaching, again, extolled simplicity, the faith in progress found its ideal in an increasing complexion. The former system of thought taught an ethics based on the natural affections, the latter system was based on an intellectualistic foundation."

Whitney refers to "ideas existing side by side which by all the rules of logic ought to have annihilated each other." Having presented some of the literary evidence, Whitney concludes: "That either group should ever have thought that they could look, Janus-like, in both directions at once, hold both their primitive simplicity and evolutionary diversity within the same system, cling to permanence and change at the same time, would seem to be an impossibility outside of a logician's nightmare. But popular thought has a hardy digestion and does not recoil from a diet of mutual incompatibilities that would send an epicure of fine philosophical distinction to his grave."[38] In fact, though, the contradictions are not restricted to popular literature. They are to be found in the philosophical prose of John Locke, William Godwin, and Jeremy Bentham (as well, of course, as we have so graphically seen, *chez* Rousseau),[39] and in the poetry of James Thomson and Alexander Pope.[40] The reality is that each of the antonyms – the simple and the complex; permanence and change; instinct and education; nature and reason; regress and progress – has much to offer. An equal reality in that they are inherently incompatible. We want both to live in harmony with nature and to control nature to improve the quality of life at the same time.

It is when we turn to the literature of respect for animated nature produced at the turn of the nineteenth century that we find the beginnings of that unilateral mode of thought which culminates in contemporary works that delight in the denunciation of the Western cultural tradition – those that depict Aboriginals as, in the words of Colin Turnbull, "infinitely wise"(3) and the West's role as nothing but, in the title of William Leiss's book, *The Domination of Nature*.[41] No longer do we encounter the Montaignes who find it necessary to introduce the evidence that counters their thesis. Balanced argument is replaced by a polemic. To be sure, the purpose of the polemic is wholly laudable – to persuade us of the worthiness of non-Western norms and to alert us to the dangers of certain Western practices. But this purpose does not justify the unidimensional and inherently misleading nature of the picture that is painted.

The nineteenth-century works to which I refer include John Oswald's *The Cry of Nature; or, an Appeal to Mercy and Justice, on Behalf of the Persecuted Animals* (1791), Thomas Young's *An Essay on Humanity to Animals* (1798), George Nicholson's *On the Primeval Diet of Man ... &c.&c.* (1801), and John

Frank Newton's *The Return to Nature* (1811). These works themselves, and the positive contemporary reviews they received (most notably in the *Gentleman's Magazine* and the *Monthly Review*) in all but the most reactionary of circles, reflect the continuing Western interest in the issue of animal protection.

Of these works, perhaps the most interesting is George Nicholson's compendium of the writings of those who have gone before him in the Western animated nature-oriented tradition – from Pythagoras, Porphyry, and Montaigne through James Thomson, Erasmus Darwin, and the Comte de Buffon to Gilbert White, Charles Bonnet, and some lesser contemporary authors. In similar vein to the message of the other, above-mentioned books, Nicholson postulates a hero who can do no wrong, and a villain who can do no right. His hero is the peaceful Hindu, his villain at first the treacherous Moslem, later the cruel Japanese, and always the arrogant European. He ignores, of course, the vast amount of evidence he himself offers – there is still no better compendium today – about those in the Western tradition who have shared his views. He also conveniently forgets, or is ignorant of the fact, that Hindus engage in animal sacrifice, and that only the Brahmin caste is vegetarian by principle. He conveniently forgets, too, that the Turks whom he compliments for their animal hospitals and the Arabians whom he commends for their kindness to horses are devout Moslems, and that many of the Japanese whom he condemns for their cruelty practise an ecologically sensitive Shintoism.

In like manner in his *An Essay on Abstinence from Animal Food*, Joseph Ritson – who reputedly persuaded both William Godwin and Percy Shelley to become vegetarians – treats the Hindu as his healthy, faultless, long-lived, ethical, vegetarian standard. Yet he concedes parenthetically toward the end of his book, and without allowing it to disturb the standard, that only a small proportion of Hindus are vegetarians by principle. For both Nicholson and Ritson, the Hindu reality was far less important than the convenience of having a standard. In several works of the era, it is the recently "discovered" Otaheite – the Tahitians – who replace the Amerindians as standard. Sympathetic yet more anthropologically sound studies of the Amerindians were now available. Joseph-Francois Lafitau's *Moeurs des sauvages ameriquains, comparés aux moeurs des premier temps* of 1724 was one of several works drawing attention to Amerindian bravery under torture from fellow Amerindians and to their courage in combat against their fellow Natives. Torture and war, especially when compared explicitly with human behaviour in the supposedly peaceful state of nature, could not be considered a part of any utopia, however brave its people. Perhaps Montaigne could get away with his exaggerated eulogy when so little was known. Now the reality was better publicized. How much better it now was to employ the Otaheite – cannibals and general carnivores, too, incidentally – or, to a lesser degree, the Hindus, about whose cultures most were still ignorant.

The greatest difficulty in employing any particular culture as the moral standard against which to measure the failings of one's own society is that, to make one's point effectively, one is constrained to idealize the standard – whether it is the Amerindians, the Otaheite, or the Hindus who constitute the standard. The reality of life in the standard becomes secondary. Indeed, it becomes a hindrance to the point one wishes to make. The reality then comes to be ignored and replaced by the utopic imagination.

Nicholson's *Primeval Diet* and Ritson's *Abstinence from Animal Food* are both delightful books, as indeed are those of Oswald and Young. They are delightful as rhetoric and moral suasion. But as anthropology and logic, they leave much to be desired. They seek to persuade not to a knowledge of empirical truth but to a particular course of thought and action.

This practice certainly does not begin with Nicholson and Ritson. Nor does it disappear after them. Indeed, the practice of restructuring the described tradition to fit one's ideological convenience has been a commonplace. And not merely in the peripheral and readily dismissed material. In fact, it has pervaded the most influential and highly praised writings.

Chief Seattle's famous ecology speech is of special interest. Its history demonstrates beyond reasonable doubt that Western interpretations of Aboriginal ecology have been more concerned with providing a standard with which to execrate the West than with any reality of Aboriginal norms. There is no better known, more frequently repeated and cited statement of the Aboriginal view of the relationship of humanity to the environment. But what does the statement owe to Chief Seattle or the Aboriginal tradition? Certainly, it is a great deal less than is commonly assumed.

The German scholar Rudolf Kaiser[42] has demonstrated that there are major discrepancies between anything the chief may have said – and we have no compelling evidence of what that may have been – and what is today reported as Chief Seattle's profound pronouncement. Chief Seattle almost certainly made an environmentalist speech of a kind, somewhere on or near the west coast of the United States sometime between 1853 and 1855. We cannot be more precise than that. A Dr. Henry Smith witnessed the oration and it is said he made copious notes on it. However, Smith probably did not understand Seattle's native tongue. Presumably his notes were a derivative rendering. Smith did not write up the speech from the notes probably based on a translation until more than thirty years after the speech was delivered. Indeed, he no longer knew in what year it had been delivered. It was published in the Seattle *Sunday Star* in 1887.

Given that the article was rendered from notes, which were probably based on a translation of a translation (Chief Seattle's native Lushotseed language was probably first translated into Chinook, then English), that more than three decades had elapsed before the notes were revisited, and that the whole was written to impress an American audience, we may have some doubts about the faithfulness of the 1887 article to the 1850s original.

Yet even if the article were Chief Seattle's words verbatim, what we are now offered as Chief Seattle is emphatically not Chief Seattle. Moreover, if the subsequent history of the article reflects anything of the preparation of Smith's article, we would have grounds for doubting its authenticity too. When the speech was republished in the *Washington Historical Quarterly* in 1931, a few mysterious new ecologically impressive sentences were added without any acknowledgment or justification. In the 1960s and 1970s, the piece underwent several further "refinements," each a rephrasing to meet a changing environmentalist emphasis. Whatever the latest orientation, by a few deft strokes Chief Seattle was presented as its embodiment.

The piece most frequently cited today as the speech of Chief Seattle is a fictional re-interpretation written in 1970 by an American university instructor and screenwriter. The piece was written as an elaboration of Seattle's theme with no intent to misrepresent. Nonetheless, what is now reiterated time and again as Chief Seattle is 1970s Western environmentalism.

The most famous phrase, quoted and requoted as the essence of the Aboriginal tradition as expressed by Chief Seattle, is that "all things are connected." Nowhere does any such statement appear in Dr. Smith's version, never mind the original speech. Indeed, the claim that "everything in nature is linked together" is to be found not in Seattle. Instead, I find it in the section on "Cosmologie" in d'Alambert's great *Encyclopédie* of 1772. So too Cézanne: "Everything is connected ... Nature isn't at the surface. It's in depth." As we have already seen, the view that "all share the same breath" is also to be found in Ecclesiastes (Introduction, 4). It is absent from Dr. Henry Smith's version of Seattle but present in most recent renderings. Given this, and given the continued Western re-interpretation of a Western interpretation of an Aboriginal speech, would it not be in line with the evidence to recognize what is now published as Chief Seattle's ecology speech to be at least as much a statement of Western as Aboriginal views?

Perhaps the second best known statement of the Aboriginal ecological worldview is that presented as the opinion of Black Elk, a Sioux elder, whose experiences ran from the period of the "Indian wars" through to late industrialism. *Black Elk Speaks*[43] was written by the American poet laureate John Neihardt after lengthy conversations with the Sioux "medicine man." Yet A. Kehoe in *The Ghost Dance*[44] has argued compellingly that Neihardt gives us a far more pristine, utopianly ecological Black Elk than he was, or would indeed have presented himself as. If in the representations of Aboriginal attitudes and beliefs what we are offered often does not conform to the ascertainable reality, we can only conclude that the portrayers of the Aboriginal position are less interested in the reality of the tradition than in presenting us with a model against which to measure Western iniquities. Moreover, as often as not, Western *practices* are measured not against Aboriginal *practices* but against Aboriginal *ideals* with regard to the status of other species. Wilfully or not, we are being asked to compare apples and orangutans.

It would appear that at least in the most popular, persuasive, and enlightened statements of the Aboriginal position what we are offered is a less than faithful representation of that position. Indeed, little effort is made to be faithful to that position. The Aboriginals are not seen as they are, in all their subtleties and complexities, their contrarieties and their tensions, their yearnings and their self-doubts, their virtues and their vices, indeed in their humanity. They are reduced to a symbol, coerced into the conceptual boxes designed for them by an engagé branch of the Western intelligentsia.

And if, unlike their forefathers, some modern Aboriginals proclaim their deep-seated environmentally pure tradition, it is either because they have been convinced by Western intellectuals that it must be so, or because they perceive wisely that there is much to be gained politically and financially by broadcasting their ecological virtue – while casting a knowing wink toward each other.

It would not have been difficult for those who portrayed the Aboriginal or Hindu or Taoist or Buddhist traditions in utopian terms to have found equally worthy candidates in the West. Indeed, Gandhi acknowledged how much he derived from the primitivist animal-respecting writings of Tolstoy, how impressed he was by the naturalist message of Edward Carpenter's *Civilization: Its Cause and Cure,* how he was inspired by G.K. Chesterton's part in the resurrection of the medieval moral tradition. He wrote that "Ruskin's *Unto this Last* captured me and made me transform my life." Gandhi's primitivism had decidedly Western as well as Eastern roots. Robert Southey and S.T. Coleridge advanced "primitivist" ideals in their plans for a pantisocracy settlement on the banks of the Susquehanna. Margaret Fuller and Nathaniel Hawthorne expressed similar revulsion at the excesses of an industrializing civilization in their involvement with the Brook Farm utopian experiment. In *The House of Seven Gables,* Hawthorne pursued the "peaceable kingdom" theme in which his paradise is adorned with robins in a pear tree, a chanticleer with his hens, and "a bower in Eden, blossoming with the earliest roses God ever made." In Russia, "back to nature" discussions were frequent in the Petrashevsky circle and the Beketov circle. It was a favourite theme of Dostoevsky, present both in *Notes from Underground* and in the preparation of "Socialism and Christianity" – "The disintegration of the masses into personalities, or civilization, is a diseased state." In France, it is to be found in Gustave Flaubert's *Madame Bovary* as well as among the Fourierists. In Germany, in the writing of Fichte, Schiller, and von Schelling. And theosophy flourished everywhere. In all these writings, the virtue of the primitives' attitude toward nature and animals is emphasized.

In the Western political tradition, it has long been considered, in the words of Lord Randolph Churchill, "the duty of an opposition to oppose." The merit of the government's case is decidedly secondary. Likewise, among the advocacy intellectuals the duty of the critic is to criticize, of the academic to be a representative of the oppressed. Truth is not only the first casualty of war and politics. It is the first casualty of advocacy intellectualism.

This derogation of the Western tradition through the elevation of others without adequate evidence has a long tradition that has not failed to arouse the ire of some. Thus, in an article in *The Craftsman* (28 June 1735), Henry Fielding criticized self-important travellers who returned "home with an idle Contempt of the Manners and Customs of their *own Country.*" In the operetta *The Mikado* of 1885, W.S. Gilbert bemoaned:

> the idiot who praises with
> > enthusiastic tone,
> all centuries but this and every
> > country but his own.

Gilbert and Sullivan's patriotic audiences would have nodded sagacious approval. A sizeable portion of today's social scientists and, indeed, intellectuals in general would disavow Gilbert. For example, to cite a recent book by George Wenzel on the Inuit and animal rights, the Inuit are described as "an ecologically balanced culture." The values of those who suggested Inuit practices harmful to the environment are considered to be expressive of their "own cultural prejudices."[45] The question of whether the Inuit may have their own cultural prejudices is settled by never being raised. The answer is merely assumed. Wenzel, in fact, employs prejudice to combat what he perceives as the prejudice of others.

We read in another recent work on Canadian Native cultures by Alan D. McMillan that early ethnohistorians could not "be totally objective about practices they were attempting to eradicate."[46] Why? For no other reason apparently than the fact that they had a political agenda, a desire to change existing practices. Their goals, McMillan asserts, must perforce hinder their objectivity.

But why should that rule apply only to those who differ from oneself? McMillan welcomes intercession by modern anthropologists on behalf of Amerindian land claims. He does not appear to realize that if early ethnohistorians must have been prejudiced because of their goals, the same relativist thesis must apply pari passu to modern advocacy anthropologists. By analogy, if the relativist thesis has any value, modern advocacy anthropologists too cannot "be totally objective about practices they are attempting to eradicate." One could repeat the story ad nauseam by referring to much of the recent literature on Aboriginal society that is prejudiced in favour of the Aboriginals – as much as the writings of Darwin and nineteenth- and earlier twentieth-century anthropologists are prejudiced against them.

The current cultural self-denigration among Western intellectuals arises from the most laudatory of motives. The desire is as old as morality itself: to side with the oppressed, to resurrect the image of those unjustly maligned, to cock a snook at traditional Western conceits, to redress a historical imbalance – in short, to right a wrong – "advocacy anthropology" George Wenzel calls it, unwittingly conceding a greater concern for representation than intellectual impartiality, an attempt at which is an absolute necessity for all sound thought. One is reminded of the Maid of Orléans in G.B. Shaw's *Joan of Arc:* "The voices come first, and I find the reasons after." One must be forever wary of advocates for, on their own acknowledgment, they seek to represent their clients. Truth is at best a secondary consideration. It is sought only to the extent that it serves the client's needs. When it does not, it is ignored. "Sane hallucination," G.B. Shaw terms it. Undue reverence for the historically maligned has thus replaced an undue reverence for the purveyors of "progress." There would appear to be a – largely justified – deep-seated cultural guilt that hinders us from recognizing the cultural reality of those we have historically oppressed. Accordingly, there would appear to be less interest in finding the truth than in proclaiming it. Wenzel and McMillan are not aberrations but represent a dominant strain in Western intellectualism – a strain that in turn many other anthropologists seek to counter.[47]

One must have sympathy for such advocacy critics, for they are reacting against a traditional Western arrogance and self-proclaimed superiority – which in fact has in recent decades all but disappeared from Western intellectual writing – but they are responding to it with a no less objectionable prejudice of their own. The most striking and oft-repeated of these claims is that Amerindians contracted syphilis from the white man, a disease hitherto unknown among the Aboriginals. Not only is this claim unlikely but in all medical probability Europeans contracted syphilis from the Amerindians during Columbus's voyages of discovery.[48] Certainly, Europeans believed they did, for, until Paracelsus proclaimed its dangers in 1529, a poisonous dose of mercury and guaiacum was prescribed for the illness. Guaiacum was a drug derived from a New World hardwood tree – a New World drug intended by God, it was thought, to counter a New World malady.[49]

In whichever direction the disease travelled, however, it should not be regarded as an indication of the superiority of either culture. Unfortunately, it is often used as a means of criticizing Western civilization – as often as not by Western intellectuals – but reflects more of a desire to be on the side of the oppressed than it reflects any desire to discern justice or respect truth.

It is a horrifying fact that many Amerindians, especially from sedentary or semi-sedentary tribes, suffered serious illnesses and often death as a consequence of contact with Europeans. But we should not judge that fact as it is sometimes presented – in David Maybury-Lewis's *Millennium: Tribal Wisdom and the Modern World* and in Ann F. Ramenofsky's "The Spread of Infectious Diseases,"[50] for example – as though that outcome were a necessary consequence of nefarious colonialism or a mysterious reflection of European iniquity. It was instead a deplorable yet crimeless consequence of the presence of microbes to which immunities had not been built. In fact, to everyone's dismay, the problem still occurs. Since the previously isolated Yaminahua of Peru established contact with whites in the 1980s, the population has been reduced by 50 percent due to disease.

Ramenofsky's thesis is that the idea of the "survival of the fittest" is inadequate as an explanation of the success of European colonialism. "In the late twentieth century, such a simplistic account of the speed and success of European culture is neither accepted nor acceptable." Indeed, who would have believed otherwise? Who in the last quarter century has suggested otherwise? Surely, the purpose of Ramenofsky's thesis can only be to provide an occasion to launch into ideological invective. In writing in terms of *"predator* cells" and *"victims,"* in telling us that "Europeans *introduced* numerous infectious parasites," that "mass death has occurred throughout human history and prehistory whenever Europeans carried a foreign infectious parasite to a population that represented virgin soil,"[51] she writes emotively rather than descriptively, as though the infections were culpably inflicted, as though only Europeans, and no Africans or Asians or Amerindians or South Sea Islanders set off on voyages of discovery and settlement, and as though the infections were all one-sided.

Surely, the Europeans are no more "guilty" of carrying diseases to the places they "discovered" than are modern anthropologists for the appalling deaths of the Peruvian Yaminahua with whom they came into contact. It is an unfortunate fact that many analysts are now more concerned with ideological advocacy than with the discovery of truth. It is difficult enough to discern truth when we seek it with all the strength we can muster. When we are concerned to make a case for those we view as having been oppressed, we can be confident that a very one-sided picture will be painted. In the words of Jerry Melford in Tobias Smollett's epistolary *The Expedition of Humphry Clinker* (1771), "Without all doubt, the fumes of faction not only disturb the faculty of reason, but also pervert the organs of sense." Through advocacy, we become rationalizers, not only in our judgments but in what we imagine we witness. What matters should not be self-criticism or cultural revenge, as Western historical shortsightedness becomes increasingly apparent, but rather a concern to weave through the maze toward truth and understanding rather than victory or defeat.

Western intellectual society constantly condemns its own "possessive individualism," its own materialism, without acknowledging an earlier and equally persuasive version in the Chinese *I Ching:* "Great possession means great success."[52] Truthfulness requires that we acknowledge both. Indeed, many hundreds of years ago, Taoist sages were already finding the structured life of urban China incompatible with their search for fulfilment. East and West are not as different as our desire for intellectual novelty and mysterious heroes is wont to imagine.

As the West comes to a greater awareness of the destruction its attempted mastery of nature has wrought, solutions are not achieved but hindered by merely acquiescing in avenues suggested by Western misrepresentations of Oriental and Aboriginal realities. And in the cultural revenge of the oppressed, they are unable to recognize their own errors or Western successes and we in our guilt are unwilling to point to their failings or our own achievements.

The contradictory nature of the rejection of Western culture must be apparent, for those who reject it will often desire its fruits. Frequently, they stake their claims to the wealth derived from its technology but fail to understand that the wealth and the technology are the very foundations of the culture they reject. The spoils of capitalism and the spirit of capitalism are interdependent. We simply cannot acquire the benefits of Western technology – including broad higher secular education and an effective health system – without becoming immersed in the values of Western culture. Of course, Aboriginal holistic medicine has much to commend it. But it cannot deal effectively with physical disease and injury.

There is a curious but not surprising analogy between our attitude toward other cultures and our attitude toward other species. At one time, the West – or at least a substantial portion of it – saw itself as possessing a level of achievement beyond the capacity of other cultures to emulate. We were, some imagined, inherently more intelligent, more sophisticated, more capable, more cultured, more moral. This view began to change in the second half of the nineteenth century (following some perspectives of earlier vintage), much to the chagrin of some. Thus, for example, Charles Darwin claimed to have written in some detail "on the immorality of savages because some authors have recently taken a high view of their moral nature, or have attributed most of their crimes to mistaken benevolence."[53] Eventually, we recognized the capacities of others and came to acknowledge other races and cultures as our equals. We came, too, to recognize certain attributes of Western culture as less than wholesome, as indeed some long had, that our "progress" had entailed a certain amount of regress, and that societies we had once disparaged possessed characteristics we might be wise to adopt. Now, in our self-criticism, we have come to idealize other cultures and to treat them quite uncritically. We have striven to overcome the arrogance of our former sense of superiority but have acquired no greater objectivity.

Similarly, some in the Western tradition regarded themselves as the natural masters of all other species. Over time, many came to recognize that, as Honoré de Balzac expressed it in his 1845 Introduction to the *Comédie humaine* in what he called the "theory of synthetic unity": "There is but one animal. The Creator used one and the same principle for all organized beings."[54] In other words, humans and other species were sufficiently similar that humans owed a moral responsibility. Soon to follow was the theory of evolution by natural selection, which drew humans and other species ever closer together and showed them to be ever more alike.

Eventually, the view that humans and other species differed by degree rather than in kind came to receive general intellectual acknowledgment. But that was then surpassed by the claim that "All Animals Are Equal," a claim made not merely by the revolutionaries-in-waiting of George Orwell's *Animal Farm* but as the title of the first chapter of Peter Singer's *Animal Liberation,* the book that called the faithful together to overcome the proclaimed Western tradition of oppression. Singer has a good moral case to make, but with regard to any "equality," objectivity seems to have lost out to advocacy once again. We are left confused when "equality" is depicted as "equal consideration" rather than "equal treatment." It is, for Singer, sentience that is at issue, but because some species are clearly more sentient than others, equal consideration will lead to significantly different treatment – which is in no meaningful sense any equality at all. "Equality" is used by animal liberationist philosophers more to arouse than to describe. There appears to be a greater desire to be on the side of the underdog – in matters of both comparative culture and animal welfare – than to care about evidence, argument, and ultimately truth.

As an aspect of our recent sensitivity to those societies we once deemed "primitive," we have come to recognize that in abandoning our original character we have lost something of our essential and worthwhile character. But let us not imagine that what we have acquired in its place is without merit. Let us not imagine that we began human history totally at one with nature and became its unregenerate exploiters. History is far more complex than that.

We have acquired science and technology, which have diminished disease and poverty, but at the expense of imagination, reverence, mystery, and romance; individual self-fulfilment but at the expense of communal integration; abstract reason and greatly increased education, but at the expense of the primal emotions of loyalty, courage, and self-sacrifice. We now more readily fulfil our wants and our tastes but at the expense of our needs. Yet the fact that we recognize what we have lost and regret the passing itself indicates that we know what must be revitalized, that our primordial nature still exists within us, however obscured. The skill we must acquire lies not in abandoning the new for the old, or in entertaining a vain attempt to have all of both, for they are inherently incompatible. Nor would we want to lose the health, longevity, and education offered by modernity. We cannot, anyway, wilfully unlearn what we have learned – as individuals, as cultures, or as a species. The art of civilization lies in a balance between the centrifugal forces. It is the art of balancing competing and inconsistent but equally admirable characteristics. Today, the most important aspect of that balance lies in finding an accommodation with the natural environment. And that, I believe, is most readily accomplished by understanding human history, its errors, *and* its achievements. It requires that we view the non-Western world with the same critical stance we take to the West. It is as inappropriate to rely on Western representations of Oriental and Aboriginal traditions as it would be to rely on earlier Western rationalizations. To understand Oriental, Aboriginal, and Occidental attitudes to animals, it is imperative that we recognize and overcome contemporary anti-Western prejudice in anthropological and environmental thought.

It should not be thought that this book stands as an apology for the age of technology or as a monument to the triumphs of Western civilization. It is instead an attempt to offer a perspective somewhat different from the increasingly customary one. It is written to redress an imbalance that is itself the consequence of redressing a previous imbalance. It is intended as a synthesis to the thesis of primitiveness and the antithesis of civilization.

But before we discuss that synthesis in the concluding chapter and the details of the realities of the Aboriginal and Oriental realms in the penultimate chapter, we will turn our attention to what it is about the West that has aroused so much antipathy and to the realities of the historical continuity of the Western tradition in relation to animated nature.

2
Beastliness and Brutality

1   When he is best, he is a little worse than a man; and when he is worst, he is little better than a beast.

    – Shakespeare, *The Merchant of Venice* 1.2, c. 1596

2   No arts; no letters; no society; and which is worst of all, continual fear and danger of violent death; and the life of man, solitary, poor, nasty, brutish and short.

    – Thomas Hobbes, *Leviathan,* 1, 13, 1651

3   It is a fact, then, that in the heart of every man there lies a wild beast which only waits for an opportunity to storm and rage, in its desire to inflict pain on others, or, if they stand in his way, to kill them ... It is the will to live, which, more and more embittered by the constant sufferings of existence, seeks to alienate its own torment by causing torment in others.

    – Arthur Schopenhauer, *Parerga and Paralipomena,* 1851

4   Upon the first goblet he read this inscription: monkey wine; upon the second: lion wine; upon the third: sheep wine; upon the fourth: swine wine. These four inscriptions expressed the four descending degrees of drunkeness: the first, that which enlivens;

the second, that which irritates; the third, that which stupefies; finally the last, that which brutalizes.

– Victor Hugo, *Les Misérables*, Bk. 6, Ch. 9, 1862

5   There are in every man, at every moment two simultaneous long-ings, one for God and the other for Satan. The invocation to God, or spirituality, is a wish to ascend; the invitation to Satan, or ani-mality, is a delight in degradation.

– Charles Baudelaire, *Mon coeur mis à nu*, 1868

I

Among Aboriginals, animals are good to think with. So stated the great French anthropologist Claude Lévi-Strauss. But it is not so only in Abori-ginal society. In Western civilization, we also think some of our thoughts through animal analogy – and not only in cartoons, significant though they may be from Mickey Mouse to the Lion King, and, on a different level, from Toad of Toad Hall to Winnie-the-Pooh. The tradition is exemplified in Richard Adams's *Watership Down* and the metaphor pervaded the private, and to some degree public, writings of the Bloomsbury group. Animal anal-ogy is a primary mode of discourse in several of Anton Chekhov's plays, notably *The Cherry Orchard*. It is common in the writings of John Keats, Charlotte Brontë, Ivan Turgenev, and Nikolai Gogol. In Gogol's *Dead Souls*, the animals play a significant actual as well as metaphorical role – horses and dogs foremost, but much else besides[1] – as, of course, do the rabbits in *Watership Down*. Generally speaking, those who employ animal analogy most widely also express the greatest respect for the animal realm.

Seven of D.H. Lawrence's novels have animal titles.[2] *Kangaroo* – a novel pri-marily about Australian politics – employs human-animal analogy not only through the kangaroo but also through white ants, great and domestic cats, wombats, asses, dogs, gannets, kites, mice, emus, scorpions, jackals, rats, ser-pents, frogs, birds, bullocks, and flying fish. A volume of Lawrence's poetry appeared as *Beasts, Birds and Flowers*, which are indeed its subject matter. Nor should we deem the extraordinary extent of animal metaphor in *Kangaroo* without parallel. There is an even more extensive usage in Victor Hugo's *Notre-Dame of Paris* (1831) – from sparrows and herons through flies, spiders, cats, dogs, horses, wild boars, elephants, crocodiles, and much more. If there is a hero to the tale, other than La Esmeralda and Quasimodo, it is probably Djali, Esmeralda's white goat, which was tried for attempted murder before the Ecclesiastical Court, a case not without historical parallel in medieval France where, in one instance, a sow was prosecuted and deemed criminally responsible for its actions (which irony might venture as tantamount to recognizing animals on a par with humans!). For Hugo, metaphorical animal usage was self-conscious. In *Les Misérables,* he tells us, in distinctly Aboriginal manner, that "God displays [animals] to us to give us food for thought" – and that was decades before Levi-Strauss's pronouncement.

Nor is it merely in literature that we think our thoughts through animals. In common parlance, we talk of measuring distance "as the crow flies," and of travelling "at a snail's pace"; we have dubbed a semi-precious stone "tiger-eye"; we describe human features in such terms as "pigeon-toed" and "crow's feet lines"; and we acknowledge immediacy "in two shakes of a lamb's tail." We "walk in a beeline" and suffer "like a bear with a sore paw." We "badger," we "ferret," and we "duck." Summer has its "dog days" and some "live high off the hog." Of course, animals are not the only trope. But they are the most common and significant.

We also use terms like "animal," "beast," and "brute" to elevate the conception of the human and to demean the non-human realm. To say of someone that "he behaved like an animal" is to deride that person's behaviour as unbecoming of a human, as fit only for a "lower being" – even though we will be aware that the behaviour complained of would not usually be found among such "lower beings"! Goethe was the first to formulate the proposition that animals are individual ends in themselves (see epigraph). He also wrote home from university that he had been "drunk as a beast." We can be confident he did not imagine non-human species customarily inebriate. The vegetarian Leonardo da Vinci, who purchased caged birds to set them free, described the Battle of Anghiari as a most bestial folly – "una pazzia bestialissima." We can be confident he did not envisage nations of non-human animals in destructive combat. Despite the inappropriate uses of "beast" and "bestial," we may still recognize Goethe and Leonardo as early proponents of animal rights, as beings who possess entitlements. Clearly, their usage is paradoxical and requires an explanation.

As intimated by the five quotations with which we opened this chapter, it is not difficult to understand why the Western conception of other species has been deemed a negative one by so many scholars. In *The Merchant of Venice,* Portia describes the repulsive nephew of the Duke of Saxony in terms that elevate the worst of men over the best of animals (1). Schopenhauer describes the worst of the human disposition as "the wild beast" that inhabits all our hearts (3). Victor Hugo defines the degrees of drunkenness by a denigrating animal analogy (4) – even though, again, we know those animals do not consume alcohol. Baudelaire relates Satan to the lowest aspect of our being – our "animality" (5). Denigration indeed!

Despite this denigration, Shakespeare, Schopenhauer, Hugo, and Baudelaire all demonstrated elsewhere a deep sympathy for the animal realm. Schopenhauer, for example, wrote of our symbiotic relationship with animated nature and of the need for strenuous animal protection laws. In *Les fleurs du mal,* Baudelaire's poetry reflected his compassion for the captured albatross, the concern he felt for the swan deprived of water, and his affection for "the powerful gentle cats, pride of the house."

Already in his 1801 *Primeval Diet of Man,* George Nicholson was warning of the dangers of disrespectful language in literary and philosophical discourse. His admonitions went unheeded. But, as the otherwise respectful attitudes of Goethe, Leonardo, Schopenhauer, and Baudelaire suggest, the apparent disrespect may not be what it at first sight appears.

Of course, we should not imagine all who use disrespectful language to be somehow mysteriously and subliminally respectful. Hobbes (2), for example, deemed both human and non-human animals in a manner "brutish." Generally speaking, for Hobbes humans and non-humans shared a common animal nature: the pursuit of individual material self-interest (though there are inconsistencies in Hobbes's positions). Hobbes could be said to be disrespectful of humans and non-humans alike. For Hobbes, whatever appeared as an aspect of human spirituality was in fact no more than a subterfuge to disguise the expression of a material interest. Our rationality did not raise us above other animals, morally speaking. It provided us with a more effective means of determining how to achieve our "animal" ends.

There are also those who consider humans the pinnacle of nature owing no consideration for the interests of non-humans. While many subscribe to the first part of that proposition, I have been unable to locate any major thinker who has been willing to entertain the latter part. To be sure, in their writings, Passmore, Mason, Singer, White, and others, including Keith Thomas in his acclaimed *Man and the Natural World,* identify such thinkers: Aristotle, Augustine, Aquinas, and Descartes are among the more frequently cited offenders. But, as we shall see in later chapters, especially Chapter 6, such interpretations are clumsy. As always in matters of the human-animal relationship, we can be easily misled if we rely on the apparent implications of metaphorical or otherwise comparative language.

None of this is to suggest that disrespectful language does not matter, or that apparently disrespectful language is never "really" disrespectful. It is to suggest that the language employed needs a more careful analysis than it customarily receives.

That our language is, indeed, deeply demeaning of other species is not to be doubted. In vexation, we call a person who has annoyed us in some manner "a stupid ass," "a crazy coot," or simply "a worm." Men berate women as "dumb cows" or "ugly dogs." Women berate men as "lascivious beasts" or "filthy pigs." Indeed, one might have hoped that those sensitive to unfair treatment in general from the perspective of their own unfair treatment in particular might have found a less animal-denigrating obloquy than "male chauvinist pig."

In this and the following chapter, we will look at how we use language with respect to other species, at how we do not treat other species as all of a kind (that is, as equally "animal"), and at the implications of this usage for our understanding of non-human animals. Throughout known human history, animals have been, and remain, good to think with. This fact, more than any other, influences the way we conceptualize the animal but also produces a form of discourse that distorts the way we relate to the animal. When we are thinking through animals, the animal is a medium of thought, a tool, a vehicle, and is neither an autonomous being nor an end in itself. It sometimes serves as a standard against which to measure ourselves; it is often a metaphor. As standard, its own intrinsic characteristics are far less important than the symbol it can be made to represent. As metaphor or simile, the concern is to depict the character of that which is likened to the animal, not the animal itself. In such instances, the language *uses* the animal, but it is not *about* the animal. The animal is often no more than a character to facilitate the parable. Its characteristics are whatever is conducive to the tale, not what is explanatory of the animal. When language is directly *about* the animal, we will, by and large, find it far more considerate and respectful, if rarely considerate or respectful enough.

Of course, it can be well argued that if that usage, even though metaphorical or otherwise symbolic, contains universally negative images of the animal, then the Western understanding of other species must possess something of a negative element. And we do, as many commentators have correctly pointed out, deride animals by such phrases as "as cunning as a fox," "as evil as a snake," "as obstinate as an ox," "as ferocious as a wolf," "as slippery as an eel," and "as stubborn as a mule." Yet it is equally noteworthy – a fact that the Western denigrators steadfastly ignore – that we talk of "the loyalty of the dog," "the memory of the elephant," "the grace of the swan," "the courage of the lion," "the self-possession of the cat," and "the gentleness of the lamb." And if "chicken-livered" and "toady" are deplorably demeaning, they are more than matched by the dove as the symbol of peace and the owl as the symbol of wisdom; and by Shakespeare dubbed, by James Joyce among others, "the swan of Avon."

Moreover, we should not fail to recognize that other cultures have their negative conceptions of certain animals, too. In Islam and Hinduism as much as Judaism, some species are considered unclean. Among the Desana Amerindians of Amazonia, the scorpion, the poisonous black ant, the stingray, and the bat are held to be despicable creatures, the origin of whose antisocial behaviour is explained in the creation myths – not unlike the snake in the Bible. In Ecuador, Amerindian folklore has it that aged despised rats grow wings and become equally despised bats. It is not the West alone that derides the bat unjustifiably.[3] Certainly, in all cultures, the metaphorical role of the animal is a significant one, often a disturbing one, and sometimes difficult to interpret. We can be sure that all cultures need both positive and negative images of animals if their myths are to be told well, their metaphors to be meaningfully employed. In one of the Dakota myths, buffalo trample to death a human father attempting to rescue his daughter from captivity by the buffalo. The story's purpose is to explain the continuity of life after death. The buffalo is the villain to facilitate the telling of the story. There had to be a villain and animals are good to think with, so the villain might as well be a buffalo. No one should, or would, imagine the Dakota to be disrespectful of the buffalo because of its use as villain in the myth.

One is led to wonder why it is that when alcoholics hallucinate, it is snakes, spiders, beetles, and pink mice that scurry over the body while equally pink elephants dance on the ceiling. In Joseph Conrad's *Lord Jim,* when the apparently alcoholic chief engineer looks under the bed, it is "Millions of pink toads" he professes to see. Still, murmurs the attending physician, "Traditionally he ought to see snakes." The metaphorical can have some unpleasant practical consequences! The images occur as they do, it would appear, for no better reason than that animals are good – "useful" might here be a less misleading word – to think with. Animals are useful symbols to express our agonies through. Again, the animals contribute to the experience, but the experience is not about the animals. And that is so whether we are talking about Western hallucinatory toads or Amerindian mythological buffaloes.

It is a common error among those who decry the Western canon to imagine that the comparisons and distinctions made in Western society between humans and other species are implicitly or explicitly detrimental to other species. Both Lynn White, Jr., in his "The Historical Roots of our Ecologic Crisis" and Jim Mason in his *An Unnatural Order* mention a number of detrimental examples, and not a single positive one. And that is customary in the increasingly large body of literature that condemns the Western tradition.

Indeed, the message has become so widespread it has convinced many who, if they knew their own tradition better, would not have been so easily duped. Thus, again to take one of numerous examples, in his foreword to a new edition of Humphry Primatt's *The Duty of Mercy and the Sin of Cruelty to Brute Animals* of 1776, John Austin Barker, Bishop of Salisbury, tells us that "so far as animals are concerned, Christianity has on the whole the blackest record among religions."[4] Primatt was an Anglican clergyman and his book is treated as a welcome rare exception in the Christian tradition. In fact, a large body of writing from around the same time expresses the same message. Much of it is authored by members of the clergy and much by those not in orders but who proclaim a commitment to Christianity as well as a commitment to the well-being of non-human animals. Some of the writing, including some of the best, is by those who are unconvinced of the truth and goodness of Christianity. Those animal advocates committed to the Christian faith followed in the tradition of the saints Basil, Thecla, Isaac the Syrian, Neot, Bonaventure, Werburga, Colette, Benno, Anthony, Albertus Magnus, and Francis; and the devout if not formally saintly Leonardo, Albrecht Dürer, Thomas Tryon, Jakob Boehme, John Evelyn, Anne Finch, John Milton, William Blake, and many, many more. It is remarkable how the breadth and depth of concern for animal well-being have been downplayed.

Many of the finest scholars seem to have been persuaded by the myth of Western ogredom. Even the admirable Mary Midgley – normally a scholar of great care as well as insight – writes denigratingly of the time when people "thought of animals as incarnations of evil."[5] In reality, only *some* people thought *some* animals so on *some* occasions. In the thirteenth century, often noted as one of the worst epochs, some of the French thought of the cat in such terms; it was after all a witch's customary familiar, and just as the witch was feared, so was her familiar. Yet not all women were deemed witches and not all cats familiars. We note, in contrast to the occasional derision of the domestic cat, that around the same time *coeur de lion* (lion-hearted) was about the highest compliment one could bestow, even on a king. Indeed, the king of France was known as the lion and the king of England as lionhearted. In the medieval period, too, according to Norse legend, "Chief Hardrada, like a lion from his lair; / His the fearless soul to conquer, his the willing soul to dare."[6]

In Europe generally, but especially in the first half of the nineteenth century, the much maligned wolf received almost universal bad press. (There is a graphic instance in Dostoevsky's *Diary of a Writer.*) Yet in the same era, the eagle was revered (in Keats's *Endymion* and in the chapter on "Prison Animals" in Dostoevsky's *House of the Dead,* for example). Perhaps the eagle was no more deserving of its adulation than the wolf of its defamation. If some animals some times were indeed seen as "incarnations of evil" – wolves, rats, and snakes were always good candidates – other animals were seen equally on other occasions as incarnations of grace, courage, and power. Dolphins, horses, leopards, swans, eagles, and lions – "magnanimous Beast" Henry Fielding dubbed the species in *Joseph Andrews* – were among the favourites.

Often in the Western tradition the comparisons, analogies, and metaphors involve a deep respect, even an affection. And this respect and affection is ignored by most who comment adversely on Western norms. For example, T.H. Huxley praised his good friend Charles Darwin with the assertion that "there is a marvellous dumb sagacity about him like that of a sort of miraculous dog"[7] and C.G. Jung described his mother as possessing "a hearty animal warmth."[8] Charles Dickens addressed his fiancée, Catherine Hogarth, interchangeably and ever affectionately, as "My dearest life," "My dearest love," "dearest Pig," or simply "Mouse." (After several years of marriage, he called her "donkey" with rather less affection.) Robert Louis Stevenson called Fanny Osbourne "Most high and mighty American Eagle" and referred to himself as "the British lion." Virginia Woolf wrote to her cousin Emma Vaughan almost invariably and always lovingly as "Dearest Toad." Evelyn Waugh thought of his favourite daughter, Meg, as his "ewe-lamb," and, with no less affection, as "my pig." The Reverend Dr. Andrew Bell addressed Mary Wollstonecraft with kindliness as "dear antelope." Nathaniel Hawthorne proclaimed his beloved Sophie his "little

Dove" as did Dostoevsky call Anna Grigoryeva his "golubchik" ("little dove"). And the marine biologist Ed Ricketts named a woman he loved "wormy." Not surprisingly, the woman didn't like it. But Ricketts meant, according to John Steinbeck, that she was pretty, interesting, and desirable.

In Jon Winokur's compilation of quotations *The Portable Curmudgeon Redux,* there are unfavourable comparisons of humans with other species – unfavourable to humans, that is – in three of the five entries under "human race," four of seven under "man," and one of two under "mankind." Jonathan Swift made similar comparisons in *To Mr. Congreve, Gulliver's Travels, A Modest Proposal,* and *The Beasts' Confession,* in which last he claimed to do "a great honour to his own species almost equalling them to certain brutes." This comparison constituted, of course, Swift's revenge on overweening human pride. The same theme underlines Emile Zola's *La Bête humaine* (though his understanding of animal nature leaves a lot to be desired). The great art critic John Ruskin claimed that a "good, stout, self-commanding Animality is the make for poets and artists." If, on the whole, there is a duality of attitude in the Western canon, it is captured in Thomas Hardy's phrase in *Tess of the d'Urbervilles:* "The serpent hisses where the sweet birds sing." In like vein in Samuel Richardson's *Pamela* (1741), the eponymous heroine is described "as innocent as a dove, yet ... as cunning as a serpent."

Sometimes we are misled by apparent pejorative usage because, over time, the connotation of a word may have changed. Today, if we hear a reference to "a dumb animal," we may be confident the usage is derogatory, "dumb" having been employed as a synonym for "stupid." We may then infer mistakenly that the expression has always reflected disrespect for other species when in reality the very reverse has more often been the case.

In past usage, "dumb" was used to refer to the lack of human language and hence the inability of the animal to express its needs to humans. Sometimes this inability was seen as a positive attribute, as in Florence Nightingale's dictum: "Dumb beasts observe you so much more than talking beings." Sometimes it was the source of compassion, as in Thomas Hardy's poem "Last Words to a Dumb Friend." Hardy writes affectionately of his beloved companion: "This speechless thing, / subject to our mastering." Sometimes it was a stimulus to mirth, as in Evelyn Waugh's *Black Mischief* (1932), in which he refers sardonically to the animal welfare organization of the mythical Azania as "The League of Dumb Chums." Those familiar with Waugh's writings will know he thought animal protection important. Any scorn was directed at undue sentimentalism, not at the animals.

In fact, traditional animal advocates have used "dumb" at will without any disrespect. *Our Dumb Animals* was the name of a magazine first published by the Massachusetts SPCA in the 1870s. There was an "Our Dumb Friends League" founded in England in 1897. The Reverend Thomas Jackson wrote *Our Dumb Companions* and *Our Dumb Neighbours* in the mid-Victorian era. S.W. Partridge & Co., the publishers, described these books as "publications on kindness to animals." In the past, "dumb" was used not to denigrate but to express precisely the same message as that intended by both animal welfare and animal rights organizations today when they claim, to use the words of PETA (People for the Ethical Treatment of Animals), "to speak for those who cannot speak for themselves."[9]

Thomas Jackson intended his books to encourage youth to treat both wild and companion animals with "pity." Today, of course, "pity" is often used to suggest an attitude almost bordering on contempt. Again, we are likely to be misled by its usage. In the Victorian era, and for some time thereafter, "pity" was synonymous with "compassion." The novelist John Galsworthy deemed "pity" to be "a pearl in a diseased oyster"; it was humanity's saving grace. It enjoined an active concern for the well-being of others. If we read yesterday's language with today's meanings, we will derive a mistaken impression of the past's prevailing attitudes, as so many critical commentators have.[10]

Sometimes our language is inherently misleading. When, for example, we talk of "bestiality," the reference is to an act with a beast, not a quality of the beast. Indeed, as Plutarch opined in his essay "Beasts Are Rational," "Nor do animals force themselves sexually upon men as men do animals." Yet the customary subconscious conception of the term is one of acting without reasoned morality, that is, as we imagine a beast to act. And we use "brute" in a similarly disparaging manner. Incongruously, we may talk of someone being brutally stabbed, even though we know non-human animals do not use knives. By "brutally," we mean "viciously," that is, as we imagine some animals to act in some circumstances. The usage may be misleading as a generality – certainly neither cows nor butterflies would suit – but it does relate to a subconscious conception we possess of "the beast." Language does, after all, reflect both our own personal conceptions and values and our culture's conceptions, sometimes consciously, often subconsciously. Given such conceptions of "the beast" and "the brute," it is not surprising that many scholars have concluded that a negative conception of other species is inherent in the traditions of our language, and hence of our culture. Indeed, there is some truth in the claim, but left unanalyzed, the claim distorts more than it describes.

Initially, we might note that we are not alone in our negative usage. It is also present in that culture deemed the most positive in its estimation of animated nature: Hinduism. Thus, the widely differing Hindu sages Rabindranath Tagore and Mohandas Gandhi – the one the cherisher of beauty, the other the ascetic – used words in that way. The deeply compassionate Tagore referred in his poem *Arogya* to the "brutal night," a phrase as objectively misleading as "brutally stabbed." Nor was this a one-time aberration. He remarked that "when men turn beasts they sooner or later tear each other."[11] Clearly, it was the Bengal tiger and not the zebu, zebra, or gnu that Tagore conceptualized as the beast – and even then one would note that tigers do not normally "tear each other." Hindu usage does not appear very different from Western usage.

Sometimes words like "beast" and "brute" may be used descriptively and no more pejoratively than "dumb." Thus, for example, that eighteenth-century lyric friend of the animals, Oliver Goldsmith, wrote in his *History of Earth and Animated Nature* of "Ruminating Animals" that it is "neither their interest nor their pleasure to make war upon the rest of brute creation." He also composed the compelling plaintive words about carnivorous animal sympathizers: "They pity, and they eat the objects of their compassion." He did not consider other species as "brutes" in any demeaning manner. In like manner, there is nothing derogatory in Virginia Woolf's description of a cat she befriended as "a superb brute," or in D.H. Lawrence's reference to a fine dog as "a handsome brute." In "Hart-Leap Well," Wordsworth is full of praise and compassion for the stag hunted by a knight: "This Beast not unobserved by Nature fell; / His death was mourned by sympathy divine." And a forerunner of the RSPCA in Britain was the Society for the Prevention of Wanton Cruelty to Brute Animals (1809), which promoted what was sometimes inelegantly called "philobrutism" (the love of brutes) in that era.

Less descriptive was the usage of Michel de Montaigne who chastised humans for their conceit in imagining their own superiority over animal creation, yet who also wrote of human "brutal stupidity" and "brutish carelessness."[12] Given Montaigne's perspective, and indeed given that of Tagore, neither "brutal" nor "brutish" can be thought to refer to the essential nature of non-human animals. For Montaigne and Tagore, the usage must be in some manner metaphorical.

When we use "animal," "beast," or "brute" pejoratively rather than descriptively, we would appear to be using the words to convey certain characteristics present in some species and decidedly absent from others. If any one species embodies this negativity, it is the bowerbird. Its behaviour exemplifies our conception of the brute within.

Male satin bowerbirds build impressive bowers to attract females. They go to great lengths to adorn their bowers, even using perishable decorations such as flowers, which they replace daily. Some paint their bowers blue, black, or green, using crushed fruit, charcoal, or even laundry detergent as paint and a wad of bark as a brush. J. Diamond, however, writes of "the invariable sequel to successful mating: the male bowerbird savagely attacks the female, picks and claws her, and chases her from the bower. Mating itself is so violent that often the bower is partly wrecked, and the exhausted female can scarcely crawl away." It is not only with regard to sex that the satin bowerbird is so "brutish": "Bowers, like flags of possession, may serve as symbols of males' property rights in their wars with other males. An adult male spends much time repairing his own bower, protecting it from raids by rivals, and attempting to steal ornaments or destroy rivals' bowers."[13]

Diamond suggests that the rivalries "make the European Thirty Years' War seem straightforward by comparison."

Analogous behaviour in humans is a frequent theme of the novel and the cinema: man desires woman, he goes to elaborate lengths to get her, but once he has had his way with her, he becomes either indifferent or aggressive, even "brutal," and sometimes inflicts physical harm. (Daphne du Maurier's short stories and early novels exemplify the tradition.) The message, of course, is of the human potential to behave like the bowerbird, like the brute. If we do not so behave, it is civilization we have to thank: effective socialization, good family upbringing, "the love of a good woman" – as in Elizabeth Gaskell's *Mary Barton* (1848), in which John Barton, once widowed, relinquishes "the ties which bound him down to the gentle humanities." If we do so behave, so the story goes, we point to the thin veneer of civilization so readily penetrated. Describing the barbarity of the behaviour of "white Gaucho savages" of the South American pampas toward their Amerindian captives, Darwin deemed "the former a little superior in civilization, as they are inferior in every moral virtue." Even civilization, if it is shallow, cannot save us from our baser selves. Even sophisticated civilization is, as Havelock Ellis wrote, "a thin crust over a volcano of revolution." Animals, we tend to conceptualize, *though not believe,* are "brutes" by their intrinsic nature, but humans can, though often will not, rise above their "brutish" potential. The human-animal parallel was used extensively by Emile Zola, Honoré de Balzac, George Eliot, and Virginia Woolf in their novels to demonstrate the oneness of animality despite its significant diversity. The "bowerbird" character was only a part of that animality. Throughout his writings, Jonathan Swift employed the satiric theme of human-animal comparisons customarily to the animals' advantage but always with the purpose of demonstrating human failures to achieve their greater potential than that of instinctive animals. Few animals appeared in "bowerbird" guise. The animals were treated as complex wholes, their "brutality" being only a part of their species nature, and that brutality was most apparent in the human.

Of course, whether animal behaviour is as genetically programmed, as instinctive, as we sometimes imagine is a moot point. Even more moot is the depiction of the bowerbird as the quintessential "animal." By contrast, jackdaws, as so well depicted by Konrad Lorenz in *King Solomon's Ring,* are loving, caring, mutually supportive, faithful partners, whose mourning at the loss of a loved one can only arouse our deepest sympathies. Why, we must ask, is it the bowerbird that represents the "animal" archetype rather than the jackdaw? Or the pelican? Already in the sixteenth century, we can read in Sir John Hawkins's *Second Guinea Voyage* of "the Pellicane, which is faigned to be the lovingeste bird that is: which rather than her yong shoulde want, will spare her heart bloud out of her bellie, but for al this lovingness she is very deformed to beholde." At around the same time, Michel de Montaigne was asking of arrogant Man, "By what comparison from them to us doth he conclude the brutishness he ascribeth unto them?" The curious anomaly is that we tend to employ "animal" or "beast" or "brute" emotively and demeaningly but at the same time delight in, and acknowledge the reality of, Lorenz's depiction of the jackdaw, Hawkins's depiction of the pelican, and Montaigne's view of animal character.

It was the view of Havelock Ellis, the noted author of *The Psychology of Sex*, that "it has taken unknown millions of years to evolve Man, and to raise the human species above that helpless bondage to reproduction which marks the lower species." And, certainly, prima facie much of the behaviour of the bowerbird appears to support Ellis's claim. However, G. Borgia's findings of 207 copulations at 28 bowers in one season, ranging from zero to 33 in each bower, give us reason to reconsider.[14] Even the bowerbird may not be entirely "a brute." Certainly, many humans could boast a greater proficiency, at least over the least successful of the bowerbirds! Even 33 times in a season would not appear excessive. In fact, as with humans, the bowerbird spends more time in courtship than in sex – and courtship for both bowerbirds and humans encourages the finest of behaviour. Moreover, the violence of the bowerbird is so beyond the animal norm that it is distinguished by the bowerbird's Latin name of *violaceus*.

It would appear that we tend to use the terms "animal," "beast," and "brute," especially in their adjectival forms, not to describe or depict other species in general but to denote those aspects of the purported character of other species that are the least spiritual, compassionate, and altruistic. What we seem to have in mind is not animals per se but specific purported characteristics of *certain* animals, including humans. And, oddly, while we continue to use the terms in a negative way, we are nonetheless able to think in a positive manner about many species. For example, Virginia Woolf had a soft spot for marsupials in particular, and the animal realm in general, but she was not above using "animal state" to mean lower consciousness, describing herself in an ugly mood as "a crazy tempered Beast" and insulting her employer as a "longshanked reptile." What is clear is that commonly used words may eventually lose much of their descriptive content; their usage will become predominantly habitual. Atheists will frequently use the word "creature" (that is, created being) without any sense of inconsistency and intending to suggest no more than "animal." Few today, believers or otherwise, use "creature" as though it implied creation.

We require great care in understanding what the Western tradition – or, for that matter, any other tradition – has meant by "animal" and analogous words and what their import may be for understanding Western attitudes to the animal realm. Often, the purpose of the usage has been to create a standard against which to measure ourselves, either flatteringly, as, say, with Aquinas, or disparagingly, as, say, with Jonathan Swift. But just as the real characteristics of the Natives or the Hindus were unimportant to the likes of Montaigne, Nicholson, and Ritson in creating a standard against which to measure the West's iniquities, so too the real characteristics of animals have been less important than the very convenience of having a standard with which to congratulate or chastise human behaviour. The characteristics of the bowerbird rather than those of the jackdaw or the pelican serve as standard in such usage, not because we deem the bowerbird more truly representative of animal nature, but because it suits our metaphorical and otherwise symbolic convenience.

To describe a person as an *animal,* as beastly, or brutal, is less to suggest the possession of characteristics common to animals than the possession of characteristics inappropriate to humans. While negative conceptions of certain other species may have stimulated some such usage initially, it would be quite erroneous to imagine continued usage to relate in any manner at all to attitudes to other species. The users of such terms will almost always be concerned with the human. The animal analogy is a tool of convenience, not a comment on animals themselves. It bears considerable similarity to the employment of myths with animal characters. Whether Aboriginal, Oriental, or European myths, the animal characteristics depicted are intended to teach us about human foibles rather than animal nature. The animals are no more than a convenient vehicle for the telling of the moral tale. The owl may symbolize wisdom. But no one imagines the owl to be especially intelligent. In like manner, no one expects a koala, a zebra, an ox, or an emu, to be "brutal" or "beastly." They expect it of a hyena, a scorpion, or a snake.

There are frequent instances too, especially in fable, where animal behaviour is offered as an appropriate model for humans to copy – faithful birds, loyal dogs, courageous members of the great cat family are legion. But not in fable alone. In at least two instances in philosophy, "beasts" are offered as models to follow. Thus, in the first century, Philo-Judaeus offers the filial devotion of the storks as worthy of human emulation (*De decalago*). And Machiavelli claims in *The Prince:* "There are two methods of fighting, the one by law, the other by force: the first method is that of men, the second of beasts; but as the first method is often insufficient, one must have recourse to the second. It is therefore necessary for a prince to know well how to use both the beast and the man." For Machiavelli, there were occasions when wisdom required humans to don the garb of the beast: "One must ... be a fox to recognize traps, and a lion to frighten wolves."

To be sure, Machiavelli was writing not only against the pervasive trends of the Western philosophical tradition but more specifically, and provocatively, against the popularity of Cicero who had maintained the more traditional view: "In fine, to close up this discourse of justice, there are two ways or methods, whereby one man may injure or oppress another, the one is *fraud* and subtlety, the other open *force* and violence; the former of which is esteemed the part of a fox, and the latter of a lion; both of them certainly very unworthy of a reasonable creature, though fraud, I think, is the more odious of the two."[15]

In reality though, neither Cicero nor Machiavelli is writing about the characteristics of lions or foxes. That the fox symbolized cunning or fraud was a conception that bore only the vaguest resemblance to Reynardian reality. And in medieval folklore, the lion appeared somewhat in favourable light – as a merciful and just creature, a vigilant guardian who symbolized Christ – and other times quite unfavourably, as the representative of evil, the devil, or the antichrist. The mythical griffin, too, could appear in art as either a symbol of valour or a symbol of oppression and persecution. Lambs and doves would appear to be uniformly favourable symbols; snakes, rats, and scorpions, almost universally unfavourable.

Both those who stressed positive features and those who stressed negative features were little concerned with the realities of those species. Their primary concern was to promote, criticize, or correct some aspect of human behaviour. Indeed, the Cicero who associated fraud with the fox and violence with the lion was the same Cicero who, according to Pliny the Elder, spoke approvingly of the feeling of fellowship between the human race and the animals mistreated in the Roman circus. In similar paradoxical vein, John Keats in *Endymion* writes of "men slugs and human serpentry." Yet, within half a dozen lines, he is describing the nightingale as blessing "the world with benefits."

For most philosophers of history, "the bestial" was equated with the lack of civilization. Thus, for example, Giambattista Vico (1668-1744) claimed that "the Bestial Age" was the initial human historical stage, followed by the Age of Religion and the Gods, the Age of Heroes, the Age of the Peoples (the rule of law), before collapsing into chaos and becoming "bestial" again. "The beast," for Vico, is the human without the trappings of culture. While such usage may appear less than complimentary to the beasts, it would be unwarranted to jump to hasty conclusions. Not only did Biruté Galdikas name one of her beloved orangutans of Borneo "Beast," but she captures the essence of male orangutans in general in telling us: "In his eyes we see a precarious balance of ruthless strength and brutality on the one hand, and gentleness and serenity on the other. The eyes of the male orangutan remind us of the awkward combination of angel and beast that characterizes the human soul."[16] Clearly, for the animal-embracing Galdikas, as for most of us, the concept of "beast" is generally a negative one, but it does not equate to the descriptive use of "animal." Rather, it refers to certain behavioural characteristics found among many, if not all, complex species, including, and perhaps even especially, the human. Indeed, for Galdikas, "beast" is one of the characteristics of "the human soul," not that of the animal. In the preceding quotation from Galdikas, "brutality" is a specific characteristic of a particular orangutan matched by its gentleness. Each was a part of the orangutan whole. Had "brutality" referred to an *essential* animal quality, Galdikas's statement could only have confused. As is, it enlightens.

As must be clear, usage is in fact complex and inconsistent. Prima facie pejorative uses of "beast," "brute," and "animal" cannot, despite repeated attempts, be offered as convincing evidence that the Western conception of the non-human animal is preponderantly negative. Indeed, negative usage by any major thinker will invariably be found to be balanced by other irreconcilable examples. The particular emphasis is chosen on each occasion to facilitate the point to be made; it tells us very little about the author's attitude toward non-human species. Thus, in *The Merry Wives of Windsor*, Shakespeare's usage shows some sympathy: "O powerful Love, that in some respects makes a Beast a Man; in some others a Man a Beast." (5.5.5). But there was none in *Measure for Measure:* "Oh you beast, oh faithless Coward, oh dishonest wretch" (3.1.137). In *Julius Caesar,* he went the whole hog with "brutish beasts" (3.2.109) and in *Hamlet* he reiterated the Thomist (and then almost universal) view with "a beast that wants discourse of reason" (1.2.22). If we were to conclude that these examples reflected Shakespeare's lack of respect for the animal realm, we might consider it curious to find, in Reuben Halleck's classic *History of English Literature*, William Shakespeare offered as a profound respecter of animated nature, in contrast to Dryden and the Restoration poets, who "pay but little attention to the charms of nature." Indeed, Halleck expresses the view shared by almost all who read English verse that "poetry which affects a contempt for nature is lacking in an important element of greatness."[17] Wordsworth claimed for the poet the role of priest of nature. In regarding Shakespeare as the greatest of all poets, Halleck certainly believes him to possess a ready love of nature, and John Keats concluded, "How much more Shakespeare delights in dwelling upon the romantic and wildly natural than upon the monumental." Indeed, Shakespeare's assertion in *Troilus and Cressida* that "One touch of nature makes the whole world kin" may be taken as a signal part of Shakespeare's philosophy. He certainly possessed an unusual knowledge of nature in which he evidently delighted, being aware of the rarity that a barn owl may bring down a kestrel (*Macbeth* 2.3) and fully conversant with the lapwing's elaborate mating display (*Measure for Measure* 1.4). To be sure, a portion of the animal lore he relates reflects only the Aesop he studied in school, but there are some impressive additions. Moreover, he demonstrates a consistent sympathy for the hunted animal, especially in his early poem "Venus and Adonis." In fact, if we are to regard Shakespeare's writings as internally consistent, we must regard Shakespeare's use of "beast" as having little reference to estimations of animal nature in general but to aspects of behaviour shared by humans and certain other species alike.

Sometimes "beast" has been used to denigrate the human, as in Elinor Hoyt Wylie's "This man, this mongrel beast" in *Hymn to Earth* and in Thomas Percy's "A man is but a beast" in *Love Will Find Out the Way,* but even here "beast" is being used emotively rather than descriptively. Indeed, since the thirteenth century at least, "beast" has been used as a pseudonym for the antichrist and the devil.[18] And in the eighteenth century, the word was used to reflect perceived distinctions among humans. Thus Voltaire: "The common people is between man and beast." The *canaille* was, strictly speaking, not entirely human, so the *philosophes* thought, for the masses lacked the benefits of culture. Their immediate precursor, John Locke, held to the same view, fearing the "beasts" who constituted the majority.

In sum, while "beast" has descriptive content, meaning "animal, quadruped, ... bovine animal, animal for riding or driving,"[19] the word is often employed prima facie pejoratively and, of equal importance, quite misleadingly, as though different species were all of a piece and could be appropriately described generally in terms that, at most, could only be appropriately applied to a few. However, whatever the apparent linguistic implication may be, in fact "beast," "brute," and "animal" are customarily used emotively without more than the vaguest reference to non-human species. When we are offered instances of pejorative usage to demonstrate the iniquities of the Western tradition, we should recognize that what we are being offered is a far from complete picture. At such times, we may wish to recall that in Nathaniel Hawthorne's "The Artist of the Beautiful," there is conflict between the Beautiful and the Brute. It is the Beautiful and not the Brute that is represented by an animal: a butterfly. The Brute is a boy.

II

We have been exploring the emotive and metaphorical usage of animals predominantly in Western literary discourse, which has proven to be so easily misinterpreted. We might expect philosophical discourse to be more readily reflective of an objective reality. But again things are not always what they might appear at first blush.

Certainly, traditional philosophical discourse has raised humans above other species. While this tradition begins with some of the Presocratics – others were far more circumspect – it reached its apogee in Aristotle. He thought of all species, including humans, as animals in common, which thus share an essential similarity in their animality. Humans, however, possessed capacities to make them special. What distinguished humans was their level of evolutionary development and thus the possession of a far greater potential for thought, morality, and cultural refinement – in short, civilization. He believed, however, that human potential was not always actualized. The veneer of civilization was truly fragile for, as Aristotle remarked in the *Politics:* "Man, when perfected, is the best of animals; but if he be isolated from law and justice he is the worst of all ... man is furnished from birth with arms [such as, for instance, language] which are intended to serve the purposes of moral prudence and virtue, but which may be used in preference for opposite ends. That is why if he be without virtue, he is a most unholy and savage being, and worse than all other [animals] in the indulgence of lust and gluttony."[20]

Again, "animal" reality was treated as a symbolic standard rather than a description. Aristotle, as the first of the empirical natural scientists, must have known that "savage" could not describe the essential squirrel, "lust" the essential deer, or "gluttony" the essential sheep. Lust and gluttony were deemed – for metaphorical convenience – characteristics of animals that civilization could, but not necessarily would, overcome in humans. It was in the possession of a moral sense that one could promote justice, inhibit lust, and practise moderation, but civilization also gave one the knowledge of how to pervert and destroy justice, how to exceed the moral imperatives of the Golden Mean. With Aristotle, and even more emphatically from the age of science onward, Western civilization recognized not so much its necessary superiority over other species as its *potential* to exceed them. As Blaise Pascal opined, insightful people "find both greatness and wretchedness in man. In a word, man knows that he is wretched; he is therefore wretched because he is so; but he is very great because he knows it" (*Pensées*, no. 237). Increasingly, Western civilization prided itself on what Pascal called the sense of self-consciousness, what others termed "rational power" and "power over nature." Although the West became increasingly self-confident, we should not assume that other species were thought not to matter at all. Indeed, many of those who welcomed and participated in the scientific and rational revolutions (Sir Francis Bacon and Sir Isaac Newton, for example) were among those who recognized the worth of other species. While the West came increasingly to consider itself different from, indeed in some respects superior to, other species, it does not follow that it treated other species less benevolently than those that the distinction between themselves and other species.

The seventeenth-century materialist Hobbes's use of *Leviathan* (customarily a synonym for whale, occasionally another "sea-beast" [Milton]) and *Behemoth* (literally, "water-ox," and customarily a synonym for hippopotamus) as the titles of his books on political power reflects his difference from Aristotle in his understanding of the nature of political community and human moral potential. Whereas Aristotle considered the polity a moral community engaged in the pursuit of the public good, Hobbes deemed the state an instrument of power devoted to its own ends and devoid of moral purpose. Both Hobbes and Aristotle understood the animal as an autochthonously self-interested creature, but whereas Aristotle viewed the *polis* as the means by which humans are raised out of their animal natures, Hobbes considered such elevation a naive and forlorn hope. For Hobbes, not only is the animal a "brute," so too is the human. It is no wonder that the poetic protagonist of "the permanent things" of a mystical humanity, T.S. Eliot, described Hobbes as "that presumptuous little upstart." Nor is there any wonder that philosophical attempts to compare animal and human natures invariably came – and still come – to grief, for there is considerable disagreement on the nature of the human with which the animal is being compared. One cannot demonstrate x via the properties of y when the properties of y are in dispute. The concept of "human" for those who think like Aristotle has a very different connotation than it does for those who think like Hobbes.

For Hobbes, civilized humans possessed the "animal" characteristics of other species, but, unlike other species, they possessed sufficient reason to understand that they could escape the worst of brute life by respecting the rights of others to pursue their self-interest, provided their own rights were in turn respected. For Hobbes – Epicurus, too, incidentally – other species lacked the power of reason to enter into such a social contract and thus could not escape the war of all against all. Humans were like all other species in their "animality" but differed by dint of the capacity to reason – a capacity that did not alter their self-interested animal nature but permitted them to achieve their self-interests without resorting to the destruction of other humans. Of course, most animals do not behave in the manner Hobbes conceptualizes. There is probably more intra-species strife among humans than almost any other species. Moreover, there is no reason to assume that Hobbes was unaware of this fact. For Hobbes, "leviathan" and "behemoth" are tools of convenience, not means of identifying animal behavioural characteristics.

In Hobbes's words: "During the time men live without a common power to keep them all in awe, they are in that condition which is called war; and such a war, as is of every man, against every man."[21] Because non-human animals lack political organization (that is, lack the state, which maintains order and ensures the maintenance of contracts), they lack the means to escape continual conflict. The "animal" is a being at war. Hobbes might be thinking of the nature of animals like the bowerbird, but clearly his concept includes neither Lorenz's jackdaw nor Hawkins's pelican. Again, "leviathan" and "behemoth" have nothing to do with essential animality but are abstract standards, useful as a contrast with the disputed human capacity for spirituality, altruism, and love. Certainly, some of the statements sympathetic to animals Aristotle makes elsewhere, as we shall see, suggest that his notion of "animal" in the *Politics* is devised to facilitate the description of the human potential rather than to describe the real world of other species.

If neither Hobbes nor Aristotle has made his conception of the *real* animal clear, other than in the simplest possible – and rather misleading – terms, at least we can recognize that, for the one, it is the lack of reason and political organization that accounts for the difference from humans, while, for the other, it is lack of human moral potential and political organization. For both, however at odds their conceptions of human nature and of justice itself may be, the state is the common factor that permits humans to escape "animality." For both, the differentiating human characteristic is the potential for civilization – which is purportedly absent from the lives of even the least "beastly" or "brutish" of all the other species.

In "A Voyage to the Houyhnhnms" of *Gulliver's Travels,* Swift distinguished between the "falsity of that definition" of the human as *animal ratione* – the rational animal – and the appropriateness of *rationis capax* – a being capable of reason but who only rarely achieves it. Civilization remains the human potential denied by the human reality. If other species cannot reach the heights of which humans are capable, neither do those other species, Swift opines, degenerate to the level to which humans are capable of falling. Although Aristotle and Swift engage in quite different forms of discourse, they share a similar conception of human and non-human animals. For Aristotle, too, humans, if they fail to achieve their best, readily descend to the worst of animality. Indeed, who could imagine that any non-human animal could match the "corrupt" and "depraved" Svidrigailov or the "base, malicious" Luzhin in Dostoevsky's *Crime and Punishment,* or the innkeeper and the vicar in Daphne du Maurier's *Jamaica Inn*? Readers find Heathcliff's hanging of the little dog in Emily Brontë's *Wuthering Heights* the lowest to which any animal can descend. In D.H. Lawrence's *Kangaroo,* Somers asks, "Is the tiger your principle of evil?" "Oh dear no," replies Cooley, "The jackal, the hyaena, and dear deadly humanity."

III

If we are to understand the Western tradition, we must accustom ourselves to differentiate symbolic, allegorical, and metaphorical language – even, perhaps especially, when it appears in philosophical or scientific guise – from language that talks directly about the animal as animal. Here, any careful reader of the Western cultural tradition will be struck not by its opposition, or indifference, to the well-being of the non-human animal realm – even in many of those instances that at first glance suggest antipathy – but by its ambivalence, indeed outright contradictoriness. For example, we can read in Davies's *Naturalist's Guide* of 1858 about the nature and use of collections of mammals, birds, nests, eggs, insects, and so on. Animals are thought appropriate beings to be killed and stuffed or dissected for educational purposes. Yet: "In killing animals, the shortest way is always the best. To the humane naturalist, and it is to be hoped that all who pursue the science are really humanized by it, nothing can be more distressing than to see a creature writhing under pain ... It is well in all cases to lean to the side of mercy; to kill only where a decided object is in view, and then in the quickest manner."[22] Is this not equivalent to the "respect" with which Aboriginals are seen to kill animals for alimentary and sacrificial purposes?

Even today, of course, millions of frogs and other animals are killed in school laboratories. The ecologically sensitive Ed Ricketts, close friend of John Steinbeck, did much to keep the body and soul together of a small

Monterey intellectual entourage in the 1930s by collecting and selling marine specimens for school dissections. More strikingly, Leonardo da Vinci was a vegetarian who killed animals for his art.[23] John James Audubon's famous paintings appear to indicate a deep respect for his subjects. Yet he shot the birds in order to paint them. Gilbert White, author of *The Natural History of Selborne* (1788),[24] the first detailed ethological study, at least since Aristotle, kept his home filled with killed and stuffed examples of the animals he studied. Yet we should not imagine such apparent contradictoriness a purely Western phenomenon. It is no more contradictory than vegetarian Hindus who hunt tigers for a trophy of their ears, Amerindians who hunt eagles for their feathers, or Koreans who pay to have bears killed for their gall bladders or their paws. Nor is it any more contradictory than the behaviour of the Inuit who supply the bear parts.

Robert Louis Stevenson wrote to a friend in 1887, a year after the publication of *Dr. Jekyll and Mr. Hyde,* that the "hypocrite let out the beast of Hyde ... who is the essence of cruelty and malice and selfishness and cowardice, and these are diabolic in man."[25] The "beast" was not animal but the devil within humanity. By contrast, Stevenson claims, "dogs will be in heaven long before any of us." The beast was diabolic. Animals were not. Indeed, according to Stevenson's biographer, he "had a lifelong horror of cruelty to animals" (somewhat tainted by his treatment of Modestine, one might add). Certainly, he refused to hunt or fish on the grounds of the cruelty unnecessarily inflicted on animals. Significantly, he "detested ... laboratory experiments with guinea pigs [that were infected] with tubercular bacilli,"[26] even though he suffered from the illness for which the experiments were designed to find a cure. That is a significant aspect of the Western tradition of which one must not lose sight, especially when one recognizes that Stevenson was not in any manner involved in the animal protection or anti-vivisection movements. I do not recall his name receiving anything more than a brief mention in any of the animal rights literature. For Stevenson, it was simply an aspect of natural humanity to care for the well-being of other animals, even if one did not always live up to one's precepts. In *That Hideous Strength* (1945), C.S. Lewis, the Oxford don renowned as a Christian apologist rather than as an advocate for the animals, expressed a similar instinctive revulsion at animal experimentation, which anticipated much of the thinking of the modern animal rights movement. And Tertullian had brought humanity down to size in the third century by asking us to "imitate, if you can, the hive of the bee, the hill of the ant, the web of the spider, the thread of the silkworm ."[27]

George Bernard Shaw, in part from his association with the naturalist Henry Salt, has been more frequently recognized as an animal advocate. He was an avid anti-vivisectionist and declared himself "a vegetarian purely on humanitarian and mystical grounds" who had "never killed a flea or a mouse vindictively or without remorse."[28] Yet that self-same Fabian could refer without any sense of contradiction, but nonetheless with a decided ambivalence, to the welcome historical change "from the brutalizing torpor of Nature's tyranny over Man into the order and alertness of Man's organized dominion over Nature."[29] Shaw's socialist faith was in a technology that would allow us to overcome the degradation that the nature of disease and oppression and competition for scarce resources had imposed on us. It was victory over the deleterious aspects of nature that, Shaw believed, would allow us to live in harmony with other species.

Nor was Shaw an exception. Thomas Hardy, whose animal sensibilities were sufficiently well known that he was invited to become a vice-president of the Animal Defence and Anti-Vivisection League, cared enough for wild animals to condemn sport-hunting as barbaric. And, it is said, he was attracted to his reputed lover Florence Henniker in part because of her love of animals. On one occasion, on seeing a blackbird emerge from a hedge with a broken wing, he asked his cycling companion to kill it. He was unable to perform the merciful act himself. His acquaintance complied with the request, for which Hardy thanked him profusely, noting that otherwise the "poor thing" would have been "tortured by a cat or a stoat." Hardy often expressed the view that life was not worth the living of it and this "mood," we are told by Hardy's biographer, "was invariably prompted by nature's apparent cruelty."[30] Indeed, in *Two on a Tower,* Hardy referred explicitly to "nature's cruel laws." It was nature itself that prevented our living at one with the other species. Occidental ambivalence to nature is epitomized by Wolfram von Eschenbach's Parzival who was ashamed at having killed the beautiful and faithful swan instead of exulting in the death of the dangerous and malevolent dragon. Not all of nature was deemed to be wholesome. Indeed, justice for other species was thought to require us to take a critical stance toward nature in general. This view is to be found in Hinduism, too. In a poem by the 1913 Nobel literature laureate Rabindranath Tagore, we can read of the "terrible mirth of brute Nature" ("Shindhutaranga," 1887), echoing and amplifying George Eliot's "the presence of Nature in all her awful loveliness" (1859).

There is also a curious paradox in the behaviour of many who claim to possess a love of nature. Benjamin Disraeli in his *Endymion,* for example, tells us of a country rector who had written an essay on squirrels and who showed his guests "a glass containing that sportive animal in all its frolic forms." Nonetheless, Disraeli insists that the rector possessed a readily recognizable "love of nature."[31] In Keith Thomas's *Man and the Natural World,* we are told that the family home of the historian George Macaulay Trevelyan reflected "the nature-loving preoccupation of its owners."[32] The presence of stuffed birds is offered as evidence for that love. Nature-lover, too, was the Nathaniel Hawthorne whose parlour mantel's centrepiece was a stuffed owl. Michael Shelden informs us of Eric Blair (George Orwell) and his respect for one of his school teachers: "What really drew him to Mr.

Sillar was their shared love of nature." As evidence of that love, we are told of the "butterfly-hunting trips"[33] they took together. It is this contradiction – hunting, killing, and collecting the objects of apparent love – that is a more persistent phenomenon in human behaviour than any rejection of our relationship and responsibility to the natural realm. As we shall see, especially in Chapter 7, the same kind of paradox is present in the Aboriginal and Oriental worlds as well.

In fact, the paradox is not merely an occasional discomfort but an inescapable moral dilemma for all. Michael Shelden states that Kay Welton, a friend of George Orwell, "was frequently impressed by his sharp observation of nature, and found that he was a storehouse of information about trees and plants. She also discovered that he knew a great deal about birds and was 'passionately fond' of them. To her amusement, she later learned that he was equally fond of cats, but that he could 'never square the fact that cats killed birds.' "[34]

Nature provides no convenient passage for allowing itself to be used as a moral standard. One cannot love nature without also deploring some of its laws. Or by postulating an idealized *Nature,* a Platonic form of "Nature," which differs substantially from the practical reality of nature – nature without the "beasts" and "brutes." It is Eden before the Fall rather than Tennyson's "Nature, red in tooth and claw." The Bible (Genesis I and Isaiah XI, 6-8, for example), no less than George Bernard Shaw – no more varied could thought be in the Western tradition – and no less than Rabindranath Tagore, recognizes the iniquities of nature and the natural human desire to overcome them. One is compelled to ask whether to be "at one with nature" is of necessity to be at odds with justice. We will return to this theme, particularly in the concluding chapter.

3
Animals All?

1   In most of our abilities, we differ not at all from the animals; we are in fact behind many in swiftness and strength and other resources. But because there is born in us the power to persuade each other and to show ourselves whatever we wish, we not only have escaped from living as brutes, but also by coming together have founded cities and set up laws and invented arts; and speech has helped us attain practically all of the things we have devised.

– Isocrates, c. 374 BC

2   Man differs from the animal in eating without being hungry, drinking without being thirsty, and engaging in sex at all seasons.

– Pierre de Beaumarchais, 1784

3   One Law for the Lion & Ox is Oppression.

– William Blake, *The Marriage of Heaven and Hell*, 1793

4   All the operations of Nature, great as they are, become in general so familiar to us, that in a great measure they cease to attract our notice. Thus above all the usual powers of animal life, which, were they but adverted to, could not fail to affect the mind with the most powerful impressions, are suffered to operate unheeded, as if unseen.

– W. Bingley, *Animal Biography*, 1803

5   Let man visit Ourang-outang in domestication, hear expressive
    whine, see its intelligence when spoken [to]; as if it understands
    every word said – see its affection. – to those it knew. – see its
    passion & rage, sulkiness, & very actions of despair; let him look at
    savage [man], roasting his parent, naked, artless, not improving
    yet improvable & let him dare to boast of his proud preeminence.

    – Charles Darwin, *Notebook C,* 79, 1838

6   I have endeavoured to show that no absolute structural line of
    demarcation ... can be drawn between the animal world and our-
    selves; and I may add the expression of my belief that the attempt
    to draw a psychical distinction is equally futile, and that even the
    highest faculties of feeling and of intellect begin to germinate in
    lower forms of life. At the same time, no one is more convinced
    than I of the vastness of the gulf between civilised man and the
    brutes; or is more certain that whether from them or not, he is
    assuredly not of them.

    – T.H. Huxley, *Man's Place in Nature,* 1863

7   Besides love and sympathy, animals exhibit other qualities con-
    nected with the social instincts, which in us would be called moral.

    – Charles Darwin, *The Descent of Man,* 1871

8   Man is the only animal who blushes, or has need to.

    – Mark Twain, c. 1890

9   Go, go, go, said the bird: human kind cannot bear very much reality.

    – T.S. Eliot, *Four Quartets: Burnt Norton,* 1944

I

With Isocrates (1) and Huxley (6), writing over two millennia apart, we
encounter examples of what is perhaps the most prevalent Western view:
there are great similarities between ourselves and the other animals. There
are also great differences. Whichever is to be emphasized depends on the

point to be made. Charles Darwin (5, 7) emphasizes the similarities, albeit (5) in a manner that stresses the supposed differences among classes of humans. Elsewhere Darwin commented on the necessity of continuing animal experimentation, implying a significant difference in value between humans and other species.[1]

De Beaumarchais (2) and Mark Twain (8) follow Montaigne and Jonathan Swift in propounding the merits of non-human animals. It is a reminder to those who boast of their pre-eminence that, despite human reason and manual dexterity, other species demonstrate their greater worthiness by not succumbing to the human frailties, not engaging in human vices.

William Blake (3) reminds us of the great variety among different species. To treat them (including humans) all as one, as an unvariegated animality, would be to ignore the requirements of justice. Justice involves treating each person, each being, in terms of the very character of that being. To treat the lion and the ox as one would be to ignore their respective needs.

Bingley (4) notes how much we miss of importance to us in the natural realm, for, although it happens in our presence, we do not see it. We judge by our preconceptions, not by the objective reality. Similarly, T.S. Eliot (9) points out how much we miss of the reality of our environment as a consequence of human emotional incapacity.

From Isocrates to Eliot, members of the philosophical, scientific, and literary worlds have concurred about the importance of the animal to the human realm but have disagreed – sometimes vehemently – about the particulars of the relationship. What is clear is that no simple view of the Western tradition will suffice. It is complex and diverse. It cannot be summarized in pithy apothegms.

In the last chapter, we looked at how our usage of animals in discourse may sometimes provide a misleading impression of our attitudes to animals. In this chapter, we will be more concerned with why we talk about animals the way we do and what it *does* tell us about our attitudes toward other species; and, indeed, what it tells us about our attitudes toward ourselves.

It is sometimes said, with some justice, that the West does not see humans as animals in the same way that other animals are animals. Humans are often seen as somehow special and superior in their animality. Yet seeing ourselves as special has encouraged us to recognize the special capacities of others, too. Thus, Aristotle saw all beings in terms of their *telos,* their species being. While humans were superior, each being was, Aristotle implied, entitled to respect as the being that it was. It was Blake's view (3) that each being was entitled to treatment according to its nature. And Mary Midgley has told us, "We are not the only unique species. Elephants, as much as ourselves, are in many ways unique; so are albatrosses; so are giant pandas."[2] Each species has its own unique *telos.* (*Telos* is better rendered as "species being" or "nature" rather than the more literal "purpose," which last serves to confuse the issue by raising the question of who or what determined the purpose. To be sure, "nature" has its own problems. Arthur Lovejoy listed sixty-six different meanings of the term.[3] It may still be used with effect as a means of distinguishing the characteristics of one species from those of another. Seen in this way, Aristotle's *telos* comes to approximate Plato's *Form*, both being capable of being rendered as ultimate nature, with the addition for Aristotle that the *Form* includes life development, as from the potential of an acorn to the fulfilment of an oak tree. I shall treat the Platonic and Aristotelean "essences" as compatible throughout this book – a now fairly customary treatment in philosophical analysis.)

The alternatives to the view of each species as the possessor of its own special qualities – its "nature" – would include regarding humans and other animals as somehow the same, as in some manner "equal," and regarding humans as of an entirely different animal order, as God's chosen species, the very purpose of creation. While both these positions have their adherents, they require clarification.

Even among many of the "egalitarians," the continuing question is not whether humans are entitled to preferential treatment but how preferential that treatment should be. Many of the modern proponents of animal rights who make the case for equality don't seem really to mean it. Thus, for example, while Peter Singer asserts the equality of all animals, he also insists that neither he, nor any other prominent animal liberationist, holds "the right to life of a human being with mental capacities very different from those of the insect and the mouse" as only equal to the right to life of an insect or a mouse.[4] And while Michael W. Fox tells us in his *Inhumane Society* that "all life is equal. It is unethical to value one life over any other," and while he sees "humans and other animals as coequal, morally equivalent," we can also read in the same book that "the culling of animals ... can be justified ethically." We are told on the one hand that to "accept *any* form of violence against animals on the grounds of human necessity is, in the final analysis, chauvinistic and patronizing," and on the other that locust plagues and rabid dogs are instances where violence against animals may be justified. Fox thus deplores the "hierarchical principle" and at the same time offers us philosophical principles that support it. He claims that "all animals of similar sentience should be given equal and fair treatment,"[5] which, of course, implies that animals of dissimilar sentience should be treated differently. Fox is implicitly proposing a hierarchical principle based on the degree of sentience!

A less self-contradictory version of the egalitarian view is to be found in Chapter 9 of James Serpell's ground-breaking *In the Company of Animals*,[6] which is entitled "The Myth of Human Supremacy." Serpell discusses the characteristics shared by all animality. Similarly, in their *Shadows of Forgotten Ancestors*, Carl Sagan and Ann Druyan conclude that the jealously guarded attributes of "consciousness, language and culture" are not exclusively human attributes.[7] There is nothing chemical, physical, or mental, they claim, that sets humans apart.

What is common to most such writings – Serpell is a refreshing exception – is that, to make their points, they compare humans only with the most complex species, always the bonobos, baboons at a pinch, never the scallop, shrew, or three-toed sloth. They accept the flimsiest semblance of, say, self-awareness – restricted, as far as current research indicates, to orangutans, dolphins, and chimpanzees, though one might question the usefulness of the definition employed – or of culture in any single species as indisputable evidence for making claims about animals *per se*. For example, for Sagan and Druyan, any capacity to think creatively, however relatively trivial and however restricted to the great apes, perhaps dolphins and whales, too, is taken as conclusive evidence that non-human animals possess "culture."[8] Of course, animals learn through experience, and geographically separated groups of the same species may on occasion learn rather different techniques. Thus, in a limited sense, they may be said to possess "culture." But to use the term "culture" generically with reference to animals serves more to confuse than enlighten.

The point implicit in both the radical and the guarded egalitarian pronouncements is far more an ethical than a descriptive point. The essence of the egalitarian message is that, whatever may be the differences in rationality or accomplishments between humans and other species, such differences are entirely insufficient to justify human arrogance or the manner in which other species have been treated by humans, especially in conjunction with the development of Western technology. The point is not really that other species are in some mysterious manner equal but that they are entitled to consideration as ends in themselves. Despite the great differences in approach, those who think in terms of the *telos* of each species and those who stress equality are not as far apart philosophically as their respective choice of controlling concepts would suggest. Each side acknowledges significant similarities.

The idea of equality may indeed be said to be present in the minds of those who lack a pronounced consideration of other species. Thus, for example, Hobbes was a forerunner of that materialist utilitarian view of animality which understood that humans operate under the same natural laws as other species, of which the primary laws are those of self-preservation and the propagation of the species, understood under the general rubric of the maximization of pleasure and the minimization of pain. If that is animality, it is scarcely surprising that many had pronounced reservations about whether humans were that kind of animal. Their experience taught them that altruism, self-sacrifice, love, honour, loyalty, and courage were truly human attributes, never practised enough by anyone and studiously avoided by some, but human characteristics nonetheless. If the utilitarian view of animality denied the possibility of such behaviour, then the human was not an animal in the way that utilitarians understood animal nature. In such instances, it would be quite plausible to argue that those who denied human animality would have a significantly greater respect and consideration for other species than those who proclaimed it.

Today, few Westerners would have any qualms about understanding humans as animals, at least zoologically speaking. In the past, such a conclusion would not have always appeared so obvious. Many nineteenth-century theologians, and some naturalists of the same era, for example, would not have been so generous in their categorizations, sometimes because they deemed humans to possess capacities denied to all animality by the early utilitarians, sometimes through human pride. Given what was seen as the great mental and spiritual superiority of humanity, it was not unusual to see the organic world divided into the three kingdoms of "the Human, the Animal, and the Vegetable," thereby allotting an exclusive category to humankind.

It was Carolus Linnaeus (Karl von Linné), the eighteenth-century originator of the modern classification system for plants and animals, who first placed human beings in the same order as the Quadrumana (mammals with an opposable digit on all four limbs) under the title of the Primates,[9] thus affirming a greater proximity to other species than had customarily been acknowledged in the West. Linnaeus's classification did not remain uncontested, some demanding that humankind be classified as altogether separate from the rest of the animal realm, others conceding human animality but demanding an entirely separate order, humans being deemed too superior to be placed alongside the apes, the monkeys, and their relatives.

Nor should we consider the naysayers necessarily religious fanatics. Many naturalists followed the renowned German anthropologist and taxonomist Johann Fredrich Blumenbach (1752-1840) and the French pioneer in the science of comparative anatomy Baron Cuvier (1769-1832) in assigning humankind to a separate order of Bimana while affirming humankind's place in the animal realm.

Today, the Primate classification is readily accepted by almost all naturalists, but it should be recognized that there is of necessity some degree of arbitrariness in where to draw the line between species and between orders or even which criteria to employ for classification. It is scientifically acceptable and morally appropriate rather than objectively right to classify all humans together as one species and in the same order as other species. Blumenbach and Cuvier were not wrong. Their classifications were merely less appropriate. As Darwin put it, "I look at the term species, as one arbitrarily given for the sake of convenience to a set of individuals closely resembling each other, and that it does not essentially differ from the term variety which is given to less distinct and more fluctuating forms."[10] It should be noted anyway that even in the Primate order, Homo sapiens is assigned a separate family whereas the chimpanzees, gorillas, and orangutans are categorized together in the Pongid family.

Whether somewhat arbitrary or not, it should be clear that any attempt to determine an entirely separate order for the human being is born more of a desire to maintain the exclusivity of humankind than from any scientific considerations. As Charles Darwin wisely proclaimed, "If man had not been his own classifier he would never have thought of founding a separate order for his own reception."[11] Indeed, many apparently objective scientific questions cannot be addressed without moral and ideological implications.

Perhaps surprisingly, the gradual acceptance of the theory of evolution did not end the taxonomic debate entirely. Of course, the creation science theorists continue to expound their antiquated views,[12] but, more disconcertingly, as late as 1945 the renowned American paleontologist Professor G.G. Simpson suggested, "Perhaps it would be better for the zoological taxonomist to set apart the family Hominidae and to exclude its nomenclature and classification from his studies." As anthropologists Eric Trinkaus and Pat Shipman point out, "It is an astonishing remark that shows clearly the potency of Darwin's basic affront to Victorian sensibilities – his implicit suggestion that humans operated under the same 'rules' as other animals – one hundred years later."[13] If we recognize the original "implicit suggestion" as that of Linnaeus, Buffon, Lamarck, Goethe, Herder, and Erasmus Darwin rather than Charles Darwin, it was almost 200 years of affront to human sensibilities, but one that perhaps now, except by the purveyors of creation science, is finally accepted. If it is, we should note that it is the only issue with regard to human animality that is beyond legitimate dispute. All the other battles rage on.

Today, the vast majority readily accept the human as an animal. What remains at issue is whether humans possess attributes commonly, but perhaps mistakenly, ascribed to other species alone. What is disputed is whether the general attributes of humans are of significant similarity to those of other species or, perhaps surprisingly, what is a decidedly different question, whether animal attributes are similar to those of humans.

They are not the same question in that the first asks whether humans possess what are deemed by the questioner the defining characteristics of other animals (perhaps fierceness or promiscuity), and the second asks whether other animals possess what are deemed by the questioner the defining characteristics of humanity (perhaps reason or altruism). Implicit are likely to be other decidedly leading questions. "Are you an animal?" may well be seen to be asking "Are you rational?" or "Are you moral?" Before answering the question whether humans are animals, whether humans possess the essential animal attributes, it would be wise not only to ask which attributes, but also which species.

Virginia Woolf assigned a goodly portion of her friends and acquaintances to their appropriate niches in a bestiary. For example, the ballerina and wife of John Maynard Keynes, Lydia Lopokova, was deemed to possess the soul of a squirrel, the novelist Rebecca West was a shaggy dog, and the Fabian Sidney Webb appeared as a moulting eagle. E.M. Forster began as a mouse, was transformed into a blue butterfly, and finally, in disfavour, into a moth. Woolf occasionally reflected on what her "self" would be were she a goat, a lemur, a baboon, a butterfly, or a sparrow. On one occasion, she even saw herself as a chanticleer, on another as a sea anemone. In her novel *Flush* (1933), she attempts to present the consciousness of Elizabeth Barrett Browning's spaniel, and in her short story "Lappin and Lapinova" (1938), she has her principal characters assume the identities of a rabbit and a hare. What distinguished Woolf's writing from much of the traditional metaphorical human-animal comparison was that she had almost as much interest in the character of the animals as the character of her acquaintances. For Woolf, the appropriate question is not "Are you an animal?" but "Are you a squirrel?" or "Are you a baboon?" She did not doubt that we were animals but recognized a differing essence, a differing fundamental character, for each species.

As we noted, one of the surprising uses of the word "animal" when contrasted with "human" is that it has come to imply a commonality of character among different species as though the gazelle and the jaguar, the platypus and the crocodile, the ant and the peacock, possessed practically indistinguishable characteristics. Exasperated at her husband's proclaimed love for all animals, Sofya, Countess Tolstoy asked, "How can one love an insect which never stops stinging?" (Diary, 3 August 1862). Leonard Woolf, author of *The Wise Virgins* and *After the Deluge,* and owner of an esteemed marmoset called Mitz, wrote to Lytton Strachey from his civil service post in Ceylon, "And then there are the flies – they are bred in the millions of rotting oysters that lie about the camp ... They are crawling over one's face & hands all day long & owing to the putrid filth on which they feed every little scratch or spot on one becomes sore" (12 December 1913). To love universal animalkind in the abstract is to deny the logic of human – and animal – reality.

Whether we approve or not, we must not fail to recognize that the Robert Browning who so praised the noble character of the horse Roland – "stout galloper ... with resolute shoulders" – in "How They Brought the Good News from Ghent to Aix" was the same Robert Browning who so disparaged rats in "The Pied Piper of Hamelin."[14] Apart from the rat, "mole and toad and newt and viper" are offered by the Piper as "creatures that do people harm." Gnats, "vampyre-bats," scorpions, and mice are deplored while cats, dogs, and peacocks are treated with favour. Like Robert Browning, most people do not have a unified view of the animal realm but have likes and dislikes, attractions and fears, friends and food. This differing attitude toward different species is present at the very beginning of Western literature. In his Introduction to his translation of *The Odyssey,* T.E. Lawrence (Lawrence of Arabia) describes Homer as "a dog-lover" who also hunted, and killed, wild boars. In the eighteenth century, Dr. Samuel Johnson contrasted different species of bears. "The black bear is innocent," he opined.

Others were not. And on a visit to the Berlin Zoo when he was twenty-eight, Tchaikovsky was reduced to sobbing hysteria for the rest of the day after seeing a boa constrictor consume a live rabbit. (Charles Dickens condemned the practice of such public feeding on the grounds that it not only terrified the victim but was demoralizing to the spectators.) Virginia Woolf described the man who had molested her as a child as an "obese & obsolete alligator." By contrast, she described her maid, kindly if condescendingly, as a "merry little brown eyed mongrel." Topping the list was her sister, Vanessa, who appeared as a majestic dolphin. Not all animals were equal.

In a 1795 engraving, William Blake symbolizes corrupt materialism using "Behemoth and Leviathan." Behemoth, apparently styled on Albrecht Dürer's *Rhinoceros*, has the body and tusks of an elephant, humanoid ears, and the eyes and nose of, perhaps, a bear. Leviathan is a sea-dwelling dragon with stylized crocodile teeth. In other engravings, he depicts "Leviathan" and "Behemoth" as symbols of warfare. Elsewhere, it is the serpent that Blake uses to represent the degradation of materialism. In a watercolour painting, he portrays *Satan as a Toad, Haunting the Dreams of Eve*. In *Hecate,* he has a demon ass, owl, frog, and bat, which add to the fantastic horror of the painting as a whole. Beastly indeed! But this same William Blake writes in awe of the tiger and with love for the lamb, paints swans, elephants, horses, cats, and eagles with evident affection – even the etching of the tiger of "fearful symmetry" makes him more benign than sinister – and he laments, "How can the bird that is born for joy, / Sit in a cage and sing?" Some animals evoke a more favourable response than others.

On witnessing an octopus whose predatory activities seemed to her to symbolize Satan, the anti-vivisectionist crusader (and poet) Christina Rossetti declared that she "had to remind herself that this vivid figure of wickedness was not in truth itself wickedness."[15] All beings were entitled to respect as the beings that they are, but not to admiration or even liking, for the rapaciously predatory behaviour of the octopus made it a less commendable creature than, say, the pelican.

It was Porphyry's view that "One should never destroy or damage any animal that is not harmful to mankind." There is no similar injunction against destroying the harmful kind. In fact, in the *Tales from King Arthur,* Sir Percival assists a lion against a serpent because the lion "was the more natural [wholesome] beast of the twain," and Arthur himself in a dream killed "gryphons and serpents which burnt and slew his people, and he made war on the monsters."[16] Otherwise, he demonstrates a sympathy for horses and even the mythic "Questing Beast." And in the twelfth-century Arthurian romantic poem *Yvain* by Chrétien de Troyes, we read "in the pine tree ... all the birds sang in harmony, yet the note of each was different ... [their song] filled me with such joy ... I was lost in rapture." "Monsters" were apparently treated with less favour. Still, many animals were symbolically positive. It has, in fact, been suggested by archeologists that the great white horse carved into the hillside at Westbury on Salisbury Plain in England may have been executed to commemorate King Alfred's victory over the Danes in AD 878. Primal antipathy and primal sympathy exist side by side.

In Middle Eastern mythology, the distinction is equally apparent. Thus, according to Zoroaster, the faithful Ormuzd was the source of all good, including humans and benevolent species, while the rebellious Ahriman introduced evil and created savage beasts and poisonous reptiles and plants. In like vein, both the Maya and the Iroquois believed that harmless species were created by the Good Spirit and harmful species by the Evil Spirit. Such examples correspond to the "Manichaeism" of Mr. Tulliver in George Eliot's *The Mill on the Floss,* in which, by contrast with the good animals, "rats, weevils and lawyers were created by Old Harry," that is, the devil. In fact, the distinction among species is not restricted to the West but begins with the earliest mythologies that deem certain species to possess particular characteristics that may make them more appropriate as the vehicle of the particular mythological moral. Some animals are to be feared, some to be loved, many to be admired, and, in principle anyway, most to be respected as the beings that they are.

There is a charming, oft-repeated, traditional story about a putative fifth-century son of Ireland, Kieran, claimed as the first Irishman to embrace the Christian faith. The tale reported here is an eighteenth-century version of a very much older legend: "In the air right over him a kite came soaring and, swooping down before his face, lifted a little bird that sat upon her nest. Compassion for the little bird took Kieran, and he deemed it an ill thing to see it in such plight; thereupon the kite turned back and in front of Kieran deposited the bird half dead, sore hurt; but Kieran bade it rise and be whole. The bird rose, and by God's favour went whole upon its nest again."[17]

It is an endearing story, and one that reflects a general sympathy for other species in the Western tradition, though it is also one that depicts rather more naivety than compassion. The kite – a falcon-like bird of prey – either died from starvation, we must suppose, or repeated its attack rather more successfully on some other victim – no doubt as soon as Kieran was out of sight – or was miraculously converted to vegetarianism and expired in short order from a diet inappropriate to its constitution!

Did Kieran not recognize his futile gesture as inconsistent with his theology in which God made the natural law according to which animals behave – and which, according to Genesis 1:30 "was very good" – or did he think that the future utopia portended in Isaiah 11 – in which the wolf dwells with the lamb, the leopard lies down with the calf, and the lion with the fatling – had already come to pass? What would Kieran have thought of the swallow parent, torn between the nurturing instinct and the instinct to migrate, as it often is at the end of the season, which eventually leaves its offspring to starve? Kieran's friend and associate, so Irish legend has it, was

St. Patrick who, as everyone knows, expelled the snakes – but not the birds of prey – from Ireland. Neither Kieran nor St. Patrick had a unified view of the animal realm. When the "animal" we contrast with "human" comes to mind, it is the rat or the bird of prey, the scorpion or the jackal, the snake or the hyena, not the horse, the peacock, the small bird "sore hurt," or the lamb. Unfortunately, Kieran's compassion flies in the face of nature's cruel reality, as, indeed, does so much of the Western tradition. In the West, nature's cruelties are deplored. Indeed, they are often ignored and the perpetrators of the apparent cruelties are idealized, lions and eagles especially. In other cultures, the "cruelties" are rather more readily accepted as a part of nature's necessity.

The distinction among species in terms of their worth is certainly not restricted to the naive or the malevolent. It can be found, sometimes in a startling degree, among the most admirable of the ethologists. Thus, for example, writes the experienced elephant ethologist Cynthia Moss in her *Elephant Memories:* "Elephants are not so many rodents to be exterminated; they deserve something better than that and I am not afraid to say that ethics and morality should be essential considerations in our decisions for their future. Preserving habitats and trees and maintaining species diversity are important goals in conservation, but nothing will convince me that killing Slit Ear, Tallulah, and Tuskless and their families would be worth the achievement of these goals. The world would not be a better place if they were dead."[18] Moss prefers elephants over rodents and over species diversity. For Moss, some species are more important than other species and in some instances individual justice for animals must supersede environmental considerations.

A few pages earlier, Moss had written: "I am not against sport hunting because it brings revenue to the people who have to live with wild animals, and taking a few trophy animals each year apparently has little detrimental effect on wildlife populations."[19] The killing of animals for sport is perfectly acceptable provided it respects ecological considerations! The individual lives of lions, zebras, impalas, and waterbucks don't seem to matter while those of the elephants do – for no better reason presumably than that Moss was working with elephants! The contradiction between balanced nature as an end and individual animals as ends is portrayed starkly by Moss.

It is necessary to the story of George Orwell's *Animal Farm* that the heroes should be such animals as horses, dogs, sheep, and cows rather than alligators, bats, or weasels. If Orwell had lionized snakes, spiders, or lice, it is unlikely the book would have been published – it was rejected by four publishers as it was, including one that had published seven of his previous books – and it is certain the book would not have achieved its popularity. The generic "animal" requires some internal distinctions if we are to understand attitudes to, say, cobras, or lobsters, or vultures, both in the West and elsewhere.

A killer whale (orca) will toss a seal victim about as if in a game before devouring it; chimpanzees, orangutans, and dogs will engage in "rape" on occasion; and chimpanzees, lions, and barnyard cats will practise cannibalism. Our lovable companion cat will toy with a mouse before killing it. (The eighteenth-century poet Christopher Smart had a different, if perhaps unconvincing, explanation. In his *Jubilitate Deo,* he opined, "For when he takes his prey he plays with it to give it a chance / For one mouse in seven escapes by his dallying.") Several species of birds will abandon their fledglings when migration beckons. And these animals are among those we tend to admire the most, not those we tend to disparage, such as the scorpion, the rat, the hyena, and the jackal. It is little wonder that Darwin wrote of "the clumsy, wasteful, blundering, low and horridly cruel works of nature." For Darwin, it was appropriate to recognize our similarities to other species and our responsibilities to other species. But to be at one with nature was to participate in the clumsiness, the waste, and the cruelty. To be humanitarian was to distinguish between the wise and fulfilling parts of nature, and the cruel and destructive parts of nature.

It is not difficult to understand, then, why, for Westerners, the question of our animality involves some ambivalence. As T.H. Huxley expressed it (6), "No one is more convinced than I of the vastness of the gulf between civilised man and the brutes; or is more certain that whether from them or not, he is assuredly not of them." We share the same basic structure, the same basic feelings, the same basic reasoning with the other species. But, for Huxley, it is only the human who has the capacity to escape the worst aspects, and practise the better aspects, of animality. We are in principle like other species and owe a significant responsibility toward them, but those capacities that distinguish us from other species permit us the capacity to overcome the worst of our animal behaviour, even though many humans refrain from doing so.

For many Westerners, to accept our animality without reservation would be to condone aggressive and selfish behaviour when humans, so it is claimed, are capable of behaving altruistically. Even though animals *may* behave altruistically in some respects, it would nonetheless be an impossibility for the swallow consciously to opt in favour of protecting its endangered offspring rather than to migrate; the orca cannot contemplate, regret, or overcome the "cruelty" of toying with the seal; the domestic cat will not choose to kill only the mice it needs for survival. Thus to accept the category of animal unquestioningly would, for the Western mind in general, imply an acceptance of humans at their worst. The idea of being human, of being a *Mensch,* a deeply expressive term in Yiddish, involves overcoming not animality per se but those uncaring aspects of animality that human spirituality allows us to overcome – however reluctant we may be to do it.

It would be unwarranted to interpret the Westerner's ambivalence about human animality as a form of disrespect, a lack of concern for, other species. Many who have reservations about our animality admire and behave responsibly toward other species. In the West, we tend to have reservations about nature, including animal nature. We are inclined to want to adjust nature, to overcome its abominable cruelty. For some others, recognition, acceptance, and even participation in that behaviour which the West terms cruel come with far less soul-searching. In the West, we accept the finer aspects of nature but refuse to condone that which we find unacceptable. In other cultures, especially those closest to nature, nature's necessity, including that which we tend to regard as unacceptable, is treated as normal and appropriate. Thus, the traditional Western ambivalence about our animality may distinguish us somewhat from other cultures, but it would be inappropriate to regard it as a form of disrespect for other species as it so often is regarded.

Mary Midgley has pointed to two distinct uses of "animal," one that is inclusive of human beings (that is, the scientific classificatory use), and one that excludes humans and serves to contrast humans with other species to the detriment of other species.[20] She indicates how we have come to use the term "animal" in an *apparently* objective manner to reflect a self-proclaimed human superiority and to degrade animals by treating them as, what they are not. In the previous chapter, we discussed in some detail the degree to which such an interpretation may mislead us, even though it is in no small part accurate. What Mary Midgley's analysis entirely ignores – as ironically, do almost all sympathetic writings about attitudes to animals – and what requires equal notice and explanation, is the immense popularity in Western society of pet-keeping, of both scientific and laical television documentaries about wild animals, of involvement in animal protection organizations, of animal-related books and other literature – much more so than in other societies. In addition to the negative and neutral attitudes to animals, there is a third, a positive and pervasive if inconsistent attitude. It is reflected in a whole host of idealized statements about other species – for example, that they only eat when hungry (tell that to the owner of a cocker spaniel or the caiman's prey), or that they only engage in sex to procreate (tell that to the observer of the proverbial rabbit or just about any of the monkey species), or that they kill no more than they can consume (Australian dingoes wantonly destroy more prey than they require; domestic cats often kill mice and birds for the apparent fun of it; and leopards, lions, and cheetahs sometimes leave to rot a significant part of the prey they have killed).

The late-nineteenth-century animal advocate Henry Salt – George Bernard Shaw said his own plays were "sermons preaching what Salt practised" – argued that oppression and cruelty are invariably founded on a lack of imaginative sympathy, or on a failure to avoid the fallacy of special pleading. Unfortunately, special pleading is just as much a failing of those who oppose the oppression and cruelty. In their sympathy for the oppressed, they write as though other species possessed none of the human frailties. Thus, pet dogs are described as "unquestioningly loyal," "eating only when hungry," "not hung up about sex," possessing "unconditional love" – all of which are patent exaggerations and all of which statements are to be found in Gary Kowalski's highly regarded recent animal book, *The Souls of Animals* (1991). No understanding of animal relations can be complete if it does not acknowledge "rape" (if one may be permitted a perhaps inappropriate anthropomorphism) among the chimpanzees, orangutans, dogs, ducks, gulls, herons, albatrosses, and bank swallows (and, lest we forget, humans too). In all these instances, the "rape" is accomplished despite the strenuous efforts of the victim. For a good deal of less-than-eulogizing reality – jackrabbits, mules, and alligators in their authentic and often unattractive characters – mixed with unquestioned respect for them as the beings that they are, a reading of Mark Twain's stories is to be heartily recommended.

Despite supposedly "undesirable" characteristics in many species (bearing striking similarities to human failings), there are often differences acknowledged in Western literature that may be said to redound to the animal's credit. Thus, Walt Whitman writes in his *Song of Myself* (Stanza 32):

> They do not sweat and whine about their
>   condition,
> They do not lie awake in the dark and weep
>   for their sins,
> They do not make me sick discussing their
>   duty to God,
> Not one is dissatisfied, not one is demented
>   with the mania of owning things,
> Not one kneels to another, nor to his kind that
>   lived thousands of years ago,
> Not one is respectable or unhappy over the whole earth.

On a recent visit to a bookshop, I found over 60 percent of the material in the children's section to be animal-oriented – both, presumably, because "animals are good to think with," and because there is a natural sympathy toward them if unadulterated by experience or indoctrination. A goodly proportion of animal-related reading for adults was to be found under "Nature" – a section which was larger than "Science" or "Art," as large as "Religion" and "History," but smaller than "Biography" and "Psychology."

In the Everyman's Library Pocket Poets series, the poets covered range from Baudelaire to Whitman. Only three books in the series were, before a few recent additions, designated by topic rather than poet: *Love Poems,* *Erotic Poems,* and *Animal Poems.* In William Blake's *Songs of Innocence,* fifteen of eighteen poems mention non-human animals. In Gustave Merlet's

Anthologie classique des poètes du XIXème siècle (1890), over 20 percent of the poems listed are classified, in approximately equal portions, under "nature poetry," and "animal poetry," the other categories being "childhood," "family," "man," "work," and "patriotism." Over 300 of Emily Dickinson's poems feature animals. Clearly, the importance of the animal to the Western mind cannot be doubted.

II

However sympathetic to animal interests they might be, many will insist that humans are the only species with a moral sense (one of Aristotle's differentiating characteristics), of a religious nature (as per Edmund Burke – and also according to the creation story in the *Popol Vuh* of the Maya), capable of spontaneous creativity (Marx), or, according to Aristotle and Hobbes, the only species with a developed culture rather than solely a nature. T.S. Eliot followed Burke in distinguishing between civilized human and brute by possession of the moral imagination – the faculty of ethical perception that surpasses the barriers of private experience and is expressed most fully in poetry and art. And I would add that the human is the only species that experiences an inherent tension between its primordial nature and an acquired culture. Nonetheless, most – but by no means all – learned writings, especially since Charles Darwin, come to the same conclusion: the human is indeed an animal; differences between humans and other species are but differences of degree. However much we may differ from other species in specifics, as a generality we are entirely a part of them. Thinking in these terms, the renowned and deeply humane ethologist Jane Goodall has written: "There are many similarities in chimpanzee and human behaviour – the affectionate, supportive and enduring bonds between family members, the long period of childhood dependency, the importance of learning, non-verbal communication patterns, tool-using and tool-making, cooperation in hunting, sophisticated social manipulations, aggressive territoriality, and a variety of helping behaviours, to name but a few. Similarities in the structure of the brain and central nervous system have led to the emergence of similar intellectual abilities, sensibilities and emotions in our two species."

Despite the similarities though, Dr. Goodall is not swayed by her sympathy to ignore the differences: "Knowing that chimpanzees possess cognitive abilities once thought unique to humans, knowing that they (along with other 'dumb' animals) can reason, feel emotions and pain and fear, we are humbled. We are not, as once we believed, separated from the rest of the animal kingdom by an unbridgeable chasm. *Nevertheless, we must not forget, not for an instant, that even if we do not differ from the apes in kind, but only in degree, that degree is still overwhelmingly large.*"[21]

The Western tradition, beginning with the classical Greeks, has invested a great deal of thought and intellectual energy in understanding the appropriate relationship between humans and other species. But that has meant that one should examine the differences as well as the similarities.

Perhaps the best-known statement by any classical Greek philosopher is Aristotle's assertion that man is a *zŏon politikon* – a political animal, a political *being*. As anyone who has studied political philosophy will know, Aristotle meant that human beings are suited by their unique natures to live in the *polis* – the Greek city state – which is the root of our related words: polity, political, police, policy, and polite. He meant in part that they are only capable of fulfilment as human beings if they live in an organized community. For that reason, most modern scholars prefer to translate *zŏon politikon* as social animal rather than political animal. But that now customary translation misses Aristotle's intent; it also ignores the fact that Aristotle could readily have used a Greek word for "social" (perhaps *koinonikos*) had he so wished. To define humans as social animals is to fail to differentiate humans from bees or gorillas or caribou.[22]

What Aristotle was attempting to elucidate was the human essence, the human *telos* – that which differentiated humans from all other species – and the word "social" fails to fulfil the task. Humans, so Aristotle was arguing, are distinguished from other species by their unique capacity for civilization, which can only be achieved in a community organized as a state. *Zŏon politikon* is thus better translated as "civil animal" or in its former customary form of "political animal" in which "political" is understood by reference to the quality of life of the *polis*. Those who today claim that the human differs from other species only by degree or, conversely, in kind are thus engaging in that debate about the essence of humans and the essence of animals to which Aristotle made a most important early contribution.

Aristotle was well aware, of course, that humans had not always lived in civil communities. There were earlier, more "barbaric," stages of man – stages in which the xenophobic Greeks believed that societies more primitive than the Hellenes spoke like animals ("baa, baa," like sheep, hence barbaric) and thus were closer to the animals. Nature, or essence, for Aristotle, was demonstrated not necessarily by how things were at any given time but by their purpose, their potential, their *telos*. Humans were like many other species in that they were social but different in that their *telos*, their potential, was far greater and to achieve that potential, that human perfection of civilization, humans must first pass through more primitive, more animalistic, stages. An Enlightenment-type conception of societal development and probable progress as well as the rudiments of a theory of evolution can be readily found in Greek thought, the latter in the writings of Thales, Empedocles, Anaximander, and Epicurus as well as Aristotle. In fact, in his "Historical Sketch on the Progress of Opinion on Origin of Species," which Charles Darwin appended to the later editions of *The Origin of Species,* it is to Aristotle's *Physicae Auscultationes* that Darwin first doffs his cap in acknowledgment of an early predecessor.

For Aristotle, the route to an understanding of the perennial questions of social and political philosophy lay in an understanding of human nature that could only be attained in the context of animal nature. It was thus partly through a contrast of humans with other species that we could approach an understanding of polity and society, the state and community, sovereignty and spontaneity, authority and freedom, family and individual. Only if we could understand the nature of humans as animals could we determine the human *telos*. Indeed, for Aristotle, it is precisely on the basis of distinctions in nature between species that we can come to understand the *telos* of each species. In determining what is appropriate for each species, its welfare, its entitlements or rights, we must attempt to understand its *telos* by understanding what is necessary to it as the being that it is.

Aristotle wrote in *On the Parts of Animals* (1, 5), "in all natural things there is something wonderful ... We should approach the inquiry about each animal without aversion, knowing that in all of them there is something natural and beautiful." In the *Historia Animalium* (588, A:8), Aristotle concludes that "just as in man we find knowledge, wisdom and sagacity, so in certain animals there exists some other natural potentiality akin to these."

All animals have value, all are deserving of respect as the beings that they are, but their natures are not alike. According to Aristotle, we should recognize all animals as equal in their animality, but essentially different in their species natures. In his "Animal Welfare, Science, and Value," Bernard Rollin explained the Aristotelean position: "Animals [as well as humans] have natures – the pigness of the pig, the cowness of the cow – which are as essential to their well-being as speech and assembly are to us."

It is only when we understand animals in their species *telos* that we can really respect them as the beings that they are – through their differences from humans and each other. A bird with clipped wings, a bat without echolocation, a jaguar without its predation zone, each is in a manner no longer a *real* bird, a *real* bat, or a *real* jaguar. It is deprived of something that constitutes a part of its *telos*.

In acknowledging the import of the Aristotelean approach, the pig ethologist David Fraser suggests that the:

> genetically encoded "nature" of an animal can be seen as including two components: (1) the set of adaptations that an animal possesses as a result of its evolutionary history, as modified through domestication and perhaps the animal's own experiences; and (2) the set of genetically encoded instructions that guide the animal's normal ontogenic development. If we conceptualize *telos* in this way, then [it implies] that animals should be allowed to live in a manner to which they are adapted, and have the type of ontogenic development that is normal for the species. And these two criteria actually form the basis, implicity or explicitly, of considerable research currently being done by animal welfare scientists.[23]

Mark Twain made the point less profoundly but perhaps more piquantly. In "How I Edited an Agricultural Paper" (1870), his critic jibes, "You talk of the moulting season for cows; and you recommend the domestication of the polecat on account of its playfulness and its excellence as a ratter!" Appropriate commentary and appropriate action require appropriate species knowledge – a knowledge most of us possess in sufficient degree to avoid Twain's jesting mistakes but in far from sufficient degree to know what is appropriate for a particular species. If we do not know that a jaguar's natural predation area is some 25,000 acres, we may imagine it appropriate to confine the animal to a paddock in a zoo. More explicitly Platonic than Aristotelean but nonetheless apposite are James Joyce's words in *Ulysses:* "Horseness is the whatness of allhorse." If we do not know the "whatness" of each species, we cannot know what is appropriate for it.

It is not then enough to have fine sensibilities (though it is essential!), not enough to have myths and legends that treat other species well (though it does help!); if we are to know and respect the rights of animals we must know – ethologically and scientifically – their natures.

Beginning with classical Greece, an understanding of the nature of human and non-human animals has been central to debate. What is the nature of the animal in general – *On the Nature of Animals* was the title of a treatise written by the Roman author Aelian some 1,800 years ago, reflecting the fact that the topic was not without general interest – and what was the nature of the human animal in particular? Aristotle – though certainly not Aristotle alone – believed that an answer to such questions was a prerequisite of answering all the great questions of social philosophy. One could only answer the perennial questions if one understood humans in their unique animal nature. The human essence distinguished humans from all other species.

Not merely the polymath Aristotle – "the master of those who know," according to Dante – but also such diverse social and political theorists as Cicero, St. Thomas Aquinas, Descartes, Hobbes, Hooker, Rousseau, Marx, and John Stuart Mill, among others, considered the most appropriate avenue to determining the essence of humanity – the identifying human characteristics – to be by determining in what significant manner humans differed from other species. In his *A Treatise of Human Nature* (1739-40), David Hume has short chapters concerning "Of the reason of animals," "Of the pride and humility of animals," and "Of the love and hatred of animals." For Hume, an understanding of animal nature was a prerequisite for understanding human nature. Indeed, it would appear to have been only in the last century that philosophers have – with a few exceptions – failed to raise the question for themselves and failed further to recognize the importance of the question for philosophers of the preceding two and a half millennia.

For Cicero and Aquinas, the essential differentiating human characteristic was the possession of reason; for Descartes, it was consciousness – "bête machine" was how he referred to non-humans; for Hobbes and St. Augustine, individuality; for Hooker, speech; for Rousseau, choice; for Hume, the *degree* of reason; and for Marx, creative labour. Marx argued that what was distinctly human was what was most worthy of achievement; whatever humans did of which other species were incapable was the distinguishing human essence. It was thus that Marx would write so much of the human "species nature." Marx's materialist progenitor Ludwig Feuerbach began his *The Essence of Christianity* (1841) by distinguishing between human and brute nature. The human possessed "not finite and limited but infinite nature." "Reason, Will and Affection" were what Feuerbach called the "divine trinity in man."

For Aristotle, the distinguishing essence was a variety of factors involving reason, speech, and the possession of a moral sense:

> The reason why man is a being meant for political association, in a higher degree than bees or other gregarious animals, is evident. Nature, according to our theory, makes nothing in vain; and man alone of the animals is furnished with the faculty of language. The mere making of sounds serves to indicate pleasure and pain, and is thus a faculty that belongs to animals in general: their nature enables them to attain the point at which they have perceptions of pleasure and pain, and can signify those perceptions to one another. But language serves to declare what is advantageous and what is the reverse, and it therefore serves to declare what is just and what is unjust. It is the peculiarity of man, in comparison with the rest of the animal world, that he alone possesses a perception of good and evil, of the just and the unjust, and of other similar qualities; and it is in association in [a common perception of] these things which makes a family and a *polis*.[24]

I have quoted Aristotle at some length to demonstrate how central he thought the comparison between humans and other species, how he thought it the starting point of understanding human behaviour (the quotation is taken from the opening pages of the *Politics*), and how different he thought a human association from any other animal association.

Most philosophers thought that reason, or some related attribute such as consciousness or creativity or speech or self-conscious individuality, differentiated humans from other beings. Even those who acknowledged that other beings were capable of reason did not distinguish themselves in principle from those who claimed that animals did not reason. Following such thinkers as Porphyry and Plutarch, and in line with his contemporary David Hume, Jean-Jacques Rousseau insisted that "Every animal has ideas ... It even combines those ideas in a certain degree, and it is only in degree that in this respect man differs from the brutes."[25] Perhaps surprisingly, this view did not distinguish Rousseau from Aristotle who denied reason to the animals – but also claimed that some of them possessed a quality akin to it.

What differentiates those who ascribe reason to other species and those who deny it is the meaning of reason. Because Aristotle inappropriately denies the capacity for reason to slaves, and, with some circumspection, to women as well as other species, he is clearly not referring to the customary use of reason to determine the relationship between means and ends – a capacity he readily acknowledges in slaves, women, and other species – but in speculative reason, philosophy, and self-reflection. Aristotle distinguishes between *sophia* – philosophical wisdom – and *phronesis* – practical reason or judgment. It is only *sophia* that he regards as restricted to an intellectual elite of male humans, predominantly Greeks. The less speculative form of reason he calls "calculative reason" and he understands it to be possessed by the animals he studied as perhaps the first of ethologists. Of course, both those who acknowledge and those who deny animal rationality readily concur that the mental capacities of humans far exceed those of other species. And, perhaps surprisingly, most of those who deny animal rationality insist that animals are entitled to considerate treatment. It should be remembered that the Aristotle who is so disparaged by the animal liberationists for his denial of reason to other species is also the Aristotle who insisted that "there is something natural and beautiful" in each animal. The implication was that animals are entitled to respect as the beings that they are.

Many of those philosophers who have come to constitute the mainstream of the development of Western society's self-awareness have recognized that an understanding of human society is predicated in some degree on understanding our relationship to other species. In many instances, this recognition was understood to imply a respect for other species in relation to the degree in which they differed from us and each other. Indeed, this conception of the Great Chain of Being – from angels through humans to other mammals to amphibia to insects – pervaded much of Western thought before the materialist and rationalist age of the nineteenth century (see Chapter 6).

While most thought of reason and its associated concepts as the appropriate categories in which the human-animal similarities and differences should be understood, Jeremy Bentham, following the reasoning of Jean-Jacques Rousseau, suggested that the relevant category for acknowledgment of consideration was the capacity for suffering. In an obscure footnote made famous by the animal liberationists, Bentham claimed that animal exploitation was unacceptable not because animals could reason but because they possessed sentience: "A full grown horse or dog is beyond comparison a more rational as well as a more conversable animal, than an infant of a day or a week or even a month old. But suppose the case were otherwise, what would it avail? The question is not, can they *reason?* nor can they *talk?* but, can they *suffer?"*[26] We should not, however, interpret Bentham in what has become the customary manner as espousing an egalitarian position. Indeed, he explicitly denies it. In the *Deontology,* Bentham tells us that "We deprive [animals] of life, and this is justifiable – their pains do not equal our enjoyment. There is a balance of good."[27] It is in the tension between the claim that we are not entitled to exploit other species and the claim that we are entitled to deprive them of their life – their deprivation matters less than our legitimate satisfactions – that Western ambivalence toward other species rests. And so does the ambivalence of other cultures.

If Bentham is right that suffering is a most relevant category by which to determine exploitation, it is not enough. Explicitly, Bentham equates suffering with pain, and we know that birds whose wings have been clipped under anesthetic do not feel pain. They are nonetheless deprived of their *telos.* The lobotomized monkey is a travesty whether it suffers or not. Neither the bird nor the monkey is any longer its real self. Bentham is right, of course, that animal exploitation is unjustifiable. What is difficult to discern with any degree of accuracy is what constitutes the beginning of animal exploitation.

With the development of such ethological research as that of Fossey, Goodall, and Galdikas on primates, Moss on elephants, Fraser on pigs, Duncan on poultry, and the like, we are moving beyond the historical-philosophical concern to understand human nature by animal comparison to the concern to understand animal nature for its own sake. Just as we lack a firm understanding of human nature, so too with animal nature there is a long way to go. But if we are to determine appropriate treatment for other species, it is a prerequisite. It can, however, never be enough. Science without sensibilities is far worse than sensibilities without science.

III

Some in the Western tradition have acknowledged a compassion for other species based on our fundamental and primitive human nature, a compassion similar to, but not derived from, Oriental and Aboriginal sensibilities. Thus the founder of analytical psychology, Carl Jung, wrote in his posthumously published memoirs, *Memories, Dreams, Reflections:* "My compassion for animals did not derive from Buddhist trimmings of Schopenhauer's philosophy, but rested on the deeper foundations of a primitive attitude of mind – on an unconscious identity with animals."[28]

Jung derived his sense of being at one with the animal realm neither from reason alone nor from studying animal-sympathetic philosophies or mythologies. Instead it came, so Jung avowed, from an ancient sense of common belongingness that lies deep within the human soul, within our collective unconscious minds, and that is often obscured by discrepant cultural experiences. It corresponds to what the doyen of the Lake Romantics, William Wordsworth, called primal sympathy:

We will grieve not, rather find
Strength in what remains behind,
In the primal sympathy
Which having been, must ever be.

For Wordsworth, the identity with Nature is eternal – "Which having been, must ever be." Elsewhere he acknowledges himself:

well pleased to recognize
In Nature and the language of the sense.
The anchor of my purest thoughts, the nurse,
The guide, the guardian of my heart, and soul of all my moral being.[29]

Whether that be entitled God, Nirvana, Nature, or the Universal Soul depends more on perception than reality.

Phrases such as "the traditional Hindu respect for animals,"[30] the Taoist "seamless unity of nature,"[31] or Buddhism's "caring for the natural world ... its inherent harmony with nature"[32] abound in naturalist Western literature. Respect, caring, and harmony are usually deemed lacking in Western thought. And while what Jung calls that "primitive attitude," that "unconscious identity," may be more consistently discerned in the language of Aboriginal cultures, it has always also been present in the Western tradition. Whether respect for other species is derived from an unconscious identity, from reason, intuition, feeling, or some other faculty, it has played a significant role in Western thought. It is to be found in the writings of Pythagoras and Empedocles, Ovid and Plutarch, Pliny and Porphyry, Montaigne and Gassendi, Gay and Pope, Locke and Monboddo, Shelley and Goethe, Wollstonecraft and Macaulay, Voltaire and Saint-Hilaire, von Schelling and Dostoevsky, Twain and Wagner, Einstein and Schweitzer – and many more in varying degrees,[33] including even Plato if David Dombrowski is right in his view that "the Republic was to be a vegetarian city [which is] one of the best kept secrets in the history of philosophy."[34] (Given that Plato's metaphysics was Pythagorean in conception, and Pythagoras was an avid opponent of meat-eating, it ought not to come as a great surprise.[35]) One wonders at the response of those who imagine animal welfare issues to have been peripheral in Western thought! As Sir Francis Bacon expressed the prevalent Western attitude around the beginning of the seventeenth century, "The inclination of *Goodness* is imprinted deeply in the nature of Man; insomuch that, if it issue not toward Men, it will take unto other living creatures."[36] And Bacon is one of those treated by animal rights commentators as an animal adversary.

Is Bacon's position in fact substantially different from the Oriental and Aboriginal traditions? The famous Oglala visionary and medicine man Black Elk reiterated the Amerindian tradition by dividing animal life into the two-leggeds, the four-leggeds, and the winged. In the Native North American tradition, each type has its special character, attributes, and rights. In the two-legged category, there is only the human and, on occasion, when standing upright, the bear. The human, as in the Western tradition, thus possesses certain exclusive entitlements. What, then, is at issue in the differing traditions is not whether the human is entitled to privileges denied the other species, but how much differentiation is legitimate. Every society acknowledges, in practice, legitimate differences. In Hindu and Buddhist thought, animals are human beings in different karmic form but the human is at the apex.

In the West, the prevailing tradition, despite a few significant variations, has been to recognize the human as a very special animal while recognizing all other species as having their own identifying, unique characteristics. There is a hierarchy of worthiness in the Western mind, ranging from the rat to the ape. In *All Religions Are One,* William Blake wrote that "all men are alike (tho' infinitely various)." In *Walking,* Henry David Thoreau tells us that humans "are in the main alike, they were made several in order that they might be various." In the Western tradition, the dictum applies to animals also. There is a commonality of animality, but each species is thought to vary substantially from others. Each part of nature relates in increasing complexity to the other. Thus John Keats writes in "Hyperion":

> Say, doth the dull soil
> Quarrel with the proud forests it hath fed,
> And feedeth still, more comely than itself?
> Can it deny the chiefdom of green groves?
> Or shall the tree be envious of the dove
> Because it cooeth, and hath snowy wings
> To wander wherewithal and find its joys?
> We are such forest-trees, and our fair boughs
> Have bred forth, not pale solitary doves,
> But eagles golden-feathered, who do tower
> Above us in their beauty, and must reign
> In right thereof.

Animals are one in their animality. But not all animals are the same. To respect animals, we must acknowledge both the similarity and the diversity.

The notion of the human as animal may be used either, as with Hobbes, to reduce humans to the level of biological needs – satisfying machines – or, as with Charles Darwin, to raise non-human animals to the level of moral (7) and reasoning (5) beings. The underlying assumption of the first alternative is disparaging of the reality of humans; the second a ready compliment to the reality of much of the non-human animal world. Hobbesians and Darwinians will customarily give the same affirmative answer to the question "Are you an animal?" Their answers will have very different meanings. Moreover, the Darwinian, in responding to that question asked by a Hobbesian, will, if he or she does not wish to mislead the questioner, offer a circumspect answer. For Darwinians, the human is not an animal in the manner that Hobbesians conceive of animals. And neither are the other animals.

4
Rationalism

1   Knowledge is unsurpassed by any law or regulation; reason, if it is genuine and really enjoys its natural freedom, should have universal powers.

– Plato, *The Laws*, c. 365 BC

2   If an offence come out of the truth, better is it that the offence come than that the truth be concealed.

– St. Jerome, c. AD 347-420

3   The heart has its reasons which reason cannot know.

– Blaise Pascal, *Pensées*, 1670

4   Reason must be our last judge and guide in everything.

– John Locke, *Essay Concerning Human Understanding*, 1690

5   Our sensibility is incontestably anterior to our intelligence, and we had sentiments before ideas.

– Jean-Jacques Rousseau, *Profession of Faith of the Savoyard Vicar*, 1762

6   Man under present social conditions seems to me corrupted more
    by his reason than by his passions. His passions – I mean those
    that characterize the primitive man – have preserved for society
    the few natural elements it still possesses.

    – Sébastien Chamfort, c. 1780

7   Absolute Reason / Died last night at eleven o'clock.

    – Henrik Ibsen, *Peer Gynt*, 1867

8   I am the snake. I am the snake of reason.

    – Lieutenant Henry in Ernest Hemingway's *A
    Farewell to Arms*, 1929

9   The exercise of man's highest possession, that which differentiates
    him from the brute [is] his reason.

    – Frederick Copleston, *A History of Philosophy:
    Greece and Rome*, 1944

10 Overvalued reason has this in common with political absolutism:
    under its domination the individual is pauperized.

    – C.J. Jung, *Memories, Dreams, Reflections*, 1963

11 Our age has put its trust in reason, and reason is a whore.
    She goes with anyone.

    – Father Cyprian in Mary Gordon's *The
    Company of Women*, 1980

12 Reason is a narrow system swollen into an ideology ... Like most
    religions, reason presents itself as the solution to the problems it
    has created.

    – John Ralston Saul, *Voltaire's Bastards*, 1992

13   Whatever anyone says [reason] means, someone will argue that it
      means something else. The one thing they will agree on is that
      reason is both central and essential to our civilization, which is
      curious since they don't know what it is.

—John Ralston Saul, *The Doubter's Companion*, 1994

I

John Ralston Saul (13) tells us there is considerable disagreement in the
Western tradition about the nature of reason, but that everyone agrees it is
essential to our civilization. His is certainly a common perception. Yet while
there are indeed many of the West's primary thinkers who proclaim the
supremacy of reason (1, 2, 4, 9, for example), there are also those (3, 5, 6, 7,
8, 10, 11, 12, for example) who have expressed earnest reservations about its
efficacy for human fulfilment, or even whether it is our primary source of
knowledge. Mary Gordon (11) captures the anti-rationalist view with
aplomb: faith in reason must be at the expense of loyalty and community.
And while Machiavelli and Hobbes stressed the significance of reason, they
restricted its function to that of calculating how to achieve the ends determined by the passions: animal and human reason differed only by degree.

In fact, as the quotations reflect, the Western tradition is a complex one,
incapable of being reduced to unidimensional terms. Understanding rationalism for our purposes – the term may in general be said to possess almost
as many nuances as "nature," some philosophers going so far as to employ
"reason" as others employ "intuition" – as the view that reason is the cor-
nerstone of the human *telos,* and as that which raises humanity above the
level of other species, one may readily understand the Western tradition as
more rationalist than it is anything else. But it is nothing exclusively. There
are many who find reason to be the source of humanity's dissatisfactions.

Animal rights advocates decry rationalism as the source of Western disrespect for other species. We disparage other creatures by denying their
capacity for the supreme attribute of rational thought. And by deeming reason the supreme attribute, we fail to recognize the value of the qualities possessed by other species. There is undoubtedly some truth in such a claim.
However, while, as we shall see in the first part of this chapter, rationalism
has predominated, we shall see in the second part that both the rationalism
itself and the complexity of the Western tradition – possessing both rationalist and anti-rationalist elements – provide some surprising benefits for
our relationship to the animal realm.

In Western civilization, reason is the category we resort to when we wish
to demonstrate why we should receive preferential treatment over other
species, even though we are sometimes willing to acknowledge reason's
limitations, or even its negative aspects, when we are not using the concept

to compare ourselves favourably to other beings. Plato deemed us godlike in our natures when we allowed true reason free rein (1). Aristotle acknowledged that there were other excellences than the intellectual: the productive and the practical virtues each had their rightful place. Nonetheless, the intellectual capacities remained the most prized for Aristotle, and, generally speaking, despite numerous caveats, they have remained pre-eminent in estimation in Western civilization. Indeed, they have remained so despite biblical admonitions to the contrary. Thus, in a Buddhist vein, in Genesis 3, God warns humans not to eat of the tree of knowledge, for then (Verse 5) "your eyes shall be opened; and ye shall be as gods, knowing good and evil." But when it was recognized that (Verse 6) "it was a tree to be desired to make one wise," the fruit was eaten. Plato, Aristotle, and the Bible concurred that the acquisition of knowledge made one divine in one's nature but disagreed about its benefits. Since the Renaissance, the West has been far more a child of classical Greece than it has been a civilization based on biblical edicts. Thus, for example, Sir Francis Bacon writes in his "Essay on Atheism" (c. 1600): "Certainly man is of kin to the beasts by the body; and if he be not of kin to God by his spirit, he is a base and ignoble creature." Our possession of reason raised us, at least in potential, above mere animal nature to which other species were restricted.

To be sure, a number have resisted the rationalist clarion call of Platonic Greece. Thus, for example, the Swedish philosopher and mystic Emanuel Swedenborg (1688-1772) argued that birds have their knowledge of the things appropriate to them, including an understanding of the seasons, because they have remained true to their primordial natures and have not perverted that nature by reason. In contrast, humans have pursued the path of reason to the detriment of their souls. Much in Swedenborg corresponds more closely to the Orient than the Occident, though there is much in early Christianity in similar vein – among the Desert Fathers, for example. Clearly, thinkers like Swedenborg are somewhat of an exception in the later Western tradition, but it would be unwarranted to assume that the power of reason has gone unquestioned, as some of the opening quotations to this chapter indicate. Indeed, as John Steinbeck put in the mouth of Doc in *Sweet Thursday,* "Thought is the evasion of feeling." Notoriously, Edgar Allan Poe denounced the feebleness of reason. "Hundreds of people can talk for one who can think," wrote John Ruskin, "but thousands can think for one who can see." For Oscar Wilde, "The only way in which truth can with certainty be discovered [is] by evolving it from one's inner consciousness." Emphatically, John Keats declared that "Men of Genius" come to truth not through "consequential reasoning" but by "the submission of their intellect to intuition and imagination." The list is legion.

Yet even some of those who express their sincere reservations about reason use the concept to distinguish us from other species when it is convenient. When we domesticate food species, use animals in medical experiments, take other creatures' habitats for human ends – be they for hospitals, homes, food production, or recreational pursuits – destroy "vermin," incarcerate fauna in zoos or circuses, or engage in sport hunting, we usually justify our behaviour by an appeal to human rational superiority. We are entitled, so we claim, to save our sick at the expense of the lives of other sentient beings, to build our homes on the homes of, say, foxes, antelope, or rabbits, to enclose space for food cattle production, even though the enclosures destroy the natural habitats of other species, because we are superior beings. Because we are clearly inferior to many species in, say, courage, or loyalty, or speed, or strength, we deem the appropriate comparative category to be reason. Or we resort to an appeal to religion or nature that, on closer examination, entails the idea of human superiority (for example, being made in the image of God, or having a greater capacity to feel pain or suffering).

In his *On the Senses* (c. 300 BC), Theophrastus reported the view of Diogenes of Appollonia (c. 425 BC) that:

> We think by air that is pure and dry; for moisture inhibits the mind. That is why when we are asleep or drunk or full we think less. There is a sign that moisture destroys the mind in the fact that the other animals have weaker intellects; for they breathe air from the earth and the food they take is moister. Birds breathe pure air, but their nature is like that of fish; for the flesh is firm and the breath does not pass through the body but comes to a stop in the belly. Hence they digest their food quickly but are themselves stupid. In addition to their food, their mouths and tongue contribute to this; for they cannot understand one another. Plants, because they are not hollow, and do not take in air, are completely incapable of thinking.[1]

Clearly, the speciousness of Diogenes's claims indicates that rationalization was present in the early days of Western philosophy to explain the human rational superiority that entitled humans to preference over their fellow creatures. It was not, however, reason alone that exemplified that superiority. Thus we read in Hesiod's *Works and Days* of the eighth century BC: "For this was the rule for men that Kronos' son [Zeus] laid down: whereas fish and beasts and flying birds would eat one another, because Right is not among them, to men he gave Right, which is much the best in practice."[2] The moral sense in humans raises them above other species and requires them to behave better than other species by abstaining from flesh-eating. (Hesiod seems not to have recognized that most mammal species are vegetarian, which is curious because Hesiod was himself of farming stock and must have been aware that little farming livestock is carnivorous.)

The vegetarian tradition was a significant one in classical Greece, arising from a respect for other beings based on kinship. Thus we read in the work of Sextus Empiricus that: "Pythagoras and Empedocles and [others] say that we have a fellowship not only with one another but also with the irrational animals. For there is a single spirit which pervades the whole world as a sort of soul and which unites us with them. That is why, if we kill them and eat their flesh, we commit injustice and impiety, inasmuch as we are killing our kin."[3] The Pythagoreans recognized human rational superiority, even sometimes deeming other species irrational, but they did not consider that superiority sufficient to entitle human use of other species for solely human ends, for example, as food. This idea of fellowship and the universal spirit bears considerable similarity to Oriental[4] and Aboriginal conceptions, with the significant exception that in the latter cases kinship is not taken to imply that one should refrain from consuming one's kin (Jains, Brahmins, and certain Buddhists excepted).

Increasingly, the importance of the universal spirit in classical Greek thought gave way to individual rationality, which thereafter dominated Western philosophy, even though it was not exclusive. Indeed, as we can recognize from the thoughts of Diogenes, Hesiod, and the Pythagoreans, the varieties and complexities present in later Western philosophy have their origins in classical Greece. It is perhaps with Philolaus (c. 420 BC) that we encounter what later became the Western "common sense" view of the animal realm, acknowledging its rationality but positing its significance beneath that of the human. In his *Logical Arithmetic,* pseudo-Iamblichus reported that Philolaus in his *On Nature* had proclaimed, "There are four first principles of *rational* animals ... brain, heart, navel, genitals. Head of thought, heart of soul and perception, navel of rooting, genitals of depositing of seed and generation. Brain signifies the first principle of man, heart that of animal, navel that of plant, genitals that of all together (for all shoot and sprout from seed)."[5] Brain and thought were deemed the defining human characteristics.

Certainly, it is today difficult for many Western minds to conceive of acquiring knowledge other than in some manner through reason, although in the nineteenth century one would still occasionally encounter the view expressed in Robertson's *Sermons* of 1872 that "there are two ways of reaching truth: by reasoning it out and by feeling it out." The idea of knowledge through inspiration pervades Blake's writings. It is especially pronounced in his *Milton* (though paradoxically Milton himself thought reason the route to *Paradise Regained*). Victor Hugo queried, "Why does the mind say so poorly what the heart feels so well?" And mid-twentieth-century American literature is filled with anti-rationalist sentiment. Indeed, D.H. Lawrence remarked that the "best Americans are mystics by instinct." Still, in the East such views are more commonplace. Zen Buddhism eschews "reason" alone in favour of what is called *Prajna* – a "wisdom-intuition" in the mind of the person being awakened to awareness. In *Foundations of Tibetan Mysticism,* Lama Angarika Gorinda writes that the way of Mahayana Buddhism "is not a way of running away from the world but of overcoming it through growing knowledge (*Prajna*), through active love (*Maitri*) toward one's fellow beings, through inner participation in the joys and sufferings of others (*Karuna, Mudita* [compassion, sympathy]), and through equanimity (*Upeksa*) with regard to one's own weal and woe."[6] It is revelation more than reason that is the source of our knowing and our love for other beings. Truth and justice lie in a search within, not without.

One of the earliest consequences of the self-conscious pursuit of reason in the West was the distancing of the human from other species. It was perhaps Alcmaeon (c. fifth century BC), again as reported by Theophrastus in *On the Senses*, who first expressed the view explicitly "that humans differ from the other animals because they alone understand, whereas the others perceive [that is, sense or feel, perhaps] but do not understand."[7] It is, then, with Alcmaeon that we first encounter the later common belief – at least, I can find no explicit earlier instance – that humans differ *in kind,* rather than *in degree,* from other species and that difference consists essentially in the possession of reason, although there are undoubted hints in that direction in earlier myth and legend. Still, explicit expression had to await the philosophical awakening of the Presocratics in classical Greece. Alcmaeon's assertion is to be understood as a reflection of the emergent dominance of reason, and consequently of humanity over other species, which accompanied the development of Western philosophical thought. The impact of such thinking retained its force throughout Western history, exemplified by the Russian philosopher Nikolay Strakhov in 1860: "The secret of human life is contained in itself, and we lose its significance as soon as we do not separate man from nature, as soon as we place him on the same level with [nature's] creations and begin to judge him from the same point of view as animals and plants."[8]

By contrast to the Western concern with reason, in the Hindu *Upanishads* – several of which were composed around the same time as, and some a little earlier than, the origins of Greek philosophy – we read, "Into deep darkness fall those who follow action. Into deeper darkness fall those who follow knowledge."[9] Neither alone suffices. Each must be in harmonious balance and neither must be pursued for its own sake. Truth and understanding come from the testimony of revealed scripture (the Veda). Appropriate external knowledge requires prior spiritual awareness. The sage Rabindranath Tagore referred to "the inner voice that goes beyond the boundaries of words."[10] That inner voice reflects the truths of the scriptures. There are more trustworthy paths to the human essence than through abstract reason. Reason differentiates us from everything around us. The inner voice is in harmonious balance with nature. Philosophical reason alone leads us away from understanding our relationship with nature and fulfilment within it.

It is thus that the Occidental and Oriental paths diverge and not only produce different cultures, but also encourage different roles for humankind –

the one above, the other within, if at the apex of, the world of nature. One must stress, however, that these are different emphases, different tendencies, not opposites. The East never denounced all reason, though it often used different words for it. Its conception of reason, however, was restricted to technical reason, which can remove obstructions to, and inconsistencies in, sound thought so that knowledge can emerge. And the West never deemed reason the sole reputable faculty of humankind; nor made it clear precisely what it meant by "reason."

In the classical Greek age of reason, the Olympic Games and the Muses are witness to the breadth of human interests, to the fact that philosophical reason played a minor role, despite the extravagant claims made for it as the defining essence of humanity. Athletics and music are as essentially human as is the province of reason. Indeed, more so. Then, as now, enthusiasm for sport and light entertainment far exceeded any interest in philosophical or scientific endeavour, despite Plato's and Aristotle's (and later John Stuart Mill's) insistence on its pre-eminence, on its being the defining human attribute. Indeed, Xenophanes, Euripides, and Diogenes, as well as Plato, warned against idolizing athletes in preference to patriots and thinkers – but to as little avail in classical Greece as in Bulls-worshipping Chicago or Eagles-worshipping Philadelphia. "In the blessings of the mind athletes have no share," wrote Galen, the most eminent physician of the Roman Empire, but again to no avail. Indeed, after researching on five continents, Abraham Maslow reported that music and sex were the two most universally acknowledged peaks of human experience. As Robert Louis Stevenson wrote after listening to steerage passengers merrymaking during a transatlantic voyage, "Humanly speaking it is more important to play the fiddle, even badly, than to write huge works on recondite subjects."

And if we are tempted to include music in the realm of reason, let us not forget how that would require the elevation of the birds. As Alexander F. Skutch wrote in *Origins of Nature's Beauty*, "the aesthetic sensibility of birds" is reflected in their seeming "delight in hearing themselves and probably also their neighbours. When a versatile singer invents a new tune, he repeats it over and over; his neighbours may copy it. Jays who lack loud songs sometimes rest in solitude and continue to sing pleasantly in an undertone. Such *sotto voce* medleys appear *to lack social or biologic significance;* the jay sings for his own comfort or enjoyment, as a human hums a tune when alone."[11] Charles Hartsthorne in his *Born to Sing* developed an objective method of bird-song assessment, giving some birds as many as forty-eight points out of a possible fifty-four.[12] Melody is as much avian as it is human.

The horrors of the Roman Circus are no less witness to the breadth of human interest, even in a self-professed age of reason and of enlightenment. There were seventy amphitheatres in the Roman Empire which saw four centuries of grave atrocities committed against both animals and humans. While the young and still benevolent Nero forbade contests in which blood would be shed, the edict died long before its ultimately blood-thirsty author. Eight thousand animals are reported to have been slaughtered in two days to celebrate the opening of the Colosseum in Rome itself, eleven thousand to celebrate Trajan's conquest of Dacia (modern Rumania). Elephants, hippopotamuses, rhinoceroses, crocodiles, lions, tigers, bulls, leopards, chamois, deer, giraffes, and bears were butchered for entertainment alone. Aghast at ancient Roman incongruence, Voltaire remarked that they "built their greatest masterpiece of architecture, the amphitheatre, for wild beasts to fight in."

Such barbarisms often – there were exceptions – aroused the greatest pride, rather than shame, in the Roman populace. Thus, for example, in the document attached to his will, the Emperor Augustus boasted that he had exhibited 8,000 gladiators and 3,510 wild beasts – such was his private generosity to the Roman people. The "fury of the circus, the atrocities of the amphitheatre, and the cruel orgies of the games" was the judgment of Queen Victoria's chaplain, Frederic Farrar, reflecting the changed values of a later Western epoch.[13] Both classical Rome and Victorian England thought of themselves as supremely rational societies, however much they may have differed in their moral evaluations. Reason and morality are in fact independent attributes. As Arthur Schopenhauer expressed it in *The World as Will and Representation,* "It is as little necessary that the saint be a philosopher, as that the philosopher be a saint." So, too, Victor Hugo: "Virtue and philosophy are separate things." Obvious perhaps, but it is remarkable how often we refuse to acknowledge it, assuming reason to be the prerequisite of moral action. Perhaps again it is a consequence of our self-distinction from other species, coupled with the assumption that other species lack a morality as well as reason. Yet reason is used in two distinct senses – the one as the primary source of philosophical, including moral, knowledge; the other as the instrument of achievement for goals derived from some other source, such as "self-interest," "convention," or "the passions." On the second usage, one may argue the Romans were being perfectly "rational" in their slaughtering of the beasts, rational in their immorality – at least if "reason" is understood as no more than a tool of the passions. While the former sense – reason as the path to ultimate truths – prevailed until the scholastic age, the latter – reason as mere instrument – has predominated since Machiavelli, overwhelmingly since Rousseau (Kantians excluded). It is to overcome the rationalist error – the belief that morals are subject to rational discovery and explanation – and the relativist error – the belief that morals are merely conventions – that the *Tao Te Ching* insists that we stop analyzing morality and get on with being moral. Our intellectualism leads us astray. Both reason as the source of moral knowledge and reason as the appropriate path to implement moral conventions are, for Taoists, a misunderstanding of the nature of morality. We know our morality instinctively just as the animal knows its morality. Philosophical investigation serves to obfuscate what we already know as the animals that we are and hinders our capacity to *feel* our moral nature. In the Western tradition, Emanuel Swedenborg, William Blake, and William Wordsworth are among those who recognized the truth of the Taoist understanding. Fichte, Emerson, and Thoreau, too. But not the rationalists. For them, reason is sufficient to demonstrate morality or to deny its existence; in short, to lead us away from what we already know in our souls. And a part of that natural morality would be to recognize ourselves as a part of the natural order, kin to the other beasts of the natural realm.

Before the sixth century BC – or thereabouts – Western society remained in the realm of myth and epic. It had not yet discovered reason and philosophy, or, for that matter, the meekness of soul of some religions. Traditionally, Greek philosophy is said to have replaced myth, and life according to myth, in 585 BC when Thales of Miletus in Asia Minor (a Greek colony) is reported to have predicted successfully an eclipse of the sun. Of course, Thales had his predecessors in Sumeria, Babylonia, and Egypt, for example, and with Hesiod among the Greeks – and many even doubt that he could have predicted an eclipse with any degree of accuracy at all. Nonetheless, despite the customary cavils and caveats, it is as fruitful a point as any, and less arbitrary than most, to acknowledge as the beginnings of philosophy and the dominance of Reason. (Moreover, Aristotle said it was so!)

Still, the prior flourishing of Sumerian medicine, however mixed with the acknowledgments of evil demons as a causal agent of sickness, encourages one to choose a different point. Egyptian architecture, medicine and hieroglyphics, Babylonian physics, astronomy and mathematics, and the bloody *science* of war of the predominantly vegetarian Assyrians, along with their mathematical mastery, are even more tempting alternatives.

Nearly all the ancients concur in ascribing the invention of technological science to the Egyptians, and their own legends claim its origins lay with their god of wisdom, Thoth, at a time that is now some 20,000 years in the past. But it is not a matter of legend that we owe to the original inhabitants of Egypt – the current population is descended predominantly from later immigrants – the invention of glass, ink and paper, clock, calendar, and alphabet. We may be even more impressed by the Central American Mayan achievements in the scribal arts, mathematics, astronomy, and architecture, admittedly their classic period not coming until the third century AD, but accomplished, apparently, without the aid of the wheel, metal tools, and, most significantly, without beasts of burden. (By contrast, by the first century BC, Greco-Roman technology employed animal power for grinding grain via the "hourglass" mill and the water mill, raising water by capstan in a geared-bucket chain, crushing olives or metal ore in an edge-runner mill, and even for kneading dough.)

What was different about Greek philosophy was that it stimulated a pervasively rationalist mentality, which, despite its dearth in the centuries of the Greco-Roman gloom, the so-called dark ages, continues to suffuse the modern educated mind. While the scientific and technological achievements of the Middle East raised human achievement inexorably above that of the rest of nature, Greek rationalism gave us the consciousness to imagine ourselves a separate and essentially superior existence.

Following the success of Plato and Aristotle, above all, in elevating human rationality to godlike stature, most Westerners, especially the educated, acquired a mode of consciousness in which humans were essentially separated from nature and the other animals. One must, however, note that there continued to be some – exemplified by Pythagoras, Empedocles, Plutarch, and Porphyry, but found more frequently in the "common man," and even more frequently in the "common woman" – who acknowledged themselves an intrinsic part of nature. Moreover, the idea of human superiority is certainly not confined to classical Greece, but is found just as completely in the Middle East in both Christianity and Islam. The difference between Greece and the lands of the Bible is that in the former reason elevates us, and in the latter, God. Both, however, have the same impetus to their conceptions – the scientific and mythological inheritance of the Middle East. We cannot ascribe the idea of human superiority, exclusivity, and separation from nature to Greek rationalism alone. Nonetheless, the New Testament strikes an accommodation between Greco-Roman rationalism and the more mythological and more explicitly animal-friendly manner of the Old Testament, and predominantly in favour of Greece.

Claims have been made for the origins of philosophy in an earlier period than that of classical Greece. One hears the claim for the Hindus and the Chinese, in the *Rig-Veda* and the *I Ching* respectively, while some claim its beginnings to be found already with ancient Egyptians almost 5,000 years ago in the *Instructions of Ptahhotep,* which included inter alia advice for dealing with rebellious children. The core of the Egyptian ethic of the Fifth Dynasty (c. 2400 BC) was the concept of *ma'at,* meaning justice or balance, and bearing a striking resemblance to the later Greek *dikê.* The Mesopotamian *Epic of Gilgamesh,* also of the third millennium BC, may be understood as a dialogue between proponents of hedonism and proponents of the work ethic, thus in a manner being a forerunner of both Homer's *Odyssey* and the dialogues of Plato.

The *Epic of Gilgamesh* was followed by the famous law code of Hammurabi of Babylon (c. 1700 BC), in which is asserted the moral responsibilities of ensuring that "the strong might not oppress the weak" and of maintaining economic justice, although it also promoted hierarchy in proclaiming that injuries to the aristocracy alone called for the *lex talionis,* an eye for an eye. In several respects, this code was a reiteration of the code of King Unikagina of Lagash in Mesopotamia about 2350 BC, in which he claimed to have a covenant with the city god Ningirsu to "not deliver up the weak and widowed to the powerful man." Even animal welfare was in the minds of at least some of the ancients. In the Egyptian *Book of the Dead*, dating back to the sixteenth century BC, perhaps earlier, which deals predominantly with the symbolic passage of the soul through the afterlife, the journeyer is warned that worldly ill-treatment of animals will prove a detriment to the quest for heaven.

None of these codes, however, should be equated with philosophy, at least in its Greco-Western form. Those who make philosophical claims for these codes confuse philosophy with speculation and moral philosophy with moralizing. What differentiated Greek thought – at least in its dominant strain; there was another side – was its elevation of philosophical reason to the status of the sole route to knowledge, and philosophical knowledge as the human potential that makes us godlike in our natures, which, indeed, separates us from the rest of nature, and which encourages us to treat animals as legitimate interests of our human ends.

The Chinese do offer something in some significant respects comparable to Greek philosophy, beginning with Confucius in the sixth century BC, very similar in time to the origins of Greek philosophy, and followed by Mozi and Yangshu. But even here, not unlike in the writings of Hesiod, is a recognition of the prime importance of the origins of one's historical culture. The Golden Age, the age to be emulated, lies in the past. It is an ideal, the offering of a utopia to be recaptured. Confucius, Mozi, and Yangshu *represent* a tradition. They regard themselves as expounders of traditional truths, not as discoverers of philosophical novelty. For them, the wisdom of the past needs to be expounded, to be filled out, at most to be explored, not to be replaced by the products of individual reason. They are filling out ancestral archetypes, not inventing them. They are at most developing, not discovering. "I transmit rather than create," wrote Confucius, "I believe in and love the ancients."

Only with Mencius (c. 300 BC) do we encounter a more individualistic reason-based philosophy – and not entirely unlike Aristotle's criticism of Plato – in which practical wisdom is preferable to philosophic wisdom, that is, wisdom relevant to the doing of things rather than the knowing of things. While philosophical elements are increasingly evident in the Chinese tradition, to claim, say, that Confucius is a philosopher is like claiming that Moses or Gautama Buddha is a philosopher – which is true only at a superficial level, even though they do not espouse superficial philosophies. They are decidedly not metaphysicians within the Greek conception of philosophy – which is concerned with "the truth" rather than "the way." Buddha would have been insulted by any equation of his teachings with a rational philosophy.

While grand generalizations must always be exaggerations, we may nonetheless say that Western society, as a consequence of the Greek experience, building on Middle East experience, pursues knowledge as an end in itself, in almost wilful disregard of societal traditions and mythological origins. Non-Western societies pursue knowledge to the extent that it contributes to the fulfilment of traditional human purposes and is consistent with societal traditions and mythological origins. The West pursues external truth, the East pursues inner understanding. The former is essentially alienating from the traditional conception of self, and the latter essentially integrating. The traditional Chinese credo insists that "it is not well for a man to know more than is necessary for his daily living." Knowledge of "the way" is knowledge of how we may develop fully our inner realities to live well our daily lives. Knowledge of "the truth" is sought independent of any benefit to the soul, and even when it is detrimental. It becomes an end in itself. Walt Whitman recognized that a rational science stands for an absolute surrender to the truth: "It never asks us: Do you want this thing to be true? Is it ugly, hateful? If it is true that settles it." Neither Orientals nor Aboriginals would consider the scientific question a wise one. For the Oriental and the Aboriginal, the "way" is to be pursued, "rational truth" to be cast out. Abstract knowledge will not make you free. It will enslave you. It will alienate you from your essential self, the self engendered by primordial nature. When you pursue knowledge through philosophic reason, you separate yourself from that which is known internally and intuitively. Hence, in Western thought, nature and other species are estranged from the self and understood as "other," as something alien. In this manner the sense of kinship with nature and other species is lost.

Nonetheless, we should not fail to recognize that while the West may have sometimes imagined itself above nature, the Aboriginal and Oriental worlds have imagined themselves the apex of nature, even though they acknowledge themselves a part of it. While the East may have escaped the worst self-aggrandizing consequences of rationalism, it has in its technological and intellectual development come to see humans as the zenith of nature. In her discussion of the Buddhist idea of the "evolution of the ego-centered state of being" in the introduction to Guru Rinpoche's *Tibetan Book of the Dead*, Francesca Fremantle explains its five components:

The first component is form (*rūpa*), the beginning of individuality and separate existence, and the division of experience into subject and object. Now there is a primal "self" aware of an external world. As soon as this happens, the self reacts to its surroundings: this is the second stage, feeling (*vedanā*). It is not yet fully developed emotion – just an instinctive liking, dislike or indifference, but immediately it grows more complicated as the centralized entity asserts itself by reacting not only passively but actively. This is the third stage, perception (*samjñā*), in its fullest sense, when the self is aware of stimulus and automatically responds to it. The fourth component is concept (*samskā*), covering the intellectual and emotional activity of interpretation which follows perception. It is what puts things together, and builds up the patterns of personality and karma. Finally, there is conscious-ness (*vijñāna*) which combines all the sense-perceptions and the mind. The self has now become a complete universe of its own; instead of directly per-ceiving the world as it really is, it projects its own images around it.[14]

Buddhism's message here is that it is through the "dissolution of the sense of self" that one is fulfilled. The import of the Buddhist view is that any heightening of individual ambition to pursue knowledge will lead toward a disengagement from all that surrounds. The search for an objec-tive knowledge of nature separates one from nature. Science and belong-ingness are in tension (as Mary Gordon also emphasized [11]). In the Buddhist view, secular education is in essence alienating from both nature and the authentic self. In reality, of course, because most humans must pass through the stages set out by Fremantle, at least to some substantial degree, and because all societies have undergone some form of technological devel-opment, all will be alienated from nature.

However, with the Greek approach to reason, the substantial degree is increased and the conception of separation becomes self-conscious. Indeed, it reaches its apogee in the philosophy of John Stuart Mill, who avowed in his *Utilitarianism* of 1863: "It is better to be a human being dis-satisfied than a pig satisfied; better to be Socrates dissatisfied than a fool satisfied."[15] Knowledge is the ultimate goal of humankind. We are fulfilled not through grace, or love, or belongingness, or being in harmony with nature, but through reason. Finally, the hedonistic elements of utilitarian-ism were transcended, but at the expense of the status of other species and less intelligent humans. This transcendence did not mean that we should disregard the interests of other species. We should instead protect them as beings needful of our concern. In *The Principles of Political Economy* (1848), Mill argued, "The reasons for legal intervention in favour of children apply no less strongly to those unfortunate slaves and victims of the most brutal part of mankind – the lower animals." Similarly, Mary Wollstonecraft asked, in her *A Vindication of the Rights of Woman* (1792), "In what does man's pre-eminence over the brute creation consist?" Unequivocal was her own reply: "The answer is as clear as that a half is less than the whole; in Reason." Nonetheless, she considered it an essential part of education to teach the virtue of consideration for other species. While rationalism may have distanced us from a sense of kinship with other species, it encouraged us to recognize our responsibilities to them as autonomous, even if inferior, creatures.

We should not imagine the human-animal value distinction by contrast inimical to the Oriental mind. Thus, in the *Tibetan Book of the Dead,* we can read of the warning to those about to be reincarnated: "If you are going to be born as an animal, you will see, as if through a mist, rock-caves and holes in the ground and straw huts. Do not enter there." It is better for you if you can avoid becoming an animal and remain at the apex of life as a human. And, yet again, a few pages further on, we are warned of becoming "the lowest of the low, like beasts."[16] Clearly, reincarnation as an animal is a fate to be avoided if at all possible. Both Orient and Occident acknowledge the human a decidedly superior being, but, in principle at least, with responsibility toward the "lower animals."

What is different is that in the Western tradition the grounds for the distinction are made clear. Human superiority is predicated on superior reason.[17] Indeed, Mill, goes so far as to claim the intellectual pleasures superior to all others. In a wonderfully circular argument, Mill offers as his ground the fact that intellectuals, who alone are in a position to choose intellectual or non-intellectual pleasures as a consequence of their exclusive experiences, will choose the intellectual pleasures.[18] Mill's claim is rather like arguing that human meat-eaters should have the exclusive right to determine the superior diet because they alone have experience of both meats and non-meats. Indeed, such logic will allow rapists to determine whether sexual assault should be a crime and burglars ordain the rules for property acquisition – and those who possess reason, but not grace, or speed, or strength, to determine the categories of relative animal values.

Few Western intellectuals have recognized the potential problem of knowledge, as understood by Taoists, Buddhists, and Hindus. To be sure, there was both a patristic and medieval anti-intellectualism that included Tertullian, St. Anselm, and Bernard of Clairvaux, but this tendency had little influence on later Western philosophers. Schopenhauer was a notable exception in his reiteration of the Ecclesiastes doctrine that "he who increases knowledge increases sorrow," echoing Byron's "Knowledge is sorrow," which evoked John Keats's "Sorrow is Wisdom." Blake proclaimed education "the great sin." In his *Life and Habit,* Samuel Butler praises instinct as the basis of right conduct. But it is Rousseau above all who blames our decline from noble savagery on the acquisition of knowledge. Tolstoy echoed him in *A Confession,* proclaiming that "rational knowledge does not provide the meaning of life, but excludes it." He adds that one must first understand life through faith, "then one may use reason to elucidate it." Nonetheless, these instances belie the more rationalist Western norm. Of course, there have been many university courses, going back probably into the nineteenth century, entitled "The Problem of Knowledge" or something similar. But the "problem" dealt with is how we know what we know, or whether we know what we know. Whether what we know is worth knowing is almost always assumed in the positive, at least by the intelligentsia. Indeed, Aristotle opened his *Metaphysics* with the claim that "all men by nature desire to know." And Hobbes added: "Man is distinguished, not only by his reason; but also by this singular passion from other animals ... which is a lust of the mind, that by a perseverance of delight in the continual and indefatigable generation of knowledge, exceeds the short vehemence of any carnal pleasure."

Of course, especially since Marx, but as also recognized in embryo by James Harrington in his *Commonwealth of Oceana* some two centuries earlier, there has been constant acknowledgment of the dangers of technology – in the recent words of John A. Livingston, "the accumulating *knowledge of how-to-do-it*" is "downright devastating."[19] It is remarkable how Bacon's "knowledge is power" has been constantly applauded by intellectuals who have at the same time been dismayed by the domination produced by technological knowledge, which is also power, and will produce the same kind of control as knowledge itself. In the Oriental view, both pure and practical reason unaccompanied by a nature-embracing spirituality are essentially alienating. Both remove us from our natural kinship with other species.

Such a judgment is clearly alien to the traditional Western conception that has recognized Greek rationalism as the harbinger of a self-conscious humanitarianism. Certainly, Greece is what Hegel called "the native land of cultured European man." Its culture stimulated H.D.F. Kitto to write of "the reason and humanity of the Greeks," who, according to Edmund Husserl, were noted for their theoretical knowledge based on objective truth, which, for the Greeks, was itself the absolute value. "The Greek is the bearer of Reason," concurs the French student of classical mythology Marcel Detienne, writing on behalf of "the new Enlightenment." By consensus, we owe to Greece both our rationalism and our humanity. And by "humanity" is meant the willingness to be kind, tender, considerate, and compassionate toward others.

Yet, given the distancing of ourselves from nature, we may wonder whether "humanity" had any implications for the benevolent treatment of other species. What might astonish us, and what cries out for an explanation, is that those who insist on a significant human superiority exemplified in reason are often precisely those who insist on our responsibilities to the animal realm. Earlier in this book, we encountered that view with Jeremy Bentham, Francis Bacon, and Jane Goodall; in recent pages, we met it with John Stuart Mill and Mary Wollstonecraft. It is incumbent on us to ask whether this view is an illogical aberration or a direct consequence of the rationalist and scientific mentality.

II

Whatever the detriments to the life of reason may be, however wise the Orient may have been in recognizing its limitations, the reality of scientific reason is that it encourages us to distinguish between subject and object and thus come to understand the object as an autonomous entity with its own *telos*, quite independent of our own. Impartiality and objectivity are encouraged (if almost never *entirely* achieved) by the scientific mind.

While the life of reason may separate us from nature, it also allows us to recognize the intrinsic merits of things in themselves. Thus, reason allows us to understand other species, as well as other humans, not merely as interdependent parts of nature, subject to all the cruelties of nature, not merely as extensions of ourselves, but as ends in themselves that are entitled to be considered independently of nature, and that may even possess rights against nature when it is purposelessly harmful. While other civilizations may more readily perceive how we are an intrinsic part of nature, we may more readily recognize the worthiness of a being for its own sake, rather than that of the relationship to ourselves and to all else. Indeed, the perception extends beyond animated nature. D.H. Lawrence explained the achievement of Cézanne as one in which his "apples are a real attempt to let the apple exist in its own separate entity, without transfusing it with personal emotion. Cézanne's great effort was, as it were, to shove the apple away from him, and let it live of itself." Cézanne's insight extended scientific consciousness into the world of art. The apple was understood for itself, and thus understood far more fully. Novelists and poets frequently acknowledge their need to "distance" themselves from the object of their attention to depict it accurately.

One should not imagine, of course, that these possible consequences of the recognition of the rights of other species through scientific objectivity are always followed in Western thought. Only occasionally are they. Nonetheless, it is by treating animals as objects and understanding them as entities in themselves rather than the source of human lessons that David Hume could write:

'Tis evident that *sympathy,* or the communication of passions, takes place among animals, no less than among men. Fear, anger, courage and other affections are frequently communicated from one animal to another, without their knowledge of that cause, which produc'd the original passion. Grief likewise is receiv'd by sympathy; and produces almost all the same consequences, and excites the same emotions as in our species. The howlings and lamentations of a dog produce a sensible concern in his fellows. And 'tis remarkable, that tho' almost all animals use in play the same member, and nearly the same action as in fighting; a lion, a tyger, a cat their paw; an ox his horns; a dog his teeth; a horse his heels: Yet they most carefully avoid harming their companion, even tho' they have nothing to fear from his resentment; which is an evident proof of the sense brutes have of each other's pain and pleasure.[20]

Having shown the similarities, Hume goes on to mention the commonly recognized differences that revolve around the rational and aesthetic life, each species possessing both a common animality and a separate species being. By understanding animals as objects, we can acquire a greater appreciation than when we see only the interdependence. If they are understood primarily for the lessons they have for us, we will miss their significance for themselves. And if we do not recognize both their similarities to us and differences from us, we will not understand them as the beings that they are. There is a significant difference between Goethe's dictum that each animal is an end in itself and the claim of Black Elk that "the buffalo were the gift [to the Oglala] of the good spirit." For Goethe, animals are ends; for Black Elk, at least sometimes merely means, because they are only understood in their relationship to us. By understanding animals as ... objects, we can recognize more readily the similarities to, and differences from, ourselves.

What objectivity does not itself provide is a positive attitude toward the object, a recognition of the object as a worthwhile entity in itself. And without that attitude, the object is merely a separate and autonomous being in its own domain. Without a sympathetic attitude toward a living being as object, there is no distinction between an animal and a stone. For the animal to be valued for itself, there must be a recognition of that animal as a self-directed end with its own entitlements. As the preceding quotation from David Hume reflects, that recognition is not a rarity.

In anthropological literature, much is made of the distinction between a "thou" and an "it." It is customarily argued that Aboriginal societies have a significantly greater respect for other species, regarding them as "thous" whereas the West regards other animals as nothing more than "its." Indeed, the very use of "it" in English to refer to an animal is seen as reflective of disrespectful attitudes (by Schopenhauer, for example, as well as by modern anthropologists). But if we wish to make that point, we would have to recognize that other European, and thus equally Western, languages with masculine, feminine, and sometimes neuter nouns do not commit the same faux pas. Moreover, the use of "it" in English may reflect gender uncertainty rather than any non-human animal-oriented attitudes.

Certainly, the use of "thou" may be said to imply one kind of respect, but we should recognize that "you" implies another kind. Indeed, we might consider the distinction to be threefold in attitudes toward animals: those who regard them as a "thou" (the Aboriginal perspective, at least among hunter-gatherers)[21]; those who regard them as a "you" (respectful objectivists, such as David Hume); and those who regard them as an "it" (disrespectful objectivists, such as the Cartesians).[22]

In English, German, and French – indeed in Western languages generally – where and when familiar and formal distinctions were, or are still, made, the "thou" form (*du, tu*) implies a relationship, a belongingness, an informality, a familiarity, a similarity, and an affection. By contrast, the "you" form (*Sie, vous*) implies a respect for an autonomous being with individual, autonomous, and distinctive rights. In fact, it is often known as the respect form. A "you" is more distant and distinct from ourselves, which permits us a recognition of others in their uniqueness. It is thus that the West does not see other species as humans in different karmic form, as do Hindus and Buddhists, or as other beings with their own replicas of human society, as do the Makuna, but, at least potentially, as distinctive entities with their own forms, their own characteristics, their own entitlements, their own *telee.* "Thou," by contrast, may be said to reflect a respect for a being seen to exist primarily in relation to the observer and as a part of nature along with ourselves rather than as an autonomous rights-bearing being. Aboriginals respect other species as beings like ourselves; compassionate Westerners respect other species as beings different from ourselves with their own worthy characters and essences. It is thus that scientific objectivity permits animals to be seen as individual ends in themselves. Indeed, the language of individual rights applied even to humans does not arise in tribal society where humans exist primarily in their relationships rather than their autonomy. An Aboriginal more readily experiences empathy, a Westerner sympathy. For a complete respect, though, for other species, they must be addressed as both a "thou" and a "you." Each alone ignores the fullness of individuality and community, of separateness and similarity, of subjective relationship and objective independence. The fact of the significant anti-rationalist strain in Western thought allows for the addition of the intuitive communitarian element. The empathetic strain is witnessed most clearly in Rousseau's question in *Emile:* "How do we let ourselves be moved by pity if not by transporting ourselves outside of ourselves and identifying with the suffering animal, by leaving as it were, our own being to take on its being?"[23] The anti-rationalist and rationalist elements together allow for a synthesis of empathy and sympathy.

Unfortunately, as a consequence of its objectivity, Western science has often missed the interdependence because rationalism leads so readily to an acceptance of the ultimate reality of individuals alone. Nonetheless, it is important to emphasize the fact that the Western mind, *through its separation from nature,* has achieved a measure of objectivity greater than that of other civilizations and is able to view other species as ends in themselves rather than as contributors to a common good alone. Our alienation from nature proved a surprising benefit to the treatment of other species and a recognition of their rights, however incomplete and however much animals continued frequently to be abused. Abuse continued not from a failure to recognize that animals have rights but from a steadfast belief that humans mattered more. Humans were considered to be entitled to so much greater consideration that animal interests often received short shrift where they were in conflict with human interests. And the fact is that, as a consequence of its technological capacities, the West has put itself in fundamental conflict with the animal realm through animal experimentation, factory farming, and, now, genetic engineering, for example.

The reality is that neither Western nor non-Western cultures treated other species with appropriate consideration, but Western thought retained the capacity to treat them as ends in themselves as a consequence of the implications of Western scientific mentality – and the capacity to treat them as a mere means because of the power of Western technology. It should scarcely surprise us, then, that from the sixteenth century to the present, many reports by travellers of the actual treatment of other species in other societies have commented on the abject cruelty. If they have been aware of proclamations of identity with the animals by the Native populations, they have invariably noted that the claims are contradicted by the reality. Of course, one might conclude that this observation is a consequence of a cultural prejudice whereby the Westerner has failed to comprehend the Aboriginal or Oriental way. Yet the pain and suffering experienced by the animals are real, not cultural. If the travellers have failed to recognize the premises of tribal and Oriental myth, they have not failed to recognize the reality of the torment undergone by the animals. They were not treated as ends in themselves.

Until recently, Occidentals have been less willing to acknowledge the cruelties of Western hunting for pleasure, certain animal husbandry techniques (for example, gelding), the abuse of furbearers, and the like. As with most societies, the West has traditionally considered itself superior in its attitudes. In recent years, it has come to recognize its failings and lauded others instead. It has, however, also failed to understand the complexity of its own traditions and the practical reality of others. While its technological capacities have been to the detriment of the animal realm, the concomitant objectivity of the scientific attitude is the necessary precursor of appropriate treatment of other species. The Mark Twain who wrote pamphlets against vivisection and avowed in Swiftian manner "that now and then / Beasts may degenerate into Men" is every bit as much a part of the Occidental tradition as any white-veal farmer.[24] Mark Twain may be said to represent the anti-rationalist tradition in Western thought. The rationalist and scientific tradition may be said to be best represented by the physicist Albert Einstein, who argued that "our task must be to free ourselves from this prison [the delusion of being separated from the rest of the universe] by widening our circle of compassion, to embrace all living creatures and the whole of nature in its beauty."[25] In *The Outermost House* (1928), Henry Beston took the sympathetic objective idea to its logical conclusion: "Animals are not brethren, they are not underlings, they are other nations, caught with ourselves in the net of life and time." All, at their best, extend their objectivity through their sense of belonging; and they add to this sympathy a recognition of the independent worth of the other being in its own selfhood.

5
Alienation from Nature

1. Prepare for war with peace in thy soul ... Hate and lust for things of nature have their roots in man's lower nature.

   – *Bhagavad Gita*, 2, 38; 3, 34, c. 500 BC

2. What a piece of work is a man! How noble in reason! how infinite in faculties! in form, and moving, how express and admirable! in action, how like an angel! in apprehension, how like a god! the beauty of the world! the paragon of animals; And yet, to me, what is this quintessence of dust? man delights not me, no, nor woman neither.

   – Shakespeare, *Hamlet* 2.2, c. 1600

3. Wild and untaught are Terms which we alone
   Invent, for fashions differing from our own:
   For all their Customs are by Nature wrought,
   But we, by Art, unteach what Nature taught.

   – John Dryden, *The Indian Emperour*, 1.1.11-14, 1675

4. O be a man! and thou shalt be a god!
   And half self-made! Ambition how divine!

   – Edward Young, *Night Thoughts*, 1742-4

5   This is a good day to die.

> – Plains Indian warrior Fire Thunder on attack-
> ing the US cavalry, 1876

6   All the nations that have roots or legs or wings shall fear you.

> – Gift of the ancestral spirits to Black Elk

7   Only individuals matter, never the race or the nation.

> – Rabindranath Tagore to Leonard Elmhirst, 1924

8   The whites only see with their eyes and hear with their ears.
     We Indians can see and hear with our minds.

> – Ignacio, Makuna Indian of Colombia, c. 1980s

I

Western society's alienation from nature is now so commonly acknowledged it has become a truism. Indeed, its acknowledgment has a lengthy
history but with conflicting interpretations. While Shakespeare (2) and
Dryden (3) reflect on the high price of our cultural development away from
our original nature, Edward Young (4) delights in our divine capacity to
remake ourselves, even if only in part. In this chapter, I propose to investigate the origins of the West's alienation from nature, and to ask whether
Aboriginal and Oriental societies differ in principle (though a more explicit
investigation of those traditions will be left for Chapter 7).

A case can be made for the similarities between West and East and the
Aboriginal world – and the similarities are certainly greater than is customarily recognized, as the Benthamite utterance of Tagore (7) exemplifies. But,
however good a case can be made that their differences are only matters of
emphasis – Ignacio's cultural self-congratulation (8) is little different from
that of Charles Darwin (Ch. 3 [5]) – authority has spoken on behalf of
Greece not merely as the home of Reason and the source of later European
rationalism, but also as the starting point of a decidedly different human
adventure. Both those who revel in the triumph of Reason and those who
denounce it concur in their recognition of its origin.

To counter such time-honoured beliefs would be both to mislead and to
court dismissal. Suffice it to say, then, that what is important to understand

is that the rationalist and individualist dominance epitomizing Greek thought is already recognizable in embryo in earlier Sumeria, Assyria, Babylon, Egypt, India, and China – and even in primitive form in the earliest of cultures as they began to develop tools. While rationalism may be more pronounced in the West, its technological attributes are also present everywhere else.

Human divorce from the *primordial* natural condition of benevolence toward other non-harmful species raged everywhere apace, which culminated in the West in the organized cruelty of the Roman ampitheatres and the vile vivisection of the seventeenth-century age of science. Animals were but machines, their cries "only the noise of a little spring that had been touched," according to Jansenist Seminary scientists at Port-Royal.[1] In the East, this perspective produces barbarities toward the beasts of burden, and in tribal societies, killing without any apparent concern to diminish the suffering of those killed. While Gandhi abhors it, he acknowledges mistreatment of cows and animal sacrifice a recurrent Hindu malady. While Black Elk abhors it, he acknowledges stone-throwing at birds and shooting of squirrels as customary Sioux pastimes. If there is, as Oriental and Aboriginal languages suggest, a *natural* human respect for other species, it has been long transgressed in practice.

What differentiated West from East and from the Aboriginal world was not the abuse of other species but the intellectual conception of one's place in nature. Western philosophy justified a sense of superiority over other creatures. David Hume, for example, shows how similar we are to other species, and acknowledges our responsibilities to other species, but nonetheless adds, "Men are superior to beasts principally by the superiority of their reason."[2] He assumes rather than argues that reason is the most relevant capacity to overall superiority. The influence of Greece was such that it never seems to enter Hume's head that reason might not be the only category worthy of consideration. And while Western philosophy offered "reason" as a justification for having a sense of superiority, the Oriental and the Aboriginal worlds did little to prevent the oppression of other creatures. For the one, superiority is a matter of power, expressed as a natural consequence of rational self-conception. For most others, it is a matter of power, expressed as respect toward nature's rules of hierarchy, nature's "will," justifying the hunting, killing, eating, and sacrificial and agricultural usage of other species.

Although it is in Presocratic Greece that we first encounter predominantly rationalist minds, the preconditions are already to be found in the literate civilization of the Tigris-Euphrates valley. There, in Sumeria, the focus of myth had already shifted from the living and growing world of the animals, and occasionally plants, of primary societies to the impersonal and unsocial cosmic order of the planets – as later but independently among the Meso-American Maya and the Dogon of Mali with their highly sophisticated stellar cosmologies, as well as in the Orient.

Indeed, historically, there would appear to be three stages of awe – the initial stage, toward the realm most like ourselves, that is, other animals; a secondary stage toward more distant natural objects such as the strength and suppleness of trees, the grandeur of mountains, and the mysteries of the watery depths; and a third to the heavens, whose magical stellar and planetary workings appear at first beyond all human comprehension. As we acquire mastery of other animal species as hunters, especially through the development of superior weapons, then of vegetal nature as cultivators, so we move on from that toward which we have diminished our awe and respect in the direction of that deemed ever more worthy of our adulation. Power breeds contempt. And hunting power is just as much an aspect of power as is the power exercised in, say, herding or farming. Lord Acton's famous dictum that "all power tends to corrupt and absolute power corrupts absolutely" is not without merit. Human glory was finally complete when we could claim to understand the movements of the stars – which explains the magnificent stories of the passage of the sun from dusk to dawn in most pre-scientific societies.

Among hunter-gatherers and incipient states, animals usually were worshipped, but we should not imagine that those worshipped must of necessity have benefited from the worship. Nowhere were animals worshipped more assiduously than in Egypt – from scarabs through crocodiles to antelopes, snakes, and baboons. Yet the "worship" was of no benefit to the animals. So many "worshipped" animals have been found in human graves in Egypt that we can be confident that the animals must have been acquired in the neighbouring lands specifically for the purpose of sacrifice. Let us not make the customary error of imagining that treating animals well in myth, drawing pictures of them on cave walls, or making statuary of them meant for one moment that they were well treated. More often than not they were sacrificed for their divinity. Animals were useful symbols, sometimes religious ones, to help humans develop rules for living their own lives. Only rarely did they matter as ends in themselves.

As Aesop and Aristophanes (and before them the Egyptians and all tribal societies) understood so well, animals are ideal tools for moral tales – almost three quarters of Aesop's fables employ animals – and no one seems to be concerned that the descriptions of the behaviour of the animals are highly improbable. In Aesop's tales, the foxes, monkeys, lions, bears, donkeys, boars, hare, bulls, wolves, sheep, and the like possess emotional and behavioural characteristics entirely appropriate to an understanding of human behaviour. In Aristophanes's plays *The Birds* (414 BC) and *The Frogs* (405 BC), we meet nightingales, hoopoes, kestrels, widgeons, flamingoes, cuckoos, falcons, amphibia, and the like, but we learn lessons for humans not the birds or the frogs. Little consideration is given by Aesop and Aristophanes (or the Egyptians, or tribal societies) to whether the descriptions represent with any degree of accuracy the characteristics of the species employed. Indeed, the true characteristics are scarcely relevant to the story. The fables may *employ* animals. But the fables are entirely *about* people. (The medieval story of Reynard the Fox may be an exception.) Collections of Amerindian and African folklore lead to the same conclusion (if nowhere near as emphatically, for here at least sometimes the fables *are* about the animals). And precisely the same point may be made about modern cartoons, in which the animals almost always speak and are often understood by humans, just as they were for Geoffrey Chaucer and are for the Amerindians. The same is true of more recent literature in general, although there are notable exceptions, including Jack London's *White Fang* and Richard Adams's *Watership Down*.

As we move further away from using animals as explanation and justification for human mores and move ever increasingly into the realm of the abstract, so we diminish our identification with the natural world. Humans were transformed in the rising civilizations of the Middle East from understanding themselves through their relationships to other species to understanding themselves in terms of rational abstraction, numbers, and ratios, ultimately in terms of scientific laws – the path from the communal creature at one with nature to the autonomous individual. They undertook the journey away from a prehistoric earthly animal order – in which humans were but one species among many – and placed themselves in the heavenly order. They deemed humans rational, the rational to be divine, and humans to be made in the image of the gods (or, at least, so Plato finally confirmed it in the fourth century BC, at about the same time as the prophet Ezra was also affirming, for the writing of Genesis, the credo that man was made in God's image). The human was no longer an animal like other animals but, if not exactly a god, at least a master of all other creatures, and that for which the heavens and earth had been made by God.

In Mayan astronomical mythology, in like manner to that of the Dogon and the Sumerians, the Path of Awe elevated the sky and its contents, as once animals were elevated. In the *Popol Vuh,* the K'iche" Maya congratulated themselves on their abandonment of the animal nature cult for the worship of the heavenly bodies. For the Maya, their scientific abstractions indicated their superiority as a people to those who still worshipped animals. Now, "the voracious animals, the puma, the jaguar, the snake, and the *cantil,* as well as the hobgoblin" had been "turned into stone by the sun."[3] No longer needing to fear the "voracious" species because of Mayan technological superiority, they no longer needed to worship them. Their superiority over nature was ensured.

The Mayan experience should reinforce a fairly obvious but important point frequently ignored by some panegyrizing writers on Aboriginal culture. The belief system and social structure of a culture are related fairly closely to the type of economy and technology it enjoys, for example, hunter-gatherer, pastoral, or feudal. As the Maya, and also the Aztecs and the Incas, acquired the capacity for scientific and technological abstraction, so their manner of thought, their identity with nature, their culture, changed. They remained Indians every bit as much as the Iroquois or the Sioux, but they thought in a very different way. They now had the power to master the animals. They no longer held them in quite the same awe; they had confidence in their capacity to provide enough food without praying to the animals to return. There was no longer uncertain conflict among equals in bravery. In becoming agriculturalists rather than relying predominantly on the vagaries of the hunt, they elevated themselves above other species. The sun turned the jaguar, the snake, and all else to be feared, into stone.

Both rationalism and technology induce substantial cultural change. To those who demand that tribal societies should be entitled to the fruits of industrial development, to the delights of democratic participation at the level of the state rather than tribe, and to the benefits of Western-style education, one must emphasize that any such changes will involve an inevitable loss of solidarity, increase in conflict, and alienation from traditions. Precisely that which makes such societies admirable will disappear if they attempt to achieve those technological comforts and the rationalism encouraged by the secular education that the West possesses. This view is not at all to deny the opportunity for such achievements. It is to insist that one knows the price to be paid – and indeed to note that the dislocation for the current West may well be less, for it took place over many centuries. A greater speed of change is likely to increase both the contradictions and the alienation.

Ideas are not independent possessions of particular tribes or societies. They are in substantial part reflections of their lifestyles, which, in turn, are in substantial part reflections of their economies and technologies. Just as the myths – the belief systems – of hunting societies alter dramatically if and when they become agricultural societies, so too if Canadian Cree become oil producers as a consequence of land distribution, or if the Xhosa join the petit bourgeoisie as a consequence of the democratization of South Africa, so they will cease to think and behave as traditional Cree and Xhosa. They are likely to think and behave instead as capitalists and merchants, certainly as *Cree* and *Xhosa* capitalists and merchants, but nonetheless in a significantly different manner from the way they thought and behaved before. They will lose much, but not all, of their traditional culture. Because all societies retain some of their past beliefs as they enter new stages of development, so there is always some ambivalence, if not outright contradictoriness, in their belief systems, which in turn is often reflected in contradictions between behaviour and professed belief.

By the time of Darwin, the West had long flourished under its boast of superiority not only over other species, but, like the Maya before the arrival of the conquistadors, and like the Japanese before military defeat, and like the Amerindians to the Inuit on occasion, over "lesser" cultures, too. It is no wonder that the Victorian civilized world railed against Darwinism, for it threatened the whole edifice of our exclusive self-conception, as, indeed, had the Lake Romantics already, but now it was not merely with soul but with empirical evidence and scientific rigour. Moreover, poetry was subject to the vagaries of interpretation and, anyway, no one could doubt the reverential spirit of a Wordsworth or a Coleridge. It was Thomas Hardy who proclaimed that you could get away with things in verse that would have 100 Mrs. Grundys on your back if said in prose – and no doubt 100 exclusivist, anti-evolutionist, Christian literalists, too. "If Galileo had said in verse that the world moved," so Hardy noted, "the Inquisition might have left him alone." But then the Inquisition and the public would have said "how beautiful" instead of "how dangerous" and ignored the scientific relevance.

Poetry and the novel were not the way of science, which appeared to turn humans into materialist monkeys. The poets made humankind an intrinsic part of Nature – if sometimes only half-heartedly so (4). When humans rose above nature, they lost something of their worthwhileness (2, 3). Nature was, mostly anyway, to be revered. Certainly, that was the message of Blake, Shelley, Keats, Coleridge, Christina Rossetti, Browning, and, above all, Wordsworth. That, too, was the message of Darwin, or at least with regard to the glories rather than the cruelties of nature. But as a scientist, Darwin possessed no poetic licence. By many, he was read not as one who glorified Nature but as one who had tried to kill God. If the Victorians had doubted Nietzsche before, Darwin appeared to affirm his conclusion that the gods were dead. And, for many Victorians, this affirmation implied that humankind must be worthless and no longer had any purpose.

Only a belief in ourselves could replace a belief in God, which, fundamentally, had been the message of eighteenth-century utilitarianism and the Enlightenment. Indeed, the "Man-God" of Feuerbach's materialist anthropotheism in his *The Essence of Christianity* (1841) was the culmination of the process. It is indeed strange that Darwinism had the impact it did. For well over a century, the essential similarity of human and beast had been proclaimed. David Hume had noted quite clearly that animals possessed reason, pride, humility, love, and even a tiny smattering of virtue. "Every thing," Hume tells us, "is conducted by springs and principles, which are not peculiar to men, or any one species of animals."[4] Darwin had far more influence than Hume because of the greater ease of confirmation – or rather, greater difficulty of refutation – of the natural sciences over the humanities. Darwin demonstrated our kinship with other species and a recognition of our non-exclusive nature. What Darwinism succeeded in doing, however, was precisely what Darwin feared. It provided us with an ever greater sense of self-importance and removed the last vestiges of humility. It confirmed Feuerbach's boast. God was indeed dead. We were no longer in the image of God. We were gods, and even more divine in our nature than we had imagined ourselves to be before.[5]

For many, Darwin's theory threatened to remove us from our perch in the lower pantheon of gods, and threatened to return us to our animal origins on the savannah, where we feared other creatures, were jealous of their attributes, and longed for their skills. The need for us to claim the priority of reason over other faculties was never greater if we were not to come tumbling to earth. But if the conception of rational creatures in God's image was threatened, we could now portray ourselves as the superior beings of secular reason. Indeed, if God was dead, the need for us to proclaim our superior rationality was ever greater. We no longer possessed an infallible protector on whom we could rely. We must now rely on ourselves. "We have stopped believing in God," wrote Emile Zola in 1886, "but not in our own immortality." William Butler Yeats affirmed that "Men will no longer separate the idea of God from that of human genius, human productivity in all its forms." Whether Darwin himself believed in God is uncertain. His closing of *The Origin of Species* with a vision of life "having been breathed by the Creator into a few forms or into one" may be read as religious belief or as an earnest endeavour to minimize the dangers of persecution and even prosecution. What is clear is that for many, whatever Darwin's own beliefs, Darwinism implied either the necessity of agnosticism or the irrelevance of the customarily worshipped God. In such circumstances, who could now complain, or inflict retribution, if we proclaimed, as did Feuerbach, our own rational divinity? If God had not made the world for us, we had made it for ourselves, and were entitled to both its mastery and its fruits. God's death, or at least his mortal illness, extinguished our already severely diminished humility. The *logic* of Darwinism should have led to a recognition of the human as an animal like other animals in most respects. That was, indeed, Darwin's conclusion. Psychological imperatives, however, were stronger than logical ones. It was Feuerbach rather than Darwin who triumphed.

In such an epoch, Edmund Burke's lessons on the prudential requirement for humility and the folly of reliance on human reason were readily cast aside. Human reason could now reign untrammelled by any recognition of a superior power. Only direct evidence of our own failings in our mastery of nature, failings that would threaten our own existence, would bring us back to our senses to understand ourselves once more as an intrinsic part of nature.

When we finally acknowledged our failings, epitomized by the publication in 1962 of Rachel Carson's *Silent Spring,* Western civilization became more aware of human limitations and our natural responsibilities than has any society since the origins of civilization as we understand it some seven or so thousand years ago. We finally married scientific objectivity with Darwinian naturalism. Yet, oddly, we have, in our shame, pointed to others as being without our sins, when, in fact, their sins have only been less in that they have lacked the technology to make them greater – and let us not forget that we have sometimes used technology wisely, to create sewage systems, or to provide disease-resistant crops, for example, when less technological societies suffer the problems of open waste-disposal systems and inadequate sustenance, and their rivers suffer no less than ours, where the populations are equivalent, from corresponding water pollution. The pollution of the Ganges by dead bodies and of major Indian cities by smog is as bad as anything achieved by corporate capitalism.

It is not Western ideology alone that itself brings about the dominance of nature with its attendant miseries. It is the technological and industrial capacity to do so. It is not Western society alone that desires the material possession provided by Western technology – as has become abundantly apparent throughout the world where other societies have been given, or have taken, the opportunity to do so. The error is to imagine that one may partake of the fruits and still retain the purity of primitive collectivity. The essential collectivist message of Fire Thunder's "This is a good day to die" (5) or Black Elk's conception of "the shape of all shapes as they must live together, like one being" must of essence diminish in a world dominated by secular education and secular technology. Indeed, since the Sioux ancestors, Black Elk tells us with pride, have made all other creatures fearful of him (6), the dominance of nature has long begun. It is far from an exclusively Western phenomenon. Black Elk already expresses the attitude which, when coupled with Western technology, moves us beyond self-glorification and control of other species to a general and devastating environmental degradation.

Literacy, astronomy, mathematics, urbanization, and the attendant preeminence of reason, as well as technology, were at once contributing factors to our sense of superiority and also the catalyst for the loss of our communitarian self and the rise of the autonomous self-fulfilling individual. While Darwinism encouraged us to treat other species well, because of their similarity to ourselves, the greater consequence was to imagine ourselves superior because of our scientific and technological achievements.

It would, however, be an error to imagine that, either historically or currently, reason alone has been deemed the faculty most worthy of merit in the West. Even John Locke, who, more often than any other philosopher, is labelled the prime exemplar of Western rationalism, thought of reason as only one of the most worthy attributes. Thus, in his *Second Treatise of Civil Government,* we read: "God gave the World ... to the use of the Industrious and Rational (and *Labour* was to be his *Title* to it); not to the Fancy or Covetousness of the Quarrelsome and Contentious." While reason is to be admired, it is through labour that one achieves one's entitlements. Indeed, it is not difficult to interpret Locke here as denying rights to the intellectuals, that is, "the Quarrelsome and Contentious"! "The *Labour* of his body, and the *work* of his hands ... are properly his. Whatsoever then he removes out of the state that Nature hath provided, and left in, he hath mixed his *Labour* with, and joyned to it something that is his own, and thereby makes it his *Property*."⁶ This labour theory of value not only is the source of the more sophisticated liberal versions to be found in the writings of David Ricardo and Adam Smith, but is also the spring to Karl Marx's labour theory of value. Indeed, it is the very source of what Max Weber termed the Protestant ethic. It lauds reason but puts ardour above it. It would be remiss to demean the role of reason in Western thought, but equally remiss not to mention other values that may help to distinguish Western society. We justify our acquisition of property at the expense of others, both human and non-human, as an entitlement of our industry and labour. In the West, we tend to laud industry for its own sake – a practice explicit as early as St. Ambrose's fourth-century *Hexaemeron,* and intimated still earlier. For the West, this practice has reinforced the sense of superiority over other species. While other species labour only to survive, we labour to produce, and in our productivity we have created what we imagine a vastly superior world in which to live. It is not only reason but also industry that raises us above the rest of nature. (For a literary example of the industrious rationalist, the character of St. John Rivers in Charlotte Brontë's *Jane Eyre* [Chs. 34, 35] may be consulted.) By contrast, both Taoism and Buddhism warn of the excesses of industry that disturb our tranquillity, our relationship to nature.

In the traditional Oriental view, humankind is not fulfilled by labour but is alienated by it if the labour exceeds that which is necessary for our spiritual fulfilment and the maintenance of primary needs. For the Oriental, Western industriousness encourages the manipulation and control of nature, and results in an alienation from nature. Yet, at the same time, despite the admonitions, the Oriental world has employed elephants and oxen as beasts of burden for centuries, has engaged in clear-cutting, and, least comprehensible of all in terms of an identity with nature, has practised extensive animal sacrifice.

If the Western desire to acquire property through industry alienates us from nature, disturbs our inner tranquillity, and provides a justification for our use of other species, so too does the industrious desire to acquire knowledge, to be "educated." The desire for property and the desire for knowledge remove us equally from the primordial conditions for being at one with nature. In the Oriental and the Aboriginal worlds, the concern in literature and myth with the exclusively human capacity for spiritual enlightenment performs a similar function of alienation from untrammelled animal nature. This spiritual enlightenment leads directly to animal sacrifice. All cultures are alienated from nature, even if the source of the alienation is different, and even if Oriental and Aboriginal languages suggest an identity with nature. The suggestions are more aspiration than reality.

II

Certainly, the West is alienated from nature, and certainly the elevation of reason is a primary source of that alienation. But the West does not stand alone. We should not imagine that our conception of reason necessarily differentiates us radically from those, such as the Buddhists, who laud intuition. Thus, for example, in the *Meno* and the *Republic*, Plato treats reason as an illuminated immediate perception, something very close to intuition, and for David Hume, "reason is nothing but a wonderful and unintelligible instinct in our souls, which carries us along a certain train of ideas, and endows them with particular qualities, according to their particular situations and relations."[7] Joseph Butler, bishop of Durham, explaining the views of St. Paul in 1729, claims: "Every man is naturally a law to himself ... Every one may find within himself the rule of right, and the obligations to follow it."[8] Deist sceptics (such as Hume), Christian advocates, and Platonic idealists would find common ground in an antinomian notion of reason that did not differ too significantly from the Buddhist sense of intuition. It is certainly worthy of note that the Greek word for "idea" is derived from the word for "seeing," not the word for "reasoning." The Dissenters' conception of the "inner light" denies the premises of rationalism and is evocative of Taoism. The eighteenth-century evangelical dictum *"Intra te quaere Deum"* (look for God in thyself) is evocative of all forms of Oriental religion. Western and Eastern conceptions are closer than we sometimes imagine. It would be unwise to make too much of this, for the distinction between East and West is real, but it serves as a reminder not only that we sometimes exaggerate the difference, but that there is an underlying common humanity, with common human ideas. It was popular at one time to make the differences proclaim Western superiority, later to insist on the importance of nurture over nature, now to eulogize Aboriginal and Oriental cultures. All too readily the emphasis on cultural distinctiveness allows us to forget that we share our biologically driven natures, our needs, our primal memories, our collective unconscious, indeed our very humanity. As C.S. Lewis wisely wrote in *The Screwtape Letters,* humans "constantly forget ... that they are animals and that whatever their bodies do affects their souls." And if the West is removed from a recognition of humanity's animal nature by its explicit rationalism, Oriental mysticism and Aboriginal myths ultimately, if less dramatically, serve the same ends. Nonetheless, none of them eradicates our primordial conception of an identity with the rest of the natural world that inhabits our primitive souls.

While we may be appalled at the history of Western arrogance and the sense of superiority over the rest of nature, let us not imagine it an exclusively Western conception. In the creation myth of the Pima Amerindians of southern Arizona, man (and "man" rather than "human" appears to be implied) wanders through the darkness until he begins to reason. He then knows himself and knows that he is a man and has a purpose. For the Pima, reason is the defining essence of mankind and mankind is the creator of the world. In the *Popol Vuh* of the K'iche" Maya of Guatemala, the creator gods Tepeu and Gucumatz exclaim that they will acquire glory and honour for having formed a human – "the creature with reason endowed." "Great was their wisdom," announces the compiler of the *Popol Vuh* in describing these first humans. In the Abenaki story of "The Coming of Gluscabi," man forms himself out of the dust left over from God's creation. Surely, if the message of the Amerindian creation stories were contained in Genesis, we would denounce the message as a reflection of Western arrogance, as a reflection of the Western sense of human superiority over nature, and of men over women. It is a curious reflection on modernity that we do not customarily recognize their implication for Aboriginal attitudes. What is important to understand is that, in all of these conceptions, there is a sense that whereas other animals are, generally speaking, what they were in their species origin, humans have made themselves more than their merely animal selves – and reason has accomplished this great feat. Edward Young's boast (4) is not an exclusively Western arrogance. In the Aboriginal traditions, as well as the West, reason is recognized as the essential defining and differentiating characteristic. At the same time, all are pulled toward an understanding of essential humanity as present in primordial nature. The conflict between nature and culture is the source of the alienation and ambivalence present in all human societies.

Earlier we mentioned Rousseau as the quintessential exemplar of Western ambivalence, indeed downright contradiction, of the conflict between nature and culture.[9] We may offer Rabindranath Tagore as his Oriental counterpart. Tagore deplored untouchability, the bane of India, but cherished the sacred thread that proclaimed his elevated caste; he castigated the Indian practice of child marriage, but arranged such marriages for two of his daughters; he banned meat-eating in his school but was himself not only not a vegetarian but, almost unthinkable for a devout Hindu, let alone a Brahmin, he ate beef; he recognized that India had much to do to rescue women from their tormented status but treated his own wife as an inconsequential appendage; he was an elitist attached to the fascists (as were George Bernard Shaw, T.S. Eliot, and W.B. Yeats; and even Gandhi momentarily), yet was an advocate of Indian democracy.

I do not choose Tagore as the Oriental example of ambivalence and contradictoriness to condemn him. Despite the ambivalence, he is (like Rousseau) one of the most admirable and accomplished of men. Both Tagore and Rousseau represent their cultures while they try to improve them, fail to live up to the standards of their cultures while they enjoin them, and are constrained by the cultural realities of the aspects they reject. Ambivalence and contradictoriness are central not only to individuals but to the cultures they inhabit. If we look only at the ideological pronouncements and fail to compare them with the realities of both individuals and cultures, we will understand neither. Tagore and Rousseau epitomize the title of Nietzsche's *Human, All Too Human*. Both Tagore and Rouseau are essentially all too human, in both their utopian philosophical yearnings and their quotidian failings. It is not ethical abstractions but Tagore and Rousseau who represent Eastern and Western realities. They are not realities awaiting a transcendence to some quasi-utopia. They represent the human condition. And not at its worst but at its finest, for they at least understood the paradoxes of their own lives. Moreover, they help create the conditions in which their own failings may be, if not overcome, at least ameliorated.

Beyond ambivalence and contradiction, there is also perversity. In *The Black Cat,* Edgar Allan Poe presents the sadism of a supposed animal lover toward his cat. The narrator of the story attributes this behaviour to "the spirit of PERVERSENESS. Of this spirit philosophy takes no account." Nor does it. It is this perversity that contradicts so much of ideology. As the *Bhagavad Gita* put it, "Hate and lust for things of nature have their roots in man's lower nature" (1). "Man's lower nature" is to be found even among the Tagores and Rousseaus and, as we saw earlier, the Robert Louis Stevensons of the world. It is to be found also in the fox-hunting Anthony Trollope who nonetheless recognized in *The Eustace Diamonds* that these are men "in whose love a great deal of hatred is mixed; – who love as the huntsman loves the fox." It is to be found in the Russian dramatist Anton Chekhov, who shot goldfinches with abandon in order to sell those he only winged. It was in revulsion against his own cruelty that he later became a resolute opponent of all bloodsports. To understand both East and West, we must understand the tension between thought and thought, and between thought and action. A recognition of that permanent tension is expressed in the *Bhagavad Gita*'s wise admonition to "prepare for war with peace in thy soul." (1)

When we read nature-embracing pronouncements in Oriental and Aboriginal cultures, we should be more circumspect in our interpretation of them than has become customary, recognizing that ambivalence, contradictions, and perversity are a permanent part of the human condition. We must recognize, too, that Orientals and Aboriginals as well as we have deviated substantially in our cultural development from that primordial stage in which we will have felt an affection for those beings with whom we did not compete for the necessities of life and awe for those species that possessed the characteristics of which we were envious or that were a threat to our lives. Instead of acknowledging the "at one with nature" pronouncements without further question, it behoves us to contrast them with competing and perhaps contradictory proclaimed principles and to check those principles against behaviour. After all, that is precisely what we do with Western proclaimed principles.

Certainly, if we were to hear the claim that "Westerners are altruistic and peace-loving," we would be highly sceptical and demand to know on what evidence the claim was made. Perhaps the answer would be that in Matthew 7:12, we read, "Therefore all things whatsoever ye would that men should do to you, do you even so to them." And in Matthew 5:39 is stated, "Whosoever shall smite thee on thy right cheek, turn to him the other also." No one would accept this as appropriate evidence for the proposition asserted. How absurd, one would suggest, to draw a correlation from the exhortations of the Bible to the behaviour and attitudes of Westerners. Yet, at the same time, we blithely quote from the *Tao Te Ching*, the *Bhagavad Gita*, the *Dhammapada,* and Aboriginal mythology as evidence for Oriental and Aboriginal attitudes. When Amerindians proclaim themselves at one with nature and chant a reverential prayer for the animal they have killed, we are inclined to accept this action as confirmatory evidence. We should at least be willing to ask whether the assertions are perhaps unrealized ideals or ideological obfuscations of a rather more pernicious reality. We should be willing to treat others with the critical objectivity we currently reserve for analyzing ourselves. We must look to the words of Beaumont and Fletcher in *The Lover's Progress:* "Deeds, not words shall speak me." Nonetheless, we must not ignore the fact that all societies, the West included, acknowledge in principle our responsibilities to other species, even though those principles are often ignored in practice. This circumstance reflects the fact that, despite the cultural deviations from our primordial condition, the original human sensibilities of that condition continue to play a role. The moral task in all societies must involve a regeneration of our primordial sensibilities consistent to the degree possible with the cultures we have developed. That complete consistency will be forever impossible is a cross all humans will always have to bear. Ambivalence and alienation are necessary and permanent consequences of our deviation from our primitive animality.

In general, but with some circumspection, we may say that Western civilization, but not Western civilization alone, has elevated individual self-fulfilment and achievement in such a manner that we have separated ourselves as individuals from society, as societies from primordial humanity, and as humans from the rest of creation. By continuing to maintain reservations about reducing the role of individual self-fulfilment, Oriental and Aboriginal philosophies have made it somewhat easier in practice to recognize oneself as a part of the natural world. Again, though, it must be well recognized that some, especially the Romantics, within Western philosophy have overcome its inherent limitations with regard to Nature. Indeed, in his introduction to the *Bhagavad Gita*, Juan Mascaró describes Sanskrit literature as "on the whole, a romantic literature," and he tells us that the romantic "Wordsworth in 'Tintern Abbey' gives us the spirit of India."[10] And Darwin, too, as Peter Bowler insists, is fully a part of the Romantic tradition.[11]

We must be forever wary of treating Buddhism or Hinduism or Aborig-

inal society as some utopian ideal – a practice common among environmentalists, naturalists, and animal sympathizers. Where there is oppression within a society toward fellow humans, it is unlikely that it will be
absent toward non-humans. In some South American Amerindian nations,
women are excluded from the place of worship. In others, women must use
separate entrances to homes. The Mayan *Popol Vuh* (Pt. IV, Ch. 4) provides a
justification for class and metropolitan domination of the plebeians. For
some two and a half thousand years, Brahminic Hinduism has given its
blessing to a caste system in which there are four *varna* (literally, "colour";
the irony should not be ignored): the *Brahman*, whose tasks are religious
and instructional (corresponding to Plato's philosopher kings); *Kshatriya*,
the warriors, whose tasks are protective and military (corresponding to
Plato's auxiliaries); *Vaishya*, who perform agricultural and business functions (corresponding to Plato's artisans); and *Shudra*, who are involved in
menial labour (such tasks being undertaken by non-citizens in Plato's
Athens). While most of Western philosophy, beginning already with Plato's
student, Aristotle, has condemned Plato's system as too restrictive, even
though it allowed for movement between classes, caste and lack of social
mobility have remained the Indian norm, albeit somewhat relaxed of late.
Only occasionally has the caste system been seriously criticized by Hindu
philosophers, and even Gandhi went no further than to criticize its caste
rigidity, while accepting the basic class-controlled social order. And while
we might note again that the intent of the caste system is functional rather
than hierarchical, so indeed was Plato's societal structure, which was
posited as the prerequisite for the maintenance of justice. The effects of
both were nonetheless hierarchical. Joseph Campbell concluded from his
research in India that as a consequence of "the caste principle ... no one is
an individual – everyone is but a fraction." Indeed, the very success of
Islam on the subcontinent may be attributed to its rather more egalitarian
appeal to those who perceived themselves oppressed through caste. Caste
was such that, in the tradition of Sankara, one was deemed truly fortunate
who was born a Brahmin and a male, for only he was eligible to achieve
moksa – the ultimate of the aims of life: release, detachment, other worldli-
ness. And while such hierarchies may permit affection for lowly humans or
non-humans, especially if they know their place, disdain is more customary and a genuine respect more difficult of achievement. In practice, Hindu
ambivalence differs little from that of the West.

In the Hindu *Shatapatha Brahmana*, we read: "Friendship is not to be
found in women, / For they have hearts like half-tamed jackals."[12] This suggests that there is another face to the sometimes genuinely animal-friendly
Hinduism than that frequently presented. The passage also reinforces the
classical Hindu disdain for gender equality, which is to be found in addition in the Buddhist scriptures where a Bhodisattva – an enlightened one –
has five advantages over lesser mortals, one of which is that he is no more

to be reborn as a non-human, another of which is that "he is always a male, and never a woman."[13] Neither other species nor women were treated with the respect their natures deserved. The human male was of a distinctly higher order.

While the Western reliance on Reason has certainly succeeded in distancing Western society from Nature, let us not make the customary error of assuming that those who have not taken that step, or have not taken it in the same manner, are somehow at one with the animal realm and treat it better than we. Although it is an assumption to be found in much of the recent literature on Oriental and Aboriginal societies, there are good conceptual and empirical grounds for imagining the distinctions less stark than they are frequently portrayed. If other cultures are less rationalist than those indebted to the Greek legacy, they still have a sense of themselves as godlike and at the apex of the rest of creation. Ultimately, one must investigate whether the behaviour of Oriental and Aboriginal societies corresponds to their rather more nature-friendly ideological pronouncements, or whether those pronouncements are belied by their practices.

The ambivalence present in all societies with regard to nature arises from the fact that the cultures adopted are incompatible with our primordial condition and the values we held as the animals that we once were; and beneath the surface still are. While intrinsic belongingness within nature may remain as an acknowledgment and aspiration of many cultures, their hunting, farming, herding, and cultivating practices are in conflict with it. They may retain aspirations to remain at one with nature, but the practical dictates of their lives are in conflict with those aspirations.

III

With Thales and his philosophical successors (customarily known as the Presocratics), Western civilization came to place its trust in *logos* – in words, reason, logic. A *logos* is something stated, an account of something, an explanation, a reason. Parmenides (c. 470 BC) urged his audience to test his argument by *logos*, by reason, not by their senses, nor by feeling, custom, and experience.

The Presocratics, as a whole, emphasized rationality, announced rational argument as the sole means to truth, and treated perception, the senses, feelings, and intuitions as fundamentally illusory, at best flawed, or incomplete. They replaced old ways of knowing – feeling, legend, communal memory, myth, and judgment – with a new way of knowing: individual rationality and scepticism of tradition, that is, of the wisdom of ages. This novelty encouraged the movement of Western civilization away from community and inwardness toward self and science, away from an identity with nature toward human exclusivity. The purveyors of such rational knowledge limit themselves to *explicit* logic and thus lose from their ken what they once held by other and usually implicit means, and, because human reason is so limited, they often delude themselves about what they believe they know. In place of feeling their identity with animated nature, they examine it. They thus begin to make distinctions that counter their natural impulses.

"In the beginning was the Word" is the opening to the Gospel according to St. John. In the Greek from which our standard versions of the Bible are translated, "the Word" is rendered by *logos*. St. John was, I would venture to guess, reacting against the rationalist tendencies of his day. The *logos*, the divine wisdom, lies in the *arche*, the beginning. That is, the rationality, the meaning, the essence of things, lies in their origins, in their archetypal nature. If my interpretation has any merit, St. John was reacting against the rationalist innovations introduced by the Presocratics. (And if my interpretation is without merit, one may still identify many in the early Christian tradition – the Desert Fathers of the fourth century, for example – who were well aware of the devastation wrought by rationalism on veneration and reverence.)

In favour of my interpretation, I would point (in recognition of the fact that all religions share a common message about the significance of human origins) to the fact that the sound "Om" or "Aum" (pronounced ar-oo-mm) is believed by Hindus to be the sound that brought creation into being. In the *Rig-Veda* (11:29), we read that "When the ancient Dawns first dawned, the great Syllable was born in the footsteps of the Cow." The opening message on stela C at the Quirigua Maya site in Guatemala is the same as that found in the *Popol Vuh,* and, as David Freidel informs us, in "almost all classic period [Mayan] Creation texts ... Creation began with the uttering of a word and the thing embodied by the word" – the primal message is present at creation, or, to use more modern idiom, in the nature of the human animal in its species conception. As David Freidel, Linda Schele, and Joy Parker wrote in their *Maya Cosmos: Three Thousand Years on the Shaman's Path,* "For the ancient Maya, Creation was at the heart of everything they represented in their art and architecture." [14] The essence of things, so the Maya believe, lies in their origins.

In like vein, in his translation of the Bible into Chinese, the Zen Buddhist expert Dr. John C.H. Wu translated the opening lines of St. John's gospel as "In the beginning was the Tao." [15] For Wu, the message of how to live our lives according to our nature was present at human inception. It did not need to be discovered by philosophic reason, and it may indeed be harmed by it. Or at least this idea was the message of St. John, he was implying, as does Aldous Huxley in *Island* (Ch. 5). In Buddhist thought, p'u – the uncarved block – is the human without alien imposition, without the destruction of the worth of original humanity. Modern rationalism is a deviation from our primal nature, as understood by Buddhism, the Maya, and St. John alike. Of modern Western thinkers, Edmund Burke has come closest to retaining the pre-rationalist tradition in his assertion that a society consists in "a partnership not only between those who are living, but between those who are living, those who are dead, and those who are to be born." This partnership is "in all science ... in all art, ... in every virtue, and in all perfection."[16] He understands, as the Enlightenment did, our obligations to the present and the future, but, unlike the Enlightenment, he understood also that we have an obligation to the past that contains "the wisdom of ages" and is the source of who we are. In *Four Quartets: Burnt Norton,* T.S. Eliot offers a modern version of the relevant conceptual framework: "Time present and time past / Are both perhaps present in time future, / And time future contained in time past." In *East Coker,* he writes suggestively, "In my beginning is my end." Of course, "end" refers both to finality and to purpose. In his *Notes toward the Definition of Culture,* Eliot is more explicitly Burkean (and Buddhist/Hindu/Taoist) in telling us that the societal bond embraces "a piety toward the dead, however obscure, and a solicitude for the unborn, however remote."

Before the supremacy of Greek philosophy, early civilizations looked to a Golden Age in antediluvian culture. Our earliest animal nature, it was thought, is the source of our finest nature-oriented values. Homer idealized the mythical Arcadians; and the Greek myths of Prometheus, Pandora, and Cronos, the Roman of Saturn and Jupiter, make reference to the Golden Age, as does the verse of many classical poets. The idea of the Golden Age played a major role in Indian and Chinese thought, too. Still today, the Pitjantjatjara Aborigines of Australia revere *tjukurpa,* the mystical past and its legendary heroes. A similar conception is present in many contemporary foraging societies. Islam, too, holds to a conception of the highest of all humans as the *insan-I-kamil* – "the primordial man of fully realized spiritual qualities."

Indeed, almost all religions look back in awe and reverence to the life and teachings of one or more prophets and saviours. Etymologically, *re-ligio[n]* means a linking back. It is a uniting of the present with human archetypal origins. It is not only in China that we encounter what is perhaps misleadingly called "ancestor worship." Alex Haley, in his novel *Roots,* offers us a convincing description of the reality of 1750s West Africa: "One by one, the arafang recited the names of the Mauretanian forefathers of whom the baby's grandfather, old Kairaba Kinte, had often told. The names, which were great and many, went back more than two hundred rains. Then the jaliba pounded on his tan-tang and all of the people proclaimed their admiration and respect at such a distinguished lineage."[17] The worth of the present was spoken through the descent from the past. Our worth lies in our heritage. It bears comparison with the attempt by Sir Robert Filmer in his *Patriarcha* of 1680 to trace the lineage of British royalty back, in circuitous manner, to Adam via King David. Similarly, the Aksum kings of Ethiopia claimed descent from the biblical King Solomon and the Queen of Sheba. Why was such a demonstration relevant? Because of the lingering conception that authority, justice, right, and our fundamental nature lie in the source of our humanity, not its future or its reason. Even in an increasingly rationalist, forward-looking society, the appeal of the past continues to draw – as so eminently exemplified by current interest in archeology, antiques, anthropology, ancient history, and genealogy.

Some of the less rationalist of the Presocratic philosophers saw their goal as the re-creation of a golden age of peace and vegetarianism. Vegetarianism, which was a practice of the cult of the Orphic mysteries, remained a prominent and respected part of Greek life at least until the time of Plato. It was not until Diodorus Siculus in the first century BC that we encounter an entirely negative view of the retrospective golden age and of principled vegetarianism, which is assumed in many cultures to be the original human condition. This time should perhaps be seen as the point of no return from a retrospective man-in-nature philosophy to a progressive human-exclusivity philosophy, from the solidarity of primitive community to the selfhood of civil society, from an identity with nature to a human separateness.

It is in the as yet unattributed *Aetna*, written just a few years later, that we read the first of many later satirizations of the utopianism of "Golden Age" conceptions, in which "no one sowed wheat in the plowed fields or kept wheat out of the future crops, but brimming harvests yearly filled the granaries." If, for Locke, Ricardo, and Marx, labour was the prime human value, for the primitivists it was a life without labour, or at least so they were ridiculed in *Aetna*. The beginnings of the work ethic suffused the later classical period and confirmed our difference from other species. Other species and primitive humans were alike in their living as nature had made them. Only civilized humans were capable of exceeding the limitations of the natural life, life unaided by philosophical reason and productive labour. We were, we imagined, essentially different from other animals.

If it is only with the Renaissance that forward-looking ideas come to pre-eminence, their Western foundation was becoming firmly established in fifth- and sixth-century BC Greece, even if there was still a venerable tradition to contest. Thales essayed to replace reflective memory with creative reason. Thales's contemporary, Xenophanes, regarded customary religious beliefs as worthless because they lacked rational foundations. He advocated instead a rational theology to replace custom, tradition, and memory. The advent of reason appeared to require the renunciation of all other means to knowledge, and a renunciation of a golden past replaced by the potential for a golden future, a renunciation of the human animal replaced by the human as quasi-divine, the human as a being unlike, and indeed distinctly superior to, other beings.

It was Archelaus (perhaps c. 450 BC) and then Democritus and Socrates who rang the death knell of an intuitive, naturalistic ethic – and thus altered the moral foundations of human relations and of human-animal relations. They believed that right, goodness, and justice were either merely conventional – which appears to have been Archelaus's view – or were subject to discovery by reason alone – which was Socrates's view. Traditionally, right was known directly, and was acknowledged and illustrated in legend. Rational elucidation was unnecessary either to prove what was ethical or to cast doubt on its objective reality. Our natural kinship to other species went unquestioned. As late as Plato, the intuitionist view was still subscribed to, but with increasingly less frequency. More and more, reason was seen as a deductive or inductive process rather than as an immediate insight. Increasingly, knowledge was something we achieved through the individual process of reasoning, rather than something we discovered already present within us, a gift from the gods, or at least a memory from our original self, the being in harmony with unaggressive nature. Increasingly, the knowledge we possessed was seen as a product of the reasoner for which the reasoner was entitled to credit rather than as a datum previously bestowed on us. The path to reasoning out rather than discovering within was also the path to pride and self-satisfaction rather than humility and gratitude, the path away from an identity with nature and with our own origins. And not only was reason the prime object of respect but that which purportedly lacked reason – lesser cultures and other species – was seen as intrinsically less worthy.

The time for the discovery and development of "Reason" was no accident. The development of a culture so at odds with primordial humanity was the almost necessary occasion of a distinctly different mode of consciousness, one in which self-conscious arts had replaced our primordial unreflected conditions. Reason became necessary to discover a human ethic because humans were divorcing themselves from their primordial nature; archetypal memories were obscured and were no longer congruent with civilization's increasingly self-conscious nature. As we divorced ourselves even more than Greece's predecessors from our primordial nature, from our identity with other species, it became increasingly difficult to find relevance in our archetypal memories (which informed us, for example, which berries were poisonous), and which through disuse became increasingly obsolete, just as unused organs – the incisor teeth of ruminants, the subsidiary hoofs of pigs and oxen, and the remnants of the tail in humans, to borrow Darwin's examples – became obsolete through evolutionary adaptation.

While Aboriginal and Oriental societies continued to find relevance in their creation myths, in their human origins, in their societal foundations, increasingly the West looked to progress, to originality, to individuality, to glory in change, especially from the Renaissance onward. Leonardo da Vinci exhorts us to "imitate no one – Let thy every work be a new phenomenon of Nature." Michelangelo warns us that "he who follows another will never overtake him." "Sapere Aude! Dare to think! Think boldly!" was

Beccaria's "motto of the Enlightenment." Rainer Maria Rilke avowed, "I believe in everything that has never been said before." Even Schopenhauer, no friend of the Enlightenment, claimed that "the task is not so much to see what no one has yet seen, but to think what nobody yet has thought about that which everyone sees." It is difficult to escape the conclusion that originality was to be admired for its own sake, quite independently of whether it provided for human fulfilment, or even moved toward the discovery of truth. In Oliver Goldsmith's novel *The Vicar of Wakefield*, George, desirous of becoming a respected author, acknowledges that he "drest up three paradoxes with some ingenuity. They were false indeed, but they were new. The jewels of truth have been so often imported by others, that nothing was left for me to import but some splendid things that at a distance looked very well." Enlightenment and intellectual pretensions had been taken to heart. In Oriental and Aboriginal cultures, the opposite would have prevailed – respect for the traditionally sacred view and abhorrence of philosophical innovation. Unfortunately, the traditionally sacred view involved animal sacrifice.

Because other cultures have remained rather closer to their psychological archetypes than has the West, they do not require critical reason to know what is appropriate for them. Their culture lies closer to the universal human archetype. However, all humans acquired culture because they had subverted their primal nature. Emigration from the natural conditions of our East African origins required it. The cultures they acquired, some more than others, took them away from nature and from natural fulfilment. The elevation of reason as the sole route to knowledge was the culmination of the process. But before that stage is reached, Reason is used to justify animal sacrifice. After that stage, it is used to denounce animal sacrifice. Even if the former stage allows for a greater identity with the animal, the latter stage involves a greater respect for its life.

In the optimism of the Enlightenment, it was a commonplace to hear of human *perfectibility*, to be achieved through the application of human reason. The concept was coined by Christian Wolff (1679-1754) but given greater standing through the writings of Immanuel Kant (1726-1804). Common sense and experience later encouraged a withdrawal from such extremes. Nonetheless, Marx continued to believe that the revolution would allow "the complete emancipation of all human senses and qualities." Human reason will finally be allowed to achieve its unlimited potential. Leon Trotsky went even further: "Man will become immeasurably stronger, wiser, and subtler; his body will become more harmonized, his movements more rhythmical, his voice more musical. The forms of life will become dynamically dramatic. The average human type will rise to the heights of an Aristotle, a Goethe, or a Marx. And above this ridge new peaks will rise."[18] Reason freed from the oppressions of traditional authority and traditional mores would allow for the emergence of a human beyond previous conception. All of human animality would disappear. Human-kind's alienation from nature would be complete.

There is an incompatible tension between those who see a future human perfection in some utopia from which all oppression has been removed and those who see the human ideal contained at least in embryo in a long-forgotten past. Those who see the potential for a future human perfectibility remove humans from the lands of the animal and place them as gods in heaven. Those who see humans fulfilled in the archetype of their origins recognize humans as animals, albeit most frequently as very special in their animality. It is unrealistic expectations of fulfilment as something inconsistent with the biological animals we are that completes our alienation.

Yet if that foolish progress toward "perfectibility" completes the journey of alienation from nature, we need still to understand the impetus to its origin. According to the great Swiss historian Jacob Burkhardt, in his classic *Civilization of the Renaissance in Italy* of 1860, in the dark ages "man was conscious of himself only as a member of a race, people, party, family or corporation – only through some general category." With the onset of the Renaissance, however, "man became a spiritual *individual* and recognized himself as such. In the same way the Greek had once distinguished himself from the barbarian, and the Arab had felt himself an individual at a time when other Asiatics knew themselves only as members of a race ... at the close of the thirteenth-century Italy began to swarm with individuality; the ban laid upon human personality was dissolved; and a thousand figures meet us each in its own special shape and dress."[19]

Taking up the same theme a century later, Michael Seidlmayer offers us the philosophical background:

The perceptive judgement of Bishop Marbod of Rennes (d. 1123) that a man could either "stand there in himself," or "be given back to himself" or "let himself be drawn out of his own being" and thereby "lose cognizance of his own self," seems to herald a new epoch. A full century later Thomas Aquinas reduced this simple, personal experience to an abstract scientific formula – namely, that each and every being is a unity which stands on a higher or lower plane in life according to the degree to which his words and deeds proceed directly from his true self, which is the foundation of this unity. John of Salisbury (d. 1180), the great English scholar, probably the best educated man of his century, returns again and again to this same problem – the problem of the true development of individuality, even as a way to a just and happy life in this world. According to him the greatest danger is the estrangement (*alienatio*) of man from himself, whereby he loses all "dignity of his nature and of his person" – in other words his personal identity. A man then plunges into a "land of oblivion" (*terra oblivionis*), in which he is unaware of himself, and finally succumbs to simple "human degeneration" (*degeneratio hominis*).[20]

Marbod, Aquinas, and Salisbury can be readily recognized as precursors of Hegel and Marx in their understanding of alienation and of John Stuart Mill in the emphasis on individual authenticity. Marx takes up the same theme of overcoming individual estrangement from the self and society – a transcendence seen as fulfilling the natural human potential that remained unsatisfied. For Marbod of Rennes, Aquinas, John of Salisbury, Hegel, Marx, and John Stuart Mill, the human was already alienated before the predominance of individual reason. Reason was seen as the faculty that could emancipate the oppressed human from the fetters of prior civilizations, from the limitations of our animal origins. Most in the Western philosophical tradition, certainly with undue optimism, saw reason as that which could overcome traditional and earlier alienation. While Oriental and Aboriginal societies failed to recognize the failings of the traditional worlds in which the individual counted for very little, the West was unduly optimistic in its expectations. Certainly, though, the West recognized that the individual was an alienated being in primitive and pre-rationalist societies. If the West has failed in its endeavours, we would be foolish not to recognize the very real limitations to individual fulfilment present in other societies. William Blake, in frustration at Western pretentions, insisted in his *Jerusalem* that "In Selfhood, we are nothing." It would have been wiser to understand that in selfhood alone, we are unfulfilled – just as in community alone, we are unfulfilled. Balance is always appropriate. The utopian socialist Charles Fourier, in his *The Passions of the Human Soul* (1851), went to great if sometimes comic lengths to adumbrate the details of the individual and communitarian sentiments necessary to human fulfilment. Burke offered as a compromise between the organicists and the individualists the view that "art is our nature." He might have added that art has of necessity become our nature because we have all lost the solidarity of primordial life. And, given that we cannot unlearn what we have learned, it cannot be entirely regained. Assuredly, we should not imagine individualism to have been entirely fulfilling even when and where it was most forcefully proclaimed. As Peter Ackroyd informs us, "In fact it sometimes seems that late eighteenth-century London was awash with mysticism and millenarian yearnings, complementing its appetite for commerce and power."[21] Late-twentieth-century New Age orientations constitute a similar response to Western rationalist excesses; as did, in the nineteenth century, Nikolai Gogol's *Dead Souls,* which glorified traditional rural practices and condemned the rationalist and individualist innovation that, Gogol argued, was destroying the pristine spiritual purity of peasant communitarianism – a view that met with considerable applause.

While there is a decided emphasis on rationalism, progress, and individualism within the Western tradition, all of which have contributed to our alienation from our primordial nature, and have left us unfulfilled in significant respects, we must recognize that our adoption of individuality was seen as a means to overcome the existing alienation of previous societies. We must also recognize that the victory of individualistic rationalism remained incomplete in the West. There were sometimes faint but always persuasive voices countering the predominant trend. This naturalist and Romantic counterpoint to Western rationalism encouraged an animal-oriented dimension within the overall framework of a scientific rationalism.

IV

Many modern anthropologists will be inclined to discount the conception I have posited of communitarian and corporate pre-rationalist, including Aboriginal, society. With considerable justice, and not inconsiderable empirical evidence, there has been a reaction against the armchair anthropology of Emile Durkheim, who, in his *Division of Labour in Society* (1893, English translation 1933) coined the notion of "mechanical solidarity," which until recently remained the defining conception of foraging society. Today, by contrast, we are more frequently offered an image of hunter-gatherers as autonomous persons. The emphasis is on individualism and individuation, the looseness of institutions and values, and the maximization of self-interest.[22]

Sound as this re-orientation may be in eradicating Durkheim's excesses, it can be almost as misleading as the conception of invariable communitarianism to describe tribal society. Certainly, in making conceptual distinctions among types of society, of ideology, or of culture, we customarily attempt to distinguish, to separate, to compartmentalize, ultimately to divorce the types we are analyzing. Type A will be deemed to possess certain characteristics that identify it; let us call them qualities 1, 2, and 3. Type B will be identified by qualities 4, 5, and 6. And type C by 7, 8, and 9 perhaps, and so on. Each type will thus customarily be seen as qualitatively distinct from its neighbour. What we almost invariably tend to forget is that the members of all three types are also members of the same species with common needs who indeed share their humanness in common and who are thus far more alike than dissimilar; moreover, they also share a cultural deviation from life in the East African forests, perhaps the savannah, in which human animality began. The very notion that humans in tribal societies are in essence fundamentally different from, say, humans in feudal societies or in capitalist societies involves imagining erroneously that we are entirely cultural creatures with no common species characteristics. In reality, then, a more appropriate taxonomy of human societies will involve a recognition that type A has qualities 1, 2, and 3; type B has 1, 2, and 4; type C has 1, 2, 4, and 5, for example – and, moreover, that there may be significant individual, association, moiety, or other variables within those categories. It is always a temptation to imagine that if type A has certain attributes, type B must be understood not to possess those attributes, and if type A is categorized by its possession of a specific attribute, it must be assumed not to possess the antithesis of that attribute in substantial degree. Both assumptions are wrong. All societies possess significant communitarian and individualistic elements, albeit in different manners, degrees, and emphases.

While it is sensible to identify Western society as individualistic, what we need to understand by that is that there are today stronger individualistic strains in Western society than in its historical pre-Renaissance identity. But we would miss a great deal if we relied on that individualistic understanding alone and did not also recognize significant communitarian emphases – people sharing their identities as members of a nation, as members of a family, a clan, a sect, an established church, or even as supporters of a football club (a factor that can, in some instances, consume a person's identity and give life a meaning). Indeed, who could fully understand Basque or Welsh or Serbian nationalism without a recognition of the power of community. The individually competitive orientations of Western society, especially in its economic aspects, are sufficiently striking that it is wise to identify the West in individualistic terms, but it serves to mislead if the categorization persuades us to ignore the significantly communitarian elements. It is nonetheless the peculiarly individualistic forms that afford us the most meaningful ways of distinguishing Western society from other societal forms.

In not dissimilar manner, an emphasis on the individualistic and libertarian elements of tribal society uncontaminated by alien influence permits us to recognize significant aspects of that society that went unnoticed when it was categorized solely in communitarian *Gemeinschaft*-type terms. Nonetheless, when we recognize the importance of unquestioned loyalty to fellow tribal members in times of conflict, when we recognize the belief in the superiority of their own time-honoured and invariable traditions over those of others, when we see their commitment to their tribal lands, when we see that they regard their law as inviolable and sacrosanct and rather less subject to individual will and individual reason, when that law is recognized as the basis of order for past, present, and future societal members, when their mythology is perceived to function as a unification with significant others and significant places, when we understand that they prefer to seek answers in traditional past practices rather than with a lust for innovation, when we acknowledge their preference for the wisdom of experience over rationalist insight, when we witness their reliance on, rather than continual questioning of, their habits, mores, and customary values – then we must acknowledge that they have somewhat greater internal communal identity. Certainly, the emphases offered here are neither uniform among Aboriginal societies, nor do they tell anywhere near the whole story. But they do serve to distinguish tribal societies by degree from other societies in the contemporary world.

Of course, we will also see individualistic elements in such societies.

Indeed, its individualism is no less real than in the West, but in primary Aboriginal society, individuals identify themselves through their relationships, in the West through their selfhood. Those who acquire security through their traditional mores respond to that order with individualistic self-expression to the degree that it does not interfere with the integrity of the order itself. As John Locke understood, liberty is to be defined in terms of order. It is order that sets you free. Communitarianism and individualism are not in principle antithetical; they exist in permanent tension as irreconcilable aspects of the human condition. As John Donne wrote in *Devotions* (1624), "No man is an Island, entire of it self," and that significant truth applies to hunter-gatherers even more than to the seventeenth-century English about whom Donne was writing. Moreover, if the image of a footloose and fancy-free forager is *overall* appropriate, it is difficult to reconcile this image with an image of the Aboriginal at one with nature, identifying with other species, for to identify with another is to share one's identity with that other. Certainly, individuals in some tribal societies commune with their own individually determined animal relations, but moieties and societies also have general animal representatives. Foraging societies with little external contact possess significant communitarian elements that permit not only a ready identification but a means of illuminating contrast with other forms of society, especially those of the Western world.

It is a consequence of their greater communitarianism, their closer identity with their own origins, that Aboriginals may have a greater identity with the animal realm, may see animals and humans predominantly alike in their natures. Equally, it is a consequence of its alienation from nature and its consequent rationalist individualism that the West can respect other species in their differences and treat them as individual ends in themselves. Neither alone offers a sufficient respect for other species. Taken together, they offer a prospect for a saner human-animal relationship.

6

From the Great Chain of Being to the Theory of Evolution

1   The Thracians to this day, when they design to pass a river that is
     frozen over, make use of a fox to try whether the ice will bear or
     no. For the fox, treading gently, lays his ears to the ice, and if he
     perceive by the noise of the water that the stream runs very close
     underneath, conjecturing from thence that the congelation is not
     deep but thin, and no way steadfastly solid, he makes a stop, and
     if he be suffered, returns back again; but if he perceives no noise
     he goes on boldly. Nor can we say that this is only an exquisite-
     ness of sense without reason; but it is a syllogistic deduction from
     sense, concluding that whatever makes a noise is moved; what-
     ever is moved, cannot be frozen; what is not frozen is moist;
     what is moist, gives way.

                    – Plutarch, *On Water and Land Animals*,
                       c. AD 100

2   Since from the Supreme God Mind arises, and from Mind, Soul,
     and since this in turn creates all subsequent things and fills them
     all with life, and since this single radiance illumines all and is
     reflected in each, as a single face might be reflected in many mir-
     rors placed in a series; and since all things follow in continuous
     succession, degeneration in sequence to the very bottom of the
     series, the attentive observer will discover a connectionof parts,
     from the Supreme God down to the last dregs of things,
     mutually linked together and without a break.

                    – Macrobius, fifth century AD, *Commentary on
                       Cicero's "Dream of Scipio"* (though, in fact, an
                       abridgment of the ideas of Plotinus)

3　God willed that man should in some measure know him through his creatures, and because no single created thing could fitly represent the infinite perfection of the Creator, he multiplied creatures, and bestowed on each a certain degree of goodness and perfection, that from these we might form some idea of the goodness and perfection of the Creator, who, in one most simple and perfect essence, contains infinite perfections.

> – Cardinal Bellarmino (1542-1621), *De ascensione mentis in Deum per scalas creatorum*

4　For if a man imagine that beyond the heavens there exist nothing but imaginary spaces, and that all the heavens are made solely for the sake of the earth, and the earth for the benefit of man, the result is that he comes to think that this earth is our principal dwelling place and this life the best that is attainable by us; and also that, instead of recognizing the perfections which we really possess, he attributes to other creatures imperfections which do not belong to them, in order to raise himself above them.

> – René Descartes, letter to Princess Elizabeth, 1645

5　And, since the law of continuity requires that when the essential attributes of one being approximate those of another all the properties of the one must gradually approximate those of the other, it is necessary that all the orders of natural beings form but a single chain, in which the various classes, like so many rings, are so closely linked one to another that it is impossible for the senses or the imagination to determine precisely the point at which one ends and the next beings – all the species which, so to say, lie near to or upon the borderlands being equivocal, and endowed with characters which might equally well be assigned to either of the neighbouring species.

> – Gottfried Wilhelm, Baron von Leibnitz (1646-1716), *Correspondence*

6　[An account by Mr. Justice Fielding of a reunion between an ass and itsowner, following the theft of the former and the apprehension of the culprit]

"Sir, this is my Ass." [avowed the owner] "I should know him

among all the Asses in the World, and he would know me, wouldst
not thou, poor Duke? Sir, we have lived together these many Years,
ay that we have, as a Man and Wife, as a Man may say; for Sir, I
love my Ass as my Wife; the best twenty Horses in the World, no
nor a King's ransom to boot, should not buy my poor Ass. Poor
Duke! ... We shall never part more, I hope, whilst I live."

Then followed [according to the magistrate] a Scene of Tenderness between the Man and the Ass, in which it was difficult to say,
whether the Beast or its Master gave Tokens of the higher Affection.

– *Covent-Garden Journal*, 15, 22 February 1751-2

7   Vast chain of being! which from God began,
     Natures ethereal, human, angel, man,
     Beast, bird, fish, insect, what no eye can see,
     No glass can reach; from Infinite to thee,
     From thee to Nothing ...
     Connects each being, greatest with the least;
     Made Beast in aid of Man, and Man of Beast;
     All serv'd, all serving! Nothing stands alone;
     The Chain holds on, and where it ends, unknown.

     – Alexander Pope, *Essay on Man*, I.8.5-9, and
       3.1.22-6, 1734

I

The idea of the Great Chain of Being or *scala naturae* (the scale of nature)
had its origins in classical Greece, but it was first systematized by the vegetarian Plotinus in the third century AD. It came to the fore in the early
Middle Ages where it dominated Western thought until the latter half of
the nineteenth century. According to the doctrine, everything in nature is
arranged in a hierarchy from high to low, everything having its appropriate
niche – from God through the angels to humans to higher mammals to the
lowest insects. Indeed, the interconnectedness of animals, humans, and
plants, of all of nature, which is so emphasized in Hindu, Buddhist, Jain,
Taoist, and Aboriginal thought, can be readily seen to have here its Western
counterpart. In his groundbreaking *The Great Chain of Being*,[1] Arthur
Lovejoy described the idea as "one of the half-dozen most potent and persistent presuppositions in Western thought."

Despite Lovejoy's meticulous analysis, most modern writers on animal
welfare history have ignored this central theme of the Western tradition, thus
neglecting the import of the ideas of Macrobius and Plotinus (2), Leibnitz (5)
and Pope (7), among many others. Others have considered the idea of the

chain an oppressive one in which the lower animals are treated with contempt, subject to the whims and misuse of humankind.[2] And *sometimes* it is. In fact, Descartes, who is customarily derided by animal liberationists for thinking of animals as no more than automata, chides some of his contemporaries for failing to recognize human-animal similarities and the animal's rightful place in the scheme of things (4). The words of Cardinal Bellarmino (3) should remind us that many were not guilty of that offence, as should Edward Young's phrase in *Night Thoughts:* "Long golden chain of Miracles." But the words of John Locke may be seen to be even more emphatic: "There are some Brutes, that seem to have as much Knowledge and Reason as some that are called men; and the Animal and Vegetable Kingdoms are so nearly join'd, that if you will take the lowest of one, and the highest of the other, there will scarce be perceived any great difference between them; and so on until we come to the lowest and most inorganical parts of Matter, we shall find everywhere that the several *Species* are linked together, and differ but in almost insensible degrees."[3] For Locke, humans are in general superior and that superiority is demonstrated through reason, but some of the other species are seen to proximate the human rational condition.

Of course, there are many who thought nature or God provided the other species for human use. Thus, we can read in Aristotle's *Politics,* "Plants exist to give subsistence to animals, and animals to give it to men. Animals, when they are domesticated, serve for use as well as for food; wild animals too, in most cases if not all, serve to furnish man not only with food, but also with other comforts, such as the provision of clothing and similar aids to life. Accordingly, as nature makes nothing purposeless or in vain, all animals must have been made by nature for the sake of men."[4] However, as we have seen, this view is only one side of Aristotle. There is also the Aristotle who claims that there is "something natural and wonderful" in all animals, and that there is a property akin to reason in some that grants them certain considerations. Indeed, in *On the Parts of Animals* (2, 2), Aristotle insists that animals have souls, that some are more intelligent than others, that some possess nobility and some wisdom – thus indicating that the purported animal lack of reason is a lack of something other than that which we today customarily call reason. For Aristotle, in fact, some animals may even participate, if only minimally, in divinity: "For of all living beings with which we are acquainted, man alone partakes of the divine, or at any rate partakes of it in a fuller measure than the rest" (2, 10). In the *Poetics* (Ch. 7), Aristotle recognizes the potential for beauty in animals. Again, it would appear unwarranted to depict Aristotle as one who lacks respect for other species. While not using the chain analogy, he clearly accepts it.

Aristotle's view in fact appears to resemble that of Samuel Taylor Coleridge in his *Aids to Reflection,* in which he claims that both animals and humans possess understanding whereas only humans possess reason. "Reason" here refers to a refined form of cogitation. Plutarch went to the heart of the matter in his essay "On the Use of Reason by 'Irrational' Animals." He tells us that "if you want to deny the name of reason or intelligence to what animals have, then it is time for you to find a more attractive and distinguished name for it, since there is no doubt that the faculty it constitutes is both practically better and more impressive than human intelligence." In *On Water and Land Animals,* Plutarch attempted to demonstrate that animals perform sequential reasoning in the same manner as intelligent humans (1). There is certainly some degree of substantial dispute between Plutarch and Aristotle and his allies, but much of the disagreement appears to be semantic. Both acknowledge calculative and "instinctive" reason in other species. This should not persuade us to ignore Aristotle's positing of a human superiority that permits us the use of other species for our own ends. But it does point to the ambivalence of the usage, some would say exploitation, in conjunction with a respect for other species to the extent that their interests are not in conflict with our interests. When Aristotle tells us that "all animals must have been made by nature for the sake of men," he is offering us the same message as Black Elk when he tells us with pride of the fear of animals for humans (Ch. 5 [6]). However worthwhile animals may be, they also serve for human use.

Aristotle's ambivalence may be thought to be less pronounced in others. Thus St. Thomas Aquinas, disciple of Aristotle, states: "Things, like plants which merely have life, are all alike for animals, and all animals are for man. Wherefore it is not unlawful if men use plants for the good of animals, and animals for the good of man, as the Philosopher [that is, Aristotle] states."[5] The natural, wonderful, and quasi-rational elements of other species mentioned by Aristotle receive short shrift. In like vein, we can read from François Fénelon (1651-1715) that "in nature not only the plants but the animals are made for our use." While he acknowledges that predators may be considered an exception, he concludes, "If all countries were peopled and made subject to law and order as they should be, there would be no animals that would attack man."[6] Nonetheless, even for Aquinas and Fénelon, animals have their own entitlements. They are both ends and means.

The Immanuel Kant who developed the ethical conceptual framework of treating individuals as ends, which Goethe later extended explicitly to include individual animals, could still proclaim "Animals are not self-conscious and are there merely as a means to an end. The end is man." And as late as 1984, the Catholic Church was still reiterating Kant's message. Pope John II claimed, "It is certain that animals are intended for man's use." Nonetheless, there is often another side to such stories, the implication of the argument involving little more than that humans by nature and with justice are carnivores who are entitled to hunt and domesticate other species to provide the necessities of life; and who are entitled to use animals as an aid to the plough and as a means of transportation (all uses, incidentally, in which many Aboriginals and Orientals engage). After all, the Kant who insisted that animals are merely "a means to an end" also tells us that the "more we come in contact with animals the more we love them, for we see how great is their care for their young. It is then difficult for us to be cruel in thought even to a wolf." It is remarkable how often books on animal philosophy castigate the Kant who declares animals to be for human use – and don't bother to mention the Kant who writes of our love for other species. A careful reading of Kant would suggest that, like Goethe, he thought of animals as means in some respects and as ends in others, as both objects and subjects, just as he thought individual humans to be both means and ends. To be sure, animals were, for Kant, lesser beings but still worthy of our love.

Unfortunately, in several books concerned with the history of Western attitudes toward animals and nature – to add a couple to the lengthy list, we might mention Alfred W. Crosby's *Ecological Imperialism* and Richard D. Ryder's *Animal Revolution: Changing Attitudes toward Speciesism*[7] – we are treated to a predominantly one-sided story in which the negative aspects of the tradition are emphasized, together with an occasional sop to the author's favourite philosophers who are treated as a welcome aberration in the Western tradition. A careful reading of that tradition would suggest that we need to recognize a complex and inconsistent whole, rather than merely a tradition of abuse. Indeed, it is one with an ongoing perspective of respect.

In all Western nations, numerous legends testify to a bond of friendship between humans and non-humans, reflecting a recognition that mutual respect and compassion were deemed both appropriate and laudable. Perhaps the best known of such tales is that of Androcles and the Lion. A second-century version of that story appears in the *Attic Knights of Aulus Gellius*. Gellius quotes Apion Plistonices:

> In the Great Circus a battle with wild beasts on a grand scale was being exhibited to the people. Of that spectacle, since I chanced to be in Rome, I was an eyewitness. There were many savage wild beasts, brutes remarkable for their huge size, and all of uncommon appearance or unusual ferocity. But beyond all others did the vast size of the lions excite wonder, and one of these in particular surpassed all the rest because of the huge size of his body ... There was brought in ... the slave of an ex-consul; the slave's name was Androcles. When that lion saw him from a distance he stopped short as if in amazement, and then approached the man slowly and quietly, as if he recognized him. Then, wagging his tail in a mild and caressing way, after the manner and fashion of fawning dogs, he came close to the man, who was now half dead from fright, and gently licking his feet and hands ... Then you might have seen man and lion exchange joyful greetings, as if they had recognized each other.[8]

Apion Plistonices then relates how Androcles explained to the emperor Caligula that, while hiding from his owner in a remote cave, he chanced upon the lion, wounded with a huge splinter in his foot, which Androcles removed. (Other versions have it as a thorn.) The two became fast friends living together in the cave for three years, the lion hunting for both. The generality of the story can be seen in Dostoevsky's *The Brothers Karamazov*. Father Zosima preaches to a young peasant about the innocence and sinlessness of animals in all of nature. He uses the traditional Russian story of St. Sergey and the bear to teach the moral: St. Sergey, patron saint of Moscow, befriends a bear; they become inseparable and share their meals together. The story is as well known, and as endearing, to Russian Orthodox youth as St. Francis is to Catholic youth, and Androcles's lion is to Roman and medieval European youth.

What is significant about the stories is that they have been repeated generation after generation, reflecting the sympathetic attitude toward other species prevalent in Western society. What is reflective of Western ambivalence is that the Romans continued to delight in the story and recognize its moral imperative while also continuing to attend the circus, and that medieval (and later) Europeans repeated the story ad nauseam to their children while continuing to bait bears and bulls. The reality is, of course, that there are both higher and lower aspects to human nature, both playing a significant role in all human societies. That human attitudes around such matters are complex is reflected in Lord Macaulay's statement that the seventeenth-century "Puritan hated bearbaiting, not because it gave pain to the bear but because it gave pleasure to the spectators. Indeed, he generally contrived to enjoy the double pleasure of tormenting both spectators and bear."[9] Of course, the implication of the Whiggish historian is that, unlike Puritans, persons of refined sensibilities would both enjoy their own pleasure and refrain from tormenting other species. And while the Romans customarily enjoyed the cruelties of the "games," we should take note of the fact, as we have before, that, according to Pliny the Elder, Cicero declared that, on at least one occasion, the crowd showed pity for, and a sense of fellowship with, the animals rather than taking any pleasure in the contests. In 55 BC, when the Roman general Pompey, rival of Julius Caesar, staged a public contest between gladiators and elephants, the Roman populace found the event morally repugnant. Just how much revulsion there was at the slaughter of the games we shall never know. But we do know that the Stoic philosopher Seneca and the Roman priest Novation protested loudly. As well, the eighteenth-century historian Helen Williams insisted on the superiority of the laws of Rome with regard to animals over those of her own time.[10]

It is worth bearing in mind that the television spectacular of World Wrestling Federation events – which are both fraudulent and ghoulish – are today extremely popular. Yet most people with any degree of education and sensibility find the performances degrading and offensive. It would be inappropriate to interpret the popularity as a reflection of North American culture in general, and perhaps the same may be said of the Roman circus.

In most cultures at most times, there are demeaning practices subscribed to by a proportion of the population and rejected by others.

Again, it is significant that the Androcles story is about a lion – a creature of great grace, power, and strength, for which humans generally express awe and admiration. It could not have been told of a crocodile or a scorpion. Certainly, there is a hierarchy of animal values, but it is not always precisely what one might expect. Thus, in his *Phaedo,* Plato has Socrates and Cebes discuss reincarnation and the universal soul. Socrates expresses the view that "men who have followed after gluttony, and wantonness, and drunkenness ... will pass into [that is, be reincarnated as] asses and animals of that sort ... And those who have chosen the portion of injustice and tyranny, and violence, will pass into wolves, or hawks and kites: – whither else can we suppose them to go?" On the other hand, Socrates insists, the second-best humans – "those who have practised the civil and social virtues which are called temperance and justice, and are acquired by habit and attention without philosophy and mind" – will be accorded a preferable fate. They "may be expected to pass into some gentle social nature which is like their own, such as that of bees or ants, or even back again into the form of man, and just and moderate men spring from them."

However, the greater reward comes to the thinker – "he who is a philosopher or lover of learning, and is entirely pure at departing, is alone permitted to reach the gods."[11] In the pantheon of animals, those creatures that possess the characteristics we admire in humans are deemed preferable, of higher status, than those that possess the characteristics we deplore in humans. However, the scale is not entirely simple, and, more frequently, complexity of structure plays a significant role, thus elevating the horses over the bees. The point on which almost all seem to agree is that there is a hierarchy of animal value and that most animals are entitled not to equal respect with humans but to respect as the animals that they are deemed to be. Indeed, Plato's version of reincarnation bears a striking resemblance to its Hindu and Buddhist counterparts.

The idea that our kinship to other species obligates us to them pervaded not just the work of some of the early Greek thinkers[12] but also played a significant role in the Christian tradition. Thus, for example, Pope Urban II, at the Council of Clermont in 1095, extended the right of sanctuary to oxen, plough horses, and harrowing horses, as well as the men who worked them, because of their relationship. St. Francis was "a Nature mystic, a devoted sacramentalist [who] envisaged all Creation, man supremely, as worshipping the Creator." The thirteenth-century scholastic theologian St. Bonaventure, in his *Life of St. Francis,* tells us that St. Francis urged the brethren "to praise God in all things and through all His creatures." "He called all animals 'brother' or 'sister,' " St. Bonaventure tells us in a sermon delivered in 1255.[13] All creatures, including humans, were related through God and owed a consequent obligation to each other.

Nor are such conceptions a rarity in the early church. Of the saints, many can lay their claim to spiritual fame on their love and respect for other species. Ailbe is the patron saint of wolves, and is perhaps of less significance for his protection of wolves than because he was praised and elevated for it. Amalburga escaped her persecutors with the aid of a sturgeon. Andrew Corsini is depicted in art with a wolf and a lamb at his feet. Bernard of Clairvaux declared that "we can learn more from the woods, from stones and trees, than from teachers and books." Blaise, patron saint of sick cattle, lived in a cave in the woods to which wild beasts would come for sanctuary and medical treatment. A wolf protected the burial site of St. Edmund. Eloy blessed a horse and rid it of demonic possession. Gall, patron saint of birds, shared his cave-dwelling with a bear. Harvey charmed animals with his music and is invoked to protect flocks and herds. Hugh of Lincoln and his pet swan were inseparable. Modomnoc was accompanied by wild bees. Roch was kept alive by the actions of a friendly dog. Sylvester restored to life a dog killed by an evil wizard.[14] Of course, we might wish to characterize many such stories as predominantly legendary folk tales. But if that is so, we must apply the same criteria to the myths of Aboriginals in which their respect for other species is also expressed.

Again, in several books that touch on the topic of the history of animal welfare, we are given a predominantly negative interpretation of the Christian tradition, St. Augustine and St. Thomas Aquinas being among the customary villains. Peter Singer, for example, quotes St. Augustine's statement that: "Christ himself shows that to refrain from the killing of animals and the destroying of plants is the height of superstition, for judging that there are no common rights between us and the beasts and trees, he sent the devils into a herd of swine and with a curse withered the tree on which he found no fruit ... Surely the swine had not sinned, nor had the tree." Singer's conclusion is that "Jesus was, according to St. Augustine, trying to show us that we need not govern our behaviour toward animals by the moral rules that govern our behaviour toward humans."[15]

To understand the implications of St. Augustine's statement, however, we must recognize the context. St. Augustine had been a Manichee who converted to Catholicism (or re-converted, since he was raised a Catholic by his mother). The Manichees were vegetarians who believed that humans had no right to kill animals for human consumption. In the mystic world of the fifth century, such a doctrine was persuasive. Augustine was merely proclaiming the carnivorous rights of humans, as do almost all Aboriginals and most Orientals. He was arguing in favour of the doctrine to which he had been converted against the doctrine from which he had been converted. He was not so much arguing against treating other species well as he was against what he saw as the vegetarian excesses of his former fellow believers.

Moreover, to take this statement as the defining position of St. Augustine, as has become customary, is to miss much of the complexity of his thought. The picture we derive from St. Augustine's *Confessions* is very different from that offered to us by Singer. There, we read of Augustine being appalled at the suggestion that he should offer an animal sacrifice to gain a prize he covets. "Though the crown were of an undying lustre, I would not permit a fly to be killed to gain me the victory," Augustine tells us.[16] Later in the *Confessions,* he offers us a position entirely consistent with the idea of the Great Chain of Being, in which each niche is filled by a creature of significance, albeit not of equal significance. Thus, he tells us that "All Things, which are, are good ... beasts and all cattle, creeping things, and fowls of the air ... praise Thy Name ... I decided that all things above were better than those below, but that both together were better than the things above alone."[17] In Augustine's view, other species make the world a significantly better place than it would be without them. In *The City of God,* he proclaimed, "In no wise is anything in nature bad."

In like vein, we customarily read of Aquinas who declared that animals did not possess souls, and that they could be possessed by the devil and used for evil purposes. Rarely does the commentator bother to mention that at the time "soul" was such a restricted conception – perhaps something akin to Aristotle's "reason" – that it was doubted women possessed it, too. For example, St. Thomas, following Aristotle, believed that males were ensouled forty days after conception, and females eighty days after conception, reflecting the latter's lower status. And, of course, to declare animals capable of being possessed by the devil was to claim no more than what was customarily believed also of people.

Occasionally, we are told that Aquinas argued that charity was owed to all of God's creation, including "the creatures without reason ... fish and birds, the beasts and plants." When we are given this information, however, we are usually informed that Aquinas believed that the only argument against cruelty to animals is that it may lead to cruelty to people.[18] However often this claim is made for St. Thomas, there is nothing in his writings to suggest it. Certainly, St. Thomas tells us that "if a man practice a pitiable affection for animals, he is all the more disposed to take pity on his fellowmen" (*Summa Theologiae*, Vol. 2, 1, 102, 6). But nowhere does he suggest this point as the *sole* reason for compassion toward other species. Charity to other species was, in fact, simply a part of Aquinas's moral law. It was the view reiterated in William Hogarth's eighteenth-century didactic engravings *The Four Stages of Cruelty*. Hogarth depicted cruelty to animals as the precursor of cruelty to humans, the latter being the major vice, but the former equally an aspect of human injustice.

To offer us only one side of Aquinas and then to tell us that "if any single writer may be taken as representative of Christian philosophy prior to the Reformation, and of Roman Catholic philosophy to this day, it is Aquinas" is to ignore the complexity of both St. Thomas's thought and Catholic thought in general. Surely, St. Francis's *Canticle of the Creatures* is better known to Catholic youth than the *Summa Theologiae*. However much St. Thomas may be regarded as the intellectual pillar of the Catholic church, it would be misleading to ignore not only St. Francis but also the plea of St. Bernardino: "Look at the pigs who have so much compassion for each other that when one of them squeals the other will run to help ... And you children who steal the baby swallows. What do other swallows do? They all gather together and try to help the fledgling ... Man is more evil than the birds."[19] In his *A History of Christianity,* Owen Chadwick tells us that the devout "Dante loved nightingales singing, geese squawking, eagles soaring, frogs leaping, pigs pushing, ants hurrying down the track, goats on the mountainside; the light at dawn and sunset, the rainbow and the storm." He revelled in the wonders of nature. In *Les Misérables,* Victor Hugo tells us that according to St. Matthew, "duty to all living creatures" is one of the four duties of humankind. Unfortunately, Hugo does not indicate the precise source in the gospel (and I, for one, am unable to locate it with confidence), but it is significant that Hugo deems it an accepted interpretation of the Christian tradition.

None of what I have written in these pages should be read to suggest that the Christian tradition has been one of unwavering respect for nature. It has not. But neither has it been one in which the interests of other species have been ignored. There is a much greater diversity and complexity in Western thought than we are sometimes led to believe. And it is a complexity in which animals have customarily been treated as worthy of moral consideration, of having a respected but not equal place in creation, and of being entitled to be treated well by humans, limited by the extent that animal interests and purportedly legitimate human interests are in conflict.

Aristotle was the first to engage in systematic empirical research on other species. He maintained a fairly substantial menagerie to further his research and spent two years on the island of Lesbos studying marine mammals. He wrote the remarkable *Historia Animalium* – for many centuries the most profound work on natural history, although, as should scarcely surprise us, it contains also some hearsay nonsense as well as controversial truths. Some of his claims – such as the method of generation of the cephalopods (for example, squid and octopus), males having "a kind of penis in one of [their] tentacles ... which is admitted into the nostril of the female" – were long disputed before being confirmed finally in the nineteenth century. It is in fact only in the last two centuries that we have progressed much beyond Aristotle in our knowledge of biology. And because most of the writings of Aristotle were lost to the Western world from the heyday of Rome to the twelfth century, when they were re-acquired from Arabic sources, Aristotle's science was also lost. To be sure, we had Pliny the Elder's *Natural History,* which was known to at least some medieval scholars and which was based in part on Aristotle. But, unfortunately, pride of place in Pliny went to 300-foot-long eels, 150-foot-long sharks, three-acre whales, religious elephants, merciful lions, and an octopus that climbed trees!

Later Western understanding of other species was based not on the science of Aristotle, nor even on the half-wisdom of Pliny, but predominantly on the bestiaries – "medieval moralizing treatises on beasts," the *Concise Oxford Dictionary* calls them. During the Middle Ages, the popularity of the bestiaries was exceeded only by that of the Bible, a fact itself reflective of continuing interest, almost fascination, with the animal realm. The bestiaries were derived from a single ancient original, the work of a certain Physiologus ("Naturalist"), a Greek scholar about whom little is known but who is probably of late-second-century vintage. However, the bestiaries were embellished over the centuries, adding new information, or, quite often, misinformation to some of the already dubious accounts.

Along with some accurate descriptions, Physiologus concocted a whole host of misbegotten biologically monstrous fancies – as well as such absurdities as that leopards have sweet-smelling breath – which plagued our understanding of natural history for well over a millennium, strongly influencing later writers as well as church masons, much to the chagrin of St. Bernard of Clairvaux, who denounced these inventions in the twelfth century. Nonetheless, they were still accepted by the compilers of medieval bestiaries and the most reputable of scholars. Thus, for example, in Konrad Gesner's five-volume *Historia Animalium* (1551-8, 1587), we still encounter the satyr (a woodland spirit man-beast) as well as several other of Physiologus's fantasies. In the fourteen-volume *Natural History* of Ulisse Aldrovandi (1599-1602 and posthumously), we can still find a harpy (part bird, part woman) as one of his imaginings. In Edward Topsell's *Historie of Fovre-Footed Beastes* of 1607, we meet the hydra, a seven-headed, two-taloned, curly-tailed monstrosity – a fairly similar image also appears in Albert Seba's eighteenth-century *Locupletissimi*. John Jonston's *Historia naturalis de serpentibus* of 1653 contains dragons and basilisks (reptiles that are able to kill men with a look, but that are harmless to women), and his *Historia naturalis de quadrupedibus* of 1655 depicts three types of unicorn (as well as a zebra supposedly from India). Science and mythology were inextricably confused. Indeed, at the University of Leyden in the eighteenth century – then one of the most reputable institutions of learning in Europe – there was a hall called the Indian Cabinet filled with numerous purported "curiosities," among them a winged cat, the hand of a mermaid,[20] a monster hatched from a hen's egg, and a "vegetable Priapus."

Despite the "monsters," however, a favourite quotation of the bestiaries was the passage from Job on how we should learn from the beasts, the fowls, the earth, and the sea. Just as with Aboriginal myths the purpose of the learning was for the sake of human life, so too one of the implications of both Occidental and Aboriginal myths was respect for the source of the learning. Thus Gesner described the rhinoceros as "the second wonder of nature ... as the elephant was the first wonder."

It is notable that the fish is the image of divinity, and not only for Jesus

Christ, but, reflective of cross-cultural similarities – indeed, of universal archetypes – also in Turan, in India, and the Far East, in Chaldea, Babylonia, Mesopotamia, Egypt, Sumeria, Mexico, and a host of other places. Discussing the wings of the four mysterious animals of the Tetramorph, the sixth-century pope St. Gregory the Great indicates that: "An ingenious and penetrating description shows us these four animals which the prophet's spirit foresaw in the future: each had four faces, each had four wings. What can the face mean but knowledge; and what the wings, if not flight? It is by the face that each person is known, and by the wings that birds lift themselves into the air. The face then refers to faith, the wing to contemplation, for by faith the almighty God knows us. By contemplation which raises us above ourselves, we lift ourselves into the air."[21] And if this elevates the ox, bull, and eagle (the fourth animal being "man"), a customary depiction of the devil is with bat's wings, of vampires and dragons with membranous rather than feathered wings. Such depictions denigrate those creatures, real or fancied, that meet our disfavour.

Certainly, in the so-called dark ages of Western civilization, it was customary to encounter the view that there was an interdependent Nature in which humankind lived in harmony with an ordered universe. Thus, in the seventh century, we meet Isidore of Seville's *Liber de natura rerum* (*On Nature*), the commentaries of Remigius of Auxerre in the tenth, Byrhtferth of East Anglia's *Enchiridion* in the eleventh, and Alan of Lille's *Plaint of Nature* in the twelfth. In each, humankind is depicted as a microcosm of Nature.

However, stories of "monsters" and the seemingly less "wholesome" parts of nature abounded, providing more fear than respect – though the two are clearly related – more amazement than awe. Thus, for example, we read in *Mandeville's Travels*, composed in the middle of the fourteenth century:

Thence went men toward the land of Bactria [an ancient Greek kingdom in central Asia] which is filled with evil and cruel people. In that country there are trees which bear wool, as though they were sheep, where from men make clothes, and all things that may be made from wool. In that country there are many hippopotamuses that dwell partly in water and partly on land; and they are half man and half horse, as I have said before; and they eat men when they may catch them. And there are rivers and waters that are full of salt, thrice as much as in sea water. In that country there are many gryphons, more plentiful than in other countries. Some men say their upper body is that of an eagle and their lower body that of a lion; and they say indeed with certainty that they are of that shape. Yet the lion half of the gryphon has a larger and stronger body than eight lions; [and the remainder] is bigger and stronger than a hundred eagles such as we have amongst us. For there a gryphon will carry in flight to his nest a great horse, if one is to be found, or two oxen yoked together, as at the plough. For he has talons so long and so large, and great upon his feet, as though they were horns of great oxen, or bullocks, or cattle, such that men make drinking cups from them. And from their ribs and the feather quills of their wings, men make full-size bows to use with both arrows and bolts.[22]

Of course, there are no hippopotamuses in Asia; they are vegetarian and not "man-eaters"; gryphons are the product of human imagination and not nature; and so on. Animals were in part a source of awe and affection, in part creatures to be despised, in part to be feared, in part sources for wondrous inventions of the imagination. Just as all of life was a complex of good and evil, of joy and misery, of greed and altruism, so if animals were to be the source of our learning, they must also correspond to all the goodness *and* badness, real or imagined, in the world.

Clearly, the Western relationship to other species has been a complex one. Swallows and nightingales have been revered. Lambs have been loved; tigers have struck us dumb with awe. On the other hand, some animals were deemed so low they were thought not to have been created by God on the sixth day along with the other animals. Cornelius a Lapide (1567-1637), a Flemish Jesuit, claimed that "lice, flies, maggots and the like were not created directly by God but by spontaneous generation, as lice from sweat."[23] Such animalcules were so despicable God would not have deigned to create them, Lapide imagined. This was quite by contrast, Lapide thought, with His creation of all the nobler species, from bulls to birds, predators to prey, all filling the niches assigned to them and each and every one necessary to the grandeur of God's creation. (This was the doctrine of plenitude, an integral aspect of the *scala naturae* or *scala creatorum* – scale of creatures – as it was alternatively known.)

The age of science and technology did little at first to diminish the Great Chain, but it did have a perhaps surprising impact on giving a more honourable place to the insects. The development of the microscope allowed such scholars as, for example, Jan Swammerdam (1637-86), to show in his *Historia insectorum generalis* that insects, like the "higher" animals, possessed an intricate anatomy and did not reproduce by spontaneous generation. While the Great Chain had allotted the insects the lowest link, some thinkers had endeavoured to rob them even of that. The researches of the new scientists ensured that the insects were entitled to a legitimate place in the chain, even if at the bottom, and that all of the animals in the chain would be elevated.

When the great Dutch scientist Antoni van Leeuwenhoek acquired a microscope in 1674, he turned it on a drop of pepper water and wrote: "The whole water seemed to be alive with these multifarious animalcules. This was for me, among all the marvels that I have discovered in nature, the most marvellous of all; and I must say, for my part, that no more pleasant sight has ever yet come before my eye that these many thousands of living creatures, seen all alive in a little drop of water, moving among one another, each several creature having its own proper motion."[24] Leeuwenhoek's pleasure and marvel are witness to the capacity of science and technology to elevate nature. Unfortunately, it did not always do so. Yet it did so perhaps more frequently than we are customarily led to believe. Certainly, in his *Book of Thel,* Blake emphasized the community spirit that unites all forms of being, from the earthworm and the clay in which the worm dwells all the way up to the seraphim Thel herself. Science's discoveries encouraged even those who despised science – as Blake did – to treat even the animalcules with awe. Writing in 1713, Alexander Pope asked, when considered "with an eye to eternity," "Who knows what plots, what achievements, a mite may perform in his kingdom of a grain of dust, within his life of some minutes?" A century later, Emily Dickinson could write that "the Gnat's supremacy is large as thine." It was not an unusual conception. Thus Abraham Lincoln, recoiling at an instance of cruelty to a terrapin: "An ant's life is as sweet to it as ours to us."

Certainly, the Great Chain of Being, a concept that played a vital role in the development of Western thought, has denied equality between the non-human beings of the natural world and the authors of the doctrine. Nonetheless, there is no reason to assume that it implied a disrespect for those non-human beings. Indeed, generally speaking, regard for other beings as the creatures that they are was the predominant message of the teaching. This regard followed Aristotle's principle that self-realization in its own nature was the goal of every organism. And depictions of well-treated animals in medieval paintings (see, for example, the miniatures of the Limbourg brothers in *Les Très Riches Heures* of the Duc de Berry or the masterpieces of Sandro Botticelli such as *The Youth of Moses*) reflect the fact that it was deemed a significant part of one's humanity to recognize the intrinsic worth of other creatures and our responsibilities toward them.

II

While we should be cautious in our interpretation of Western medieval myth – or for that matter any other myth – there are important hints to be gleaned from them on the status of the animal. Swans and horses were in particular favour. In *Gudrun,* a swan assists the eponymous heroine to claim her lover. In his search for the Holy Grail and the rescue of fair Else, Lohengrin too is aided by a swan. In the *Niebelungenlied,* we read of the swan-maidens who are "wise-women" and come to the aid of a princess. In *The Ettin Langshanks,* Dietrich has a noble horse that saves him from death. El Cid's faithful charger Babieça was held in great honour, even after his master's death, was well-cared for, and no other was allowed to bestride him. In several of the legends surrounding the historical figure of Charlemagne, we encounter Papillon, Ogier's magical horse, "famed for his skill and wisdom." Veillantif, Roland's equine "comrade" of "mighty heart," is frequently eulogized in *chansons de geste,* though we might have qualms about Roland's choice at his own death at the Battle of Roncessvalles to have Veillantif killed rather than allow it to fall into "heathen captivity." We also read of Aymon's marvellous steed, Bayard, which is stolen by the devil and without which Aymon's valour comes to naught. Having been recovered, the horse passes to Aymon's youngest son, Renaud. It saves his life several times but is sacrificed in great anguish by Renaud to save the lives of his brothers. Full of remorse at his own perfidy to his horse, Renaud leaves home and joins the crusades.

Beyond horses and swans, we find in the Norse *Ràgnar Lodbrok Saga* Krake dispatching her faithful pet magpies to spy on her lover. In Wolfram von Eschenbach's *Parzival,* the eponymous hero kills a bird as a child, is reduced to tears by his cruelty, and is remonstrated by his mother for his impious behaviour. In the poem of *Ortnit* – known since the ninth century – a faithful dog mourns his master's passing.

Not all is positive, however. In the *Niebelungenlied,* Siegfrèd catches a bear alive and then releases it for his hunting guests to sport with. In *The Ettin Langshanks,* Wildeber slays and flays a bear to provide himself with a disguise. Generally, in hunting stories, little concern is evinced for the object of the chase. Both the positive and the negative aspects must be taken into account if we are to understand the status of animals in medieval legend. It is equally important to note there is far more cruelty to humans in these stories than to animals, along with many episodes of the slaying of "monsters" – especially "dragons," as witnessed in both Gottfried von Strassburg's *Tristan* and the *Ràgnar Lodbrok Saga.*

There are also a number of specifically animal epics, the most famous of which is the Flemish-German story of *Reynard the Fox,* where, as in animal tales in general, H.A. Guerber tells us, "We see described the delight which the child of nature takes in all animals."[25] *Reynard* is a tale about the manner in which the animals of the forest arrange their relationships and attempt to seek a form of mutual justice. Primarily, the story has lessons for human society rather than that of the animals but at least a subsidiary aspect is to recognize that animals behave according to their God-given natures and are to be respected as such.

III

If we have a natural propensity to treat other species well, limited to the extent that we see our legitimate interests in conflict with theirs, then our technological developments will serve to separate us from our common belongingness, our fellowship, with them by differentiating our perception of our interests from theirs. As our technological experiences serve to alter what we regard as legitimate – from domestication to vivisection – so our capacity to dominate other species serves increasingly to oppress them. But it is not without regret, as Robert Burns's "To a Mouse" (1785) reflects. Having turned the mouse up in her nest while ploughing, Burns rues, "I'm truly sorry man's dominion / Has broken nature's social union." In *A Sentimental Journey* (1768), Laurence Sterne wrote of the disconsolate peasant, full of guilt that his own usage of the animal had shortened his poor ass's days. In admiration, the narrator exclaims: "Did we love each other, as this poor soul but loved his ass – 'twould be something."

Certainly, the development of more sophisticated hunting tools and methods, such as the bow, the atlatl, and the buffalo jump, will have distanced us from our earlier respect and affection for other species, as too will the invention of the yoke, the general accoutrements of domestication, and the use of beasts of burden for transportation. As soon as Amerindians were accorded the opportunity to employ the horse as means of transportation, they took it. The use of the animal as a means was not seen to offend their value system.

The tendency to think of an animal as an instrument rather than a live being becomes strongest when an operation becomes routinized and mechanized. Clearly, the object of predation in the hunt is being treated as a means, but one for which the hunter may have some respect, especially if the prey is courageous or graceful or beautiful. And both Westerners and Amerindians developed affection for the horses they used – while they kept them often in conditions quite inappropriate to their unbroken character. Indeed, both Westerners and Amerindians domesticated wild horses in contravention of respect for nature. However, when, beginning with Roman technology in the first century AD, the animal was used to turn a capstan to operate a mill, its behaviour became entirely routinized and even respect in the use of animals was lost. The animal's life became worthless, perhaps even for itself, and it was likely treated as worthless by the operator. If all animal usage contravenes nature, some contraventions are clearly far worse than others.

Just as certain nineteenth-century Romantics, Utopians, Marxists, and Tories concurred in showing that the process of mechanization and industrialization was dehumanizing for the worker and for the relationship between employer and employee, so too the routinization of the animal's tasks served to alienate the operator from the animal and resulted in an oppressive relationship in which those who possessed power dominated those who lacked it – and to the detriment of the fulfilment of both. The one was dehumanized, the other "de-animalized," to coin an ugly and uncomfortable, if meaningful, term. It was alienated from its authentic animal nature, from its *telos*.

Worst of all, however, is that the alienation, along with the distancing of human/animal interests, led to a situation in which the animals were treated as instruments of production. They were nought but machines. This kind of relationship in first- and second-century Rome led not only to the horrors of the games but to the dissection of animals for human ends.

Galen (AD 131-200) was a Greek scientist who resided chiefly in Rome from about the age of thirty and was the imperial court physician to Marcus Aurelius. Galen correlated extant medical knowledge with his own theories derived from dissection of animals, predominantly apes and pigs. Thus, in the classical period, the view was firmly established that human superior reason gave us the right to use other animals to further our own ends. As a consequence of our superiority, we were entitled to experiment on "inferior" creatures provided the human value, either in knowledge or in health, was thought to justify it.

With the collapse of the Roman Empire and the onset of the dark ages, the advancement of learning declined – and to such a degree that by the four-teenth century, according to Chaucer, medical students still spent their time studying the works of Hippocrates (c. 460-370 BC) and Galen, and little of more recent date. In fact, the church had forbidden dissection of human cadavers shortly after the adoption of Christianity as the official state reli-gion of Rome. The practice of medicine thus relied on extant knowledge.

It was certainly not the edict alone that brought medical research to an end for over a millennium but rather the loss of will for secular learning that suffused the dark ages. There was no edict against research on animals, but almost none was conducted. Only with the resurrection of learning fol-lowing the rediscovery of reason and the individual in the Renaissance did minds turn to the acquisition of secular and useful knowledge once more.

In 1543, the Flemish anatomist Andreas Vesalius, working at the University of Padua in Italy, published *De humani corporis fabrica* (*The Structure of the Human Body*). The research for the book was based on human corpse rather than animal dissection (much to the chagrin of the Church) and corrected many of Galen's errors. Vesalius's work stimulated a significant if spasmodic scientific and medical research industry, much of which was performed on animals (to the chagrin of some members of the public). This in turn produced a new philosophy of mind that provided rationalization to justify the research.

According to most of the literature concerning the history of animal wel-fare, René Descartes (1596-1650) is the most sinning of the new breed of philosopher. Descartes, it is claimed, hypothesized a duality of matter and spirit. While all else consisted of matter, so Descartes is said to have indi-cated, human beings possessed consciousness, and because consciousness could not originate in matter, only humans had a soul, which was given by God. In most of the animal welfare literature, we read that Descartes's view was that because animals had no consciousness, they could experience nei-ther pain nor pleasure. They were not sentient. Therefore, we were entitled to use them in whatever manner we wished.

In fact, Descartes is less than clear on the matter. In his *A Descartes Dictionary,* John Cottingham concludes a thorough investigation with the claim that "to deny thought to animals [as Descartes does] is not *eo ipso* to deny that they *feel;* and Descartes sometimes talked in a way which suggested that animals might have sensations like hunger, or passions like fear, hope and joy." Cottingham cites a letter to the Marquess of Newcastle as evidence. He nonetheless acknowledges that "Descartes' account of the nature of SENSATION is highly problematic." Still, according to Cottingham, Descartes is not the mind-body dualist he is assumed to be, but identifies a "third category of sensation." And he writes often as though animals possessed this third category. In fact, in his *Descartes' Philosophical Letters,* A. Kenny cites the French philosopher's assertion that "all of the things which dogs, horses and monkeys are made to do are merely expressions of their fear, their hope, or their joy; and consequently, they can do these things without any thought."[26] It would appear probable that by defining the human as the *res cogitans* (the thinking being), Descartes is postulating "thought" in the same manner that Aristotle postulated "reason" – as that speculative and self-reflexive capacity that humans do indeed appear to possess exclusively.

Whatever Descartes may in fact have thought about animal sensations, it is clear that his work and that of contemporaries such as Malebranche (who does appear to hold the mechanistic view of which Descartes is accused) provided rationalizations for the scientists of their day. And even for Descartes himself, for he too engaged in invasive research on animals.

An eye-witness account of experiments at the Jansenist seminary at Port-Royal in France at the end of the seventeenth century tells us that the scientists "administered beatings to the dogs with perfect indifference, and made fun of those who pitied the creatures as if they felt pain. They said the animals were clocks; that the cries they emitted when struck were only the noise of a little spring that had been touched, but that the whole body was without feeling. They nailed poor animals upon boards by their four paws to vivisect them and see the circulation of the blood which was a great subject of conversation."[27] Appalled as we must be at the willingness of the scientists to discount the compelling evidence of their senses, we must not fail to recognize that the account indicates that some so pitied the creatures that they apparently lodged complaints about the experimentation.

Writing around the same time, the reputed English chemist Robert Boyle complained, "The veneration wherewith men are imbued for what they call nature has been a discouraging impediment to the empire of man over the inferior creatures of God: for many have not only looked upon it, as an impossible thing to compass but as something impious to attempt."[28] Boyle had invented an air pump, which he gratuitously tried out on animals to show that they could not live without air. Not all, as Boyle notes, were overly impressed by his scientific endeavours. This may not surprise us if we read his *Medical Experiments* (1692), in which he proposed as a sore throat remedy "a drachm of white dog's turd" worked up with honey of roses into "a linctus, to be very slowly let down the throat." For colic, he prescribed a concoction of "four or five balls of fresh horse dung" steeped in white wine, to be drunk "from a quarter to half a pint" at a time. Let us then not be surprised at the complaints of the diarist Samuel Pepys against the "petty experiments" of the new amateur "physiologists" who tortured animals for the amusement of their guests. In his *To Mr. Congreve* (1693), Jonathan Swift, certainly no sentimentalist, reflected public antipathies to the scientific passion for dissecting animals dead and alive. Henry Fielding (both novelist and magistrate [6]) was sufficiently galled by what he regarded as the perverse experimental preoccupations of the Royal Society that in his *Miscellanies*, 1 (1743), he wrote a satirical parody on an account in the *Philosophical Transactions* of the society (407, January 1742-3) of experiments by a Swiss naturalist, Abraham Tremblay, on the freshwater "Polypus." And Robert Browning remarked that he would "rather submit to the worst of deaths, so far as pain goes, than have a single dog or cat tortured on the pretence of sparing me a twinge or two." Both Christina Rossetti and Tennyson applauded Browning's stance. While some scientists and the physicians may have accepted the purported implications of Cartesian rationalism to justify their invasive and destructive research, it would appear on Boyle's own evidence as well as the statements of others, both then and later, that many continued to question its validity.

Thus, for example, the popular and influential kabbalist Robert Flood (1574-1637) proclaimed souls to inhabit animals, plants, and minerals, as well as humans. Richard Overton, more famous as a revolutionary Leveller and Cromwellian intriguer than an animal advocate, nonetheless argued in *Man's Mortality* (1643) that the difference between human and other animals was but one of degree. Moreover, his view was that "all other *Creatures* as well as man shall be raised and delivered from Death at the Resurrection." Despite our current prejudices, there is every reason to believe that the Floods and the Overtons were at least as, if not more, representative than the Descartes and the Boyles.

The prevalent view was in fact that of the popular and influential Anglican divine Richard Hooker, who had written at the close of the sixteenth century: "The chiefest instrument of human communication ... is speech, because thereby we impart mutually one to another the conceits of our reasonable understanding. And for that cause seeing beasts are not hereof capable, forasmuch as with them we can use no such conference, they being in degree, although above other creatures on earth to whom nature hath denied sense, yet lower than to be sociable companions of man to whom nature hath given reason."[29] By "beasts," Hooker meant complex mammals that stood above the other creatures but below humankind. Such standing implied that they were entitled to certain considerations. What scientists like Boyle and the Port-Royal seminarists were challenging was the degree of consideration to which they were entitled. The question was whether the advancement of learning, the benefits to human health, and the quality of human life were worth the cost to the animals. Of course, if one could argue that the animals felt no pain and were incapable of suffering, the question could be settled so much more readily.

We should not, however, imagine that the scientists cared little for the animal realm. Most notably, Sir Francis Bacon (1561-1626), the primary exponent in his day of the scientific method, proclaimed our responsibility to other species: "In *Charity,* there is no excess, neither can Angel or Man come in danger by it. The inclination of *Goodness* is imprinted deeply in the nature of Man; insomuch, that if it issue not toward Men, it will take unto other living Creatures."[30] Certainly, there is also the Bacon who claims that "in scientific investigation man must put nature to the rack in order to wring from it an answer to his question," but animated nature is entitled to significant consideration. Perhaps the Italian physiologist Marcello Malpighi expressed the contradiction best in a letter to his associate Giovanni Borelli. He lamented the fact that "I have sacrificed almost the whole race of frogs, something that did not come to pass even in Homer's savage battle between the frogs and the mice." His only justification was that "I chanced to see such wonderful things that I could with greater aptness than Homer exclaim with him, 'Mine eyes beheld a certain great work.'" If our conclusion has to be that there is little consistency and much contradiction in the Europe of the sixteenth and seventeenth centuries, let us not imagine this phenomenon is exclusively Western. We can read already in the Egyptian *Book of the Dead* of over three and a half millennia ago that "Amen-Rã ... president of all the gods, beautiful god, beloved one ... careth for the welfare of his animal creation."[31] We can then read example after example of prescribed animal sacrifice and irrefutable cruelty! Ambivalence and contradiction are the nature of humankind.

The seventeenth century witnessed the popularity of philosophical materialism, a resurrection of the ideas of Democritus and Epicurus of fourth-century BC Greece. One might have expected such a relativist doctrine to have produced an attitude of carelessness of the rights of other species – one of the implications of a materialistic determinism is the impossibility of altruism. It did not. In fact, Pierre Gassendi, primary reviver of the determinist, materialist, and relativist doctrine avowed: "There is no pretence for saying that any right has been granted to us to kill any of those animals which are not destructive or pernicious to the human race."[32] It is startling how often philosophers come to the moral conclusion they find within their souls, however logically incompatible these conclusions may be with the theoretical doctrine they espouse.

Animal experimentation remained isolated and occasional until the publication of Claude Bernard's *Introduction to the Study of Experimental Medicine* in 1865. This publication established the principle of the laboratory rather than practice as the foundation for medical knowledge. It was Bernard who convinced the medical community of the value of the artificial production of disease by chemical and physical means through reliance on animal models. Such models, according to Bernard, were "very useful and entirely conclusive of the toxicity and hygiene of man. Investigations of medicinal or of toxic substances are wholly applicable to man from the therapeutic point of view."[33] Following Bernard, the capacity and propensity to use animals as a mere means of human welfare grew rapidly. Indeed, it came to be accepted by most as a natural state of affairs. Humans, on account of their superiority, were entitled to use animals for experiments to improve the human condition. This practice reflected and furthered the view that humans were entitled to the experimental use of animals if and only if there was sufficient justification in terms of medical benefits and the ends of knowledge. (Of course, then as now, in the West and elsewhere, there were always those who through ignorance, evil, or thoughtlessness paid no heed to the animal-oriented sensibilities customarily subscribed to.) Animals were ends as well as means, but human superiority, considered an aspect of nature itself, was deemed adequate entitlement to treat animals as means when the potential benefits warranted it. Spinoza held the view that all species work to their own advantage – "We have the same rights in respect to them as they have in respect to us." But he then added that on account of our "virtue, or power ... men have far greater rights over beasts than beasts have over men." Lord Shaftesbury was not so sure. In *The Moralists* (1709), he surveys the various orders of animals, plants, the earth, and the stars before concluding that "these Rural Meditations are sacred ... I sing of Nature's Order in created beings." The extent to which humans possessed rights over others was constantly disputed.

IV

At best, we might consider Western claims of consideration for animals inconclusive or ambivalent, if not downright contradictory. Why, we might ask, in the light of Port-Royal and Boyle, would it be appropriate to consider the West to have recognized the worthiness of other species and their right to considerate treatment? In a word: legislation. Before the second quarter of the nineteenth century, the prevailing view was that the law was there to be discovered, not innovatively enacted. Parliaments were more debating arenas than they were houses of legislation. Legislation, it was thought, was required only to meet novel and unusual contingencies. Even the most advanced liberal thinkers, such as Joseph Priestly in 1786, avowed that government should not interfere "without the greatest caution, in things that do not immediately affect the lives, liberty or property of the members of the community."[34] Government needed to be controlled, not given freer rein. Most radical thinkers of the time, including Priestley and William Godwin, even thought public education an undue interference in private rights that would bring more evil than good. Parliaments spent considerable time from the early nineteenth century onward (that is, as soon as the "talking shop" belief began to fade and the justice of government intervention was increasingly recognized) debating animal welfare issues and sometimes enacting legislation. This development reflects the seriousness with which animal welfare was taken. Long before Darwin, our proximity to other species was thought to entitle them to be treated as possessing legal standing.

Already in the reign of Henry VIII (1509-47), legislation had been passed to protect the eggs of certain birds in the breeding season and in 1616 a proclamation was issued in Bermuda "against the spoyle and havock" perpetrated against the cahows threatened with extinction, but also to protect all birds subject to "stoneing, and all kinds of murtherings." A law was passed to protect nesting birds in 1621, albeit to no avail. Within a decade, the birds were gone forever. In these instances, the threat of extinction was considered an extraordinary occurrence warranting legislation.

If Puritanism was unkind to bears in England, at least in Lord Macaulay's opinion, it nonetheless decreed in the Massachusetts Bay Colony in 1641 that "No man shall exercise any Tiranny or Crueltie toward any bruite creature which are usuallie kept for man's use." Further, in 1670, 1671, and 1722 in Britain and in Nova Scotia in 1768, legislation was passed to protect owned animals, in part from the emergency situation of an increase in armed marauders at night, but more to protect the interests of the owners than out of any consideration for the animals themselves. In 1800, legislation to restrict bull-baiting was introduced in the British Commons but defeated by two votes, in large part, according to contemporary parliamentary reports, not because the cruelty was condoned but because it was thought not the responsibility of Parliament to limit the few pleasures of the lower classes. "Savage sports do not make savage people" was the defence of the status quo, thus acknowledging the cruelty while denying the need for change. Nonetheless, *Gentleman's Magazine* listed with approval "preachment" against bull-baiting among the major events of the turn of the century; the attitude to the promotion of justice through legislation was changing. George Nicholson, in his 1801 *The Primeval Diet of Man*, noted that "petitions in favour of [the legislation] were signed by long lists of the most respectable names of the nobility, gentry, clergy, freeholders, and manufacturers, as well as magistrates, within the circles where it is most practiced, namely Shropshire and Staffordshire."

In 1809, a bill to prevent "wanton and malicious cruelty to animals" was passed in the House of Lords and defeated in the Commons, again on the presumed limitation of Parliament to restrict the activities of citizens, however inappropriate, if they were not disruptive of the basic social order. An opponent argued the bill ought not to be entitled "A Bill for preventing cruelty to animals" but "A Bill for harassing and oppressing certain classes among the lower orders of the people." Government was still not generally trusted.

Finally, in 1822, Richard Martin's bill was carried as "An Act to prevent the cruel and improper Treatment of Cattle." The title of the act has led some recent commentators to misinterpret the purpose and range of the legislation, imagining it restricted to farm animals. The act began with the words: "Whereas it is expedient to prevent the cruel and improper Treatment of Horses, Mares, Geldings, Mules, Asses, Cows, Heifers, Steers, Oxen, Sheep and other Cattle." Here, "cattle" does not have its modern usage but is equivalent to "chattel," that is, movable possession, though in this instance restricted to animals. The use of the term "cattle" implied that the act applied to all non-wild or feral animals, that is, citizens were not to be restricted in what were seen as their legitimate hunting practices. Whatever the apparent implications, some magistrates determined that neither bears nor bulls were cattle. The Middlesex magistrates determined otherwise. Contradictions still reigned! The penalty on conviction was a fine of from ten shillings to five pounds, with a jail term of up to three months if the fine was not paid. Those who rode horses, who used them to convey passengers in carriages, or who employed donkeys to pull carts, as well as farmers, were among those who felt the effect of the legislation, at least once the validity of the legislation had been ensured by legal interpretation.

In 1824 in Nova Scotia, similar legislation was passed, entitled "An Act to punish Persons guilty of maliciously killing or maiming Cattle," with a similar meaning for "cattle." But the punishment was to include "treble the damage which ... the Party aggrieved [that is, the owner, not the animal!] ... shall sustain." Also, anyone "duly convicted of such offence ... shall suffer such punishment by imprisonment, or Public Whipping, as such Court shall in their discretion adjudge." Public whipping or an unlimited term of imprisonment as punishment suggests that cruelty to animals was not considered a trivial offence. Protection of property was still a major consideration of the legislation, but contemporary legislative reports indicate that the animals mattered, too. Indeed, the authors of the legislation were primarily concerned to protect the animals, but they recognized that including the protection of ownership would ensure a smoother passage for the legislation.

To put the recognition of the rights of animals into perspective, it should be noted that Martin's bill was enacted a full decade before the passage of the great electoral Reform Bill of 1832, which first extended the franchise from the gentry and the uppermost middle classes, with a strong rural bias, to the educated, propertied, male members of the upper middle class in general, though far from completely. Animals were protected ten years before cities like Manchester, Birmingham, and Liverpool were represented in Parliament, seven years before Catholic emancipation, twenty-six years before the first Public Health Act, even several years before the practice of displaying the bodies of executed criminals outside Newgate prison was terminated – and a whole forty-six years before public executions were prohibited.

Slavery was only brought to an end throughout the British Empire in 1834, an act prohibiting employment of women and children in coal mines in Britain was passed in 1842, and one establishing a ten-hour day for factory workers in 1847. The Factory Act of 1819 limited the hours of employment for child labour. The fact that elementary but important animal welfare legislation was contemporaneous with these reforms reflects the relative significance of animal welfare to early-nineteenth-century reformers.

In 1819, the purportedly effeminate John Keats fought and beat a butcher's lad who was bullying a kitten. In 1838, a London *Times* headline ran "Charles Dickens in Witness Box." He was witness to a case of public mistreatment of a horse and he spoke out heatedly against the offender. The fact that the case made the headlines had more to do with the popularity of Dickens than with any recognition of the significance of animals. But it is worth noting that this case brought Dickens further good repute. Animals were deemed worthy of defence. And legislation now enshrined it.

The failure to act on these matters until the nineteenth century had more to do with the view of the purposes of legislation than with views regarding the appropriateness of child labour or acceptance of cruelty to animals. Until the effects of the Philosophical Radicals on parliamentary reform in the early nineteenth century, the laissez-faire view had prevailed. It was generally argued that the greatest public good would emerge from less governmental interference. It was generally assumed that law was a long-settled matter requiring only occasional adjustment rather than radical reformulation. In the early nineteenth century, all that changed.

In 1835, further legislation was passed in Britain, consolidating and extending existing statutes. The act referred to the prevention of "cruel and improper Treatment of Cattle and other Animals." For the first time, legislation was thus extended beyond chattels to animals in general. "Running, baiting or fighting Bull, Bear, Badger, Dog, or other Animal (whether of domestic or wild Nature or Kind) ... and Cock-fighting" were outlawed (though zoo and circus animals had no protection until 1900). Regulations were introduced for the keeping and feeding of work horses, asses, and so on, and for the operation of slaughterhouses. Again, the significance of the measures may be estimated in terms of the accompanying legislation. The immediately following measure on 9 September 1835 was "An Act for carrying into effect a Treaty, with the King of the *French* and the King of *Sardinia* for suppressing the Slave Trade," which had been signed the previous year. The reformist intentions of suppression of the slave trade and improvement of conditions for other species went hand in hand.

It was certainly notable that the continuing parliamentary debates and press reportage had profound impact. While some had ridiculed the early nineteenth-century attempts at legislation, by 1835 the measures had few opponents. The bill was opposed minimally during passage, and predominantly on prudential grounds. Once passed, its appropriateness was fairly soon taken for granted. By 1838, the *Lincoln Gazette* was referring to the baiting act outlawed as "this relic of feudal barbarism" and the *Stamford Gazette* called it "an unlawful and barbarous custom." Even the stodgy *Times* was converted to the cause, and the illustrious and elitist *Gentleman's Magazine* even helped promote it.

In 1866, New York State enacted legislation making it an offence "to maliciously kill, maim, injure, torture, crowd, or cruelly beat any horse, mule, cow, cattle, sheep or other animal belonging to himself or another." The wording ensured that an accused could not use as a defence the fact that he was treating of his own property. Unfortunately, however, the offence was only a misdemeanour.

Shortly after confederation in Canada, "An Act respecting Cruelty to Animals" was introduced and it received assent on 22 June 1869. The legislation was notable for its generality, if only to domesticated species. "Whosoever wantonly, cruelly, or unnecessarily beats, binds, illtreats, abuses or tortures any Horse, Mare, Gelding, Bull, Ox, Cow, Heifer, Steer, Calf, Mule, Ass, Sheep, Lamb, Pig, or other Cattle, or any Poultry, or any Dog, or Domestic Animal or Bird" shall be subject to a fine of between one and ten dollars, plus costs, plus damages, and in default of payment be imprisoned for up to thirty days. Clearly, the Canada of 1869 applied "cruelty to animals" more broadly than before but was a great deal more lenient than the Nova Scotia of 1824.

If the legislation passed in the first half of the nineteenth century was favourable to animals, though perhaps not quite as far reaching as its proponents might have wished, must there not have been a favourable public climate in which there was a recognition of the rights (entitlements) of animals? Certainly, many of the books on animal welfare and evolution refer to the profound effect that Darwinism had on attitudes to other species, suggesting, sometimes stating, that before Darwin, attitudes were generally less than favourable.

Yet almost all the legislation mentioned here was passed decades before Darwin published *The Origin of Species* in 1859. And many of those involved in the founding of the Society for the Prevention of Cruelty to Animals in 1824, the Vegetarian Society in 1847, and the development of anti-vivisectionism in the 1870s were not evolutionists but were devout Christian reforming members of the establishment. Among those who founded the SPCA were the wealthy (later impoverished) Irish landowner Mr. Richard Martin, MP, who had introduced the animal welfare legislation into the British Commons in 1821; William Wilberforce, a Tory reformer and friend of Prime Minister William Pitt, who was best known for his efforts to abolish the slave trade – an activity in which Martin was also involved for twenty years – but who was also influential in parliamentary reform and Catholic emancipation; Sir James Mackintosh, Whig advocate of penal and parliamentary reform who wrote the influential *Vindiciae*

Gallicae: Defence of the French Revolution and its English Admirers, against the accusations of the Right Hon. Edmund Burke – a position he recanted before taking up the cause of the animals; and Lewis Gompertz, an eccentric though highly respected philanthropist who refused to eat meat or ride in horse-drawn carriages. He also wrote *Moral Inquiries on the Situation of Man and Brutes,* published in the year of the founding of the SPCA. (The prefix "Royal" was added by grace of Queen Victoria in 1840 – a fact that itself attests to the general acceptance of animal welfare principles by even the most exalted.) There was also a bevy of eminent clergymen and parliamentarians. Certainly, the cause of the animals was taken up by responsible and highly regarded members of the social and political establishment long before Darwin wrote his revolutionary thesis.

In the preface to Reverend Thomas Jackson's mid-nineteenth-century book *Our Dumb Companions,* dedicated to the Earl of Harrowby as president of the RSPCA, the author tells of his intention to supply "a book which might present to young persons, in simple and attractive form, the solemn doctrine of the justice due to animals ... The work, it is hoped, will be ... offered as a reward to peasant boys and girls distinguished for their gentleness toward the lower creation. Such rewards are bestowed in France, Holland, and Germany, with very happy results."[35] Presumably, Reverend Jackson was well aware, as eighteenth-century Eton College historians remind us, that watching cockfights and bull-baiting had its place among the "admirable variety of diversions" that occupied the schoolboys' recreation time. Moreover, at Eton itself, once a year the boys had engaged in the rite of "Hunting the Ram" – a practice abolished in 1747 – in which the college butcher provided a ram that was hunted, ritually bludgeoned to death, and consumed. No wonder ex-Etonian Henry Fielding opined in his novel *Joseph Andrews* that "Public [that is, private] Schools are the Nurseries of all Vice and Immorality." The duty of kindness to animals might be recognized but assuredly it was not always practised. In Jackson's view, a modicum of socialization and reward could overcome these ills. Indeed, to put these cruelties in context, we should remember that the crowds at public hangings would laugh, jeer, and roar in triumph at the condemned while pelting them with missiles. If cruelty to animals was a commonplace, cruelty to humans was no rarity. Both cruelty to humans and cruelty to other species was in principle repudiated and in fact practised.

Certainly, more than occasional kindly sentiments to other creatures were not restricted to Britain, nor was Britain the only country with an animal protection movement, although it was the first. Still, by mid-nineteenth century, there were significant organizations in most European countries, Italy being the most notable exception, where Pope Pius IX (1846-78) forbade the opening of a proposed animal welfare centre in Rome on the grounds that it would divert attention from human welfare concerns. This action was part of Catholicism's rear guard, a vain but concerted effort to stem the tide of progress and commerce and to discourage the welcoming of change. Nonetheless, some Catholics, notably Cardinal Manning, were deeply sympathetic to animal protection. And in the 1908 *Catholic Encyclopedia*, we read that "while Catholic ethical doctrine insists upon the merciful treatment of animals it does not place kindness toward them in the same place of duty or benevolence toward our fellow men." And nor, of course, did the RSPCA. Certainly, matters were sufficiently well developed in Europe that Arthur Schopenhauer (1788-1860) could write an essay on the *Geschichte des Tierschutzes* (History of Animal Protection) toward the end of his life that helped arouse further public sympathy for the non-human realm.

In the United States, Mr. Henry Bergh founded the New York Society for the Prevention of Cruelty to Animals in 1865 after he had visited with the Earl of Harrowby while en route to the USA from a diplomatic appointment in Moscow – where he had been noted for his "active," albeit unofficial, "interference on behalf of the right of animals to kind treatment," according to a contemporary newspaper.[36] Nine other animal welfare organizations were instituted in other states in the succeeding three years. In Canada, the first organization was in Montreal in 1869.

Such societies were in fact giving legal and organizational status to the protection of animals – long before similar societies were established for the protection of children – and they were based on prevalent ideas and values that were no less extensive and no newer than the belief that children deserved to be protected.

It would thus seem apparent that there was an underlying consensus sympathetic to consideration of the interests of other species. We must then be prepared to interpret the views of those who argued for a substantial difference between humankind and animalkind, in the main, and with notable exceptions, as acknowledging that it was still appropriate to treat the animal realm humanely.

V

There were many of status and influence who were persuaded not only that animals mattered but that it was important to ensure a general recognition of their entitlement to benevolent treatment. Certainly, we would have little difficulty in finding animal-sympathetic statements in the writings of the great literary and philosophical figures. For example, we would find in Sir Thomas More's *Utopia* of 1516 that the Utopians "count hunting the lowest, the vilest, and most abject part of butchery; and the other parts of it more profitable and more honest as bringing much more commodity, in that they, the butchers, kill their victims from necessity, whereas the hunter seeks nothing but pleasure of the innocent and woeful animal's slaughter and murder."[37] John Locke not only proclaimed the substantial reason of other species but insisted that children should be raised to abhor the mistreatment of "sensible," that is, sentient, creatures. John Wesley, the founder of Methodism, maintained a belief in animal souls and believed that this entitled other species to considerate treatment. The philosopher Pierre Gassendi, the botanist John Ray, and the naturalist John Evelyn thought humans by nature vegetarian and the killing of food animals an unnecessary evil; in 1713, Alexander Pope published an article in *The Guardian* entitled "Against Barbarity to Animals," and his *Essay on Man* of 1734 is in part an argument against the human propensity to imagine itself above the rest of nature; in 1740, Henry Fielding contributed a piece against cruelty to animals to *The Champion* (56); in 1766, Dr. Humphry Primatt wrote *A Dissertation on the Duty of Mercy and the Sin of Cruelty to Brute Animals,* the first of many books that dealt exclusively with animal welfare issues, including John Oswald's *The Cry of Nature* (1791); and in 1798, Thomas Young penned *An Essay on Humanity to Animals.*

Voltaire castigated those who conducted invasive research on other species. "Answer me, mechanist," he wrote in anger, "has Nature arranged all the springs of feeling in this animal to the end that he might not feel?" The Tory David Hume insisted that we are "bound by the laws of humanity to give gentle usage to these creatures."[38] But he did not mean, as the animal liberationists inform us, that "we were entitled to use animals"[39] as a means to our ends. Rather he meant that they were entitled to fair consideration as the beings that they are. The conservative Whig Edmund Burke wrote of "other animals" as giving us "a sense of joy and pleasure," as inspiring "us with sentiments of tenderness, and affection toward their persons."[40] The hero and scourge of the Enlightenment, Jean-Jacques Rousseau, understood that humans, as intrinsic parts of nature, as "noble savages," maintained a kinship with the other animals. In Alexander Pushkin's *Dubrovsky* (1833), the blacksmith risks his life to save an unknown cat from a burning house, for it was "one of God's creatures perishing." In *Yeast,* the popular Christian socialist, novelist, and cleric Charles Kingsley described in chilling terms the "ghastly discord" of fox-hunting. In the 1850s, Thomas Hardy was appalled at "the horrors and cruelties" of Smithfield Market and was "haunted" by the memory of his father killing a fieldfare with a stone, "possibly not meaning to hurt it." In *Les Misérables* of 1862, Victor Hugo reminded us of the importance of all animal life when he wrote of the good bishop of Digne who hurt himself "in avoiding treading on an ant" and whose "heart was given to all suffering" of whatever species. Charles Dickens wrote in his "Inhumane Humanity," an article in his magazine *All the Year Round* in 1866, of the importance of humane treatment of both animals and children. In *The Brothers Karamazov* (1879-80), Feodor Dostoevsky argued that "When you love every creature you will understand the mystery of God in created things." Wilkie Collins, the celebrated author of *The Moonstone* and *The Lady in White,* wrote his later novels as explicit condemnations of Victorian social ills. Prominent among them was vivisection, which is the primary focus of *Heart and Science* (1883). In the years before the First World War, the poet Rupert Brooke and his (almost) vegetarian entourage practised a back-to-nature primitivism that declared a kinship with animated nature. In Mikhail Sholokhov's *And Quiet Flows the Don* (1929), "The old general was fond of birds, and even kept a maimed crane." Even the disabled of other species possessed an entitlement to protection. If the Jansenist seminarians and the Robert Boyles are a significant and disturbing aspect of Western experience, and one of which we should be ashamed, there are many deserving of our whole-hearted approbation.

VI

The prevailing theological spirit of eighteenth- and nineteenth-century Protestant Christianity was to be found in "the argument from design," an extension of the idea of the "Great Chain of Being," best exemplified by William Paley's *Natural Theology* (1802) (but long before first argued, if neither so well nor so fully, in John Ray's *Wisdom of God Manifested in the Works of Creation* [1691]). Like the "great chain" idea, it is customarily interpreted as disparaging of other species. Paley argued inter alia that all beings are exquisitely adapted to their surroundings, animals are complex mechanisms designed by God, and each species is perfectly fitted for its niche in this world. Everything shows undeniable evidence of superb design. Therefore, there must be a Designer. Of course, such reasoning is tantamount to proclaiming that whatever is, is right. Human dominance is justified. This type of reasoning has persuaded recent analysts that eighteenth- and nineteenth-century thought was unkind to animals. But that misreads the import of the argument from design, at least as understood by many of those who espoused it.

Without doubt, most of those involved in the founding of the animal welfare movement would have applauded Paley – as did at least one poet who desired consideration for the animals. In *The Task* (1785), William Cowper insists:

> I would not enter on my list of friends, (Though
> graced with polish'd manners and fine sense,
> Yet wanting sensibility), the man
> Who needlessly sets foot upon a worm.[41]

He also subscribes elsewhere to the argument from design:

> How sweet to muse upon His skill displayed,
> (Infinite skill!) in all that He has made;
> To trace in Nature's most minute design
> The signature and stamp of Power Divine;

Contrivance exquisite expressed with ease,
Where unassisted sight no beauty sees;
The shapely limb and lubricated joint,
Within the small dimensions of a point:
Muscle and nerve miraculously spun;
His mighty work who speaks, and it is done:
The invisible in things scarce seen revealed;
To whom an atom is an ample field.[42]

H.G. Adams, the author of *Beautiful Butterflies* (1854), who glories in the beauty of the objects of his study, closes his paean to the butterfly with those words from Cowper.

As we have noticed, throughout the history of Western civilization, many have recognized animal value. And despite Descartes, Malebranche, Hobbes, and their ilk, there were many even in the rationalist age who recognized animal reason. Thus, for example, John Milton:

Is not the earth,
With various living creatures, and the air
Replenished, and all these at thy command,
To come and play before thee? Knowst thou not
Their language and their ways? They also know,
And reason not contemptibly.[43]

Even the language of animal rights has a history from the late seventeenth century – not much later than the explicit development of human rights theory – when Thomas Tryon, in his *Complaints of the Birds and Fowls of Heaven to Their Creator* (1688), wrote of the "natural rights and privileges" that humans break when they "assault and destroy" other species.

From the time of Carolus Linnaeus, who published his classification system in 1735, there was a growing scientific recognition of the organizational similarity among species. Scientific thought has not derided other species as much as often imagined. Long before Darwin, Linnaeus confessed that he "could not discover the difference between man and the orangutan ... It is remarkable that the stupidest ape differs so little from the wisest man, that the surveyor of nature has yet to be found who can draw the line between them." Such ideas at least in embryo had a very lengthy prior history. Starting with the Sumerian schools of around the third millennium BC, it was taught that originally people walked with limbs on the ground and ate herbs with their mouths like sheep. We came, in other words, from vegetarian apes. Thereafter, subscription to some vague type of evolutionary theory, or at least to one that recognizes our considerable similarity to some other species, was not uncommon. But while the majority did not so subscribe, they still recognized, at least customarily, that

humans owed something to other species on account of our common animality. Some went so far, as Davies complained in his *Naturalist's Guide,* to
insist, in the words of Shakespeare, that "The poor beetle that we tread
upon, / In corporeal sufferance, finds a pang as great / As when a giant
dies." Certainly, Shakespeare was not here in line with the dictates of the
argument from design. Davies argued against Shakespeare that "on the
contrary, it is a pretty well recognized fact, that the lower the development
of the nervous system, the less intense is the creature's sense of pain."
Nonetheless, Davies insists, "It is well in all cases to lean to the side of
mercy."[44] The pre-Darwinian argument was not between those who proclaimed and those who ignored the animals' well-being, but between those
who thought the differences among the species merited great difference of
treatment and those who believed they merited little. Generally speaking,
both theological thought, as in the *scala naturae* and the argument from
design, and scientific thought found animals worthy of consideration
because of our similarities to them, though few would have gone as far as
Shakespeare.

Certainly, if we look to many of the finer representatives of European literary culture, we will find them expressing a sympathy for the natural
realm. Because philosophers were often engaged in discourse to discover
the relevant differences between human and animal in the Great Chain of
Being, circumstance encouraged them to write of rational humans and cor-
respondingly of less rational or irrational animals, even when animals were
loved and respected. Poets and novelists did not always face the same limitations. The freedom of their arts and the relationship to nature they discussed offered them a greater variety of expression. A superficial reading of
the argument for the Great Chain of Being or of the argument from design
might leave the reader with a faulty impression of the status of other
species, as the arguments constantly referred to human superiority, not
because of any disdain for the animal realm but because of the nature of
the question they addressed. One is much less likely to be misled by a reading of the poets, dramatists, and novelists.

Certainly, if we were to return to Plutarch it might not surprise us to read
that although we have superior reason, "in all other respects, we are more
unfortunate than the beasts." We might be a little more surprised to read in
Jonathan Swift's fantasy, *Gulliver's Travels,* of the Laputans who are offered as
an example of the world gone mad, a place where philosophy, abstract reason, and intellectualism govern. A "rational" world, for Swift, is one in which
the human superior reason does not play an excessive role. In the land of the
Houyhnhnms, the horses govern the uncivilized Yahoos (humans) and do
a rather better job than when Yahoos govern Houyhnhnms.

Alexander Pope in *An Essay on Man* of 1734, which was as popular in his
own day as it is renowned today, argues the case for a basic human-animal
similarity:

Not Man alone, but all that roam the wood,
Or wing the sky, or roll along the flood,
Each loves itself, but not itself alone,
Each sex desires alike, 'till two are one.
Nor ends the pleasure with the fierce embrace;
They love themselves, a third time, in their race.[45]

Given Pythagoras's and Plutarch's recognition of a universal soul shared by the animal world, Chaucer's belief in a time when all species were at one, Montaigne's understanding that humans possess no exclusive characteristics, and Pope's acknowledgment of similar emotional characteristics among species – to mention some of the more obvious but not more striking instances – it is difficult to escape the conclusion that, before the age of utilitarian dominance, there was a *fairly* common understanding of a spirituality shared by all animals and one most commonly recognized by those who did not feel the need to follow the enveloping strictures of scientific and philosophic method. And once utilitarianism predominated, there was a recognition of the animal as a self-directed end, and there were always the Romantics, from Shelley through Byron to the Lake Poets, to counteract the lack of recognition of animal spirituality. When we read the Romantics, we can have little doubt that they shared the conception with the Great Basin Indians (for example, the Shoshoni and the Paiute) that all of animate creation was imbued with *puha*, spirit, soul, to which we owe a reciprocal obligation – a belief in fact shared in different forms in almost all tribal societies, in the Orient, and indeed in the historical West, too. Of course, the materialism, hedonism, cynicism, scepticism, and commercialism of Western society have dimmed and obscured those recognitions, but reputable and respected, as well as the more obscure, voices have always acknowledged animal spirituality; and many of those belong to the heady realms of a spiritual literature.

In the seventeenth century, we can read from the pen of the Duchess of Newcastle her poem on "The Hunting of the Hare." After a moving account of the hare's desperate attempts to outrun the hounds, she then turns on the hunter:

Yet man doth think himself so gentle, mild,
When he of creatures is most cruell wild.
And is so Proud, thinks onely he shall live,
That God a God-like Nature did him give.
And that all Creatures for his sake alone,
Was made for him, to Tyrannize upon.

In fact, the duchess's poem of 1653 is repeating the argument of Michel de Montaigne in his *Essays* of 1595:

Let him shew me, by the most skilful argument, upon what foundations [man] has built these excessive prerogatives which he supposes himself to have over other existences. Is it possible to imagine anything so ridiculous as that this pitiful, miserable creature, who is not even master of himself, exposed to injuries of every kind, should consider itself master and lord of the universe, of which, so far from being lord of it, he knows but the smallest part? Who has given him this sealed charter? Let him shew us the "letters patent" of this grand commission ... Presumption is our natural disease. The most calamitous and fragile of all creatures is man, and yet the most arrogant.

In *The Miser* (Act III, Sc. I) of 1688, Molière arouses our sympathy for Maître Jacques by telling us that the coachman not only cared well for the horses in his charge but that when they were hungry, he fed them from his own meagre provisions.

In the eighteenth century, Lady Anne Finch, countess of Winchelsea, wrote "A Nocturnal Reverie," which includes the enchanting but ominous lines: "Their short-lived jubilee the creatures keep, / Which but endures whilst tyrant man does sleep." She was putting in poetic form ideas similar to those of Thomas Tryon who, some decades earlier, had expressed his "spiritual affinity with the lower powers" in his *Complaints of the birds and fowls of heaven to their Creator* of 1688: "But tell us, O men! We pray you to tell us what injuries have we committed to forfeit? What laws have we broken, or what cause given you, whereby you can pretend a right to invade and violate our part, and natural rights, and to assault and destroy us, as if we were the aggressors, and no better than thieves, robbers and murderers, fit to be extirpated out of creation. From whence did thou (O man) derive thy authority for killing thy inferiors, merely because they are such, or for destroying their natural rights and privileges."

When we turn to the great poets, the immediacy and effectiveness of the message exceeds anything that might be expressed philosophically or scientifically. Thus, Byron's poem about his companion Boatswain, *Inscription on the Monument of a Newfoundland Dog*:

When some proud son of man returns to earth,
Unknown to glory, but upheld by birth,
The sculptor's art exhausts the pomp of woe,
And storied urns record who rests below;
When all is done, upon the tomb is seen,
Not what he was, but what he should have been:
But the poor dog, in life the firmest friend,
The first to welcome, foremost to defend,
Whose honest heart is still his master's own,
Who labours, fights, lives, breathes for him alone,

Unhonour'd falls, unnoticed all his worth,
Denied in heaven the soul he held on earth:
While man, vain insect! hopes to be forgiven,
And claims himself a sole exclusive heaven.
Oh man! thou feeble tenant of an hour,
Debased by slavery, or corrupt by power,
Who knows thee well must quit thee with disgust,
Degraded mass of animated dust!
Thy love is lust, thy friendship all a cheat,
Thy smiles hypocrisy, thy words deceit!
By nature vile, ennobled but by name,
Each kindred brute might bid thee blush for shame.
Ye! who perchance behold this simple urn,
Pass on – it honours none you wish to mourn:
To mark a friend's remains those stones arise;
I never knew but one, and here he lies.

Newstead Abbey, Oct. 30, 1808[46]

If we take Byron seriously, if feelings and morality are of a higher order than reason, if faith comes before philosophy, perhaps the dog is the superior creature. Or perhaps humankind has so lost its primordial human character that it is simply overwhelmed by the contradictions between reason and passion. Indeed, what is poetry but a recognition that the deeper truths known to passion are obscured from pithy prose and pure reason? Pascal urged, "Let us labour, then, to think well; this is the foundation of morality." Perhaps, instead, it is, as Hinduism would insist, the foundation of moral confusion. Certainly, to those who think that "this is just poetry," it is important to point out that before the twentieth century, poetry was deemed a reputable, by some the most reputable, form of advancing a philosophical argument, for poetry could extend the philosophical imagination beyond the limits of science and pithy prose. And most educated people then read poetry. Certainly, Lucretius (*de rerum natura*), John Dryden (*Religio Laici*), Abraham Cowley (*Davideis*), Daniel Defoe (*Jure Divino*), and Alexander Pope (*Essay on Man*) employed what was called "Greater Poetry" to establish and advance "a philosophy of man."

With a wisdom perhaps obscured at the turn of the millenium, William Blake used to engage in what is known as Menippean satire (from the Greek cynic Menippus), the joining of poetry and prose to advance an argument. It was the method employed most memorably by Boethius in his fifth century AD *The Consolation of Philosophy,* which remained a highly persuasive and widely read tome until the end of the eighteenth century, when we still find the method practised by Ann Radcliffe in her *The Romance of the Forest* (1791). This practice Blake probably borrowed from the members of the Scriblerus Club – Pope, Gay, Swift, Arbuthnot, and Parnell – who deemed each form to have its unique virtue, the one stimulating the moral imagination, the other the more pedestrian but equally necessary faculty of reason. George Eliot accomplished something similar in her *The Spanish Gipsy* (1868). Poetry, she says, is superior to other art forms because "its medium, language, is the least imitative, & is in the most complex relation with what it expresses." Equally inimical to the modern rationalist mind is Wordsworth's assertion that "poetry is the first and last of all knowledge – it is as immortal as the heart of man." Indeed, Wordsworth announces boldly, poetry is "the most philosophic of all writing." Likewise, Robert Browning says of art, in which he includes poetry, that it "remains the one way possible / Of speaking truth." For W.B. Yeats, "Whatever of philosophy has been made poetry alone is permanent."

Perhaps most of all, the literary figures chose their art form because in the pursuit of truth they did not wish to be restrained by the acceptable forms of philosophy and science. Though those forms may have a surer path, they also have a path limited by, perhaps even dominated by, their restrictive languages. If the language of poetry leads to flights of the imagination, the languages of science and philosophy limit the imagination in the search for truth by reducing everything they study to a consistency with the terms they employ. While science may succeed more readily in depicting a truth, literature seems to draw our attention, our sentiments, and our behaviour toward an acknowledgment of other truths. Science and philosophy are concerned with "the truth"; literature more readily embraces "the way," is more readily in accord with Eastern and Aboriginal wisdoms. When philosophy functions to proclaim truth rather than to seek it, as in the works of Marx and Engels, it functions more as poetry than science. No one became a Marxist because of its scientific determinism but because it offers answers – even if hopelessly inadequate, indeed counterproductive, answers – to the problems of humankind. There can be good and bad philosophy in terms of its logic, good and bad literature both in terms of its beauty and of the worthwhileness of its message. As art, literature offers us beauty alone. But literature goes beyond beauty to offer us examples and understanding, rather than analyses, of justice and injustice. Dostoevsky's refutation of utilitarianism in *Crime and Punishment* is, to most people, far more convincing than any profound philosophical treatise written to the same end; Voltaire's *Candide* is a readier refutation of Leibnitzian optimism than the most learned of abstractions. They succeed because they proceed by way of human example in a societal context rather than as a logical search for universal truths expressed in abstractions. Philosophy relies on a degree of reason humans at best only rarely possess.

The language of poetry leads us to an opening up of the self. The language of science teaches us about the world we are opening ourselves up to. Poetry enlivens the imagination and frees the soul. Science allows us to understand better the world into which our soul is released. Whereas philosophy and science draw distinctions and tend to separate us from nature, literature discusses relationships and draws us toward nature.

Certainly, when Byron elevates his dog, he invites us to ask questions about the human-animal relationship that traditional science has suppressed by dealing predominantly in terms of human rational superiority. In fact, the terms in which science has discussed the human-animal relationship is itself tendentious. Thus, Charles Darwin in writing *The Descent of Man* encourages us to look to our similarity to other species. Jacob Bronowski, by contrast, entitled his justifiably renowned tour de force *The Ascent of Man*. *Descent* and *Ascent* are more didactic than descriptive terms. They influence our attitudes more than they depict a situation. Bronowski entitled his opening chapter "Lower than the Angels," an allusion to the *scala naturae*. But not much lower was the implication of the opening lines: "Man is a singular creature. He has a set of gifts which make him unique among the animals: so that, unlike them, he is not a figure in the landscape – he is a shaper of the landscape. In body and in mind he is the explorer of nature, the ubiquitous animal, who did not find but has made his home in every continent."[47] Whereas Balzac insisted there is but one animal and Darwin emphasized the similarities between humans and other species, Bronowski asserts that we are "singular" and "unique." He assumes rather than argues that other animals are not "singular" and "unique."

Although the titles of Darwin's and Bronowski's works are antithetical, there is no need to assume that Bronowski was in practice less considerate of the interests of other species than Darwin himself, though, in this instance, he employs a language inimical to a perception of their interests. In fact, without any inconsistency, one may recognize the value of thinking in terms of both the ascent and the descent of humanity. The emphasis that one gives is influenced by the points one wishes to make. Against those who would exaggerate the ubiquity of human sins and foibles, it is important to emphasize human achievements. Against those who would denigrate other species, it is important to emphasize the evolutionary relationship to other species, as well as to note the uniqueness, say, of the dolphin or bat echolocation systems, the "dance language" of honey bees to communicate the location of food, the protective swimming formation of anchovies, tuna, and dolphins, the navigation system of homing pigeons, the perception of electric currents by sharks, and the use of electricity to stun or kill by electric eels. All these animals possess capacities beyond the reach of humans. Their uniqueness does not make them any less animals than does any human uniqueness. To write of the *ascent* or *descent* of humans may be to write in ideological rather than scientific terms, but sometimes ideology is appropriate.

What Byron's poem encourages us to consider is whether reason is the relevant category of distinction – a question not answerable by science, not even by philosophy. Perhaps only a species that prides itself on reason or rational choice would claim rationality as the sole superordinate category of worth. Which category do we imagine of greater significance for a bat, a tuna, or a shark? For a shark, no doubt the dexterity permitted by the lack of bones would be significant, for the tuna swimming range would be important, and nocturnal navigation would be a vital consequence of echolocation for the bat. And surely newts and salamanders, and now a certain type of mouse, possess a "superiority" in their ability to regenerate amputated organs (for example, a leg or a tail). Even the lowly freshwater hydra is capable of regenerating itself when cut in half, both parts becoming whole organisms. Indeed, the hydra, like the amoeba, have discovered the secret of eternal life. Through bifurcation, they live on in their progeny far more than we who merely pass on our genes. No mere human can pretend to such capacities, nor to the feat of the duck-billed platypus that both lays eggs and gives milk. And if we wish to stress our bipedality, we might note it also as a feature of common poultry as well as of the Megolosaurus and Iguanadon some sixty-five million and more years ago. Moreover, if finally we have learned to fly, we do it with less grace and more cumbersome equipment than the swallow (like all birds, also bipedal incidentally). But most of all, our greatest lack appears to be our incapacity to live the kind of family loyalty practised by the wolves. What ought to be stressed is a question not answerable in its entirety by science; one's emphasis must itself reflect one's philosophical stance. Scientific answers have ideological implications. And, historically, poetry has served best to raise the issues assumed, against its own principles, as self-evident by science.

VII

The scientific development with the greatest impact in the last century and a half has been Darwin's theory of evolution. However, its moral impact on our attitude to animals was not as great as is sometimes claimed. Certainly today we tend to look back to Darwin and recognize the values implied in the theory of evolution by natural selection, but we seem to forget that they were recognized well enough long before Darwin.

Proponents of the Great Chain sometimes used the chain to suggest a close relationship with other species with corresponding obligations. Thus Edward Tyson wrote an influential book on the *Orang-Outang* (1699)[48] – as the link between the ape and Homo sapiens. The Scottish judge Lord Monboddo went so far as to place the orangutan very close to the human, and indeed almost in an evolutionary manner in his *Origin and Progress of Language* (1770). And while William Blake would no doubt have been astonished by evolutionary theory, he wrote, in the last decade of the eighteenth century, "I have said to the Worm Thou art my mother and my sister" ("For Children: The Gates of Paradise").

An interesting late-eighteenth-century example of the Great Chain is offered by Priscilla Wakefield in her *Instinct Displayed:* "Quadrupeds and birds are assimilated to each other by the bat; the inhabitants of the waters to those of the land, by amphibious animals; animals to vegetables, by the leaf insect, and by plants that appear to have sensation; and animate to inanimate by the oyster, the molluscae, and sea anemones."[49] The difference between Wakefield's typology and that of evolution was more a gap than a gulf, as was that of Oliver Goldsmith who tells us that the beaver "is the only animal that in its fore parts entirely resembles a quadruped, and in its hind parts seems to approach the nature of fishes, by having a scaly tail." In 1680, Giovanni Borelli had written *On the Movement of Animals,* in which he demonstrated the unity of life by showing how the same laws governed the wings of birds, the fins of fishes, and the legs of insects. It was this kind of evidence that stimulated evolutionary ideas. Thus, in similar vein to Goldsmith and Borelli, we can read in *The Origin of Species* of "the Mustela vison of North America, which has webbed feet and which resembles an otter in its fur, short legs and form of tail; during summer this animal dives for and preys on fish, but during the long winter it leaves the frozen waters, and preys like other polecats on mice and land animals."[50]

With the publication of his *System of Invertebrate Animals* in 1801, Lamarck, long before Darwin, gave the *scala naturae* its immanent evolutionary twist in a doctrine he called transformism. He developed this more fully in his *Philosophical Zoology* of 1809. Lamarck's was the first fully developed theory of evolution and animal continuity. And while his early research was devoted primarily to invertebrate animals, Lamarck did speculate – not entirely successfully – on the erect bipedal human evolved from the stooping chimpanzee and the giraffe's long neck developed from a shorter form for browsing on the leaves of tall trees.

A few years later, Geoffroy Saint-Hilaire was developing a thesis he had first conceived in 1795 – a year after Erasmus Darwin, Charles's grandfather, and in the same year as Goethe – that the same biological forms had not been continued in perpetuity and that what we call species are various representations – descents – of the same type. He announced, "There is, philosophically speaking, only a single animal," and Honoré de Balzac was stimulated to repeat the story to the whole world in the series of novels he wrote under the generic title *La Comédie humaine.* In the preface to the series written in 1845 – some thirteen years after the series was begun! – he claimed "the study of human life in comparison with the life of animals" as the "leading idea of this human comedy." He acknowledged "the lasting glory of Geoffroy Saint-Hilaire, the conqueror of Cuvier" (permanent secretary of the Academy of Sciences, chancellor of the University of Paris, favourite of the French establishment, and steadfast defender of the fixity of species). He also repeated the claim "There is but one animal."[51] However important Darwin was to science, and however much he advanced the acceptance of our relationship to other species, the essential moral message was there long before Darwin. When in turn Goethe (1783), Herder (1784), Saint-Hilaire

(1795), Ralph Waldo Emerson (1836),[52] and Balzac (1845) declared the principle of unity (all borrowing somewhat, if unknowingly, from Borelli over a century earlier), that all beings should be seen as variations of a single principal type, they did every bit as much as Darwin for recognition of our responsibilities to, and the justice of our respect for, other species. While Leo Tolstoy believed that our responsibility to animals required a conversion to vegetarianism, he also warned his son, Sergei, against "Darwinism," which "won't explain to you the meaning of your life and won't give you guidance for your actions."[53] Tolstoy's animal sensibilities were quite secure without Darwin. So too were those of the Jesuit nature poet Gerard Manley Hopkins, who was more impressed by numerology than evolutionary theory but nonetheless risked serious injury by rescuing an imperilled monkey, and who wrote about animals with both sensibility and sensitivity, notably in "Pied Beauty" and "The Windhover." In *In Memoriam* (1850) and again in *Maud* (1855), Tennyson, who was a minor authority on birds, entertained a pre-Darwinian notion of evolution. In "The Owl," "he recalls, and obviously wants to relive the moment," his biographer tells us, "when the owl really came to his window and sat on his shoulder. Of all the magnificent moments in his life, that one surely must have ranked very high."[54] Tennyson is not only here in harmony with nature, he rejoices in it. Indeed, he tried, albeit vainly, to become a vegetarian.

Mark Twain thought Darwin unduly harsh on non-humans. In "The Damned Human Race," he renounced his "allegiance to the Darwinian theory of the Ascent of Man from the Lower Animals; since it now seems plain to me that that theory ought to be vacated in favor of a new and truer one ... the *De*scent of Man from the Higher Animals."[55] In the poem *Divinity,* Goethe deems a self-reflexive morality to be the only difference between human and animal – "For that alone / distinguishes him / from all beings / that we know."[56] In *Adam Bede* (1859), George Eliot emphasized the similarity of all intelligent beings: "There are various orders of beauty, causing men to make fools of themselves in various styles, from the desperate to the sheepish; but there is one order of beauty which seems made to turn the heads not only of men, but of all intelligent mammals, even of women. It is a beauty like that of kittens, or very small downy ducks making gentle rippling noises with their soft bills, or babies just beginning to toddle and engage in conscious mischief – a beauty with which you can never be angry, but that you feel ready to crush for inability to comprehend the state of mind into which it throws you." However important Darwin was in advancing the recognition of the moral implications of human animality, the essential moral message was present in the minds of both many precursors and opponents of Darwin as well.

Weimar, where both Goethe and Herder lived in the 1780s, should be as much a sacred venue for naturalists as Downe in Kent, the home of Charles Darwin in 1859. From 1783 onward, Goethe deemed the supreme religious issue not to be the relationship between humankind and the gods but between humankind and the animals.[57] So too pre-evolutionary Concord, Massachusetts, in the 1840s, gloriously alive to the natural sensibilities of Ralph Waldo Emerson, Margaret Fuller, Nathaniel Hawthorne, and Henry David Thoreau – the last described by Hawthorne as "a young man with much of wild original nature still remaining in him ... and Nature, in return for his love, seems to adopt him as her special child, and shows him secrets which few others are allowed to witness."[58]

It is certainly important to recognize that the power of science and technology has afforded the West the opportunity to manipulate and manage other species solely for human benefit, and that the opportunity has often been taken to the detriment of the interests of other species. It is, however, equally important to recognize that the Western moral tradition, including the scientific aspects of that tradition, has limited the excesses of that potentiality and provided a moral framework that has been in some degree, if nowhere near enough, of benefit to our recognition of the rights of non-human animals. To improve the treatment of that realm, the relevant moral conceptual framework is already at hand. It needs only to be refined and actualized.

Primarily, disputes with regard to animal welfare issues continue to occur not because the rights of animals are not recognized, at least when the issue is raised in the public consciousness, but because there is an ongoing dispute between the relative weight of animals' rights and those of humans. When the Plumage Bill, which sought to bar the import into Britain of exotic birds and feathers, was temporarily defeated in the House of Lords in July 1920, "Wayfarer" (H.W. Massingham), writing in the *Nation,* ascribed the setback to the vanity of women. Virginia Woolf responded to Massingham with the claim that such imports were due to male greed. Certainly, unemployment and loss of income must have been of concern to those who made their livelihood from the trade. Woolf closed her piece thus: "I have said more about [Wayfarer's] injustice to women than about the suffering of birds. Can it be that it is a graver sin to be unjust to women than to torture birds?" While most would have recognized it as unjust to harm the birds, the practical issue was where one placed the birds' interests in comparison with the interests of those who lived and exuberated at the birds' expense. Employment considerations, competing gender claims, freedom of expression and trade, as well as sheer indifference, combined to complicate the issue. In this case, the birds won, for the measure was passed in July 1921.

On other occasions, the birds lost. Virginia Woolf would scour the woods for birds' eggs to feed her husband's pet marmoset. While she found it inappropriate to wear birds' feathers – the cost to the birds was too great – she had few qualms about robbing their nests to feed an animal that nature would have placed thousands of miles away. Woolf had competing concerns: the oppression of women; the misuse of animals in general; loyalty to her husband; and affection for his marmoset. The competing claims were irreconcilable. Some must win and some must lose. Nature itself offered no suitable standard, other than to accept injustice. As Lao-Tse wisely warned, "Nature is not human-hearted." To seek justice, one must, at least on occasion, rise up against nature. On other occasions, one must acquiesce. On still others, rejoice.

7

Aboriginal and Oriental Harmony with Nature

1   There is apparently in this [West African] people a physical delight
     in cruelty to beasts as well as to men. The sight of suffering seems
     to bring them an enjoyment without which the world is tame ...
     In almost all the towns of the Oil Rivers, you see dead or dying
     animals in some agonizing position.

                        – Richard Francis Burton, *Wanderings in West
                          Africa from Liverpool to Fernando Po*, 1863

2   Some savages take a horrid pleasure in cruelty to animals, and
     humanity is an unknown virtue ... Sympathy beyond the confines
     of man, that is humanity to the lower animals, seems to be one
     of the last moral acquisitions. It is apparently unfelt by savages,
     except toward their pets.

                        – Charles Darwin, *Descent of Man*, 1871

3   One thing is certain that the all-embracing poverty which has
     overwhelmed our country cannot be removed by working with
     our hands to the neglect of science.

                        – Rabindranath Tagore, "The Cult of the
                          Charka," 1925 [Tagore was incensed by "the
                          moral tyranny" of the cult of the charka (that
                          is, spinning wheel) as advocated by Gandhi,
                          because, in Tagore's view, the back-to-nature
                          approach would merely perpetuate existing
                          ills.]

4   "The fish is my friend too," Santiago [the Cuban fisherman] said
     aloud. "But I must kill him. I am glad we do not have to try to kill
     the stars ... If you love him, it is not a sin to kill him. Or is it
     more?"

                              – Ernest Hemingway, *The Old Man and the Sea*,
                                 1952

5   How we bleed her to take the last drop of milk from her. How we
     starve her to emaciation, how we ill-treat the calves.

                              – Mohandàs K. Gandhi, *How to Serve the Cow*,
                                 1934

6   Indian society is not a function of Indian philosophy, but on the
     contrary Indian philosophy is a function of *one* section of Indian
     society. Consequently, Indian society as a whole does not illus-
     trate ... the ideals of Indian philosophy.

                              – Joseph Campbell, *Baksheesh and Brahman:*
                                 Indian Journal 1954-1955, 1995

7   Attuning themselves to everything in creation of which they con-
     sider themselves a spiritual part, [Aboriginals] have learned the
     ultimate art of existing in harmony with their universe.

                              – Timothy Severin, *Vanishing Primitive Man*,
                                 1973

8   The self-eulogizing attempts of expatriates to impose the notion of
     wildlife as a treasured legacy overlook the reality that to most of a
     local impoverished and inert [African] populace wildlife is consid-
     ered an obstacle – tolerated only as long as it proves economically
     valuable on a practical basis in the form of tusks, meat, or skins.

                              – Dian Fossey, *Gorillas in the Mist*, 1983

9   An [Ecuadorian] Indian trotted past us thrashing a donkey. It was
     an old donkey and it slipped on the cobbles and fell under its load

of charcoal sacks. The Indian began beating the animal, who
closed its eyes. You couldn't help noticing that its flesh was
scarred where ropes had bitten into its hindquarters. Well, it was
as though something snapped inside the German. He caught the
Indian's arm and wrenched the stick away ...

– Johanna Angermeyer, *My Father's Island: A
Galapagos Quest*, 1989

10   In Indonesia there is a phrase *"negara hukum,"* meaning that
Indonesia is a "country of laws" ... Many of these laws, such as
those protecting orang-utans, stemmed from Dutch colonial days;
they were not grounded in local norms and customs.

– Biruté M.F. Galdikas, *Reflections of Eden: My
Years with the Orangutans of Borneo*, 1995

Aboriginal Thought and Practice

I

In 1972, the United Nations organized a conference on the environment at
Stockholm. The calling of such a conference reflected the fact that technological societies were slowly beginning to recognize that all was not well,
that the much-vaunted progress of technology may have some shortcomings. This recognition was not in itself new. The degradation wrought by
industrialism, the smog, and dying rivers, and the dangers inherent in
atmospheric changes had not gone unnoticed – indeed remedial action
had long begun – but the answers were customarily sought in new and better technology to replace the old. Now voices were being raised to suggest
that technology itself might be the vice and that the problems were so serious that nothing short of a cultural metamorphosis would suffice.

Rachel Carson's 1962 book *The Silent Spring*[1] is customarily acknowledged
as the catalyst of the environmental movement, although that is perhaps
to ignore the wisdom of the conservative voices of the nineteenth century,
which, if heeded, would have radically diminished the severity of the problem in the twentieth. It is also to ignore the ecological sensibilities of John
Muir, Aldo Leopold, Ed Ricketts, and John Steinbeck, among others. Nonetheless, the force of Carson's thrust and the detail of her evidence inaugu-
rated a new era. She castigated the employment of synthetic materials to
control insects. Pesticides, she claimed, were the harbingers of natural
destruction – "the elixirs of death," she called them. They augured a world
in which spring would bring no new life but only a chilling silence.

The effects of Carson's book were startling. It stimulated many to action, not least, via the book's many disciples and a remarkable CBS documentary on her findings, the United States Senate, which introduced ameliorative legislation. Within a decade, the United Nations was calling for a re-evaluation of the relationship of science and technology to nature. But a decade was not long enough for a recognition of the metamorphosis that was required.

Tribal peoples from Africa, America, Asia, and Oceania travelled to Stockholm to appeal to the technologically advanced societies to regain a spiritual bond with all of creation, to live at one with nature – as they, and their intellectual supporters (7), claimed that Aboriginals did. Most of the participants listened, many nodded sagely, but few acted on their recognitions. It is one thing to acknowledge the wisdom of the admonitions, quite another to renounce the science and technology on which modern comforts, conveniences, delights, and successes are predicated. But if the admonitions went unheeded by the conference participants and Western governments at that time, they have since been given the greatest recognition – perhaps still more verbal than practical – by the environmentalists, the advocacy anthropologists, the supporters of animal rights, and, cautiously but increasingly, Western governments.

Little attention, however, has been given to precisely what this spiritual bond, this oneness with nature, consists in or really implies. In what manner may tribal cultures be said to be in harmony with nature? Sir James Frazer had argued famously in *The Golden Bough* of 1922 that all religion, including tribal religion, originated, like magic, in an attempt to explain and control nature, rather than to be in harmony with it. Prima facie, one might wonder how those who kill animals, whether in sacrifice to the gods, for raiment, or for hunting pleasure, can claim to live in harmony, to have a spiritual bond, with those they kill. One may ask in what manner tribal attitudes are more reverential than those expressed in the Western conception of the Great Chain of Being in which every species has its honoured and legitimate niche. To ask Ernest Hemingway's question again (4), is it more of a sin to kill an animal if you love it, or is it less? Indeed, if you kill a healthy animal, can you really love it? Undoubtedly, a case can be made for Aboriginal harmony with nature, but the Western intelligentsia has failed to explain both what is meant by such a harmony and what is in error in Frazer's finding.

It is frequently less than helpful to write of Aboriginal societies in generic terms, for there are significant differences among them. Generalized statements can be misleading. Nonetheless, it is important to respond to statements by and on behalf of Aboriginal societies, especially the latter, which in themselves treat such societies as essentially similar in their relationship to nature and to other species. In reality, Aboriginal societies *qua* Aboriginal societies do not possess a single type of relationship to nature. Some are decidedly not "at one with nature," others are very much more so – though even here we must make such statements with some significant reservations. Much depends on the type of Aboriginal society under discussion.

It is customary to find included within the Aboriginal concept, when claims about non-exploitation are being made, a wide variety of societal types, from small-scale nomadic hunter-gatherers through all kinds of agro-pastoral tribes and chiefdoms to expansionist urban state empires (such as the Maya or Aztecs). When, for example, Knudtson and Suzuki in their *Wisdom of the Elders* tell us about contemporary "native peoples' profound ecological wisdom" and "the age-old wisdom of indigenous peoples around the world" with regard to nature and spirituality, they include such widely differing peoples as the Hopi and the Inuit, the Chewong and Dayak of Malaysia, the Mnong Gar of Vietnam and the Murngin of Australia. They treat widely differing *types* of society as though their cultures could be categorized without discrimination, and they accept unquestioningly as reflective of behavioural reality the moral prescriptions of the society's religious belief systems. All of the societies they discuss are deemed to live in wholesome harmony with nature.

When I open John Eadie's *The Classified Bible* (1856) and read that hunting is "illustrative of persecution," I would be foolish to imagine that in the Western tradition hunting was demeaned. And if I read a little further on that "wild asses [were] regarded as untameable," I would be naive to imagine that wild asses had not been tamed and were not widely used. When I note the exhortations to mercy, to faithfulness, to charity in the Bible, an impartial observer would consider me foolish if I then concluded that these exhortations were indisputable evidence of Western norms. An understanding of any society requires that we recognize the economic and cultural reality of that society and the relationship of ideology to practice. General "at one with nature" statements do not offer us such necessary discriminations.

Of the Aboriginals, it is only the nomadic hunter-gatherers who display a consistently custodial, conservationist and anthropomorphistic relationship toward nature and non-human animals – and not as much as they would have in a distant at least quasi-vegetarian past (perhaps grubbing and scavenging but not killing sentient creatures) when their behaviour would not have required the development of a respectful but, from the perspective of the hunted animal, harmful attitude. Because of foraging characteristics, the low population density, limited technology, nomadic, or transhumant ways – which allow foraged areas to regenerate – the way of life of hunter-gatherers is significantly less detrimental to nature than that of other societies. Nonetheless, we should note that they do kill other creatures, albeit often respectfully, indeed with gratitude to the animals they have killed. The fact that they have developed a sophisticated ideology to justify the "necessity" of such killings reflects a "wish-it-were-otherwise" attitude, a recognition that in a perfect world the killing would not be necessary. The respectful prayer to the slain involves an apology for in principle unacceptable but in practice unavoidable reality.

The other types of food-producing societies of larger size and complexity have, like Western society, all become variously alienated from nature. Many, however, in their guilt at their alienation, indeed in an attempt to obscure their alienation from nature even from themselves, have maintained and developed a justificatory language that proclaims an apparent, but ultimately unconvincing, sympathetic relationship to nature. The reverential, if harmful, attitudes of hunter-gatherers toward the animals they hunt are repeated in the belief systems of more complex, pastoral, agricultural, and non-subsistence hunting societies, but here the reverence is only mouthed and can be recognized as inconsistent with behaviour in the same manner that Western norms of charity, of the meek inheriting the earth, of respect for the poor, may be deemed pious aspiration rather than cultural description.

We should be wary of considering many of today's Aboriginal cultures to be reflective of the characteristics they possessed before contact with (contamination by, many would argue) European culture. Most Aboriginal cultures have today undergone some form of substantial Westernization, or have suffered from the incompatibility of their mores with a way of life increasingly influenced in some manner by Western orientations. Certainly, in my experience, traditional Inuit express despair at the loss of respect for non-human animals among the younger Inuit. Both wolf biologists and more traditional Amerindians were horrified in February 1998 that a single Native hunter in the Northwest Territories chased 162 wolves to their deaths on a snowmobile in a single season. In the same period and manner, another dozen Natives had killed a further 500 – with numerous other kills still to be counted. The wolves are chased on to the tundra, where they have nowhere to hide, until they collapse from exhaustion. Then they are shot. One biologist called the kill "local genocide."[2] Next door in the Yukon, such inhumane practices bring a maximum $10,000 fine and a possible jail sentence. Increasing "at one with nature" claims for Aboriginal societies are untrue at the present, even if they were true of a rapidly disappearing, in many instances long-disappeared, past.

Certainly, the customary contemporary image of the Aboriginal – either in pre-history or among today's tribal societies – is one of veneration for nature, and of the possession of a sense of being an intrinsic part of nature, of being but one species among many species, all of which have their rightful place. Hope MacLean offers us an example of this image. For Aboriginals: "Animals are necessary to support human life. The animal world is seen as equal to, if not more powerful than the human one – both on a spiritual level and in the physical world. The hunter reveres the animal, and asks it to make a gift of itself so that humans can eat. Animals comply and give themselves to the hunter who shows proper respect."[3] This image is certainly very different from that offered to us by Burton (1), Darwin (2), Fossey (8), Angermeyer (9), and Galdikas (10), though it must be conceded that MacLean is restricting her comments to North American Natives. Still, her statement begs a host of questions, rarely addressed in the anthropological literature. Of course, it would be unwarranted to accept the interpretations of Darwin, Fossey, and the like without question. The quotations were chosen merely to indicate there is another side to the nature-friendly interpretations we are more customarily offered. In fact, some of the quotations reflect a degree of prejudice, some an interpretation of post-contact situations – but such interpretations should warn us to treat the unabashed eulogies of Aboriginal relationships to nature with a degree of skepticism and circumspection. If we are to side with MacLean against Darwin and his allies, we must ask for the evidence.

If, as MacLean asserts, "the animal world is seen as equal to, if not more powerful than the human one," how is it that it is always the other animals that "are necessary to support human life" and not vice versa? If the hunter "reveres the animal," as is claimed, we may wonder why many North American Indians continue to use, and many continue to support the use of, the steel-jawed leghold trap, which is recognized as so cruel that it is outlawed in sixty-eight countries and which, it is claimed, was described by Charles Darwin as "the most diabolical instrument of torture ever devised!"[4] The 1949 Scott Henderson Committee instituted by the British Parliament certainly called it "a diabolical instrument which causes an incalculable amount of suffering." We may ask ourselves why Amerindians continue to use the gillnet for salmon fishing, although it is condemned as inexcusably detrimental to the environment – trapping even the smallest of fish – by many others who claim to respect other species. We may question why Harry Robinson, the renowned Okanagan story-teller, has no qualms in his "The Indians got the Power" of securing a grizzly bear, a moose, and a groundhog on the railway tracks to hinder the progress of a train. It doesn't seem to occur to Robinson that the lives of the animals might be valuable in themselves.[5] We may ask why North American Aboriginals continue to engage in and advocate the hunting and trapping of animals for their fur, even though it is neither a necessary nor an environmentally friendly commodity. Any function provided by fur can be provided more readily by manufactured garments – which, incidentally, most Natives wear in preference to fur, even in the far north – and three and a half times as much energy is consumed in the production of a fur coat made from trapped animals as in the production of a fake fur. (Ranched fur uses sixty-six times as much.)[6] How are these uses and advocacy consistent with the much vaunted "proper respect"?

Of course, it would be inconsiderate of Aboriginal cultural norms to demand a wholesale change of Aboriginal practices, but it is important to understand that these practices are not justifiable in terms of a harmony with nature; they are justifiable, if at all, only in terms of traditional rights. And, of course, the North American Aboriginal engagement in the fur trade, in conjunction with the imposition on Aboriginals of a capitalist system of land allocation, of production, capital goods, and a cash economy, have served to erode the former conservationist nature ideology and to change attitudes toward other species. The fur-bearing animals have become a commodity. However much we must sympathize with the plight of the Aboriginal, we must also recognize that current practices are not justifiable by appeals to a traditional harmony with nature. If it is traditional, it has been a tradition no longer than, and not unlike, that of Caucasians in North America. And it arises from an attempt to control, not to harmonize with, nature.

Among the Desana of the Amazon, the payé (shaman) meets with the Animal Master, sometimes in the form of a rare small lizard, to negotiate the sacrifice of a number of game animals for an "equivalent" – though not equal – number of humans whose souls would then be reincarnated, not in the customary manner for the Desana as hummingbirds, but as game animals in replenishment of the slaughtered prey. Any idea of equivalence is, however, a sham, for the humans are to live a full life and to die a natural death, before their reincarnation. The game animals are to be cut down in their prime. Human life is treated as vastly more important than non-human life. The idea of equivalency is merely an ideological tool to justify the killing. The language suggests respect and harmony. The practice does not. Respect may indeed be *felt* by the Desana. But we should not ignore the fact that the animals are getting a raw deal.

Most suspect of all is MacLean's claim that, when asked to give up their lives, "animals comply." How is it, then, that they do the utmost in their power to avoid their fate? Why is it, then, that when caught in a leghold trap, the snared animal, whether North American beaver or African antelope, will gnaw off its trapped limb rather than submit? Such behaviour hardly reflects compliance. Nor does the situation seem to have much to do with respect or reverence or equality. It would appear, once again, that very different standards are employed to measure Aboriginal "respect" from those used to measure Western lack of "respect." At the very least, if there is to be any logical consistency at all in the claims made for Aboriginal reverence for other species, the situation must be far more complex than it is customarily presented.

Surely, if "animals comply," and there is no equivalent compliance by humans, that must reflect human dominance of the natural world. And if, as is claimed, the evidence for the animals' willingness to be caught lies in the assertion that they know their own environment better than human hunters and could escape if they wished, that claim would reflect a profound ignorance of every complex animal's desire for self-preservation. Because it is highly unlikely that American Aboriginals are ignorant of one of the primary laws of nature, one can only conclude that the belief in the animal's willingness "to sacrifice itself" is based in considerable part on rationalization and self-justification. It is a justification for an act that in a better world would be unnecessary. Certainly, a case can be made that the *need* to believe that the animal is willing to submit to its fate reflects an earnest concern for the animal. Be that as it may, *in fact* the animal does not comply, and the *interests* of the animal receive short shrift.

Despite the reservations that immediately come to mind, one must acknowledge the pervasiveness of the egalitarian view among the most reputable and insightful of scholars. James Serpell, for example, tells us that "traditional hunters typically view the animals they hunt as their equals. They exercise no power over them."[7] We find a similar view expressed by Joseph Campbell throughout his works, and the classical doyen of mythology, Sir James George Frazer, asserts in *The Golden Bough* that "the savage ... regards all living creatures as practically on a footing of equality with man."[8] It would be, to say the least, unwise to dismiss such claims. Moreover, it is a view sincerely held as reflective of their own traditions by the Natives themselves. Thus, for example, in Harry Robinson's *Nature Power: In the Spirit of an Okanagan Storyteller*, nature power is offered as "a concept central to most Native cultures ... based on the understanding that a form of spiritual energy animates all things in the natural world. Human survival depends on a strong alliance with, and reverence toward, the natural beings that manifest and share this power."[9] Many of Robinson's stories feature "shoo-MISH," nature helpers, who cooperate as equals with humans to provide them with special powers.

It is nonetheless difficult to reconcile such claims with equally reputable accounts of Amerindian behaviour. Thus, for example, one may read of the Natchez from James A. Maxwell that "Sometimes deer were hunted primarily for sport." And the traps used by the Hurons to snare deer inflicted great pain and suffering.[10] Robert L. Carneiro tells us that, among the Tehuelche of Patagonia, a mare was slaughtered on the occasion of the birth of a boy (but not a lowly girl) child. The infant was placed briefly in a cavity opened in the horse's chest to help the child become a good horseman.[11] Whatever it might have done for the boy, it clearly did nothing beneficial for the horse (or for girls). This tale is scarcely compatible with Frazer's view of Aboriginals regarding "all living creatures as practically on a footing of equality with man," at least if "equality" is thought to have any ethical content. Nor was the Tehuelche practice a post-contact innovation. It would appear that while Aboriginals may be said to *see* other animals as equals, they do not *treat* them as equals. The "equality" lies in the fact that, in the Aboriginal view, humans and animals alike follow the competitive laws of nature.

On the one hand, one can learn from the Oglala Sioux medicine man in *Black Elk Speaks* that, unlike the "crazy ... *Wasishus* [whites]," who slaughter indiscriminately, "when we hunted buffalo we killed only what we needed." Yet on the other, one must weigh this claim against the evidence from Maxwell that "the Chipewayan hunters took what they needed" of the caribou. "After they had accumulated as much meat as they could possibly carry, the hunters continued to kill but took only the skins, long bones, fat, and tongues, leaving the rest of the carcasses for the wolves and other carnivores." Similarly, Inuit dispatched walruses with their harpoons but did not consume the meat, other than the flippers. The teeth they used for fish hooks, the bones for harpoon parts, and the hides for umiak hulls. "Of particular worth are the ivory tusks. Walrus ivory, with its hard marbled core and outer layer of enamel, is difficult to work, but its lustre has long attracted Eskimo craftsmen. Before carving, they soften the ivory in urine, then score it until a suitable piece can be broken off."[12] Today, Inuit justify their selling of polar bear gall bladders to Korea and other parts of the Orient on the grounds that they are using the whole of the animal (*Globe and Mail*, 6 February 1996). In light of past practice and the ends to which the gall bladders are put, the claim for respectfulness does not convince. It smacks of rationalization. In what manner does this differ in principle from Western attitudes, culture, and practices? Why should we consider the Chipewa and the Inuit in principle any different from the *Wasishus* so disparaged by Black Elk because they did not use the whole of the animal? Why should we not be as appalled at the Inuit walrus ivory carvers as at those who acquire their ivory from elephants? The walrus may not yet be endangered in the eastern Arctic, but it has already been extirpated in the marine coastal zones of Canada.[13] Endangered or not, parts of the walrus, like parts of the elephant, are left to rot.

To be sure, one may hear in rejection of my arguments that it is inappropriate, for example, to use Chipewayan evidence to counter a Sioux claim, that Amerindian nations are distinct entities with separate cultures, that my approach ignores the significant and substantial variety among Aboriginal cultures in general. And it is certainly important to recognize that variety, and to understand the danger in overgeneralization. Nonetheless, it is equally important to recognize a commonality that allows us to understand such societies as Aboriginal in the same manner as there is a commonality that allows us to recognize different nations with different traditions as "the West." Those nations have something in common that allows us to recognize an overall similarity despite the differences.

What is imperative to understand is that if we accept the argument that evidence of cultural distinctions within the Aboriginal world should prevent us from making generalizations about that world, then one of the generalizations it must prevent us from making is that Aboriginals are at one with nature. Moreover, it would then by analogy be just as inappropriate to describe the West as employing "demeaning images of animals," or Aboriginal societies as the possessors of "nature-embracing myths," as do Knudtson and Suzuki in their *Wisdom of the Elders*. If the fact of variety of culture should be deemed a disbarment to making critical comments about Aboriginal traditions in general, then, to be logically consistent, we are also disbarred from making positive comments about Aboriginal traditions in general or critical comments about the West.

In fact, in the case of the Sioux, there is significant evidence that they played an important role in diminishing the abundance of bison by over 70 percent between the beginning of the nineteenth century and the 1870s – a profligacy similar to that of the Chipewa and continued, even exacerbated, by the whites thereafter, almost extirpating the bison by the end of the century. In reality, there are not only cultural variations but a commonality about humankind that has worked to the detriment of animalkind.

In a different context, Will Durant wrote that "Today in the enthusiasm of our discovery, we exaggerate generously the value of the new revelation."[14] One has to wonder whether, in our flight from our former culpabilities, we too "exaggerate generously the value of the new revelation" that there is much to be admired in Aboriginal culture. It would be wiser, and less prejudiced, to recognize it for what it is rather than for something it is not but that we would like it to be.

II

One of the modes of tribal expression of veneration is through art. The nineteenth-century American portrayer of Amerindian life, George Carlin, copied forty-five designs from buffalo robes and other decorative artifacts of the Plains Indians of the 1830s.[15] Of these "Symbols, or Totems," as Carlin called them, twenty-nine were representations of animals, one was the mythical thunderbird, one was the Piasaw monster (a great red, green, and black cliff drawing near Alton, Illinois), and fourteen were other natural artifacts. The famous 13,000-year-old cave paintings at Lascaux in southern France are predominantly depictions of animals, as are other cave paintings in Spain, North Africa, and among the Arnhem Land Aborigines. Animal rock paintings are the imaginative and subtle pride of Southern African Bushmen and Australian Aborigines. No less an art feature are the serpent mound monuments at Marietta, Ohio, and Rice Lake, Ontario, the "earliest structure in Ontario known to have been designed for purposes of worship ... flecked in endless renewal by the light and shade of seventeen centuries."[16]

Pre-Columbian ornaments among the Aztec, Maya, and others customarily depicted birds, alligators, toads, monkeys, bats, and other animals; in the pre-Inka Andes, cayman, hawk, and anthropomorphic cat are to be found in Chavin art; and the Cunā Indians painted their bodies with pictures of birds, mammals, and other natural objects. Iroquoian Indians embellished their tobacco pipes with human and animal engravings. Siberian Inuit ivory dolls are incised with fish and bird figures. Mongol horsemen dedicated songs to their favourite steeds. Ainu altars on Hokkaido, Japan, display bear and other animal skulls. Maori wood carvings portray strange animals with bird heads while those of New Ireland Melanesians contain intricate depictions of birds and snakes. Santa Cruz islanders carved elegant sharks in mother of pearl, Ashanti craftsmen of West Africa cast detailed animal figures in brass, and bird-man sculptures are to be found on Easter Island in the south Pacific. Perhaps the most remarkable depictions are the 2,000-year-old representations of the Nasca of the south Peruvian coast. These figures which are etched into the earth include representations of a hummingbird, a spider, a whale (or shark), a fox, a monkey, a lizard, a condor, and a frigate bird. The spider is about forty-six metres across and the hummingbird about ninety-one metres long. The variety of animal representations are legion, but in some form or other they are present in all tribal societies and early civilizations. Anthropologists continue to dispute their meanings, but their significance to such societies is beyond dispute.

Yet it behoves us to ask in what manner such usages differ in principle from the naming of automobile models, military units, or football and baseball teams after animals and birds. How do Aboriginal uses differ from Aesop's fables, the medieval bestiaries, carousel animals, Walt Disney's films, the porcelain animal figurines by Royal Crown Derby, Goebel, Royal Doulton, Beswick, and so on? What of animal ornamentation in medieval church and other public architecture? The carvings of Barcelona Cathedral are spectacular though no more impressive than those of the Bastille before the Revolution. What of heraldic symbols – from bears to tigers to eagles – the names of inns – for example, The Black Swan, au coq d'or – precious metal hallmarks – for example, the leopard or lion for London, the bear for Berlin, the rooster for Paris? What of the Georgian and Victorian animalia collectibles, art nouveau and art deco animal representative jewellery, and nineteenth-century Staffordshire pottery dogs, cats, sheep, lions, and the like? On Charles Dickens's desk were neatly arranged bronzes of toads, of a man beswarmed by puppies and dogs, and a letter opener adorned with the form of a rabbit. In rabbit form, too, was Flaubert's inkstand at Rouen. Could these be any less emblematic than an Amerindian's eagle feather? Do post-contact Aboriginal uses of animal images reflect anything more reverential and meaningful than their Western counterparts? Can either be anything more than a lingering reflection of our primordial past? Only if the emblems are reflected in behaviour can we consider them symbolic of real attitudes to animals. To be sure, Aboriginal usage is felt more deeply, for it arises from religions and historical experiences that are still respected. The symbols are still closer to their convictions. Nonetheless, increasingly the symbols are no more effective in guiding their behaviour than are the lamb and the fish as Christian symbols. Continued usage of symbols should be persuasive of respect only if it is matched by behaviour. We should not, of course, ignore the importance of the representations, but we should be cautious – as, indeed, most non-ideologically driven anthropologists are – in our interpretation.

As early as the Late Bronze Age, the Scythians of the Steppes had introduced naturalistic motifs featuring horses, deer, and birds into the Germanic world, not to mention the animal representations that flourished in Middle Eastern art – such as the *sirrush* (a dragonesque creature) of the Ishtar gate and the golden-headed bull of Ur. In Greco-Roman art, we discover such animal wonders as the lioness attacking a bull, from the pediment of a building on the Acropolis, to the numerous depictions of Romulus and Remus with the wolves. The northern and southern artistic streams joined to produce a continuous animal orientation in Western art right through to the present. It is a curious fact that the immensely popular medieval bestiaries show what human traits the differing species purportedly exemplify in a manner very similar to that of tribal mythologies, but, unlike those myths, the bestiaries are not deemed by modern commentators to indicate a respect for the animal realm. Perhaps the differing interpretations tell us more about the motives of the interpreters than about that which they interpret.

The art of tribal societies in all its myriad varieties reflects the *significance* of animals for the society. Whether there was also *veneration* is less easily established. Nonetheless, a convincing case can be made that among small-scale foragers, many artistic depictions possess inter alia deep mythological and numinous significance reflective of an authentic respect for nature. Thus, for example, one may encounter some powerful evidence on the Inuit:

> On the skin of the dead bear the Eskimos hung presents in an effort to pacify its soul. Dead seals too were treated with the utmost respect. It was strictly taboo to place a seal's dead body on a dirty igloo floor and to do other work while an unbutchered seal lay in an igloo. It was taboo to have old blubber in the igloo when a freshly killed seal was brought in. Seal meat could not be cooked over anything but a blubber lamp. And if the Eskimos changed sealing camps in the winter, they would arrange the skulls of seals that had been killed so that they faced in the direction of the new campsite. In that way the friendly souls of those dead seals might follow the hunters and bring them good fortune.[17]

Yet it is legitimate to ask whether this scene was reflective of reverence and respect or of propitiation, fear and supplication. If one fears the power of the bear to inflict harm, or if one worries that the supply of seal will diminish, one might wish to offer propitiatory gifts, engage in certain rituals, without any respect or reverence for the animals. Or is it merely that the notion of "reverence" is used in a manner in which the concept is devoid of positive sentiment and affection toward the animals? One is reminded of the traditional Japanese attitude toward the 800 thunder deities – they "command the interest and respect of humans."[18] They are nonetheless considered repugnant. The reality is that, among small-scale foragers whose traditional practices have not changed, the experience of the holy entails both awe (*mysterium fascinans*) and fear (*mysterium tremendum*). In substantial part, their respect is authentic. Yet as traditional practices are subverted by the encounter with novelty, so the *mysterium fascinans* diminishes and fear rather than respect predominates.

Social mores of the tribes or clans are often patterned after their observations of the animals and personality traits are described and understood by comparison with similar characteristics displayed by other species. Amerindians depended on their special animal relatives – their totems – to warn them of impending dangers and appropriate courses of action. Indeed, the Miwok Indians of California relate stories not only of how the silver fox and the coyote created the earth, but also of the lessons they afford us on how to cope with life's trials and tribulations. Still, it is a moot matter whether shamans are truly able to divine the messages from the animal leaders. Moot or not, it is clear that these messages are *understood* as real rather than merely symbolic, rather more than the Western tradition has been willing to accord the persevering spider, brave lion, or industrious beaver. In being willing to learn in fact, rather than merely symbolically, from other species, the Amerindian has shown rather more apparent respect and a greater sense of indebtedness than that to which the West is accustomed.

Nonetheless, one is entitled to wonder how meaningful the learning is, to what degree the "respect" is translated into positive behaviour toward other species. Moreover, one should not ignore the fact that elements of totemism are present in Western traditions, too. Thus, for example, the renowned Scottish warrior Rob Roy (Robert Campbell) wrote to his friend and cousin Mr. Patrick Henderson in 1719 and sealed his letter with the sign of a stag – "no bad emblem of a wild cattaran [fighting man]" wrote Sir Walter Scott in his biographical introduction to his romance of Rob Roy.[19] Gerard Manley Hopkins thought of himself throughout his life as a rook and signed his "The Wreck of the Deutschland" with the pseudonym Brân Maenefa – in Welsh, the rook of Maenefa. In a letter to a friend about his "l'après midi d'un faune," Stéphane Mallarmé described the animal as "a symbol," a "hero," to represent what he admired in humanity. It is of significance that the "father of symbolism," as he is known, chose an animal as symbol in his best-loved poem and in his equally awesome swan sonnet. According to James Dickey, Jack London "prided himself on his 'animality' and identified with his chosen totem beast, the wolf."[20] The identification was real, even if, as is now commonly recognized, London failed to understand the true nature of the wolf.

III

"The best people I've ever seen anywhere are the Tasadays," said one visitor to the Stone Age people discovered in the Philippines in 1971. "Where did we take the wrong turn?"[21] Some claim the Tasaday to be nothing but a clever hoax. Hoax or not, the interpretation of their mores by anthropologists is instructive. Timothy Severin reported of the discovery of the Tasaday that "anthropologists were amazed to find that there was not even any animosity toward harmful insects, which were permitted to share the same rock shelter ... without any attempt by the people to destroy or evict these potentially harmful co-residents."[22] A moment's earnest consideration might lead us to some scepticism. If that were the case, the very health and survival of the Tasaday would be in serious question. But what should be of greater *logical* concern to us is the *nature* of the evidence used to demonstrate respect. This lack of hostility is, understandably, postulated as an aspect of being "at one with nature." By contrast, for Desmond Morris, "our ancestors treated other animals in a simple, straightforward manner: they hunted prey, avoided predators, repelled pests, and attacked parasites ... They killed and ate only what they needed in order to survive, and they destroyed only those life forms that threatened their well-being."[23] One might doubt the validity of Morris's assertion. According to David Steadman of the New York State Museum, a study of 4,000-year-old fossils shows that as many as 1,600 bird species disappeared within a few centuries of the arrival of humans in New Zealand, Polynesia, and Micronesia.[24] There is substantial evidence of animal sacrifice, hunting for pleasure, and hunting beyond need and to extirpation several thousands of years ago. But what should here concern us is the matter of consistency. In Severin's example, respect is demonstrated by *not* evicting the harmful co-residents; in Morris's case by evicting *only* the harmful co-residents. Would Morris and Severin at least acknowledge the behaviour of our ancestors and other contemporary Aboriginals as substantially less respectful than that claimed for the Tasaday? And would they thus acknowledge not killing as more respectful than killing, and likewise note that almost all tribal societies are carnivorous? Moreover, while there are some deplorable exceptions, Morris's account of the behaviour of our ancestors doesn't seem to differ all that much from the behaviour of modern Western society. Unfortunately, in discussions about respect for other creatures, there is neither consistency nor agreement in what is to count as evidence in favour and what against.

Nowhere is the problem of consistency of argument clearer than in the statements of Hope MacLean. As we have seen, she asserts that "Animals are necessary to support human life" and she describes how the North American hunter "reveres the animal" – taking its life respectfully. Yet she also tells us of "the Jains of India" who "carry the Buddhist and Hindu philosophies of reverence for all life to its logical conclusion and refrain from all killing."[25] If the "logical conclusion" of "reverence for all life" is to "refrain from killing," then it stands to reason that there is something less than reverential about the Amerindian killing of animals. In his 1985 Ojai talk on "Beauty, Pleasure, Sorrow and Love," the East Indian sage

J. Krishnamurti said unequivocally, "If there is love ... you will *never* kill another animal for food." For Krishnamurti, Amerindian hunting, as well as Western hunting, reflects a decided lack of love for other species.

If Jains refrain from killing, it is surely inconsistent for MacLean to write of animals as "necessary to support human life." It is difficult to escape the conclusion that "necessary" is used as an ideological tool to justify Amerindian practices without much consideration for what "necessary" might mean. Moreover, MacLean does not seem to notice that in using two quite different and indeed antithetical examples – one vegetarian, one carnivorous – to make the case for respect, she stretches the boundaries of consistent language and logic. She claims that in contrast to Jain and Amerindian thought, "Western philosophy of how humans and animals should relate seems deeply confused." Perhaps it appears confused because it is confused, but only because it treats a complex ethical problem as a complex ethical problem, instead of offering easy, dubious, and inconsistent rationalizations. This observation should not persuade us that Amerindians lack a measure of respect for their animal victims. But it should persuade us to be more discriminating in our analyses and evaluations.

The Mbuti pygmies see the forest as their friend and consider themselves its children. Needless destruction of vegetation and disrespectful behaviour are treated as insults to the forest. And among the forest cultures of the Guinea coast of Africa, M.C. Jedrey tells us, "Intercourse in the forest [is] considered to be immoral: it is said to spoil the forest, endangering its fertility and offending the spirits who dwell there."[26] We should not, however, allow ourselves to be misled into imagining these respectful views a universal and pervasive attitude toward nature among tribal societies, even among those who proclaim it. Thus, for example, tree felling in Switzerland for house construction during the Bronze Age (when European culture corresponded more closely to Aboriginal culture) involved such large numbers of trees that the effect on the surrounding environment must have been devastating.[27] Major Shinto shrines in Japan have been rebuilt every twenty years with proclaimedly great reverence for nature. At one site alone, 16,000 cypress timbers are used. Such needless destruction appears incompatible with a meaningful respect for the natural world. Easter Islanders slashed and burned their forests until there was insufficient wood left to build canoes. They were trapped by their own profligacy. The Yekuana of Venezuela, like other inhabitants of the South American tropical rain forest, engage in clear-cutting and slash-and-burn techniques for the production of yucca.[28] Their relatively small numbers ensure that the damage to the forest is not irreparable, even though harmful, but their practices are identical in principle to those castigated by ecologists when practised in the West. And when the numbers increase, the consequences are devastating. Thus the Kenyah Dayaks of Indonesian Borneo have long exhausted their swiddens (their slashed and burned fields) and have sought new habitations in Sarawak (Malaysian Borneo), which is now being similarly devastated. We should recall that Knudtson and Suzuki offer the Dayaks as a people at one with nature, living in harmony with their environment. After one to three years of using slash-and-burn techniques, the land is unusable for agriculture until it has grown back into forest and been rejuvenated. In medieval Europe, a field was left fallow every few years (seven was the norm, following biblical exhortations) to allow it to become productive again.

Seneca Indians built longhouse villages by burning the trees to form an open area for cultivation, and to secure wood for fuel and construction. After no more than twenty years, the Seneca had to move on, for the land was exhausted and the area denuded. The Mandans and Hidatsas migrated in a 400-year period from the middle reaches of the Missouri into the North Dakota heartland. Each move was undertaken because the land and wood supply had been exhausted. The Sioux are reported to have broken camp several times a month – so rapidly were resources depleted.[29] The Maya diverted waterways to satisfy royal desires, with the inevitable environmental consequences. Tribal societies customarily controlled nature as much as they were able, and often to nature's lasting detriment. Humans are far more similar to each other than those who glorify Aboriginal environmentalism would have us believe. If the term Aboriginal were reserved for traditional small-scale foraging societies with little or no contact with outsiders, then at least some, indeed a goodly sum, of the claims for Aboriginal ecological sensibilities would be justifiable. In fact, however, the claims are made for a whole variety of societies, from foragers to early imperialists, and in most of those societies the claims are untenable.

There *is* much to be admired in tribal society. I do not wish to diminish that recognition, but to attempt to redress an imbalance, to allow us to understand tribal society in a more realistic and less ideological manner than has become customary in recent decades. Thus, for example, on the positive side, among the Ainu every natural object is considered to possess *ramat* – a spiritual essence, a part of the universal soul – and must accordingly be treated with due reverence. When Laplanders (Saami) captured their prey, they sang to the dead animal, thanking it for not damaging their spears and for not harming the hunters. Similarly, the Inuit engage in incantations to persuade the hunted whale to submit to its own death. And the Aleut and Inuit traditions report the dire consequences awaiting those who abuse animals. The Inka of the Andes blamed a catastrophic eclipse on their failure to treat their domesticated animals well. Human exploitation of animals was met with divine retribution. Respect and reverence was a human responsibility. All "primitive societies" are said by Timothy Severin, to have "so efficiently organized their economic pursuits that they were able to reach and maintain an equilibrium with their environments."[30] This equilibrium is achieved through respect and reverence for their natural environment. It is a truly idyllic image. Unfortunately, it is not always a convincing one.

In her sensitive book on pachyderm life at Amboseli in Kenya, Cynthia Moss offers us the now commonplace description of tribal societies at one with nature. The "Maasai," she tells us, "have lived more or less in harmony with wildlife wherever they have roamed." However, she also informs us that, following disputes between the Maasai and the Kenyan government, "one of the results was deliberate spearing of rhinos and elephants [by the Maasai] as a form of political protest." Even worse, we are told that, as a consequence of the death of their cattle from drought, "Maasai tempers were short and they were spearing elephants and rhinos, not for their tusks or horns, but apparently simply in frustration." Further, as a consequence of Maasai requirements for their own housing and grazing space for their livestock, the "elephants, along with buffaloes, zebras, wildebeests, waterbucks, impalas, and Grant's and Thomson's gazelles were concentrated in a small area where the Maasai did not bring their livestock." The effects on wildlife were as devastating as when Caucasians put their own interests ahead of those of other species.

Moss describes at some length an unprovoked spear attack by the Maasai on the Amboseli elephants and concludes "it had been a spur-of-the-moment sport." She states that "having spent thousands of hours with the Amboseli elephants I know that what they fear most is the Maasai."[31] How the reputed "harmony with wildlife" of the Maasai can be considered compatible with the fear they instill in the elephants I am at a loss to comprehend. If Moss's point is that the Maasai were once respectful and changed circumstances have diminished that respect, one must recognize that all but the most primary of tribal societies have faced such circumstances.

Whatever explanation or justification might be offered for Maasai behaviour, it certainly seems no improvement on European behaviour toward animals in Africa. To describe Maasai behaviour as "more or less in harmony with wildlife," as Moss does, seems to be entirely contradicted by the other statements Moss makes. It is difficult to imagine any other explanation for Moss's contradictions than that she has a laudable empathy for the historically underprivileged and that she is willing to ignore their behaviour in her judgments. She is certainly willing to judge it by different standards from those she employs to judge Europeans. In response to the peccadillo of a white tour guide who occasioned a quite minor, if nonetheless annoying, instance of soil erosion, she castigated him "as someone who should know better."[32] But why, one wonders, should a tour guide be expected to know better than the Maasai warriors? There would appear to be different standards for blacks and whites, to the detriment of the whites.

In some of the former French colonies of Africa, *viande* (meat) is employed as a generic term for wild animal. Where English is the *lingua franca*, the term "beef" is often used as a synonym for wild animal. In

Kiswahili, a language of the Bantu, *nyama* is the word both for animal and for meat. In such usage, the animal is not viewed as an end in itself, nor as a respected and revered part of nature, but as a commodity, instrumental only to human use.

This fact in itself ought to give us cause to ponder the reputed identity with nature. The manner of interpreting this information might also occasion reflection. Thus, Dale Peterson postulates the possibility that the linguistic usage is "some strange inheritance from the colonialists."[33] Strange it would be, indeed, if the French and British colonialists did not use the words *viande* and beef in the manner they are employed by Africans, yet are somehow supposed to have left that usage as a legacy. And doubly strange it would be if the time-honoured usage in some African languages were inherited from colonialists who did not use the terms with the meanings given to them by Africans both in the colonial language and their own language. The *Oxford English Dictionary* records only three instances of such usage for "meat," none unambiguous and none later than the seventeenth century, and none for "beef," save with the explicit meaning of "ox," in use until the nineteenth century. *Larousse* gives no unequivocal instance of the use of *viande* as animal.

It would appear that the possible explanation of the usage as "some strange inheritance from the colonialists" fulfils an important ideological purpose. It allows us to identify a negative usage with a negative phenomenon: colonialism. Almost everyone today has a negative attitude to colonialism, and thus to ascribe something else also negative to it encourages the reader to accept the ascription unquestioningly. This in turn encourages us to avoid facing the alternative interpretation: that there may be serious limitations to the much vaunted reverence and respect of tribal societies.

One wonders too at the ubiquitous use of "sacred" with regard to tribal depictions of other species. According to the *Concise Oxford Dictionary*, "sacred" means "safeguarded or required by religion or reverence or tradition, indefeasible, inviolable, sacrosanct." As an exemplary use of "sacred" in the animal context, one might turn to the statement of Göran Burenhult about the Toraja of the highlands of Sulawesi in Indonesia: "To the Toraja, the water buffalo is the most sacred of all animals, and it is also the principal symbol of wealth. Buffaloes are bred for one single purpose: to be sacrificed during grand funerary ceremonies."[34] Whatever meaning "sacred" may have in the passage from Burenhult, it cannot include "safeguarded," "indefeasible," "inviolable," or "sacrosanct." After all, the animal is bred for one sole purpose, its own sacrifice, a practice endemic throughout the Aboriginal world. The buffalo's carotid artery is cut with a long knife and the "sacred" animal is allowed to bleed to death. As many as 250 buffaloes may be killed in a single funerary ceremony for an important person. Whatever "sacred" may mean for the Toraja, it must be the very antithesis of what it meant for Albert Schweitzer, for whom "life itself is sacred." According to Schweitzer, "A thinking man feels compelled to approach all life with the same reverence he has for his own." When the Canadian Straussian philosopher George Grant witnessed a Dalhousie University student crush a moth, he was appalled. "But it was life," he exclaimed. "Kill not the Moth nor Butterfly / For the Last Judgement draweth nigh," opined Blake. For Blake, "all life is holy." For the Toraja – and countless other Aboriginal societies – what is "sacred" is put to death, neither to furnish food, nor raiment, nor shelter, but to appease the spirits – and not, presumably, the spirits of the buffalo. It is the practice of sacrificing the water buffalo that may be described as "sacred," emphatically not the buffalo itself. The buffalo is merely a means to a sanctified end. This customary use of "sacred" by anthropologists serves to mislead. It inculcates in us a positive attitude toward behaviour we would otherwise find inexcusable. In *Through the Looking Glass,* Lewis Carroll wrote: "'When I make a word do a lot of extra work like that,' said Humpty Dumpty, 'I always pay it extra.'" "Sacred" deserves a substantial salary increase.

Some of the pictures we are painted of tribal societies supposedly treating the natural world with deep respect leave the attentive reader perplexed. For example, David Maybury-Lewis tells us of the Dogon respect for animal life. He writes of the desert fox which, according to the Dogon, "as a native of the bush ... possesses far greater knowledge than do village-dwelling beings. The fox is therefore consulted on matters of importance." The fox's advice is read via its footprints. "Should the answers on successive nights seem contradictory, a sacrifice of a chicken may be made on a nearby altar to encourage the fox to tell the truth."[35] Whether the Dogon are truly respectful of the fox is a moot point. What we can be absolutely certain of is that they have no respect for the chicken.

What, then, is the positive evidence that has convinced so many advocacy anthropologists to write of tribal cultures in rosy terms, to deplore the passing of a dulcet era, and to yearn wistfully for a return to "Mother Nature"? When the Netsilik Inuit catch a seal, they sprinkle water in its mouth to satisfy the thirst of its spirit, which is a part of the universal seal spirit. We are all, the Inuit believe – like the Ainu and many Aboriginal cultures – a part of a universal soul with corresponding obligations and rights to each other. To kill a seal does not harm seals provided one reveres and appeases the seal spirit as a part of the universal spirit. The Inuit place mittens on the carcass of the seal, in the hope and expectation that the seal's spirit will report its favourable treatment and encourage other seals to make themselves available as prey.[36]

It is imperative to understand that this is an atonement – *at-one-ment* – for the killing. It is understood by the Inuit that the killing is in principle unacceptable, but, so long as one eats meat, it is an unavoidable fact of life (and for the Inuit, meat-eating is a necessity, given the inhospitable clime they inhabit, where anything more than the most meagre horticulture is impossible). The Inuit must thus *atone* for their behaviour and become *at one* with the spirit of the animal they have killed. The logic of the situation requires that they engage in exculpatory behaviour, and that they choose a language of self-justification, which diminishes the severity of the offences committed against nature. The essence of the reverential behaviour is that the Inuit are apologizing. For all tribal societies, the killing of complex animals is a wrong that "necessity" permits, provided one acknowledges the offence and offers a justification in mythological terms.

IV

Unfortunately, the attempt is often made to analyze Aboriginal attitudes to animals and nature in isolation from more general attitudes and culture. Moreover, individual words are often misunderstood as meaning the same in the Aboriginal cultural context as they would in a Western context (as we saw at the very beginning of this book with "dominion" in regard to the Hindu context). Thus, for example, we might learn well from the words of Australian Bill Neidjie, elder of the Bunitj clan of the Gagudju language group, in his *Speaking for the Earth: Nature's Law and the Aboriginal Way*:

Law never change ...
always stay same.
Maybe it hard,
but proper one for all people.
Not like white European law ...
always changing.
If you don't like it,
you can change.

Aboriginal law never change.
Old people tell us.
"You got to keep it."
It always stays.

Creek, plain, hill.
That plan can change ...
wet season, him mud.
You get lily,
you get fish.
But, he dry up ...
that's alright.
Then people can get long-neck turtle.
Same for animal.
People look for food.

Lizard look,
bird look,
anyone look.
We all same.[37]

The key lies in the words "Law never change ... / always stay same ... / Not like white European law ... / always changing." For tribal communities, law is a matter not of abstract, egalitarian, and universal justice, but of order, integration, solidarity, communal belonging, and identity. Aboriginal law looks backward to a united and undeviating conception of tribal justice, originating in the dreamtime, a mystical golden age of the dawn of humankind in which all the great questions are settled; that of Europeans looks forward, progressively, altering laws to fit changing conceptions of human rights. For Aboriginals, law is of itself sacred; for Europeans, it is of instrumental value alone. For the one, law is the standard of justice; for the other, justice is the standard of law.

The Western conception of law is a response to the inadequacy of "golden age" conceptions for changing human circumstances, but itself becomes inadequate in losing the communal identity of the natural tribal collectivity. Changes from the sacred conception of law began with the age of rationalism. Plato offers us a conception of law as permanent and perfect, but knowable by reason, and hence subject to rational investigation, rather than being known by primal memory, tradition, and legend, and thus beyond investigation. In becoming the legitimate subject of human investigation, it loses its sacred quality. The history of Western philosophy has been a continuous, if not consistent, movement away from sacredness toward secularism, and from the divine community, ensured by the sacredness of the antediluvian, dreamtime, "golden age" message toward a rationalistic individualism, and toward cultural and moral relativism, ultimately toward understanding law as nothing other than that which legislators enact. Yet the journey began because of the limitations to golden age and dreamtime conceptions, which hindered individual fulfilment, proactive response to changing conditions, and most aspects of equality.

Long before Plato we have, however, already in the codes of Hammurabi and Manu, for example, attempts to state, declare, and expound the permanent god-given laws, but the very process of writing the laws rationalizes the elements of the subconscious known through tradition and revelation, and reduces the sacredness of the law by submitting it to rational inquiry.

In the development of Roman law, we encounter, around the second century BC, the development of *leges* – laws, statutes, man-made enactments, leading ever more rapidly away from sacredness and toward reason, from certainty toward insecurity. With the development of the Roman Empire and the need to apply different laws in the colonies, a distinction was made between the *ius civile* – the civil law – and the *ius gentium* – the law of peoples – acknowledging distinctions of "legal" practice among different peoples and thus encouraging the acceptance of cultural relativism. Further, a distinction was made between public law, that is, law that pertained to the community as such, and private law, that is, law that regulated the personal relations among individuals, which later encouraged the contractarian, voluntaristic conception of society with its individualistic emphases.

To be sure, political and legal theory until the time of Bentham continued to conceptualize society in terms of *communitas*. Suarez, Grotius, and Fichte, for example, wrote in terms of the state as an organism, and in practical politics in the Middle Ages, lawyers explained the relationship between crown, parliament, and populace in such terms.[38] Nonetheless, as Otto Gierke recognized, "In spite of all assertions to the contrary, [their] conception of the State was] no more than [as] a work of art, counterfeited to look like a natural body; a machine, invented and controlled by individuals." The contradiction reaches its apogee in the writings of Thomas Hobbes who, according to Gierke, "began by comparing the State, that great Leviathan, to a giant's body; he proceeded to expound, in the minutest of detail, its analogies with a living being; but he ended by transforming his supposed organism into a mechanism, moved by a number of wheels and springs, and his man-devouring monster turned into an artfully devised and cunningly constructed automaton."[39] Man first replaced nature as the measure of all things. And then the automaton, the machine, replaced man as the measure of all things. A similar incongruence continues today among political radicals who pronounce themselves communitarians or collectivists but espouse individual rights of social deviance, that is, rights against the state or "community." However admirable the espousal of such individual, or even group, rights may be, of one thing we can be sure: it is not collectivist, which by its nature must subjugate the parts to the whole. Although the debate between individualists and collectivists has *appeared* to continue, in fact, at least since Bentham, then clothed in more appealing terms by James and John Stuart Mill, the contest has been between competing conceptions of individualism – rugged individualism versus other-regarding individualism. The notion of the community as *the* end in itself diminished with the onset of rationalism, and today, if it is not entirely extirpated, it is certainly unrecognizable in the West (although some admirable attempts are being made to revive it).

The tribal conception of law and of justice is central to our understanding of the human-animal relationship in that the tribal conception is inward-looking. What is seen to be right is what supports the interest of the community. And if the interests of the community are always paramount, the interest of whatever lies outside the community must, at best, be deserving of negligible interest, especially if the interests of the community are in conflict with other interests. Every tribe sees itself as the chosen people, whose responsibility it is to look after itself. This view is the antithesis of egalitarianism and universalism. For the Aboriginal, the permanent interests of the tribe are sacred.

This attitude is present in all tribal societies. In a few, it extends to thinking of oneself alone as "human" and all others as "animal," that is, as unworthy of consideration, as enemy. We have already seen an elementary form among the early Greeks, who thought of others as speaking like or being like animals,[40] but it can be recognized more fully among, for example, the Makritare of the rain forests of the uppermost Orinoco, who speak the So'to language. So'to means twenty, the number of digits possessed by a human. All non-So'to-speaking people, including their immediate neighbours to the east, the Kariña, are regarded as fearsome animals, that is, non-human.[41] They are epitomized as their jaguar-shamans, which are eighteen retractible-clawed, predatory cats. Both fear and despisal result in the treatment of non-community members as beneath entitlement to consideration. This conception is diametrically opposed to the idea of being at one with nature, of "equality" with other tribes and other species. After discussing the history of geographical conceptions of different peoples, Daniel J. Boorstin concludes that "all people have wanted to believe themselves at the center."[42]

Yet, we must recognize, this "egalitarian" oneness is precisely how Bill Neidjie understands others:

People look for food.
Lizard look,
bird look,
anyone look.
We all same.

The Aboriginal conception that "we all same" does not, at least here, equate to the ethical conception that each is to be treated as one and no more than one. It corresponds instead to the early utilitarian behavioural tradition in which each being seeks to maximize its own pleasure and minimize its own pain. Humans and non-human animals follow the same principles of individual and communal self-preservation. It is akin to David Hume's and Charles Darwin's recognition that, in the words of the former, "Every thing is conducted by springs and principles, which are not peculiar to man, or any one species of animals." The law of self-preservation applies alike to all species, and in that respect we are equal. Being at one with nature here means behaving according to the same self-preservation laws as all of nature. And if nature is cruel – "clumsy, wasteful, blundering, low and horridly cruel," according to Darwin – then, to survive, we must behave according to nature's requirements. Considerate treatment, unreflective of one's communal interests, is mere sentimentalism.

V

How, then, are we to interpret the now customary statements of ecologically responsible behaviour among tribal societies? In her book *In the Rainforest,* Catherine Caufield tells us: "The Mentawai people collect forest products but they cut only one kind of tree, the sal tree (several species of *Shorea*), from which they make canoes, their main form of transport. Hunting with bows and arrows is a social activity, surrounded by religious taboos that protect wildlife stocks."[43] This fact may, however, be readily interpreted as arising not from any sense of empathy for the natural world, as the writer intends, but simply from a recognition that the Mentawai have no interest in cutting more wood than is useful to them; nor, if they hunt with bows and arrows, is it in their self-interest to expend energy in killing more than they can consume. By contrast, Biruté Galdikas tells us that the "Dayaks never found much wonder in the forest as such. Although they understood it, they were never in awe of it. They took the forest for granted."[44] Perhaps the Dayaks needed the products of the forest less than the Mentawai, or there was never any threat of scarcity. As we have already seen, there are many examples of tribal societies where, their apparent self-interest not at stake, they do act in a manner harmful both to the vegetation and to the animal world. Myths and taboos are designed to create operative rules of behaviour that maintain "nature" at a level suitable to the interests of the tribal community. In such instances, the interests of "nature" itself are not considered. Yet myths and taboos arise that are consistent with the interests of "nature," because those interests also correspond, in many instances, with the tribal communal interest. Thus there develops a sophisticated ideology, a sophisticated language of interest rationalization, which functions linguistically, but not in fact, precisely as would a legitimate philosophy of ecological balance. We should not confuse the two.

There is, however, a further dimension that the cynical view of human nature as uniformly self-preserving, as being determined by the imperatives of selfish genes, ignores. Within the human condition, alongside the principle of self-preservation, there is also a deep-seated altruistic principle – a respect and consideration for others arising from the depth of our souls.[45] Jean-Jacques Rousseau writes of two principles that inform human behaviour: self-preservation and compassion. And the principles that affect Western civilization are also those that inform tribal life. Different social, economic, cultural, individual, and developmental circumstances exert influences on the effectiveness each may have. In tribal societies as in Western society, there is a genuine affection, a natural compassion, which serves to diminish the worst effects of the rationalizations.

Which of these principles, then, tend to dominate in Aboriginal societies? The former cannibalism of the Caribs of South America and the Caribbean (from whom "cannibal" is derived), Maoris, Ontario Iroquois, New Guinea tribesmen, Northwest Coast Indians, Inuit, South Sea Islanders, Meso-american Maya, and palaeolithic Swedes, among others, along with head-hunting among the early Celts, the Jivaro of South America, the Kenyah Dayaks of Borneo, the Naga of Assam, the Eddystone Islanders, and in New Guinea and neolithic Taiwan (as well as in the Balkans until the later nine-teenth century) ought to suggest that the picture of peaceable Aboriginals in harmony with nature has been overdrawn. After all, fellow humans are every bit as much a part of the natural order as other species. How environmentally friendly is the Cannibal Dancer's song of the Northwest Coast Kwakiutl?

I went all around the world to find food.
I went all around the world to find human flesh.
I went all around the world to find human heads.
I went all around the world to find human corpses.[46]

How "at one" with fellow humans was the abject cruelty of the Maya toward their captives, as depicted in the eighth-century wall paintings at Bonampak, in Chiapas, Mexico? The cutting out of hearts, decapitations, pulling out of fingernails, drawing blood from tongues, inserting sharp objects through penises, all practised on live victims, might cause us to question the idyllic image we are sometimes offered. We might be espe-cially inquisitive not of the fact that the Maya indulged in such practices, but of the fact that they were sufficiently proud of them to immortalize them in wall paintings.

Slavery and slave-trading have not been restricted to Western imperial-ists. Slavery was a common practice among several Amerindian tribes, including the Apaches. It was rife in black Africa, where slaves were known to have slaves, and a commonplace among Arabs and in Mesoamerica.[47] Blood feuds were certainly known in Europe until the later nineteenth cen-tury but are also well attested to among the Hurons and other Amer-indians. Torture and human as well as animal religious sacrifices were customary among several Amerindian tribes, including the Seneca, and also among the Aztecs (where as many as 20,000 people were sacrificed per ritual event) and the Maya. The Caribs "sometimes killed the old and infirm [and the] wives were treated as servants," according to Irving Rouse.[48] Among the Barasana of Colombia, men and women even used sep-arate doors to their abodes. The Inkas of Peru selected the prettiest village girls for sacrifice or to be servants of the Emperor. At any given time, more than 200 were dedicated to the service of the temple. If Aboriginals were so out of harmony with fellow humans, it would be remarkable if they were in harmony with nature in general.

We should not imagine that there was no concern for nature in such soci-eties. But if, as is customary, we treat the sexism, elitism, and capitalism as integral aspects of the oppressive character of Western society, including an oppression of nature, it would be inconsistent to ignore similar characteristics in other societies. Certainly, where concern for the environment in more traditional societies arises out of self-interest, there would appear to be little inconsistency. But where it is offered to us as an example of *respect* for nature, as an example of tribal estimations of the worth of non-human species, we are entitled to be as sceptical as we would be if similar claims were made on behalf of Western civilization as such.

VI

Neanderthals, archeological evidence suggests, were wasteful and haphazard in their hunting habits, killing far more animals than could possibly be consumed. The practice continued. In his *The Archaeology of Animals,* zooarcheologist Simon J.M. Davis discusses in considerable detail the evidence for extinction later in the Pleistocene period and concludes: "In my opinion people played the dominant role in bringing about the extinctions of many Pleistocene large animals. Climatic changes, particularly at the end of the Pleistocene, may have put certain species under stress, and reduced their areas of distribution. This is no doubt what happened during the earlier Ice Ages. But it was late Pleistocene people's *advanced hunting technology and wider distribution* which acted as the last straw in bringing about megafaunal extinction. In regions such as Africa and Eurasia with a long man-animal record, species of large animals had time to adapt, and a sudden wave of extinctions did not occur."[49] In the Americas, immigrants from Asia appear to have had a devastating effect on the native megafauna they found there some 11,000 or 12,000 years ago. Simon Davis reports that in "South America nearly 80 percent of its large mammal fauna became extinct."[50] Already with the earliest Amerindians technology was proving a detriment to the natural order. We should not, however, imagine the extinctions and the devastation a peculiarly American phenomenon. Thus, for example, Jonathan Kingdon reports that when Indonesians arrived in unsettled Madagascar somewhere around the fifth century AD, they rapidly brought about the extinction of six species of giant elephant birds.[51] And Polynesian sailors ate to extinction several flightless bird species they encountered on the smaller islands they discovered. Through soil erosion, the Maoris destroyed the ecological basis for the shellfish diet they once enjoyed. They extinguished all eleven species of Moa and cut down half the forests.

We can perhaps recognize here the dangers provoked by the novelty of circumstance. Over time, often considerable periods of time, myths, legends, ideologies, and philosophies develop to provide rules or strategies, commanding or recommending courses of action appropriate to the circumstances. When the circumstances are predominantly new, when factors are present for which the myths and philosophies were not designed, dissonance, and alienation, increase. The myths of the new immigrants from

Asia to North America and from Tahiti to Hawaii, for example, had developed in circumstances in which there was a relatively stable, unthreatened fauna. On encountering new ecological conditions, the old myths must have proved inadequate. Yet the attachment of the new immigrants to the old myths must have been as strong as their identity with their community.

In times of fundamental change, dreamtime or golden age conceptions of the sacredness of myth and law are not only inadequate, they are detrimental to the capacity of the society to continue to function adequately. Bill Neidjie's "law that never changes" encourages a fulfilling sense of the sacred, but it can only be effective as long as there are ongoing conditions of stability and order.

We should not imagine this phenomenon to be restricted to Aboriginal societies. Thus, by the nineteenth century, Britain had experienced almost two centuries of resounding economic and political success by following the classical liberal philosophy of minimal levels of state intervention in the economy. Widely differing continental philosophers from Voltaire through Mallet du Pan and Montesquieu to Chateaubriand concurred in acknowledging the security, liberty, and prosperity of Britain and in advocating its constitutional, political, and economic principles as the appropriate basis on which to develop their own constitutional order. Yet, as Britain moved rapidly toward an urban and industrialized society in the nineteenth century, the prevailing and historically successful philosophy was no longer appropriate to the changing circumstances. It had become, however, so much a part of the integrating British myth, so much a symbol of British success, so much a source of British pride, that philosophers, economists, and politicians alike were blind to the need to adjust not just policies but also the philosophical myth to meet the requirements of the new conditions. Despite the warnings, perhaps already too late, of such writers as, say, Thomas Carlyle in *Past and Present* (1843), the British were as wedded to the sacredness of their classical liberal myth as much as Bill Neidjie is to the sacredness of traditional Aboriginal law. The myth is effective as long as one declines to participate in the new order, to accept neither its rewards nor its punishments, to remain essentially apart. An obsolete ideology can continue to function for a while in incompatible circumstances, but eventually it must change or provoke the greatest alienation from the new order.

The devastating industrial and urban squalor developed in later eighteenth- and nineteenth-century Europe and North America, not solely as a consequence of a lack of concern for the lower echelons of society, as is customarily argued – it is unlikely that the degree of concern diminished very much between the early eighteenth and mid nineteenth centuries – but at least in substantial part as a consequence of living with an outmoded myth, a myth inadequate to the new circumstances. The philosophers, novelists, and politicians looked at the squalor and were appalled, but their stock answers to every new problem were to be found in the old lexicon. For example, in Elizabeth Gaskell's *Mary Barton* (1848) the plight of the Mancunian working classes is described in heart-rending graphic detail, but Gaskell has no other answer than an extension of classical liberal principles.

Over time, we can alter the prevailing myths to meet the contingencies and exigences of new circumstances, but if the speed of change is too rapid, there will be an incongruence, a dissonance, between the myth and the reality. Moreover, myths are far less likely to be directed toward the health of the ecological order itself than to the integration, solidarity, and self-preservation needs of the society in which the myths are developed. Thus, when there was an abundance of bison, and no reason to imagine the supply would dwindle, Amerindian attitudes were a great deal less than ecologically sound, certainly difficult to interpret as being in harmony with their natural surroundings.

When bison were plentiful, North American Indians would drive whole herds of buffalo over a cliff to their destruction – up to 900 killed at a time according to archeological evidence. In excavations of kill sites, it was found that, Davis informs us, "Many of the limb bones were whole, some were semi-articulated, and spinal columns were often intact. This suggests mass killings and substantial waste."[52] Again, we should not imagine this overkill to be restricted to Amerindians. Timothy Flannery reported that "over the last thousand years, Polynesians in Hawaii have destroyed more than 70 percent of the island's bird species." He indicates that in Australia as a consequence of overhunting "gray kangaroos are now half the weight they were." It was the fittest and biggest who were hunted. Contrary to legend, it is not always the weak and infirm that succumb, although certainly among the Kalahari Bushmen and the Hadza it is usually they who are hunted. Many Australian animals have become extinct over the centuries, partly as a consequence of the poor soil and erratic climate. Nonetheless, Flannery does not exempt Australian Aboriginals. He concludes that "Australian animals were particularly vulnerable to the impact of humans [who] are the most efficient and largest warm-blooded predators that have ever existed in nature."[53] In fact, it is not only human immigration that creates the novelties with which nature cannot cope. Thus, for example, possums were introduced to New Zealand from Australia in the 1830s and now number some 70 million. They destroy many acres of forest each night. In Australia, the trees developed a poisonous defence against the possum. Not so in New Zealand where there were no original land mammals and thus there were no natural enemies to slow the possum's population growth nor a natural defence for the trees. Nature's balance may take many generations, usually many millennia, to develop.

In light of the facts about bison destruction, how do we explain the Indian buffalo myths that claim such an affinity between the Indians and the animal realm? While not all buffalo myths are the same, they share similar central elements. For example, in exchange for receiving an Indian princess as his bride, the buffalo Animal Master – the head of the herd – agrees to allow the slaughter of his brethren. The function here is to assuage the guilt of killing innocent animals. One is "at one with" the animals because they have permitted themselves to be killed. (One scarcely need add that in fact the buffalo have agreed to nothing of the kind.) A second part of such myths is to require a reverential attitude toward the animals one has killed, agreeing to kill only what is necessary for human survival. The function here is to instill the attitude that if one kills more than is necessary, then the future supply of meat will be threatened and the tribe's preservation may be put at risk. It should be clear that the purpose of the reverence is the benefit of the Amerindian community and not that of the animal. Were the animals' interests at issue, there would at the very least be far greater concern to minimize the pain and suffering of the animals killed. Moreover, just as Christians *in fact* fail to maintain the peaceful injunctions of their dogma, so too Amerindians *in fact* have often failed to abide by the injunctions of their myths and, as the archeological evidence clearly indicates, killed far more than their requirements.

Australian Aborigines poisoned water holes with the pituri plant to snare emus. K'iche" Maya Indians used the poisonous *barbasco* plant to catch fish, and Kaxinaua Indians poisoned the waters of the Curanjã river to the same end. Ecuadorian Indians tip their blowgun darts with curare to poison the monkeys they hunt. So too do Central African pygmies. Kalahari Bushmen (San) grind poisonous insects, the poison sacs of venomous snakes, and the larvae of the cladocera beetle to provide poison for their arrows with which to hunt large game.

Why, then, do we ascribe an identity with nature to representatives of tribal societies? According to the mythology of Southern African Bushmen, the eland is to be killed in accord with certain special rites. Joseph Campbell tells us that the "hunter identifies himself with the animal struck by his poisoned dart and, during the painful hours of its dying, observes food and behaviour taboos thought to advance the poison by virtue of their mystic identification."[54] What should be clear is that identifying with the animal does not require any benevolence on the hunter's part. Its purposes are "to advance the poison" and to enable the hunter to know the ways of the eland so that they might become a readier prey. If we are to talk of identity with nature in tribal societies, let us understand that it customarily means acting in accord with the cruel dictates of nature. Traditionally, Aboriginals have understood that reality of their own lives. More recently, they have been persuaded by Western intelligentsia to dress that understanding in ecologically friendly clothes.

Certainly, among such hunter-gatherers as the Kalahari Bushmen, there is an authentic reverence expressed toward the animal realm. The fact that the suffering of the hunted animals is genuine reflects rather less any indifference of the hunters and rather more the inefficient technology they employ. Bushmen use metre-long and unfeathered arrows that are incapable of ensuring a swift death.

One might note, too, the proffered reason that so many are killed when bison are driven over a cliff. It is said that the inordinate number of deaths reflects not a lack of concern but a lack of technology, an inability to control the numbers killed. Indeed. But if that is so, one cannot then argue that no more are killed than can be consumed, nor that all of the animal is used. Moreover, before they had learned how to corral the bison, Amerindians already possessed a less efficient but decidedly less profligate method of killing – the bow and arrow. It was less profligate in that it restricted unnecessary slaughter. Once they had learned the new technique – a pre-contact learning, one should note – the less efficient but more respectful method was discarded out of self-interest.

Technology, or the lack of it, does indeed play a significant role in our behaviour toward other species. It is one of the great ironies of life that the *capacity* to deal more humanely with hunted food animals was greatly increased with the invention of the firearm but was not realized. Instead, it led to wanton destruction of other animals both by those who invented it and almost equally by those who acquired it.

Of course, one can find numerous instances of the most intimate relationships with the animal realm in tribal societies. Thus, Biruté Galdikas tells us: "Of all my Dayak assistants, [Mr. Achyar] was the one most trusted by the orangutans. Many Indonesians called him a *pawong,* a person who has the power to call wild animals to him ... His devotion to them was obvious as he moved among them in a careful, solicitous way."[55] Yet this would appear to be individually differentiating rather than culturally representative. One could just as readily find cruel behaviour in Indonesia – indeed, Galdikas did, especially among the Moslem Melayu – just as one could in the West. Dayak behaviour is today no more undifferentiated than Western behaviour. It is just as ambivalent and paradoxical. As Galdikas herself says, "Paradoxically, these most gentle and courteous of any people were once fierce head-hunters, the 'wild men of Borneo.' "

While it is now customary to consider Aboriginal societies to have a positive relationship to nature, Dian Fossey, on the basis of her experience in Rwanda, was not so readily convinced. She deplored the constant poaching engaged in by the Batwa of the Virungas, which ignored all ecological considerations: "The main poacher prey within the Virungas are two antelope species: the bushbuck (*Tragelaphus scriptus*) and the duiker (*Cephalophus nigrifons*). These graceful animals are either killed directly by spears or arrows or they suffer a lingering death, after being caught in spring traps concealing wire or hemp nooses triggered upon the slightest pressure to catch and snare any animal's foot." The agony of the death throes can only be imagined: "Pit traps, about eight to twelve feet deep, are floored with sharply pointed bamboo stakes that impale any unsuspecting creature ... A neckrope noose structure is usually found in dense blackberry patches ... The victims caught in such traps slowly strangle to death, their futile struggles only serving to tighten the binding nooses." Fossey goes on to mention "a cleverly concealed wire-spring noose partially covered by dirt" and the use of cliff drops, similar to those employed by Amerindians, and with an equal lack of concern to restrict the kill to the numbers essential for sustenance.

Fossey reserves her greatest venom for the poachers of her beloved gorillas who "were frequent users of *sumu* [black magic] because many of their black magic ingredients came from the animals and vegetation of the forest. With courage bolstered by hashish, they killed silverback gorillas for their ears, tongues, testicles, and small fingers. The parts, along with some ingredients from an *umushitsi* [witch doctor], were brewed into a concoction reputed to endow the recipients with the virility and strength of the silverback [a mature male]."[56] For Dian Fossey, tribal practices, including tribal practices promoted by myths, were decidedly detrimental to the other species with which the Batwa shared the Virungas. Any notion of the much-vaunted spiritual bond between the tribes and the animals they shared the land with was, for Dian Fossey, a scurrilous sham.

Nor should we entertain the idea that such instances of cruelty are restricted to a few tribes on a few occasions. It is pervasive. Mbuti pygmies will drive a spear into the elephant's bladder and if the urine is seen to spurt, the pygmies will follow the wounded and suffering beast until it drops dead from its injuries some days later. Albert Schweitzer deplored the French Equatorial Africa "custom of creeping up behind elephants and crippling them by cutting the tendons of their hind legs."[57] The Ainu of Hokkaido engaged in the ritual killing of tame bears they had nurtured from infancy, which has a striking parallel in North East India, where the Khonds used the *meriah* in a similar manner – the difference being that the *meriah* were human.[58] (In 1835, the British outlawed human sacrifice in the Raj and thereafter goats and buffaloes were used instead.) The Ainu taunted the bear until it became enraged, tied it to the sacrificial stake, and after thanking it for being a welcome guest and promising it equally good treatment in the future if it returned, they dispatched it with bamboo arrows. One can be confident the bear was less than appreciative at being treated with such "respect."

The Ainu also used a pivotal hook for fishing that could not fail to inflict significant injury to the fish. But this activity palls against the practice of the Solomon Islanders, who bore a hole through the lower jaw of a live fish and thread a fine line through the hole to catch larger fish. They also employ spiders' webs to enmesh fish. One might wish to argue that fish are too insensitive to feel much pain. Perhaps. But on the principle ascribed to most Aboriginals of proclaiming an identity of human and animal emotions, one must conclude that the concept of a spiritual bond with nature includes relatively little consideration for animal suffering.

Even if it could be argued that the lowly fish do not warrant consideration as ends in themselves, one could scarcely make a similar case for warm-blooded mammals and birds. Seneca Indians celebrated a new year by strangling a white dog – one of a breed kept specially for the purpose – daubing its lifeless body with red paint and decorating it with a garland of white beads and then hanging it from a pole. The Navajo prepared an antidote to the possibility of a poisonous spell being cast upon them. It was concocted from the gall bladders of mountain lions, bears, eagles, and skunks, which were sometimes killed especially for the purpose. The Hopi ceremony of the *Niman Kachina* culminated in the ritual killing by suffocation of eagles they had previously tethered. In the sixteenth century, the Maya sacrificed jaguars, and for at least 1,000 years they captured quetzals to use their feathers for no better purpose than personal adornment. Over the centuries, the Maya of Yucatan exported jaguar pelts and bird plumage – from hummingbirds to toucans – merely for luxury use. The Xavante of the Upper Zingu in Brazil kept harpy eagles in cages to provide a supply of the prized decorative feathers, rubbing an unguent on the plucked birds to promote growth of new plumes. The Samoans kept birds in captivity to provide decorative red feathers to adorn their mats. The Paiute of the Great Basin caught magpies to decorate women's skirts with their iridescent feathers during the piñon nut dance. To develop courage for their conquest of the Arawaks, the Caribs of the Lesser Antilles practised initiation rites in which birds were ceremonially crushed over the warriors' heads and the hearts were eaten, the rest unceremoniously discarded – a practice scarcely consistent with purported notions of killing only what was necessary and leaving nothing to waste. In puberty initiation rites, a Kuikuru (Guiana) boy is expected to catch, wrestle with, and kill a hapless anaconda. Such a feat may reflect great courage, but no consideration for the interests of the anaconda. It would take considerable mental agility to deem such practices as somehow in harmony with nature.

In the fourteenth century, the city council of Cahors on the River Lot in southern France had six cats burned alive annually to ward off evil spirits and bring good fortune. In Metz, in Lorraine, cats were burned alive to prevent a curious malady known as St. Vitus Dance. The ceremonial custom continued until 1773. Today, Westerners congratulate themselves appropriately on having left such practices long behind. It is difficult, however, to distinguish these rites in principle from those of the Seneca with their strangling of the white dog, the Hopi with their suffocation of the eagles, or the Maya with their sacrifice of the jaguars. They are all sacrifices directed to maintaining or improving the health of the society but conducted at the expense of the animals.

In the early days of Western civilization in classical Greece, the sacrificed animal was either thrown – albeit ceremonially – into a sacrificial pit or was ceremonially burned. In Aboriginal North America, after the eagle is ceremonially killed, the feathers are plucked to provide human plumage. Neither seems of much benefit to the animal. The modern West seems to have little sympathy for classical Greek ritual sacrifice. It is surely inconsistent not to apply the same criteria elsewhere.

According to the log of Christopher Columbus's first visit to the "New World," on his initial landing in the Bahamas (perhaps at what is now Samana Cay), the Natives brought parrots as gifts. One could then scarcely blame modern Amerindian domination of other species on imitation of Western practices – a common but quite unjustifiable claim, as even the scantiest perusal of Aztec or Mayan customs would demonstrate. Indeed, Montezuma, the early-sixteenth-century Aztec emperor, already possessed a menagerie no European monarch could have hoped to rival when the Spanish first arrived. His enormous collection of birds and beasts was managed by some 600 keepers! "500 turkeys were killed every day to feed his birds of prey alone, and it was rumoured that his larger cats (pumas and jaguars) dined regularly on human flesh."[59] His "zoo" included crippled, dwarfed, hunchbacked, and albino humans.

Despite the ready availability of such information, the most knowledgeable and most sensitive, indeed most admirable, of analysts of other cultures have demonstrated what appears to be an almost wilful blindness. Thus, for example, Joseph Campbell describes the *Niman Kachina* of the Hopi: "In the spring, a number of eagles' nests will have been identified in the sides of nearby cliffs and marked with prayer sticks, inviting the great birds to come willingly to the villages to be sacrificed after this ceremony. The hunters, then, either lower themselves on ropes or climb by perilous ledges to remove from the nests the birds too young to fly (in former years, sometimes as many, they say, as twenty-five) which then are brought with great honor to the village and tied by the feet to eagle platforms on the rooftops."[60]

In a typical British early-twentieth-century book on birds, we read a warning to those who would harm the creatures by collecting their eggs: "A mere collection of faded eggs, lying in a drawer with labels on them, is not a very interesting thing; and the getting of it together is inevitably fraught with some suffering to the birds, for of course their loss is far greater than the collector's gain."[61] Would we truly consider the Hopi sacrificing of the eagles more respectful of them than a simple warning as in the British book not to interfere with the lives of such creatures? In what manner may the Hopi be deemed more respectful than the Europeans? Is it merely because they claim to be respectful while engaging in their sacred but harmful rites?

We have to wonder at the blatant discrepancy in Campbell's passage between "invitation" and "capture." If the eaglets had accepted the invitation, there would be no need to capture them. We are told euphemistically that "there the eaglets remain, until the Niman ends, and they are with cer-emonial reverence 'sent home.' " We can be confident the eaglets would far prefer not to be so revered. Campbell notes that "from a nearby housetop a tethered eagle screams." He does not question whether the scream is con-sistent with "the great honor" the eagles have apparently been accorded. One can be confident it is an honour the eagles would willingly forgo.

In like and what is by now customary vein, Campbell tells the story of the Huichol Peyote Hunt of "Brother Deer," in which "the deer was to be caught in a snare." Having been caught, according to the Huichol hunter, the deer "lies down, he stretches out before me of his own will." When the hunter brings home the prey, others exclaim, "Here you are with Our Brother. Now the earth will be able to bring forth once more."[62] However "respectful" the attitude may be, it must be recognized that the deer does not give itself will-ingly, that whatever "Brother" may mean it does not imply treatment one would accord a genuine sibling, or any other human being for that matter. "Brother" is more a subterfuge than a fraternal appellation.

The reality is that there is genuine regret at what is seen as the necessity of the killing. It is because of the regret that the hunter thinks of himself as a necessary participant in the cycle of nature, doing what the cycle requires. But if that were all, there would be no need for the language of justification, the sacred rites, to accompany it. The justifications are required because there is an implicit recognition that humans have devi-ated from their pristine nature, and indeed from their genuine harmony with nature, where no killings, ritual or otherwise, would be tolerated except in self-defence.

One could, of course, demonstrate the sins of the West just as readily as those of other societies, often more so. There have been periods when ele-phant feet were deemed highly desirable as the base for umbrella stands. Elephants have been killed in the thousands for their ivory alone, stags for their antlers, frogs by the millions for zoological demonstrations in ele-mentary science classes, and one could continue ad nauseam. The point is not to eulogize the West, but to show that others have been no less sinning, although they employ a language of natural harmony that makes it appear as though they are, and that has convinced a large proportion of Western intellectuals that there is something here for the West to emulate.

VII

Animal sacrifice is a pervasive characteristic of tribal societies. The highly creative Aztecs and Maya of Central America engaged in both human and animal sacrifices to appease the gods and celebrate martial victories. The Arawaks of Puerto Rico, renowned for their peacefulness, practised animal sacrifice in *el yunque*, the celebrated rain forest, to ward off the dangers from hurricanes. Goats and chickens are sacrificed in the Kivu province of Zaire to bring harm to tribal and personal enemies. The Kwaio of Malaita in the Solomon Islands sacrifice pigs in homage to their ancestors. Among the pastoral peoples of western and northern Africa, cattle are the sacrificial offering to ancestors and the gods. Cock sacrifice is an everyday occurrence for the voodoo practitioners of Haiti. In the Meo villages of Laos, pigs are sacrificed to provide magical "cures" for serious human illness, and the Lawa of northern Thailand have reduced but not abandoned their religious animal sacrifices. Indeed, animal sacrifice has been practised for at least 80,000 years.

Animal sacrifice might seem to be inconsistent with ideas of living in harmony with nature. Nonetheless, justifications continue to be offered by those who claim that spiritual oneness. Thus, in *Keepers of the Animals*, Vine Deloria, Jr., tells us that "after an eagle has been killed in a ceremony, one can look skyward and see eagles circling the site as if they were giving their approval of what had taken place." Is it necessary to note that there are rather more plausible explanations for the presence of the circling eagles – such as sorrow, despair, or hunger? It is difficult to consider Deloria's statement anything other than rationalization. One is reminded of the traditional story told of Confucius: "Tsekung wanted to do away with the ceremony of sacrificing the lamb in Winter. Confucius said, 'Ah Sze, you love the lamb, but I love the ritual.' "[63] It should strike us as self-serving and as an example of applying selective standards to find Deloria continuing with the assertion that "We must carefully accord these other creatures the respect they deserve and the right to live without unnecessary harm. Wanton killings of different animals by some hunters and sportsmen are completely outside the traditional way that Native people have treated other species."[64] What is animal sacrifice but "unnecessary harm?" If animal sacrifice is justifiable as an aspect of Aboriginal culture for no other reason than that it is an aspect of Aboriginal culture, then it follows logically that sexism is justifiable as an aspect of Western culture for no better reason than that it has been a part of Western traditions since time immemorial. If animal sacrifice is justifiable because its functions are to appease the gods, remove fear of the unknown, and encourage societal solidarity, let us acknowledge that, however worthwhile such atonement and integration may be, the sacrifice is performed not with the agreement of, but at the expense of, the animals sacrificed. Animal sacrifice flies in the face of respect for living beings.

In what manner is animal sacrifice, or any of the activities previously mentioned, less "wanton" than killings by Occidental hunters and "sportsmen" who claim that they too have respect, awe, and admiration for their prey? In Gottfried von Strassburg's *Tristan* (c. AD 1200), the hunting story reflects the reverential ritual attached to the animal in the medieval chase. In Germany, at least until the 1920s, hunters would engage in a communal prayer to the slain animal at the close of the hunt. I recall my father in Britain in the 1950s "singing" – if one could call it that! – the closing lines of a hunting lay he had learned in childhood: "Here's to the sound of a Lancashire hound, / And the speed of a Lancashire hare!"[65] Certainly, there was more identification with the hound than the hare (and more still with Lancashire), but the hare received its recognition, too. It did also in Richard Jefferies's Victorian paean to nature *The Open Air.* After the prey had been killed, Jefferies tells us that "even in the excitement of sport regret cannot but be felt at the sight of those few drops of blood about the mouth which indicate that all this beautiful workmanship must now cease to be. Had he escaped, the huntsman would not have been displeased."[66] S.R. Kellert identified three modern types of Caucasian American hunter, based on surveys he conducted: utilitarian hunters, who hunt solely to supplement their diet; dominionistic hunters, who seek to dominate animals and nature while remaining ignorant of their ways; and naturalistic hunters, who are people with close ties to, and appreciation for, nature.[67] He regards both the utilitarian and the naturalistic hunters as living in accord with, and with no undue disrespect for, nature. The naturalistic hunter may be said to be epitomized by both Ernest Hemingway's novels and his life. Despite his lack of concern for their interests, in *Green Hills of Africa,* he described the objects of the chase with great accuracy and some sensitivity. In *Moby Dick,* Herman Melville depicts a Captain Ahab obsessed with killing the white whale and fully believing in himself as a part of nature's moral order. George Orwell showed great interest in the natural realm, expressed awe toward it, yet avidly hunted its constituent parts. And John Steinbeck witnessed the cycle of life and death in nature with more morbid curiosity than concern for the fate of the victims. In *To a God Unknown* (1933), Steinbeck writes of his hero, Thomas Wayne, that "he liked animals and understood them, and he killed them with no more feeling than they had about killing each other." Human and animal alike were a part of nature and accepted and lived by its laws. In *Pagan Spain* (1937), Richard Wright expressed the ultimate paradox of the human psyche when, despite his empathy for the bull over the matador, and despite his loathing of the crowd for stamping on the testicles of the slain bull, he concludes that the bull is "deeply loved, no mistake must be made about that." Hemingway, too, in *Death in the Afternoon,* tells us that "all real hunters are in love with the animals they hunt." However, we might suggest that while it may involve the passion of a form of love, it does not include the compassion of an authentic respect. And, if we are willing to recognize that, we should be no less willing to recognize the limitations to Aboriginal respect.

We read from Deloria that "some of these ceremonies involved the bird or animal in sacrificing its life in order to ensure that the ceremony was properly done." Let us be quite clear about it. The animals do not sacrifice their own lives. People do it for them. Such obfuscations of reality from Deloria should lead to suspicion on the reader's part. Moreover, we should recognize from Deloria's statement that the animal's interests are decidedly subordinate to those of the ceremony. It is difficult to come to any other conclusion than that animals are seen as mere instruments of human ends.

In *Keepers of the Animals,* Caduto and Bruchac tell us that "with their close ties to the animals, and all parts of Earth, Native North American cultures are a crucial link between human society and animals ... Native North Americans see themselves as *part* of nature, not apart from it. To the Native peoples of North America, what was done to a frog or a deer, to a tree, a rock or a river, was done to a brother or a sister."[68] Initially, one might wonder at the identity of sensibilities toward a deer and rock. If they are both a "thou" rather than a "you," as Joseph Campbell tells us in praising Aboriginal reverential attitudes, one might wonder whether that means one should treat a deer with similar consideration as that to which a rock is entitled. Moreover, one might wonder how this seeming equality is consistent with Deloria's assertion that "the Plains Indians saw a grand distinction between two-legged and four-legged creatures." In fact, a "thou" can express reverence only if there are "its" with which it is contrasted.

Of far greater importance than these concerns, however, is the need to ask how one reconciles Caduto and Bruchac's claims with the killing of millions of fur-bearing animals by Natives with cruel traps for no better purpose than providing pelts for Europeans. Fur coats for Europeans (later for North Americans, now for the Oriental market) were frivolous and luxurious – not at all capable of explanation in terms of nature's necessity, not at all supportive of the view of the Native as somehow in a mystical bond with the animal world. Only the fur was used. Customarily, the meat was left to rot. Indeed, the number killed was far in excess of the capacity of the Amerindians to eat them. The practice was both cruel and wasteful. Of course, the European behaviour was no better, but no one is claiming the Europeans lived in a harmonious bond with the animals of their natural environment. Logic requires that one ask how plucking birds feathers for decoration, poisoning rivers, clear-cutting forests, strangling dogs, and suffocating eagles can be reflective of the claim of being a *"part* of nature," unless that means acting with the same disregard for the interests of other species as that shown by some other predators for their prey. It would be remiss to not recognize the reverence for nature expressed in the pre-contact, small-scale hunter-gatherer societies, but equally misleading to imagine that traditional societies in the modern world in contact with other civilizations have maintained their environmentally respectful cultural attitudes. Indeed, many of them abandoned those attitudes long before contact with the outside world as they came themselves to develop new technologies incompatible with the interests of other species. The most relevant criterion for judging Aboriginal alienation from nature is not, as is customarily assumed, whether it has been contaminated by contact with an alien industrial or post-industrial culture but the degree to which it has developed an efficient hunting or agrarian economy.

Eastern Thought and Practice

I

Joseph Campbell tells us that the "wonderful art of recognizing the divine presence in all things, as a ubiquitous presence, is one of the most striking features of Oriental life, and is particularly prominent in Hinduism."[69] This "wonderful art" is the philosophical spirit of Hinduism. Nonetheless, the journal Campbell kept of his six months in India from 1954-5 tells a rather different story about Indian practices (6). Entitled *Baksheesh and Brahman*, the journal tells us of how he went to discover the latter – "Absolute Reality in its macrocosmic inflection" – and found rather more of the former – begging, the demand for alms, the philosophy of "something for nothing." We can read of the Hindu *sadhus* (ascetics) who demanded the abolition of the killing of cattle for beef, but who engaged in sheep sacrifice. Rather than entering into an engagement with the world of nature, Campbell writes of Indians as "linked to nature by being linked to a principle beyond nature, through a ritual attitude: something very different from the romantic return to nature and intuition of God through nature."[70]

Lacking more than a smattering of Hindi, he feels frustrated that he cannot reprimand his driver who "kept striking his nag on the tip of its prominent spine, which was such a torture for the poor animal that it continually kicked." Given the reputed Hindu concern for the natural realm, we might be surprised when Campbell tells us that, at the prime ministerial palace, pet Himalayan pandas were kept in a cage – scarcely a ready recognition of species endangerment or the appropriateness of an animal to its natural habitat. Elephant rides were thirty rupees – the profit motive appeared to influence Indian attitudes to animals as much as in the West. And at Trivandrum on the Malabar Coast, we learn that the "zoo was a pretty but pitiful affair, full of sad and solitary bears, tigers, snakes, etc., in excessively smelly cages."[71] The similarity to Occidental roadside zoos is striking. Despite the doctrine of *ahimsa* – "non-injury," "non-killing" – not only was animal sacrifice the norm, but Campbell comments on the difficulties acquaintances sometimes encountered on trying to get a vegetarian meal in a restaurant. (On a 1994 visit, travel writer Christopher Ondaatje encountered less difficulty.) Moreover, we should not imagine Campbell out to make a case. He had a less-than-average interest in animal welfare; he *wanted* to witness a bull or goat sacrifice. His remarks about the treatment of animals were made entirely in passing, and he positively enjoyed the premieral pandas. And he wrote from a perspective of the deepest respect for Oriental, especially Hindu, thought.

From the perspective of making statements about Oriental philosophy in relation to animals and nature, the most significant of Campbell's experiences was that religious disputation dominated Indian intellectual life. Everyone who had an interpretation of any particular religious concept or doctrine had a different interpretation from many others. There was no orthodoxy, no agreement, and, therefore, in a significant sense, no possibility of making definitive statements about, say, Hindu or Jain belief systems, and decidedly little possibility of saying anything uncontroversial about Indian or other Oriental attitudes to other species. We should certainly be impressed by the Vaishnavas, the followers of the God Vishnu, who would not kill even the wild animals who daily destroyed their crops. We should certainly be impressed by the Yogis whose principles require that they avoid not only meat and fish, but alcohol, possessions, and the enjoyment (if not the practice) of sex. But we should not imagine these attitudes and practices to pervade the life of the many Indians who are as lustful, aggressive, and self-interested as most Westerners, a fact recognized by commentators such as Tagore and Gandhi, who, while in agreement on this point, disagreed about almost everything else in Indian life, including the primary principles advocated by each other. For Tagore (3), India's future lay in embracing modernity but with a respect for the past, being inspired but not bound by tradition. For Gandhi, India's future lay in rejecting modernization while retaining a respect for both the British and the lessons they had brought to India. Each espoused a persuasive and profound philosophy, and each philosophy was inconsistent with the other.

One may learn of the importance of respect for animated nature in Indian life. Yet, reminiscent of Western hunting lodges, the walls of the Sikh Laxmi Vilas palace at Baroda and the Fernhill Palace at Ooracamund are decorated with the stuffed heads of tigers and leopards. The similarities among human attitudes are everywhere more striking than the differences. If we seek only the differences, we ignore the reality.

Writing of the Jains of India, Hope MacLean tells us that they "refrain from all killing, even of a mosquito or an ant that crawls in their path."[72] They accomplish this difficult task by having someone go before them clearing the way with a brush so that there will be no insects on which to tread. It should be clear that the purpose of this endeavour must be the purity of the Jain and not the lives of the insects, for far more will be killed by having a path swept than if the Jain were to step boldly forth. Of course, one must not fail to recognize the genuine Jain sympathy for other species, but it is also important to keep their practices in perspective. It is equally important to note that the animal-respecting Jains constitute only 0.5 percent of the Indian population. One should be wary of making general inferences about India from the practices of the Jains, even though their influence on India in general has been both welcome and significant. Moreover, one should not fail to heed George Bernard Shaw's caveat. The Jains "of eight thousand years ago,"[73] he wrote, recognized God as human and animal, man and woman, black and white. But its modern practice, he concluded during a visit to India in the 1930s, had been corrupted by idolatry. This observation did not prevent him, however, from extolling Jainism as a visionary ideal.

As with the Aboriginal traditions, so too in India, and, indeed, so too in the West: whatever one's sacred scriptures or myths may say, they are belied, openly, by the reality. Thus, G. Naganathan, in expounding the Hindu tradition with regard to animal welfare, insists that "the condemnation of meat-eating has been thorough and unequivocal."[74] He refers to the holy script *Mahabharata* (22), which tells us that "everyone in the business, the one who abets, the one who cuts, the one who kills, the one who sells, the one who prepares, the one who offers, the one who eats; all are killers." Yet one finds in the Indian towns as early as two and a half millennia ago the establishment of guilds, including guilds for butchers, trappers, hunters, fishermen, leather-workers, and ivory-workers, and there are clear distinctions between acceptable meat and "unclean meat" in the Hindu tradition – which latter included the flesh of dogs, domestic cocks, camels, carnivorous animals, animals having two rows of teeth, and those with much hair or none at all. The remainder could be eaten. Describing a Hindu wedding ceremony he attended in Dewas in 1913, E.M. Forster informs us that while the Brahmins ate no meat, the rest did. During the eight-day festival of *Gokul Ashtami* in honour of Krishna, nothing may be killed for consumption, which implies, of course, that on other occasions carnivorousness is acceptable. In like vein, Buddhist prohibitions against flesh-eating were in force in medieval Japan, but archeological evidence from Kusado Sengen indicates that meat was eaten in large quantities – mainly dog and fish. The diet of Tibetan Buddhists includes significant proportions of animal fat, liver, and mutton – a dictate of the inhospitable clime. Whatever the proclamations of the scriptures, many members of society openly and proudly practised professions or engaged in carnivorous practices that belied the principles on which the pronouncements were made (and, of course, many who proudly and respectfully practised those pronouncements). Indeed, the *Shikarries*, Hindu hunters, have a reputation for killing tigers for no better reason than the display of courage. Tiger ears are collected by Hindus as *jadu*, a charm against evil spirits, sickness, and sudden death. Hindu kings kept menageries of exotic animals for no superior reason than European or Aztec monarchs. In the Hindu *Bhima Swarga* of the Balinese, one may read of the "dishonest butcher selling pork for the price of beef."[75] Such butchers were punished in the afterlife, not for promoting carnivorous activities but for cheating their customers. Whatever the injunctions against killing the sacred cow, beef was available on the open market. From childhood, Gandhi was a vegetarian by religion and by vow, yet he "wished at the same time that every Indian should be a meat-eater." It was only after reading H.S. Salt's *A Plea for Vegetarianism* that he became "a vegetarian by choice." On visiting a Trappist settlement, he was deeply impressed by the austere and devotional life of the brothers who partook neither of fish, fowl, meat, nor eggs. But he was aghast that the nuns ate meat four times a week. Even here there was no consistency.

Certainly, the British of the Raj considered Hindus cruel to animals. The prevalent view was reiterated in Flora Annie Steel's late-Victorian novel of the Indian Mutiny, *On the Face of the Waters:* "Cruel devils, aren't they?" was the frequent complaint. Certainly, the British view of the Hindu was somewhat less than impartial, but we should not allow that to blind us to the fact that the East Indian attitude to animals was almost universally derogated. Indeed, even the sacredness of the zebu cow was interpreted not as an aspect of respect for the animal, despite its continued proclamation since the Harappa culture of 2000 BC, but as an *aide memoire* to the Hindu that milk and calves and cow dung for fuel and for house floor construction were of greater value than beef. The prohibition against killing merely ensured an ongoing supply of necessities. It would be churlish to ignore the numerous instances of authentic Hindu animal sympathy, but, again, in light of the frequent panegyrics to Hindu animal reverence, some caution is necessary.

One may read in the *Padmapurana* (25) that "one who views every other living being as oneself, one who views others' wealth as a clod of earth, one who looks upon others' wives as mothers, he sees verily." Yet one may wonder why Bombay has an enormous problem of stray dogs, uncared for by the populace, and usually left to starve if they are not first rounded up and destroyed by the local authorities. If reverence for nature is pervasive, one may wonder why so many dead bodies polluted the Ganges that in 1986 the Indian government introduced 25,000 carnivorous Varanasi turtles into the river to devour the corpses. In his poem *Banshi* (1932), Tagore writes of back-street Calcutta:

In nooks and corners of the lane
There pile up and rot
                    Mango skins and stones, jackfruit peelings
Fish-gills,
Corpses of kittens,
And who knows what other trash.

Ignoring the fact that if these lines were written by a Westerner, he or she would be deemed disrespectful for calling dead kittens "trash," we must still note that the disregard for the lives of dogs in Bombay is matched by that for cats in Calcutta – of course, in New York, London, and Paris, too, but no one has suggested the West pure, in thought or deed.

Again, animal sacrifice is forbidden. Thus one may read in *Pancatantra* (17) that "in blind darkness are we sunk when we offer sacrifices with beasts. A higher religious duty than harmlessness (*ahimsa*) has never been nor shall be." Nonetheless, one can find numerous and frequent examples of animal sacrifice throughout India. We have already mentioned the Khonds in the north. The Hindu Kali Temple in Bengal was witness to frequent sheep sacrifice. In the Nilgiri hills of South India, the Todas worshipped cattle, but engaged in calf sacrifice. *At least* as late as the 1960s, among the Nagas of Assam in the extreme northeast of India, bulls were hacked to bits while still alive. *At least* until recent years, bulls and goats were sacrificed at the 350-year-old Kaligat Temple outside Calcutta. The goat was the symbol of lust, the bull of anger. By sacrificing the animals, one sacrificed one's own inappropriate passions. But what a deplorable price for the animals to have to pay. It is difficult to understand how it could ever be portrayed as respect. Certainly, still today in the practice of the Hindu Kaharingan religion of the Dayaks of Borneo, the *tiwah* – the funerary ritual – involves the sacrifice of animals to protect the living from evil spirits. The *tiwah* certainly provides no protection for the animals that are slaughtered.

Confronted with the realities of life in India, some Hindu apologists (much to the chagrin of many of their less extreme co-religionists) insist that "for nearly two centuries Indians have been estranged from their own [ecology sympathetic] culture by English education. They have been encouraged to think in Western ways and to value the things which the West values. Their own traditional values have been marginalized. In many cases they no longer know what those values were or why they were held because those things are no longer taught."[76] It would of course be less than honest to blame the fact of animal sacrifice on the English. First, animal sacrifice existed throughout India for many centuries before the establishment of the Raj; second, the British disapproved of animal sacrifice in India and tried to discourage it, though they accepted it as preferable to the continuing practice of human sacrifice. Had "English education" succeeded in its efforts "to value the things which the West values," it would have succeeded in eliminating at least this misuse of animals for human ends. Moreover, the once extensive practice of overt female infanticide among Hindus was a consequence of the dowry system, not some alien British innovation.[77] It is less than honourable to blame the decline in family values entirely on the modernity introduced to India by the British, as do the same Hindu apologists. Indeed, if female infanticide is declining, the introduction of the alien value system is to be thanked. Likewise, child marriages. And the fact that the ritual burning of widows while still alive was made illegal in 1829 is due to the same foreign source. No one should doubt the ills imposed on India by the Raj. But the fictions offered of Hindu purity reflect more indignant self-righteousness than a concern with truth.

Hinduism's appreciation of our responsibility to other species is admirable. In *Pancatantra* (13), we read, "the holy first commandment runs – not harsh but kindly be – and therefore lavish mercy on the louse, the bug, and the gadfly." However, this is not the whole story, although it is the story customarily presented. By contrast, we can read in the Vedic *Laws of Manu* that transmigration means that "people of darkness always become animals." Animals are the lowest of "the three-fold level of existence," which is itself divided into three, the lowest level including worms, bugs, snakes, livestock, and wild animals, the second including elephants, horses, lions, tigers, and boars, and, reminiscent of the classical Egyptian view that foreigners were animals, also "servants [and] despised barbarians." The highest level included birds, ogres, and ghouls.[78] Whereas Plato (*Republic,* Book 10) thought that animals possessed qualities that humans might choose to acquire in metempsychosis, and thus might choose to become animals, and while courageous Aztec warriors first dwelt with the god Huitzilpochtl after death before returning to earth as hummingbirds, sipping honey forever, for the *Laws of Manu* (and *The Tibetan Book of the Dead*) reincarnation as an animal always meant reincarnation in a lower form. Similarly, "A priest who drinks liquor enters (the womb) of a worm, bug, or moth, of birds who eat excrement, and of violent creatures ... A priest-killer gets the womb of a dog, a pig, a donkey ... A priest who is a thief (is reborn) thousands of times in spiders, snakes, and lizards."[79] Furthermore, the priest who sells sesame seed, except when *in extremis,* will be reincarnated as "a worm and be submerged in the excrement of dogs, together with his ancestors."[80] This is scarcely redolent of respect for the creatures with which we share the planet, not to mention the ultimate universal spirit. Respect is certainly to be found in Hinduism, not least with the revered Gandhi. But Gandhi too writes with evident satisfaction that "it is a rare thing in this world to be born as a human being."

Similar sentiments to those of the *Laws of Manu* are expressed in the Buddhist tradition, too. Thus the *Lotus Sutra* of Mayahana Buddhism, written no later than the third century AD, but, according to Burton Watson, it has been "over many centuries, the object of intense veneration among Buddhist believers throughout China, Korea, Japan, and other regions of eastern Asia."[81] The punishments for those who insult the Sutra are spelled out:

He will enter the Avichiheu
[who slanders the Sutra and] ...
Though he may emerge from hell,
he will fall into the realm of beasts,
becoming a dog or jackal,
his form lean and scruffy,
dark, discolored, with scabs and sores,
something for men to make sport of ...
Camel, donkey, pig, dog –
these will be the forms he will take on.
Because he slandered this sutra,
this is the punishment he will incur.[82]

In the ten levels of existence, "beasts or beings with animal nature" belong on the third level from the bottom, beneath the level of the *asuras,* the demons, and the realm of human beings. The first four levels, Watson informs us, represent the "evil paths": "the lowest, most painful and undesirable levels of existence."[83] In reality, Buddhist and Hindu attitudes to other species bear considerable similarity to that of the Western Great Chain of Being – sometimes respectful and sometimes not. In much of the advocacy literature, however, we are offered an exclusively positive interpretation of the Buddhist and Hindu material, and an exclusively negative interpretation of that of the West.

On a visit to Java, Tagore went to the great Buddhist temple at Borobudur, where he was delighted by the sculpted, loving depictions of everyday life. "I remember," he remarked, "having seen in my childhood a cow with its tender eyes, coming up and licking a washerman's donkey tied to a peg – and how I was wonderstruck! The [Buddhist temple] writer would have had no hesitation in asserting that the Buddha in one of his births was such a cow ... Thanks to Buddhism, the whole course of life has been invested with glory." These are inspiring words, accurately depicting both the depths of Tagore's own reverence and a magnificent aspect of Buddhism. In the Western world, they have their counterpart in Wordsworth and Percy Shelley, both of whom Tagore admired deeply. Yet if Tagore and the cow are a genuine part of Eastern reality, so too is the dirty, uncared-for washerman's donkey – as well, of course, as the uncaring washerman.

II

In his "journey of discovery to the jungles of old Ceylon" (now Sri Lanka), Christopher Ondaatje writes of H.H. Engelbrecht, the sadistic and hated first warden of the Yala National Park in the early years of the twentieth century, who "was known to whip villagers and [who] controlled his subordinates with an iron hand."[84] The Sinhalese Buddhists took their revenge by beheading the warden's prize bulls and murdering his pet bear cub. Understandable certainly, justifiable possibly, but scarcely the actions of people who revere other species. The animals must have been seen by the Buddhists not as worthwhile entities in themselves but solely as appendages, appurtenances, property, of the detested warden. Professor Htin Aung of the University of Rangoon, commenting on George Orwell's 1936 Burmese story "Shooting an Elephant," tells us that at that time few of the at least nominally Buddhist Burmese "attached any special significance to the destruction of the beasts – except, of course, the owners."[85]

Despite the fact that Hindu farmers do sometimes kill their supposedly sacred cows,[86] and despite the deplorable conditions of animals in general in India, Hinduism does offer a reverential attitude, but one, again, often contradicted by practice. Thus, Gandhi himself believed that cows were treated more cruelly in India than anywhere else. "How we bleed her to take the last drop of milk from her. How we starve her to emaciation, how we ill-treat the calves, how we deprive them of their portion of milk, how cruelly we treat the oxen, how we castrate them, how we beat them, how we overload them."[87] Similar stories were always told by the representatives of Raj imperialism, but are readily, and often justifiably, dismissed by intellectuals as mere prejudice. Perhaps the words of Gandhi are not so readily dismissed.

Today in Bangkok, Thailand, one may see as many as half a dozen birds crammed into a small cage and being offered for sale near the shrine of the four-faced Buddha. Devotees purchase and release the caged birds to declare their affinity with nature. But, of course, that means other Buddhists capture and cage the birds – that is, they deprive them of their freedom and incarcerate them cruelly – just for the worshippers to release. This practice is surely little different from the situation in sixteenth-century Florence when Leonardo da Vinci would purchase and release captured birds, or from the circumstances in eighteenth-century England where William Blake felt compelled to cry, "A Robin Red breast in a Cage / Puts all Heaven in a Rage."[88] Or, from when Anton Chekhov would purchase woodpeckers captured by peasant boys and release them. Or, from the occasion in 1905 when Virginia Woolf let loose a caged bird that was singing by Fielding's tomb in Portugal. Of course, there is abundant, often petty, cruelty in the West. But it is matched by the message of Tagore's *Glimpses of Bengal* (1921), in which we read of the tiny cowherd prodding a gigantic docile buffalo for no good reason – other than to assert the otherwise oppressed cowherd's ego. Even the young Gandhi's favourite pastime, according to his sister Raliat, "was twisting dog's ears." How reminiscent of so much in the novels of Charles Dickens.

Why, one must ask, is there such a discrepancy between reverential theory and less than reverential practice? Of course, discrepancy is everywhere, but sometimes in the Orient the practice appears totally at odds with the theory. Tagore, of exalted if unorthodox Brahminic stock, required the pupils in his school to abstain from flesh. Yet he delighted in explaining how he learned to capture lumbering turtles by turning them on their backs. "The meat was excellent," he reported, "as were the eggs buried in the sand." In Beijing, China, it is illegal to have a pet dog. The police kill them whenever they find them. In January 1994, the *Globe and Mail* newspaper reported Li Wenrui, deputy chief of public security of the East City district, as saying, "We beat 351 dogs to death in the past week. Our policy is to annihilate them ... My men make their own dog-beating weapons. They use metal poles with steel wires at the end ... You thrust the wire hoop over the dog's head and then you strangle it."[89] To be sure, the "dog-killing movement" only began a couple of years after the Communists came to power in 1949 – Mao Tse Tung deeming pet-keeping "bourgeois decadence" – but it is at least reflective of a less than pervasive concern with the well-being of other species. Indeed, in China at any one time, more than 5,000 Asiatic black bears are farmed for their gall bladder bile, and this practice has been going on for centuries. At a zoo near Shenzhen in China, visitors are invited (as of spring 1995) to pay a small fee for the privilege of tossing a live hen to the tigers. A sign on the chicken coop advertises: "The stronger animal will kill the smaller ones in this exciting game." Exciting perhaps, but decidedly not respectful. Nor is this attitude a recent Marxist innovation. Indeed, if consideration for other species had been an en endemic part of the Chinese tradition, the Marxists would have had to change cultural attitudes. They did not need to. Sun-tzu's *The Art of War,* perhaps of the sixth century BC but as yet of uncertain date, leaves us in little doubt that traditionally horses were treated less than reverentially in China. Indeed, for military reasons horses in combat were often "the prime target."[90] This fact is perhaps scarcely surprising, but it is the kind of information that ought to suggest that there were no essential differences between the Orient and the Occident – where, during wars, vast numbers of horses, oxen, and donkeys were used for transportation of supplies. In seventeenth-century France, a minimum of twenty-five horses were needed to tow the largest field artillery pieces, and horses were still being used for that purpose in the First World War. The misuse of military horses was so rampant both before and during the Boer War that Thomas Hardy and his wife Emma attempted to arouse public sympathy to have their use restricted to transportation. One might well be impressed by the statement of the *Dhammapada* of the third century BC that "who hurts not any living being, whether feeble or strong, who neither kills nor causes to kill – him I call a Brahmin" (Aphorism 405). But one must acknowledge that the influence of the *Dhammapada* on Oriental life is no greater than that of St. Francis on the modern West.[91]

In Bangladesh, rhinoceros, yak, and several species of monkey have been extirpated. Elephants, royal Bengal tigers, crocodiles, lizards, frogs, snakes, and dozens of species of birds are on the endangered list. While a 25 percent proportion of forest is needed to maintain an appropriate ecological balance, only 6 percent remains forested. Bangladesh is an Islamic state and hence does not profess a belief system that makes extensive claims about an identity of the human with nature. Muhammad proclaimed that "the angels will not enter a house in which there is a picture or a dog." Nonetheless, Bangladesh is only the worst example of the general trend throughout Asia to a depleted fauna and devastated flora. Certainly, we should not imagine Islam to lack all concern for the animal realm, but it is often insufficient to protect those in need of protection. Other interests are often put first, as indeed they are in the rest of the world. The complexity of the falconry problem in Islamic Pakistan reflects animal protection problems everywhere. In the nineteenth century, falconry was popular in Sindh – indeed Sir Richard Francis Burton wrote a book called *Falconry in the Valley of the Indus* in 1852 – but by the middle of this century, the practice was moribund until revived by wealthy visiting Arabs. Falcons can be trained to hunt almost anything – deer, gazelle, and ducks included – but in practice in Pakistan, the endangered buzzard is the primary object of the chase. As a consequence of Pakistani environmentalist demands, buzzard hunting has been banned for Pakistanis – but not for foreigners, who kill almost 10,000 buzzards per year. And, despite the ban, Pakistanis kill an estimated 2,000 to 3,000 more. The government, whose dilemma must evoke our sympathy, considers the vast amount of money spent by the wealthy Arabs from the Middle East oil states to be a greater boon to the Pakistani economy than the detriment to environmental health occasioned by the hunting. It is considered a rare opportunity to provide the capital necessary to raise the living standards of many impoverished Pakistanis. But abominable cruelty is the consequence. To capture the prized great falcons, smaller ones are used as bait. The Pakistanis tie weights to the smaller falcons and suture their eyes so they cannot fly. When released they become immediate prey to the large falcons which swoop down on them and are in turn captured. Thousands of smaller falcons are killed in this manner annually. As Christopher Ondaatje understated after a recent visit, "It really is quite cruel."

III

We are often chastised with the claim that other cultures have a positive attitude toward other species as a whole while the West lacks such an appreciation of nature. Thus, for example, Joseph Campbell, having commented on the negativity of the biblical serpent, tells us, "The snake in most cultures is given a positive interpretation. In India, even the most poisonous snake, the cobra is a sacred animal."[92] In similar vein, Miriam T. Gross assures us, "The Bible set the first curse on snakes: 'upon your belly shall you go,' said the Lord to the serpent of Eden, 'and dust you shall eat all the days of your life.' But not all cultures turned their backs on reptiles. In Buddhist belief it was the serpent that, coiling itself under a meditating Buddha, held him safely up out of the great flood. To Hindus, snakes were symbols of fertility and wisdom. In Egypt, crocodiles were worshipped as protectors of the Nile."[93] And in *Island* (1962), Aldous Huxley contrasts the snake – respecting views of Buddhism with the serpent story of Genesis. Certainly, the snake sheds its skin and is, accordingly, a potent symbol of death and rebirth. Indeed, even in the West, the caduceus – the herald's wand of the messenger god Hermes (Mercury) with two snakes coiled around the wand beneath a winged mount – is the general symbol of the medical arts. By the tradition of *The Mabinogian*, King Arthur's sword had "a design of two serpents on the golden hilt." It would be unwise to ignore Milton in *Paradise Lost:* "And God said: Let the Waters generate / Reptile with spawn abundant, living soul." A depiction of a serpent with its tail in its mouth, symbolizing the circle of eternity, is commonly found on eighteenth- and nineteenth-century New England gravestones. And in Voltaire's *The White Bull,* the serpent is a "wise ... handsome ... friend" who "sought to do women good," albeit unsuccessfully.

However, one should be careful not to confuse symbols with a "positive interpretation" in either the West or the East. In India, the cobra is indeed worshipped. Yet we read in F. Marion Crawford's *Mr. Isaacs: A Tale of Modern India* (1882) that "the Hindoo servant hates the cold. He fears it as he fears cobras, fever and the freemasons."[94] Fear is indeed the rational emotion. Before the religious ceremony involving the cobras, the snakes' mouths are customarily sewn shut. In 1994, the Indian government released dozens of such tortured – yet worshipped! – cobras back into the wild, after the sutures had been removed, of course. Non-killing was a fundamental principle at Gandhi's commune at Phoenix in South Africa. Yet a poisonous snake was killed without complaint from Gandhi. The Greek poet Stasinus announced that where there is fear there is also reverence. In the *Euthyphro,* Plato has Socrates proclaim that "where reverence is, there is fear."[95] Hobbes insists that all reverence, all worship, is based in fear. One certainly does not have to go all the way with the cynics to recognize that there might be apparent reverence for certain species without there being a positive evaluation of them. Indeed, that is how one is inclined to interpret the South Pacific Tuamoton worship of the shark. When one lives at the edge of shark-infested waters, experience teaches a rational fear that is *expressed* as a form of reverential respect – without there ever being a positive evaluation of the creature that has devoured or maimed some of one's relatives. Indeed, fear of the shark was such in the River Bonny region of Nigeria in the 1880s that physician and author Arthur Conan Doyle reported the practice of human sacrifice to the shark. If "reverence" or "respect" lead to human sacrifice, we might well learn to be wary of such respectful reverence.

In the Mahayana Buddhist sacred scripture *The Lotus Sutra,* there is a decided lack of respect for the snake. With reference to he who has maligned the holy text, we read:

And after he has died
he will be born again in the body of a serpent,
long and huge in size,
measuring five hundred yojanas,
deaf, witless, without feet,
slithering along on his belly,
with little creatures
biting and feeding on him,
day and night undergoing hardship,
never knowing rest.
Because he slandered this sutra,
this is the punishment he will incur.[96]

Furthermore, in the *Rubaiyat* of Omar Khayyam, we read:

> Oh, Thou, who Man of baser earth didst make
> And who with Eden didst devise the Snake;
> > For all the Sin wherewith the Face of Man
> Is blacken'd, Man's Forgiveness give – and take![97]

Buddhists, Hindus, and Moslems as well as Christians found the snake less than wholesome. In Mesopotamia's *Epic of Gilgamesh* of 5,000 years ago, the serpent plays a very similar role to the one it plays in the Bible. In Zoroastrian legend, it is the evil Ahriman who created the poisonous snakes. As we have seen,[98] the K'iche" Maya welcomed their new religion as they escaped animism for astronomy, because it turned the most vicious predators, including snakes, into stone. That is, it rendered the odious innocuous. In Buddhist Burma in the eleventh century, King Anawrahta eliminated *naga* (serpent) worship for similar reasons. And it is not only in Christianity but also among the Bassari of West Africa that the serpent is presented as the prime beguiler. In reality, the snake, especially the venomous snake, and other harmful reptiles, are seen as odious in most societies, both where they are worshipped and where they are not. The Western attitude toward snakes in particular, and ambivalence to the animal world in general, is epitomized in Arthur Conan Doyle's autobiographical *Memories and Adventures*. Again on the River Bonny, he came upon "an evil-looking snake, worm-coloured and about 3 feet long. I shot him and saw him drift down stream. I learned later in life to give up killing animals, but I confess that I have no particular compunctions about that one." The intrepid Hemingway, hunter of the most fearsome of big game, still confessed himself "scared of snakes and touching each root and branch with snake fear in the dark ... [they] scare me sick ... They always have." Saul Bellow approached the sublime in describing intellectuals as "ruling reptiles."

With regard to animal worship, it is important to distinguish between reverence and awe derived from fear or terror (from the sublime) and a reverence and awe based on love, admiration, and wonder (beauty). The latter shows a respect for the being as an entity in itself, reflecting an evaluation of its finer qualities; the former often reflects the urgency to escape the consequences of the worshipped being's wrath, while also, in some instances, admiring its powers.

Animal worship reflects a prayer to be excused one's iniquities toward the animal, a prayer to provide continued sustenance and usage, a prayer to acquire the animal's characteristics (for example, power and strength), or a prayer to escape its potential harm. Occasionally, the reverence will be reminiscent of Pythagoras and metempsychosis when, for example, the animal is thought to possess the soul of a departed human, as with the Fraser River sturgeon of British Columbia, which are considered by the Sto:lo Indians to be reincarnations of those who perished in the depths.

Rarely is the worship related to a respect and affection for the being in its own essential self, its own *quidditas* or "whatness" (to borrow Aquinas's term), its *haeccitas* (to borrow the word of Duns Scotus [1270-1308], translated nicely as "thinghood" by Gerard Manley Hopkins). The "thinghood" of the animal, Aristotle's *telos*, Plato's *Form* – allowing the compatibility I proposed earlier[99] – is usually ignored in animal worship. Worship is predominantly for the benefit of the worshipper. Animals that are neither feared nor food nor feigned are not customarily the object of prayer.

Certainly, just as in the Western tradition, there are many Asian individuals who demonstrate the greatest respect for non-human species and a horror at animal sacrifice – again, none more than the revered Gandhi himself. In his autobiography, he writes of an occasion he was visiting the Kali temple in Bengal where he engaged in conversation one of the religious mendicants he encountered:

> I saw a stream of sheep going to be sacrificed to Kali ... I asked him: "Do you regard this sacrifice as religion?"
>
> "Who would regard killing of animals as religion?"
>
> "Then, why don't you preach against it?"
>
> "That's not my business. Our business is to worship God ... it is no business of us *sadhus*."
>
> We did not prolong the discussion but passed on to the temple. We were greeted by rivers of blood. I could not bear to stand there. I was exasperated and restless. I have never forgotten that sight.
>
> That very evening I had an invitation to dinner at a party of Bengali friends. There I spoke to a friend about this cruel form of worship. He said: "The sheep don't feel anything. The noise and the drum-beating there deaden all sensation of pain.'
>
> I could not swallow this. I told him that, if the sheep had speech, they would tell a different tale. I felt that the cruel custom ought to be stopped ...
>
> I hold today the same opinion as I held then. To my mind the life of a lamb is no less precious than that of a human being. I should be unwilling to take the life of a lamb for the sake of the human body. I hold that, the more helpless a creature, the more entitled it is to protection by man from the cruelty of men ... How is it that Bengal with all its knowledge, intelligence, sacrifice, and emotion tolerates this slaughter?

Rationalization in India appears little different from the rationalization one encounters in the West: "Sure, it's wrong, but it's not my job." "They don't *really* suffer in sacrifice" in the same way that they are *really* transported humanely to, and slaughtered humanely at, the Western abattoir. In reality, there are humanitarian Gandhis countered by sacrificial rationalizers in India just as there are humanitarian Robert Louis Stevensons confronted by experimentation rationalizers in the West.

IV

Despite the contradictions both among religious pronouncements and between religious pronouncements and practice, there are probably more explicitly animal-considerate messages in some of the Oriental religious traditions than in any other traditions. Christopher Key Chapple refers to several of these in his *Nonviolence to Animals, Earth and Self in Asian Traditions*,[100] a book that deals in greater depth with this issue than any other of which I am aware. There, we can read of the Jain concept of *ahimsa* (nonviolence) and the success of the Jains in influencing other religious thought systems, especially Buddhism but also Hinduism, to incorporate the principle into their own systems. Chapple quotes the words of the *Acaranga Sutra* of the fourth century BC, which are considered to epitomize the Jain tradition: "To do harm to others is to do harm to oneself. 'Thou art he whom thou intendest to kill! Thou art he whom thou intendest to tyrannize over.' We corrupt ourselves as soon as we intend to corrupt others. We kill ourselves as soon as we intend to kill them."[101]

One is struck, though it is not mentioned by Chapple, by the similarity with the kinship ideas of Pythagoras and Empedocles among the Presocratics. Equally one can recognize here the intimations of Blake, Baudelaire, Henry Fielding, and Saul Bellow, as well as Plato.[102] The words of Henry Salt in *Seventy Years among Savages* are almost identical: "All sentient life is akin ... he who injures a fellow being is in fact doing injury to himself." The principles of altruism, of treating others as oneself, along with acknowledgment of the sins of intention as well as of action, are also present generally in Western thought, not least in the Bible. Thus: "Blessed are the merciful" (Matthew 5:7); "Love thy neighbour as thyself" (19:19); "Insomuch as ye have done it unto one of the least of these my brethren, ye have done it unto me" (25:40); "A new commandment I give unto you, That ye love one another" (John 13:34); "Greater love hath no man than this, that a man lay down his life for his friends" (15:13). Chapple leaves us with the impression of a Jain exclusivity. In fact, most religions have more in common than those who make a case for the virtues of any one of them would wish to acknowledge. Nor should this surprise us. The common moral intuitions of humankind are represented in all religions. As Tolstoy wrote in *What Is Religion?*, "Religions differ in their external forms but are all the same in their basic principles." Indeed, this belief is the very basis of the Bahai faith and has a profound impact on Unitarianism.

Nonetheless, what distinguishes the Jain principle of *ahimsa* from similar altruistic principles in other moral systems is its incontrovertible emphasis on its application to non-humans. While some, such as Andrew Linzey,[103] argue convincingly that significant non-human considerations are both implicit and explicit in biblical doctrine, and while many Western individuals have held compatible views, no other religion has been so emphatic as Jainism in its proclamation.

Again in the *Acaranga Sutra* (1.1.5), one may read that "all beings are fond of life; they like pleasure and hate pain, shun destruction and like to live. To all, life is dear." Again one is struck by Western similarities (including the palpable errors – neither lions killing hyena cubs, cats killing more mice than they need for food, nor deer ravaging deciduous forests is consistent with the notion that all beings shun destruction). Utilitarians will proclaim that all beings seek to maximize pleasure and minimize pain. Rousseau tells us that animals attempt to avoid causing injury to others, that the horse will go to some lengths to ensure that it does not tread on another animal that gets in its way. Both Tolstoy and Schweitzer proclaim all life to be sacred. What distinguishes Jainism is that as an organized entity it has sought, with some success, to influence the adoption of vegetarianism and the elimination of animal sacrifice in India and elsewhere in Asia. (It is certainly worth noting here that Western animal advocates would have had no need to engage in the latter enterprise, animal sacrifice having been abandoned, with a few exceptions, many centuries earlier.) While the Jains are small in number – around 0.5 percent of India's population – their influence has been greater than one could possibly have expected from those numbers.

Thus, Chapple argues that, as a consequence of the Jain tradition, one may read in the Hindu *Yajur Veda:* "May all beings look at me with a friendly eye, may I do likewise, and may we look on each other with the eyes of a friend."[104] With apparently similar impetus, one may read in the *Mahabharata* that "the meat of other animals is like the flesh of one's son."[105] According to the Buddhist *Mahavagga*, Gautama proclaimed: "A *bikkhu* [monk] who has received ordination ought not intentionally to destroy the life of any living being down to a worm or an ant."[106] And the principle of kinship, in a manner reminiscent not only of the Pythagoreans but also, if to a lesser degree, of Borelli, Goethe, Emerson, Balzac, and Darwin,[107] is expressed emphatically in the *Lankavatara Sutra* of Mahayana Buddhism: "In the long course of samsàra [flux], there is not one among living beings with form who has not been mother, father, brother, sister, son, or daughter, or some other relative. Being connected with the process of taking birth, one is kin to all wild and domestic animals, birds, and beings born from the womb."[108] While there are significant differences between the idea of reincarnation and those of the great chain and evolution, nonetheless the principle of kinship is present in all. Indeed, the notion that "there is but one animal" appears common to both Oriental and Western traditions – but not universal in either.

Whether or not the Jain principle of *ahimsa* is indeed, as Chapple argues, the primary source of these Hindu and Buddhist beliefs, we should certainly rejoice in their expression and the subscription they enjoy in Asia. While the Confucians and Taoists withstood the vegetarian persuasions of the Jains via the Buddhists and declared humankind entitled to its superiority,

Chinese Buddhists became even more emphatically vegetarian, and in greater proportions, than their counterparts elsewhere in the Orient, where, generally speaking, it is only Buddhist monks and the Brahmin caste who are expected to remain strictly vegetarian (though even here there are exceptions).

From the perspective of the animal, there is much to be welcomed in the *philosophies* of the Orient. It is unfortunate, however, that those who write to praise Eastern thought systems rarely recognize the worth of their Western counterparts and fail to notice the negative aspects of the Eastern traditions.

Professor Chapple is certainly less sinning than many.[109] He mentions Hindu animal sacrifice, which is still practised in Nepal and Orissa. (Animal sacrifice is still practised in Pakistan and Bangladesh, too, notably, but by no means solely, on the occasion of the Haj, the annual pilgrimage to Mecca.) He acknowledges the limitations to the practice of vegetarianism among Hindus and Buddhists. He recognizes the manner in which modern technology is welcomed by Indians for its potential bringing of wealth, even though its devastation of the environment is unparalleled. Nonetheless, he fails, as do most others who comment on benevolence toward the animal realm in Oriental philosophy, to mention the passages in the *Laws of Manu, The Tibetan Book of the Dead, The Lotus Sutra,*[110] or many other Eastern scriptures that treat other species in a far from respectful manner. He has a section on Gandhi but refrains from mentioning his strictures against Indian practices. He refrains from mentioning cockfighting and other "sporting" practices that reflect a less than respectful attitude. He refrains from mentioning that today in India some 200 sloth bears per annum are poached from their dens to endure an unwholesome life as dancing entertainers. Almost half the cubs die in their first year. The survivors suffer two nose-piercings with a carpet needle – without anaesthetic – to facilitate the attachment of a rope through their nostrils. The canine teeth are removed by hammering an iron rod into the tooth – again without anaesthetic. The bears are taught to dance by tugging and twisting on the rope, and by beating on their feet with a heavy club. They are fed an unnatural diet and spend most of their lives firmly tethered. To write of Indian philosophy – and that one-sidedly – and to ignore the less wholesome aspects of Indian reality is to mislead the reader.

Chapple has decidedly different standards for judging the West than judging the East. He tells us that "the status accorded to animals in most cultures, especially those arising from Europe and America, regards animals to have no such kinship relationship. The book of Genesis and the writings of Aristotle, Augustine, Aquinas, Descartes, and others have justified the position that animals exist solely for human exploitation."[111] Clearly his reading of the philosophers he mentions is one-sided. Moreover, one wonders why Chapple chooses these thinkers as representative of the Western tradition. Why not Leonardo, More, Montaigne, Locke, Herder, or

Schopenhauer? Why, one wonders, is the kinship principle claimed not to exist in the West when Pythagoras, Rousseau, Goethe, and Darwin, indeed many of the advocates of the Great Chain of Being, proclaim otherwise? In fact, not one major Western thinker has argued that "animals exist solely for human exploitation." To be sure, and regrettably, several have argued that they are "intended for man's use," but a close inspection of such writings will reveal that there is invariably a greater complexity in which the worthwhileness of animals is also acknowledged. Moreover, in terms of exploitation, one can find it every bit as readily in all parts of the East as in the West. Such diatribes against the West serve to paint a misleading picture. When Hindus and Buddhists use bullocks to pull their carts, they too subscribe to the doctrine that animals are "intended for man's use."

Professor Chapple continues with the claim that the Jain and Buddhist "traditions both view animals as: sentient beings. Animals are said to have feelings and emotions and to be able to improve themselves, at least in some of the various parables that are cited. While Westerners may dismiss this as merely a naive anthropomorphism, it is instead a deeply rooted cultural perspective."[112] The implication of this passage would appear to be that the Western tradition denies self-improvement, feelings, and emotions to animals. Explicitly, the Aristotle denounced by Chapple declared all species capable of self-actualization. In *Kangaroo*, D.H. Lawrence elaborated the idea: "Every creature, even an ant or a louse [is] individually in contact with the life-urge which we call God. To call this connection the will to live is not quite sufficient. It is more than a will-to-persist. It is a will-to-live in the future sense, a will-to-change, a will-to-evolve, a will toward further creation of the self." While one could make a case that some of the Cartesians and their intellectual successors (but perhaps not Descartes himself) denied feelings and emotions to animals, in general Western thinkers have readily acknowledged that at least certain complex animals do possess them. The problem of anthropomorphism is customarily less about the existence of emotions and feelings in other species than it is about assuming that animal behaviour prima facie similar to human behaviour may be explained or described by similar emotions. Indeed, we must maintain two competing principles if we are to understand other species: that "there is but one animal" (that is, all animals share certain organizational principles in common); and that each species is unique (that is, while there is common organizational principle, each species differs from the other in terms of its species-specific needs, and each individual animal is entitled to be treated as an end). Those traditions that assume only the first to be true understand and respect animals less than those that acknowledge the reality of both. To assume that other species possess similar emotions to humans is potentially to deny them their uniqueness. As Lucretius wrote appositely 2,000 years ago, "each species develops according to its own kind, and they all guard their specific characters in obedience to the laws of nature" (*On the Naure of the Universe,* v, 922-4). If we do not understand each animal in its *telos,* its *quidditas,* its *haeccitas,* its "thinghood," we cannot truly respect it.

Certainly, Chapple regards the Indian and Chinese traditions of animal storytelling as reflective of a deep Eastern concern for the animal realm. But if that is sound evidence, one wonders why he ignores the similar tradition in the West, from Androcles (St. Jerome in many medieval tales) and the lion, through the fable and fairy-tale tradition, to the stories of Jonathan Swift. Should they not be judged by the same criteria?

Chapple described the palanquin said to have been worn by Mahavira, the founder of Jainism, which was adorned with the pictures of several species: "This scene with its great variety of creatures is like that found in the Indus valley seals and echoed in later Indian iconography as well. It can be interpreted as depicting harmony with nature and, I might add, it could provide early evidence of reverence for all living beings."[113] So it can. So it could. But how, then, should one interpret the early Western artistic tradition? To take a few instances at random of not dissimilar vintage: a Corinthian jug of about 600 BC, now in the British Museum, is decorated with lions, serpents, and panther-birds; an Athenian mixing bowl of similar date (Antikensammlungen, Munich) is adorned with lions and horses; a third-century Roman mosaic of doves around a bowl is to be found in the Capitoline Museum in Rome; in the Sta Constanza in the same city, we can view a fourth-century mosaic of a peacock, a red-winged blackbird, and fruit trees. If the palanquin reflects early veneration in India, would we not be compelled, if we are to be consistent, to interpret the Western antiquities in a similar manner? And what then would we do with our image of the iniquities of the Roman games? Given what Gandhi and Campbell tell us of the realities of India, would it not be more in keeping with the evidence to recognize the divisions, ambivalence, indeed the downright contradictions of both West and East? Certainly, we should be wary of Chapple's claim that the path to animal rights is to be found in the Eastern tradition, to the exclusion of most others, especially those derived from Europe and America. Above all, what is required in any comparison between East and West is that we not be persuaded to rely on a selective and utopian representation of either.

V

Clearly, if Buddhism, Taoism, and Hinduism claim such a respect for the natural environment, one is required to ask why that respect is not generally realized in those areas where these thought systems predominate. The answer, in a word, is "Quietism." While there is much beauty, wisdom, and compassion in Oriental thought, there is also disengagement. Quietism may be epitomized by the words of the Chinese philosopher Mencius, circa 300 BC: "The principle of the [mountain sage] Yang Chu is: 'Each one for himself.' Though he might have benefited the whole empire by plucking out a single hair, he would not have done it."[114] Thus, for example, the young Thomas Mann wrote to his brother Heinrich "of a truly Indian passivity."[115] But it involves something beyond a resignation to, or acquiescence in, the inevitabilities of life – something closer to a joyous acceptance of them, much in the manner of Quakers. The Chinese concept of *wu wei* involves a non-assertion, a non-forcing, of those things discovered within the self on the world outside the self. One rejoices in the recognition of the world in both its splendours and its miseries, one accepts a responsibility of benevolence, but one leaves all others to seek their own salvation in their own recognitions. Its most complete Western counterpart is to be found in the iconoclastic Oscar Wilde who felt the poet Maurice Rollinat's drug addiction to be his own concern. Asked whether he would not help a man who had thrown himself into the river, Wilde replied, "I should consider it an act of gross impertinence to do so." In Oscar Wilde, we encounter the fullness of Epicurus's "autarkeia," a philosophy of individual self-sufficiency, offering a resounding "no" to Cain's question about being his brother's keeper. As Alban G. Widgery expressed the Oriental conception, "There is no arousing of ardent enthusiasm or strenuous effort for the general welfare of mankind. The impression is rather simply the avoidance of harm to others."[116] And if there is no "strenuous effort for the general welfare of mankind," there is similarly no strenuous effort on behalf of the animal realm. However benevolent toward other species the doctrines may be said to be, in general the animals go unprotected. There is, however, a significant exception to the Oriental quietist tradition: the Jains. Their activism has not only succeeded in changing the face of Eastern philosophy but it has also vastly improved the animal reality of the Orient. As everywhere though, much remains to be done, not least to eliminate animal sacrifice entirely.

In a striking poem about a ten-year-old boy who prefers the company of animals to people, Rabindranath Tagore wrote:

> A poet who is truly of the boy's world
> > Would put that dung-beetle into so vivid a rhyme
> He would not put it down.
> Have I ever managed to reach the heart of a frog
> > Or caught the tragedy of that piebald dog?

The answer, as Tagore recognizes, is probably "no" for both Eastern and Western poets. But the best of both may be recognized in part by their approximation to that ideal.

Cultural Relativism

Some will insist that the compilation of this evidence and argument is unjust to Aboriginal and Oriental societies, or worse, and that every instance of cruelty adduced can be explained and justified as an aspect of some economic or cultural necessity, or as something occasioned by the wrongs of others. First, if a need for justification is recognized, there is a tacit acknowledgment that there is something less than worthy in itself that requires such a justification. Second, if every instance of Aboriginal or Oriental cruelty can be explained away by reference to cultural and/or economic exigences, then, to be consistent, so can every instance of cruelty in Western civilization. If cultural and economic conditions determine behaviour, or even justify behaviour, then there is little point in positing Aboriginal cultures, Oriental values, or anything else, for that matter, as some kind of ideal. If we are willing to castigate Western society for its failure to live in harmony with nature, there can be no justification for not applying the same criteria to tribal and Oriental societies. And, surely, behaviour is more important than pious prose in influencing our judgments.

One may also expect to hear the response that individuals from one culture cannot legitimately critique the belief system or practices of another culture by their own standards, or that two different cultures cannot be judged by the same criteria. And there is a certain limited truth in such assertions. Nonetheless, we should note, as but one example of many, that the Naskapi Indians denigrated the Inuit as being no better than animals because they ate raw meat and fish. Amerindians are thus not immune to the practice of cultural denigration – and in their denigration of the Inuit and the animals, they demonstrated, against the dictates of their mythology, that they thought neither of their human neighbours, nor of other species, as their brothers or sisters. Tibetan nomads (Bhotia) look down on their neighbours who cultivate the land. They deem farmers "slaves to the endless toil of nature."[117] Western prejudice is neither more pervasive nor more objectionable than Asian or Amerindian prejudice.

If we are to take the cultural relativism argument seriously, we will be required to acknowledge that there are no adequate criteria for condemning the atrocities of Nazism, the human rights violations at Tiananmen Square, the burning of the oil wells by Saddam Hussein, or the environmental devastation wrought by any but one's own "greedy capitalists." If such judgments are legitimate – or, indeed, if any moral judgments are legitimate – it must be conceded that there are at least elements of a moral law common to humanity rather than one restricted to each culture.

As the celebrated Dr. Samuel Johnson wrote of the ethical relativist, "If he does really think that there is no distinction between virtue and vice, why, Sir, when he leaves our houses let us count our spoons."[118] In the final analysis, the relativist argument from culture implies in Leibnitzian or Spinozan manner "what is, is right." If it is legitimate to criticize Western civilization for its failings, it must be equally legitimate to criticize others. It is astonishing, in fact, given the sheer illogicality, how often the advocacy intelligentsia tell us that we cannot judge others by our standards, while insisting on judging us by the standards of others. It is astonishing too how often those who insist that we should revere nature show no reverence at all for their compatriots as a part of that nature.

In response to those who claim we have no right to judge other cultures, Wendy Doniger responds: "The agenda of humanistic scholarship argues that we do have the right to challenge their arguments as we would challenge anyone's arguments, that we cannot simply endorse their faith statements. The solution is a compromise: we must try to state fairly what they are saying, and to understand why they think they are right, but we must also say what we think, and we must try to be honest in stating why we think we are right."[119] In fact, if we do not acknowledge the validity of Doniger's claim, we must restrict commentary on fascism to fascists, on capitalism to capitalists, on Marxism to Marxists, on larceny to thieves, and on pedophilia to child molesters. If we do not accept Doniger's claim, it is difficult to understand how we could regard genocide as anything other than a cultural characteristic rather than a heinous wrong.

Let us not, however, be misled into a return to our former prejudiced cultural isolationism with its attendant disrespect for cultures other than our own. Aboriginal culture contains many truly admirable elements, from Mayan and Andean textile weaving, through Dogon communitarianism and astronomy, San egalitarianism, Mongol hospitality, Tlingit conceptions of justice, Apache horse skills, the x-ray art of Australian Aborigines, the honour of the Zulu, and the courage of the Maasai, to the great legends, tribal dignity, reverential mystique, and belongingness that are the central elements of tribal culture generally. For my own part, Hinduism, especially, but also Jainism, Buddhism, and Taoism, have been instrumental in helping me refine my Western sensibilities. Let us admire Aboriginal, "archaic," traditional, and Oriental cultures for what they are, though, not for what they are claimed to be when the claims are countered by the evidence. Respect for other cultures requires that they be treated and judged consistently with our own – and ours with theirs. The obverse of that is racism. Wilful blindness is no substitute for an honest sympathy.

The West needs to re-evaluate its relationship to nature. Indeed, it is already in the process of doing so, and has been for over three decades. But it should look first to its own traditions, marrying scientific objectivity with animal and other natural sensibilities, within a habit of activism rather than Quietism. Quietism is "the coward's way out," according to Robert Louis Stevenson explicitly, according to Gandhi by precept, and according to the Jains by centuries of proselytization. Of course, one may – indeed, one should – refine one's sensibilities through an awareness of the perceptive insights of others, but these insights should serve to arouse one's consciousness within one's own traditions.

When the West acknowledges its pride in its purported superiority over other species to be grossly exaggerated, it possesses a philosophy as capable as any other of incorporating the interests of non-human species within its edifice. It should, however, retain a pride in its own traditions, for not only are they worthy, but they are the very source of communal identity.

8
Gaea and the Universal Spirit

1   We have implanted in us the seed of all ages, of all arts.

                       – Seneca, *De beneficiis*, c. AD 40

2   Whoever is born anywhere as a human being, that is, as a rational
mortal creature, however strange he may appear to our senses in
bodily form or colour or motion or utterance, or in any faculty,
part or quality of his nature whatsoever, let no true believer have
any doubt that such an individual is descended from the one man
who was first created.

                       – St. Augustine, *City of God*, c. AD 420

3   Man is conscious of a universal soul within or behind his individual life, wherein, as in a firmament, the natures of Justice,
Truth, Love, Freedom, arise and shine.

                       – Ralph Waldo Emerson, *Nature*, 1836

4   I had one glimpse of a huge pine-forested ravine upon my left, a
foaming river, a sky already coloured with the fires of dawn. I am
usually very calm over the displays of nature; but you will scarcely
believe how my heart leaped at this. It was like meeting one's
wife. I had come home again – home from the unsightly deserts to
the greens and habitable corners of the earth. Every spire of pine

along the hill-top, every trouty pool along that mountain river,
was more dear to me than a blood-relation.

> – Robert Louis Stevenson, *The Amateur Emigrant,*
> 1880

5   Naturalists who accept the theory of evolution, consider that
every individual contains within itself, so to say, a history of
the race.

> – Sir John Lubbock, *The Beauties of Nature,* 1892

6   It is not wisdom to be only wise
And on inward vision close the eyes.

> – George Santayana (1863-1952)

7   So the swallow, if not my brother, is at least a cousin, and all life is one.

> – Louis J. Halle, *The Appreciation of Birds,* 1989

8   [The Judeo-Christian serpent] offered Eve the apple from the tree of
knowledge. That apple symbolized the beginnings of culture, hunting
and gathering, the domestication of plants and animals, and ultimately modern science and technology. For the first time, I was glad
that Eve had tasted the forbidden fruit. Nature had offered humans a
way out, through the developments of culture. We have clothes, shelter, cultivated food, medicine. As I visualized one lone [orangutan]
nest swaying somewhere in the green canopy with Carl's bones and
another with Cara's maggot-ridden remains, I wept. Nature had not
offered them a way out. [Carl and Cara were among the orangutans
Galdikas was studying and to whom she had become attached.]

> – Biruté Galdikas, *Reflections of Eden,* 1995

I

As I write, I am listening to an inspired recording of David Oistrakh playing
Beethoven's Violin Concerto in D – the music, the violin, and the audio
technology are all products of Western civilization; although it is a cold late

winter's day, I am able to watch the wonder of breaking ice floes as they rush down the river from the warmth and comfort of my brick home; I can sip a fine cup of coffee although coffee will not grow within many hundreds of miles of my home; and my wife and I can spend many wonderful moments together, attending plays, going to the cinema, or discussing the books we are reading, because modern technology has released us from many of life's burdens. We can be confident we will not contract smallpox, nor suffer from malnutrition. When the Brontës lived in Haworth, Yorkshire, the average age of death was twenty-five. The literary sisters lived relatively long lives. Anne died at twenty-nine, Emily at thirty, Charlotte at thirty-eight. Today, the average age of death in Haworth is over seventy.[1] No mean feat for a despised technology. Civilization has much to commend it as well as to cause distress. In a number of respects, justice calls out for a broadening of the benefits of technology to the advantage of the oppressed rather than a withdrawal from the control of nature – even though, of course, it must be a far wiser control. Rachel Carson of *Silent Spring* fame recognized not only the negative effects of insecticides but also that by 1962 they had almost eliminated malaria from India, where a few years previously 87 million had suffered the dread disease. The political task was to maintain the benefits while developing a wiser technology. Nature required some control, but not an ignorant and wanton devastation. In *Island*, Aldous Huxley rightly proclaims the South Sea Islands as "an Eden innocent unfortunately not only of Calvinism and capitalism and industrial slums, but also of Shakespeare and Mozart, also of scientific knowledge and logical thinking. It was paradise, but it wouldn't do. It wouldn't do."

As a consequence of modern technology, life spans have increased substantially, flowers have been made to grow more beautifully and vegetables more abundantly than ever before, and in places where they would not grow before. The gross national product has been increased so dramatically that free universal education, and even inexpensive (compared to cost) university education for millions, is provided out of its excess wealth. The grandest architecture, the sweetest music, the paper from which books are produced, the conveniences of modern living – from the tin can to the refrigerator that maintain healthy food – up to the benefits of medical research itself, are all derived from the technology that has devastated our environment – and that may be said in a number of other respects to have reduced the quality of our lives. One must recognize the significance of Dostoevsky's denunciation of those who would needlessly destroy the forests for firewood. The answer, he proposed, in *The Village of Stepanchikovo*, lay in better technology – double windows and efficient stoves. His hero, Myshkin, declaims rapturously about the wonder of the sunset, the glory of trees, and the sheer beauty of nature. We should use technology to further our enjoyment of that beauty, even though we must remain vigilant against technology's excesses. Double windows and efficient stoves constitute technological innovation designed to minimize the destruction of nature.

II

When we read that "the best people I've ever seen anywhere are the Tasadays," when Colin Turnbull announces that the BaMbuti people "are infinitely wise" and all "share in a world that is still kind and good ... And without evil,"[2] we must never forget that if they acquire the benefits of secular education, modern medicine, and, say, air conditioning, these benefits will rob them of that purported "goodness" and "wisdom," which arises from their technological simplicity. Moreover, we must retain a healthy scepticism about Colin Turnbull's evaluation. Certainly, the elephants the BaMbuti attack in such a manner as to cause them several days of horrendous torment before they finally succumb will doubt that the BaMbuti are "infinitely wise" and entirely "kind and good." And to those who say that the BaMbuti do not think in those terms with regard to their behaviour toward elephants, one can only respond that though the BaMbuti may be a part of nature, they are certainly not in harmony with all of its constituent parts.

If we are to eulogize the simplicity of tribal society and wish to acquire the benefits of that simplicity, let us be sure to recognize that the price for that simplicity is poorer health, shorter lives, and lack of secular education. Moreover, while we would be closer to nature, we would be no more in harmony with it. What modernity requires is not the impossible task of unlearning what we have learned, but learning to adapt our technology wisely, recognizing that it must not be solely the promoter of human convenience but must be subordinated to an understanding of the human as both a part of nature and at best in harmony with nature – at least to the degree that other no less significant values are not undermined. And if Aboriginals are to partake of the fruits of technology and secular education, they must do so in the understanding that the beauties and simplicities of their culture will be irreparably harmed in the process of providing them with the benefits, along with the ills, of modernity. With those benefits and ills, they will no longer be able to think as they once did, and there will be a necessary dislocation in their souls. Western experience of modern technology will, in substantial part, be repeated by all who embrace it.

Perhaps the most important lesson to be learned by all those who desire a more egalitarian world in conformity with an understanding of the human as an intrinsic part of nature is that there are no easy paths to that goal, nor even any clarity as to what the right paths might be. As Wolfram von Eschenbach began his *Parzival:* "Every human act has good and evil in its results." "Under every *Good* is a hell" is the wise message of Swedenborg's *Divine Love and Wisdom.* Every improvement in Aboriginal living conditions will be at some cost to the culture, every step toward individual human rights must be at some cost to the harmony and security of the community. The most frequent intellectual error involves the unwarranted assumption that the elimination of what is wrong will produce what is right. It is never enough to point to a societal ill and to assume that its removal will solve the societal problem the ill has engendered.

A respected friend recently returned from teaching English as a foreign language in Japan. She reports the lack of gender equality there, the manner in which she was demeaned because of her sex, and the fact that she took every opportunity to educate the young girls she instructed to appreciate the value of gender equality. While one must have a deep sympathy for her concerns, one is nonetheless led to wonder whether she was entitled to exceed the terms of her contract – she was paid to teach English not to impart Western values to her charges – whether she had the right to attempt to impose Western ideals on a non-Western society, and whether she had any understanding of the effect that such values would have on the solidarity of Japanese culture. While gender equality is indeed admirable in itself, one must always attempt to understand it in specific societal contexts, to ask what price has to be paid for its achievement and who is entitled to bring it about. Certainly, I find it very difficult to distinguish between this form of cultural imperialism and the now derided form in which the West once attempted to impose Christianity on "infidels" or the values of "civilization" on "savages." All values, even the right ones, are inappropriate as impositions but appropriate topics of discussion and persuasion among equals.

If the solution to human problems, including environmental problems, were as simple as much of the advocacy intelligentsia imagine, the problems would have been eradicated long ago, for we have no greater concern with justice than our predecessors. The writings of Chaucer, Shakespeare, Schiller, Hugo, Lamartine, Dickens, and Dostoevsky all embrace a deep sense of the just – and if they were not reflecting as well as arousing popular sentiment, they would not have been so popular. Every era has had its avenging angels, often with as little capacity for dealing with the complexities of reality as have the protagonists of current panaceas. The purported solutions to any one problem will be the invariable precursors, often causes, of the next generation of problems. The prime requisite of all societal problem-solving must be a recognition of human inadequacy to the task. That inadequacy will be diminished when we understand, as Talleyrand customarily complained to the intellectuals of his time: *"Jamais trop de zèle"* (never too much enthusiasm). Enthusiasm, Talleyrand understood, aroused spirit through pique but at a considerable cost to the understanding. In its naivety, it caused more problems than it solved. Talleyrand clearly understood the message of the Tao even if he did not study it.

If our place within nature, and the inherent limitations that place accords to human satisfactions, is to be recognized, that recognition must involve a significant measure of humility, of mutual respect among cultures, even an understanding of the lessons to be learned from other species. And that requires not merely that the West learns to respect and appreciate the values of other cultures, but that Western intellectuals come to recognize those cultures for what they are, not what is convenient to believe for the sake of argument. It also requires, though this is a far less serious and far from universal problem, that Aboriginal and Oriental societies come to recognize that they do not have all goodness and wisdom on their side. Those who went to the Stockholm Conference of 1972 to announce the superiority of their harmony with nature and those who boast of Buddhism's and Hinduism's superior attitudes to nature might want to take a harder look at their own traditions and practices. Moreover, there is something odd about proclaiming the superior wisdom of Aboriginal culture while Aboriginals drive snowmobiles, plough with tractors, hunt with guns, live in wood or brick homes, use traps made from steel, eat canned foods, and seek medical treatment in hospital. (Though, again, it is more often the Western intelligentsia making the claim on their behalf than Aboriginals making the claim for themselves.) The West has rightly been told for many decades that it must learn humility and respect. The dictum must apply every whit as much to everyone else. Aboriginal use of petroleum, steel, and wood is in principle no less environmentally harmful than that of Caucasians, even if it is, at present, far less widespread. Aboriginal and Oriental rationalizations do not appear very different from age-old Western rationalizations.

III

When Linnaeus, in his *Systema Naturae* of 1735, devised the first reputedly scientific system of biological classification, he divided humans into *sapiens* (wise) and *monstruosus* (abnormal).[3] The *monstruosus* are not those we would today count as human. Among the *sapiens,* he included "Wild man," who was "four-footed, mute," and "hairy" – probably a being bearing some similarity to Albertus Magnus's curiously contrived and ignorant thirteenth-century conception of a pygmy – lacking, according to Albertus, societal organization, a moral code, art, and philosophy – or Edward Tyson's late-seventeenth-century idea of the "Orang-Outang" or "Homo sylvestris": the man of the woods.

Among those in Linnaeus's classification we would more readily recognize as human – the *sapiens* – were the "copper-coloured, choleric, erect ... American," who was "obstinate, content, free" and "regulated by custom"; the "sooty, melancholy, rigid ... Asiatic," who was "severe, haughty, covetous," and "governed by opinion"; the "black, phlegmatic, relaxed ... African," who was "crafty, indolent, negligent," and "governed by caprice." It is customary to be appalled today at Linnaeus's prejudice, to ascribe it to the temper of the times, and to congratulate ourselves that we have overcome at least the more blatant aspects of such prejudice.

We have not. Linnaeus's prejudice differs little from, to take but one of many examples reported favourably by modern Western intellectuals, that of a Makuna Indian who claims, "The whites see only with their eyes and hear through their ears. We Indians can see and hear with our minds."[4] The even greater prejudice is that of the advocacy anthropologists, who cite such statements with approval and without the intellectual rigour they would employ to question the validity of statements made by, say, Belgians or Turks – or even without noting that the early-eighteenth-century idealist philosopher George Berkeley and his followers wrote in similar vein to the Makuna of seeing and hearing ideas. So too many of the Dissenters.

Just imagine the consternation today if one were to quote Linnaeus without mentioning that his views were bigoted and outdated. What if one were to quote Darwin's taxonomically accurate statement that the "Esquimaux, like other Arctic animals, extend round the whole polar regions"[5] without noting its tendentiousness? We would not be inclined to accept taxonomical accuracy as a defence.

It strikes me as odd that the prejudice of a Makuna Indian or of a Harvard anthropologist who quotes the Makuna Indian approvingly is considered less of a prejudice than that of an eighteenth-century Swedish botanist or a nineteenth-century English physiologist, and that it is now customary to denounce the prejudice of the latter two and applaud that of the former two. The Makuna classification of whites represents every bit as much a prejudice against, and a misunderstanding of, "European" civilization as does Linnaeus's classification of non-Europeans. Moreover, when we read George (later Bishop) Berkeley telling us that we see and hear with our minds, we are somewhat perplexed – indeed downright sceptical – and ask for an elucidation. The fact that we do not customarily ask the Makuna Indian for a similar clarification reflects our critical attitude to Western philosophy and unreflective attitude toward Aboriginal philosophy

According to Linnaeus, Europeans were "fair, sanguine, brawny ... *gentle, acute, inventive.*" And, when we read that today, we squirm in some discomfort at the prejudice he expressed in the Europeans' favour. Yet the current and commendable, if far from complete, Western intellectual success in overcoming racial prejudice is itself a peculiarly prejudiced one. While it overcomes *traditional* racial prejudice admirably, it continues to denounce the aspects of *Western* culture of which it disapproves, and to applaud those aspects of which it approves. Why is this prejudice? Because it unconsciously ignores the negative consequences of that of which it approves and refuses to apply to any other culture the standard of judgment it applies to itself – which is not a cultural but a purportedly neutral standard, for, otherwise, it could have no substantial grounds for criticism.

It is astonishing, and reflective of the ideological nature of much of contemporary Western intellectual society, how book after book after repetitive book tells us, rightly, how much tribal society suffers from dislocation through the introduction of modern technology, Western modes of commodity exchange, resource extraction, and the like. Yet there is rarely a word about how those things that Western intellectuals admire – for example,

Western-style gender equality, liberal democracy, the adoption of human rights codes – would, indeed will, produce every bit as much dislocation as would the introduction of Western technology. Both sets of values – the technological and the individual rights orientations – are incompatible with the emphases on solidarity and cohesion of most tribal communities.

Of course, many of the Western intellectuals who denounce technology also denounce individualism and commend community, but on closer inspection it is clear that it is only acquisitive individualism they denounce – that is, their denunciation of individualism is a cryptic, occasionally explicit, denunciation of capitalism – and not the individual rights of dissenters against the community or state. Despite protestations to the contrary, they are not communitarians at all when community implies, as it does in significant degree for some tribal societies, a common belief system that punishes opposition and discourages the right to deviate from the cultural norm. Solidarity implies commonality and belongingness, which must in some degree be at the expense of individual rights unless a balance between the competing principles is sought.

Rather than engaging in a vitriolic diatribe against Aboriginals and Orientals in the manner of a Burton (Ch. 7, 1) or a Flora Annie Steel (see page 202), or against the West in the manner of a Knudtson, a Ramenofsky, or a John Neihardt on behalf of Black Elk (see pages xxi, 23, 169), it might be rather more appropriate to ask what each might learn from the others in order to approach a synthesis in which thereby changed attitudes to our relationship to the natural world might lead to an improved treatment of both our fauna and our flora.

Certainly, the sense of collectivity of the Aboriginal world allows for a ready understanding of each individual as part of a related whole, in which the whole, the collectivity, comes to be seen as an end in itself. Unfortunately, the Aboriginal's conception of the whole that is the end toward which action is undertaken is often the tribe alone. Fauna, flora, and fellow humans are often understood not as individual ends in themselves but in terms of their contribution to the collective interest of the tribe. The sense of collectivity in Buddhism, Taoism, and Hinduism (though rarely in the practice of Oriental states) is a rather broader conception of the organic whole than that maintained by Aboriginals, often extending to humanity in toto, but, like that of the Aboriginals, often understanding flora and fauna as instruments of human well-being.

Most Aboriginal myths and Oriental literature have a more refined, and deeper, sense of spirituality than we find in Occidental secularism, which allows for a greater awe and wonder, for an immediate respect for the natural world, certainly for a greater sense of proximity to it. However, although that respect is "allowed for," it is often not practised. And the reason it is not practised, other than the self-interest that pervades most societies, is that neither Orientals nor Aboriginals have that sense of objectivity endemic to Western rationalism in which each individual human, and, though in lesser degree, each individual animal, is viewed as an end in itself, entitled to be treated as possessing the rights of individuality.

What is necessary for a satisfactory environment is a balancing of the interests of the collective whole with the interests of each intrinsic element of that whole. As T.S. Eliot intimated in "Prufrock," for love to endure, there must be a community of souls. In Western thought, we have come to recognize each individual as an autonomous identity while we are also – albeit slowly – coming to recognize human fulfilment in the sharing of the self with others, especially those who are loved. That view is to be found in the transcendentalism of Emerson and the "primal law" of Matthew Arnold as well as the recent writings of communitarian theorists such as Charles Taylor. Today, we are coming to recognize that two or more separate selves become integrated in their identities through the possession of essentially shared relationships, those relationships that penetrate so deeply as to constitute the identity of the separate selves involved.[6] Thus it is that we can recognize each individual self as an end and the shared identity as an end, whether that shared identity be a family, a religion, a nation, even humanity itself. But equally possibly, it may include animality and the natural world – what Mary Midgley has called a "mixed community." The novelist Joseph Conrad extended Burke's conception of belongingness to the animal realm. He referred to "the latent feeling of fellowship with all creation – and to the subtle but invincible conviction of solidarity that knits together the loneliness of innumerable hearts." Saul Bellow declared the source of this universal connection to be the soul. In *Mr. Sammler's Planet,* he tells us that the individual soul is unique, yet is at the same time a bond with all else. For Bellow, this characteristic is both the great mystery and the saving grace of life. It corresponds to what Gertrude Stein called our "bottom nature." If we share our identity, our sense of who we essentially are, with the animal world, we will more readily recognize the elements of that world as ends.

When we share our identity with the natural world, the awesome, lovable, and beautiful elements of that world will be treated with respect and reverence both because they are instrumental to our well-being and because they will be valued for themselves. A synthesis, or at least a balancing, of the Occidental, Aboriginal, and Oriental conceptions of spirituality, community, individuality, and objectivity will most readily help us realize those understandings. But because no society can retain its health while denying the very foundations of its culture – we must all recognize that who we are is derived from who we were – each will have to approach its new understanding through, and not in denial of, its own traditions.

Unfortunately, technological changes have diminished, and continue to diminish, our capacities to realize the appropriate attitudes. As the Orient and Africa seek land for towns, crops, and livestock, they do so at the expense of wildlife and their habitats. As the Amerindians of Brazil seek to improve the quality of their lives, they do so at the expense of the rain forest, on which all our lives ultimately depend. (Of course, the devastation wrought by the Caucasian landowners is far worse but only because of the technological power they possess.) In North America, the Amerindians use the cruellest of all traps – though recent international agreements will phase them out – and the least environmentally sound of fishnets because their use increases the yield. In the West, we continue to cut down trees without giving sufficient consideration to the fact that each mature tree produces some fifty to seventy litres of water per day, cooling the atmosphere in overly hot conditions, cleaning the air, and so on. All cultures think of their own interests first and only a spiritual education dedicated to a sharing of identities with other peoples, other animals, and nature as a whole can diminish the environmental destruction we face. It can be diminished by our being educated to share our identity with the natural world and thus understand it as a part of ourselves. With such conceptions, self-interest embraces the interests of others. And Aboriginal and Oriental societies need that education every bit as much as does the West. The West must re-orient its respect and its technology. Aboriginals and Orientals must orient their behaviour toward a respect consistent with the respect their myths urge them to possess.

Different cultures are much more alike in their prejudices than most contemporary social analysts are wont to imagine. From our perspective, a most relevant consideration is whether other cultures traditionally misunderstand the nature of other species as much as has Western society.

Just as it has become customary to laud the superior attitudes of tribal societies with regard to their sense of community, so too it is now de rigueur to insist on their superior attitudes to, and knowledge of, other species. Thus, to take but one of the very many instances that abound in recent anthropological literature, and to employ the example of the Makuna again, we are told, in an approving contrast to Western norms, the Makuna believe that "animals and fish live in their own communities, which are just like human communities. They have their chiefs, their shamans, their dance houses."[7] Yet this claim is precisely what other animals are not. It is neither indicative of an understanding of other species, nor respectful of other species to consider them so. Other species are not made in the image of humans, and are not lower-order humans, any more than humans are made in the image of God and are lower-order gods. Other species may have their own hierarchies, their own complexities, their own organizations. But they are not Lilliputian human organizations. The consequence of considering animals lower-order humans is to fail to recognize their true character and nature. Legend has it that Aboriginals have a deep understanding of the creatures of nature. In fact, they understand them less well than does recent Western ethology.

In the words of John Rodman, other species possess "their own character, and potentialities, their own forms of excellence, their own integrity, their own grandeur."[8] Just as we have demeaned other species traditionally by considering them, and treating them, like less accomplished humans, so too have other cultures. When we find in the myths, legends, or beliefs of a culture – or in the fables of Aesop or Aristophanes – animals described as behaving, thinking, or being societally organized like humans, we can be confident there is little interest in, and respect for, the animal in itself. It is merely a convenient tool of instruction by which to impart some important *human* moral. As human ideas, attitudes, and beliefs have changed, so the ways in which we have understood our relationship to the animal realm have changed. Humankind's treatment of the animal is an integral part of changing human culture, and it is of special significance given the prime importance of animals to human culture, to human identity, in all but the most recent history.[9] It is perhaps as a consequence of the diminution of that significance – through the change in forms of transportation, in urbanization, and in the modes of animal husbandry that have removed all but companion animals from our immediate experience – that we have lost our understanding of the significance that the human-animal relationship had for Western philosophers from Pythagoras to Goethe and ultimately Darwin. Steam power and the railway divorced the West from dependency on the animal for transportation, and urbanization removed animals from a place in our everyday lives. Thereafter, human and animal lives became slowly but constantly less interdependent, at least in our experience if not in ecological fact. Apart from pets, animals became strangers, and no longer imposed themselves upon our philosophies. Nonetheless, modern ethological study, replicating and advancing from the methods of Aristotle, has done much to change that for the better.

To understand much of human history – especially early human history but in significant degree more recent history, too – is to understand the human-animal relationship, given the importance of hunting, domestication, pastoralism, and adornment. Much of mythology employs animals as symbols. As the French anthropologist Claude Lévi-Strauss insisted, animals are used predominantly for discourse in primitive society not because they are good to eat, as his predecessors Malinowski, Radcliffe-Brown, and Fortes had argued, but because, as we saw earlier, they are good to think with.[10] (Although, as we shall see, it is also more than that.) And since they are good to think with, they occupied much of the thought of early human society. That thought involved veneration and awe, yet the practice was sometimes closer to cruelty and misuse. It was, like so much of human history, a history of ambivalence, a history of disjuncture between ideology and practice, a history of rationalization, as well as a history of concern, care, and consideration.

In discussing the views of A.R. Radcliffe-Brown on myths, Claude Lévi-Strauss tells us in his *Totemism* that "if we examine some dozens of these tales we find that they have a single theme. The resemblance and difference of animal species are translated into terms of friendship and conflict, solidarity and opposition. In other words, the world of animal life is represented in terms of social relations similar to those of human society."[11] Indeed, as we noted,[12] this approach is precisely how the Makuna depict other species – with their own chiefs, shamans, and dance houses. Animal species are customarily presented in pairs possessing common features. Among the Aborigines of New South Wales, for example, we find the use of the night owl and the nightjar. Eating meat and living in trees are common characteristics of the pair presented, offering points of comparison, now similar to, now different from, the human condition.

For Lévi-Strauss, the central element in the use of animals in primitive legend lies in the fact that "The animals in totemism cease to be solely or principally creatures which are feared, admired or envied: their perceptible reality permits the embodiment of ideas and relations conceived by speculative thought on the basis of empirical observations. We can understand too, that natural species are chosen not because they are 'good to eat' but because they are 'good to think.' "[13] As Lévi-Strauss implies, the natural relationship between humans and other species becomes obscured already in tribal societies by the development of myths. Myths, the product of speculative thought, serve to transform other species from creatures we *naturally* admire, fear, and envy into creatures we use first as symbols to instruct us about ourselves and then as instruments of the ceremonies developed in accord with those instructions. Myths, we might add (Lévi-Strauss does not), serve not only to distort the primordial human animal relationship but to convince us to understand other species as something different from their natural reality – a truth as evident in Makuna myths, as in the *Popol Vuh,* as in Aesop's fables, as in *Alice's Adventures in Wonderland.* Already in tribal societies, animals come to be understood not as ends in themselves but as creatures useful to humans. Thus, Amerindians become convinced of their entitlement to kill eagles in the furtherance of their own ceremonies. The eagles are not worthwhile entities in themselves. They are instruments of human mythological ends. If we are to understand our natural compassion toward other creatures, we must look back to the purest of early tribal societies, and, more convincingly, by reasoned speculations about the possibilities of pre-flesh-eating societies.

In fact, the myths themselves entail an acknowledgment that the manner in which the animals are treated is in principle inappropriate. The myths embody a justification for otherwise unacceptable behaviour and for which a justification is required. Without the exculpation, the killers would bear guilt for the acts performed. We have already noticed how Vine Deloria, Jr., insists that the eagles swoop in approval of the killing of one of their own; and we have suggested there might be more plausible explanations of the eagle behaviour.[14] Hope Maclean tells us of the animals giving their lives voluntarily,[15] although we can all judge from the animals' behaviour that they will do anything in their power to avoid the fate in store for them, including gnawing off their own limbs. No one could believe that the "voluntariness" bore any relationship to fact. Such myths are entirely exculpatory in nature.

In the Blackfoot buffalo myth, we hear of how the animal master of the buffalo agrees to the sacrifice of his kin in exchange for his marriage to a beautiful Blackfoot princess. Because the buffalo master itself enters into the contract and extracts a heavy price, the killing of the buffalo for food and raiment is thereby justified. The story goes further. The spirits of the dead buffalo are reincarnated in the new-born buffalo. Thus the killing is not really killing.

This story is repeated in essence in a myriad of myths around the world. The animals are seen to participate in their own demise, which turns out not to be a demise after all. By analogy with the complementary realm of vegetation, just as the fruits are taken from the trees and the cob from the corn and yet the plants grow again, so too animals are killed and yet they return. The bearers of the myths are customarily presented to us as engaging in a *participation mystique* in which the killer "identifies" with the animal and treats it with the utmost "respect." But it is not in any manner a respect that treats the animal as a worthwhile entity in itself, a being whose life is sacred in the same manner that a human life is deemed sacred. It is behaviour designed to minimize the guilt and shame one would feel if one lacked a justifying myth. *Participation mystique* is the *mea non culpa* of tribal society.

If there is felt a need for justification, for exculpation, there must be a recognition that something needs to be justified, to be exculpated. There must be a natural aversion to harming other creatures. We do not feel the need to justify behaviour that we find in and of itself appropriate. Behaviour that conflicts with the dictates of our inner nature does so require if we are to minimize, even eliminate, our guilt over the crime we commit. The fact that the exculpation is required, *and* is almost always offered, is a prima facie reason to believe that the harming or killing of other animals, or at least of other animals that are not harmful to us, is in conflict with the psychological requirements of our primal being. If Vine Deloria, Jr., felt the need to tell us that the eagles acquiesce – though no independent observer would imagine it so – and if animals are said to offer themselves voluntarily for slaughter – though no one could judge their efforts at escape consistent with such a statement – then there must be a compelling need for self-justification.

If the harming of harmless beings were not in conflict with the dictates of our souls (our primordial instincts, if one prefers), it is highly unlikely that exculpatory myths would ever have developed, almost impossible that they could have become as pervasive as they are. And, given the nature of the content of tribal myths, it would appear that the exculpation is required not merely for the killing or harming of other species for ritual or adornment purposes but even for killing for food.

However much myth, religion, science, and philosophy may have obscured our natural sympathetic relationship to other species, they have never extinguished it. There remains not merely a "primal sympathy," as Wordsworth has it, an "unconscious identity with animals," in Jung's words, "one universal brotherhood" of *"all* innocent and beautiful life," as Henry Salt wrote, but spontaneous affection is writ large in the joyous beam on the face of every untutored child at the sight of a puppy, a calf, or a lamb, even though, as we have seen and shall see again, this is only one side of a complex story.

There are two competing, indeed quite antithetical, conceptions of the universal spirit, or "primal sympathy," "one universal brotherhood." The first is derived from conceptions of primordial human nature, from the Golden Age in which, according to Plato, Chaucer, and Aboriginal traditions, humans and animals could speak to and understand each other. That is, they were essentially in harmony with each other. Their interests were one and they shared their identities as compatible parts of the natural realm. In such a world, the unity of harmless animals included humankind. The universal spirit was that which all shared in life, that to which all returned in death, and that which encouraged Pythagoras, Empedocles, Plutarch, the Jains, Buddhists, and Hindus to write of humans and other animals as kin, a fact that denied humans the right to kill other species except in self-defence.

The second conception of the universal spirit is that which instead of denying humans the right to kill provides them with a justification for killing. This concept of the universal spirit pervades Aboriginal societies once they acknowledge that humans have lost the capacity to converse with, and be understood by, their fellow creatures. We may surmise that the second concept was derived from the first in the following manner: in our primordial condition we were vegetarian, as the traditions of many societies (and some, but by no means all, recent paleontological research) contend; we lived at one with the animal realm, spoke its language (that is, our interests were in accord) and regarded ourselves as part of a common mutually respecting community. (And, if this is an exaggeration of reality, it symbolizes the greater commonality of experience.) As climatic conditions changed, depriving us of our primordial diet, and as circumstance or adventure compelled or encouraged us to find new habitats where there was an inadequate year-round supply of vegetation, so we will have become at least occasional killers and carnivores, but we will not immediately have lost what we might imaginatively entitle the "vegetarian elements of our psyche." To assuage our guilt for our new habits, we will have had to devise a new conception of the universal spirit, one that permits that which circumstance has made a necessity. We will feel compelled to proclaim that the animal has given itself voluntarily, that it is not *really* dead, that its soul is alive and well in the universal spirit. We will feel constrained to follow complex rituals to indicate that, *despite our behaviour,* we *really* respect the animal we have slain. Were we not to engage in such rituals, we would feel the guilt that *real* killing would inflict upon us. The universal spirit thus changes from an authentic identity with the animals to a mode of justification for harming animals. And respect for the animals is retained because the killing is not primarily an act of will but one of life-sustaining necessity.

From the very origins of human culture, as soon as we have deviated from our primordial nature, there will be a tension in our souls between the natural and the cultural, between that which our primitive instinct requires and that which our cultural experience teaches. Ambivalence toward other species is not an exclusively Western phenomenon but has its origins in the very early days of human society, as soon as we left our East African homeland. Nonetheless, it has some exclusively Western forms. While Aboriginals may excuse their behaviour by proclaiming that the animal does not really die, Westerners have been known to justify their behaviour by proclaiming that the animal deserves to die, not merely because it is inferior, but because it has engaged in treasonous acts, it has broken the contract of the "universal brotherhood." Thus, the vegetarian Pythagoras understood that, if humans eat flesh, they find it necessary to justify their behaviour. The pig, in Ovid's version of Pythagoras's account, "is thought to have been the first victim to meet a well-deserved fate, because it rooted out seeds with its upturned snout, and destroyed the hope of harvest. Then the goat, they say, was sacrificed at Bacchus' altars, as a punishment for having gnawed his vines. Both had themselves to blame."[16] It was because the pigs and goats broke the contract, it would appear, that humans were entitled to give up their vegetarianism and devour the treacherous culprits. The moral rules implied by the original universal spirit needed no longer to be obeyed.

We employ animals in traditional myths and modern fables not only because they are good to think with – though they certainly are that – but because we have a natural interest in, and attraction toward, them. They are good to think with, for, in the wild, we have a natural interest in them because we learn so much from them – they are good to emulate – and a natural attraction to them because we are so much a part of them – they are good to belong with. Our sense of self-identity does not end at our own body but includes kin, those who have gone before and those who are yet to be, fellow humans and fellow animals. This sense is the original conception of the universal spirit. It is an astonishing fact that it is the Aboriginal conception of the universal spirit that is driven by culture, by a control of nature, albeit a respectful one, while the Western conception – one that, as we shall see, continues to play a role in Western literature – is driven by a primordial longing for harmony with nature.

If there were no such primordial sympathy with nature, humans would be far more ready to use sources other than animals for their myths. It is true that, as our knowledge and technology changed, so we began to incorporate celestial bodies and vegetation into our myths. Yet we continued to use animals also. And as the technology developed further, and the vegetation and planets were no longer appropriate models, animals continued to play a vital role in the thoughts of the philosophers, and even more predominantly in the thoughts of the storytellers – the Western literary tradition being a natural continuation of Aboriginal myth-making. Most significantly, as we embraced the age of reason and renounced the world of myth, except for the instruction of young children, so, in those juvenile myths, it was rarely the skies and woods but almost always animals that were used, and that caught the imagination, and the love, of children. Despite having abandoned the world of traditional myth, we are still charmed to learn, for example, that, for the Olmecs of Mesoamerica, nobility stemmed from the mating of a jaguar with a human female – the synthesis of courage and grace. Animals are not solely good to think with because of the requirements of tribal society but because we identify with them as a part of our natural selves. We maintain our identity with the whole of nature, but it is primarily to the animal realm that we offer our affection.

It is most significant that tribal myths provide justification for killing even when the killing is for food. Increasingly, the paleontological evidence has been pointing to the origins of the human as a fruit- and root-eater; in other versions we appear at most as grubbers and scavengers but not killers of complex animals. Yet one might suggest the mythological evidence is even more convincing. If it had been natural to kill other animals for food, there would have been no guilt and no need for exculpatory myths. Indeed, the need was felt at least throughout the Middle Ages to offer justifications for meat-eating. In the fifth century, St. Augustine castigated the "superstition" of refraining from "the killing of animals." If there was a "superstition" against killing, even for food, then there must have been some lingering belief that such killing countered the moral imperatives of our natural humanity. In his *Utopia* of the early sixteenth century, Thomas More could still offer a credible view of the human untrammelled by civilization as one who would count the killing of food animals as murder. By the nineteenth century, arguments against meat-eating usually had to be offered as moral arguments per se rather than as replications of our natural condition, though there were numerous exceptions, as in the writings of Percy Shelley, for example. By the nineteenth century, the idea of the human as the dominant carnivore was pre-eminent. It is perhaps not too much to suggest that human alienation from nature begins as soon as circumstances impel us to deviate from our natural diet. With tongue only half in cheek, George Bernard Shaw relates in *Back to Methuselah* how "one of Adam's sons invented meat-eating. The other was horrified ... With the ferocity which is still characteristic of bulls and other vegetarians, he slew his beefsteak-eating brother, and thus invented murder." And as we invent tools, we think as the tools incline us to think. As Joseph Campbell wrote cogently, "A machine tends to impose upon its master the teleology of its own form." In other words, much of human thought is a rationalization of our self-interest as experienced through our culture and our technology. With culture and technology, we commence to alienate ourselves from our natural sympathy for animated nature.

IV

The Western attitude to nature has been as ambivalent as its Aboriginal and Oriental counterparts. Famously, Samuel Johnson observed that whoever "is tired of London is tired of life." Urban civilization was preferable to rural simplicity. Yet that same Samuel Johnson considered animal experimentation a crime against our nature-respectful humanity. Turgot and Condorcet, indeed the whole Enlightenment, the profound Rousseau excluded, saw Western progress toward a perfectible civilization as both inevitable and fulfilling. And most educated Victorians, at least the more vociferous and renowned of them, echoed the refrain. At the same time, they listened to, respected, and applauded those like Thoreau and Tolstoy who wrote of the virtues of a life lived in simple harmony with nature. Even Edward Carpenter, who, in his *Civilization: Its Cause and Cure,* argued we would be wiser to live slowly and simply, in accord with our animal nature as other animals do, was given a sympathetic hearing. (His book went through sixteen editions between 1889 and 1919.) And a whole host of commentators followed Scott, Carlyle, Ruskin, Chesterton, and Belloc in proclaiming the superiority of at least some elements of medieval natural simplicity over the excessive refinements of an artificial civilization.

In reality, we faced competing attractions to civilization and to nature, to progress, and to traditional natural order, simultaneously and incompatibly. It was rather more the irresistible power of economic and technological forces than intellectual choice that drove us inexorably to a further alienation from our natural condition. Of course, many welcomed the control of nature. But this welcoming did not imply a necessary disrespect for nature's constituent parts. Thus, Percy Bysshe Shelley, Francis Newman – a founder of the Vegetarian Society and described by George Eliot as "our blessed St. Francis" whose soul "was a blessed *yea*" – and George Bernard Shaw thought we could best return to our primitive vegetarian harmony with other species through a dominance over the harmful forces of nature. Perhaps Robertson Davies went furthest in the recognition of those harmful forces. In the words of one of his Scottish characters: "Oh, Nature, Nature, what an auld bitch ye are."

The Western tradition is indeed a complex one; like other traditions, it is imbued with utter inconsistencies. Despite its perennial concern with "progress," however, it has always possessed, especially in its literary luminaries, an abiding respect for, and an attachment to, nature; as well as, customarily, an understanding that the appeal of nature relates in some mysterious manner to a respect for the conditions of our human origins. This view is perhaps best recognized in Rousseau, but many of our esteemed cultural champions – the Western counterpart in many respects to the gurus and the shamans – have devoted a significant part of their attention to the human relationship to a primordial nature.

In her *The Way of the Earth* (1994), T.C. McLuhan argued convincingly that, as a whole, Aboriginal peoples relate to the earth as kin, revere mountains as a source of inspiration, and feel a spiritual connection to the seas and rivers. McLuhan offers us not a new thesis – the Aboriginal orientation to nature has been long recognized – but a lucid and painstaking adumbration of evidence. What is missing is a recognition that equally awe-inspiring orientations are to be found throughout the Western tradition.

To provide a Western counterpart to McLuhan's researches would require the several hundred pages she took to describe the Aboriginal traditions. Yet one may outline some very similar Western perceptions.

The West has been especially rich in its glorification of the wonders of the seas, the rivers, and the lakes. It was no accident that the Lake Poets – Wordsworth, Coleridge, and Southey – chose to live at the conjuncture of lakes and mountains that constitutes the English Lake District. Nor was it mere happenstance that they were followed there by Ruskin, de Quincey, and, to add but one of a multitude, Beatrix Potter, whose fictional animals enraptured more than one generation. The common attraction was to awesome nature.

The significance of the waters is pervasive in Western literature, even among writers who otherwise have little in common. Of course, the majesty of the sea – both its beauty and its terror – is the dominant theme of the novels of Herman Melville, Richard Dana, and Joseph Conrad. But the theme is not restricted to such literature. John Keats acknowledged that his first view of the sea entered deeply into his consciousness and changed his poetic vision. Dorothy Wordsworth burst into tears at her first sight of the sea at Whitehaven. James Joyce and Kenneth Grahame remarked how they were enchanted by the sea. Longfellow longed for "the magic of the sea" and George Orwell tells us he was "so pining to see the sea again." That man of many more meretricious affairs, Victor Hugo, announced, "There have been two great affairs in my life: Paris and the Ocean." With admittedly characteristic hyperbole, he added: "Each stanza or page that I write has something in it of the shadow of the cloud or the saliva of the sea." In several of Ernest Hemingway's stories, a river serves to represent cleansing, absolution, and healing. In T.S. Eliot's "Dry Salvages," we read that "The river is within us." Long before he moved to the Lakes, Ruskin described the rivers of his youth as "the rivers of Paradise." Byron may be said to epitomize the tradition:

There is pleasure in the pathless woods,
There is rapture on the lonely shore,
There is society, where none intrudes,
By the deep Sea, and music in its roar:
I love not Man the less, but Nature more.[17]

The Victorian poet Matthew Arnold – perhaps, apart from "Dover Beach," better remembered as an educational theorist and for his influential *Culture and Anarchy* – tells us that a fair half the function of poetry is "making magically near and real the life of Nature, and man's life ... so far as it is a part of that Nature."

Nature is not only an important theme in Western literature: it is often the primary theme. In *The Sorrows of Young Werther,* Goethe experiences "the wonderful feeling with which my heart embraces Nature." Wordsworth writes of "A universe of Nature's fairest forms ... Magnificent, and beautiful and gay." Christopher North announces "Wondrous, O Nature, is thy sovereign power," while Sir Walter Scott tells us of "the mighty Helvellyn ... When the eagle was yelling," which strikes a cord with the "gentle lover of nature." Felicia Hemans appeals to the "vale and lake, within your mountain-urn / Smiling so tranquilly and set so deep," while Matthew Arnold asks "one lesson, Nature, let me learn from thee." Coleridge is awed by "the hush of nature" in "Sea, and hill, and wood," as is Elizabeth Barrett Browning by the "solemn-beating heart / Of Nature! ... Bound unto man's by cords he cannot sever." And Gothic novels, epitomized by Ann Radcliffe's *The Romance of the Forest* (1791), express at great length, and with frequent reference to Burke and Rousseau, a delight in the sublimities of nature.

An hour or two spent among the library stacks would produce a list ten times as long, with a dozen examples for each author. It is far more difficult to find a single poet without a jubilation of nature than to find ten with one. Of course, one may insist that these are mere words. True. Yet one must be impressed by the fact that lines on nature evoke a greater response than any other theme but love. And if one suggests that, to be meaningful, such words must be complemented by action, so too must Aboriginal and Oriental myth and philosophy. The preceding quotations, as well as those to be found in McLuhan's book or any of the many that depict non-Western traditions in glowing terms, are only of ultimate significance if they can be seen to be complemented by behaviour. As it is, they reflect only our ideals and our yearnings.

For many, the attraction of nature lies in our primordiality. Fiona MacCarthy, William Morris's finest biographer, informs us that the Thames was "for him a spiritual investment, a line back to antiquity and history." On his arrival in California, the Scot Robert Louis Stevenson (4) found at the sight of the forests, rivers, and pools that he had "come home again –

from the unsightly deserts to the greens." That home was not just his beloved Scotland but primordial beauty. Thomas Carlyle claimed to possess "a sort of half-mad appetite for being left alone, in green places, within sound of the sea." It was in his primitive origins that he sought the solidarity with nature that could overcome his alienation. In *De Profundis*, Oscar Wilde testified to "a strong longing for the great primeval things, such as the Sea, to me no less of a mother than the earth." "Home" lay in one's primordial origins, which invoked the sense both of beauty and integration.

In the *Summa Theologiae*, Aquinas tells us, "We call that beautiful which pleases the sight."[18] However, we are left to ponder whether different things please different sights. Prima facie, because we all share a common humanity (2), common biological origins, and our senses are in part a reflection of that commonality, it would be surprising if we did not have a considerable amount of aesthetic appreciation in common. Certainly, there are cultural differences, but those differences are only partial deviations from a norm. As William Blake expressed it, "Knowledge of Ideal Beauty is Not to be Acquired[.] It is Born with us." In the *Poetics*, Aristotle refers to "the instinct for harmony and rhythm." In *Lady Chatterley's Lover*, D.H. Lawrence tells us of "the instinct for shapely beauty which every bird and beast has." And Thomas Mann wrote of "rhythm" as "the musical transcendency of the sea." These instincts form a part of a common humanity, albeit expressed through different, sometimes widely different, cultural traditions.

In the Western tradition, the relationship to nature in general, and secondarily to primordial nature, may be most readily witnessed in pictoral art, and to a somewhat lesser degree in literary art. John Ruskin declared the "Love of Nature" to be one of the pinnacles of creative art. He wrote of the importance to art of "the love of natural objects for their own sake." In discussing the paintings of J.M.W. Turner, he tells us that "he must be a painter of the strengths of nature, there was no beauty elsewhere than in that." Cézanne announced that "the aim of art is not to copy nature, but to express it." His concern was to discover the fuller significance of nature beyond photographic description. In like vein, Edouard Manet referred to "the delight of having re-created nature touch by touch." For Stéphane Mallarmé, the true function of art lay in its ability to express "universal truths" through "the revelation of nature." Dostoevsky observed that "art is for man just as much a need as eating or drinking. The need for beauty, and the creations embodying it, are inseparable from man." Dostoevsky's pantheism is evident in the "creations embodying" beauty drawing us back to primordial reality.

Any length of time spent in appreciation of traditional Western pictorial art must lead us to a convincing recognition of the almost universal attachment to nature. Often we find the objects of awe, the stimuli to an encounter with beauty, to lie in those conditions of nature that constitute our primordial home, such as the trees, the lakes, or what Henry Salt called "innocent and beautiful [animal] life." The vast majority of the religious works of the creator of modern painting, Giotto (1267-1337), depict mountains, trees, and animals (sheep, goats, pigs, donkeys) and the great Renaissance biographer Giorgio Vasari offers Giotto his greatest praise because he "became so good an imitator of nature."[19] The landscapes of Joachim Patinir (1480-1524), the first of the great Dutch landscape painters, are also representative of the tradition. In *Rest on the Flight from Egypt,* we see not just the human figures but a peaceful meandering river, trees, and cliffs. In *Saint Hieronymus* and *Passage on the Styx* and *The Martyrdom of Saint Catherine,* we find Patinir similarly following the Oriental tradition of placing small human figures in a vast comforting landscape. Likewise, the landscapes of the van Ruisdaels of the seventeenth century capture the tranquility of the rivers, trees, and cattle. Even if Watteau's scenes are predominantly filled with humans, one cannot mistake the reverence for the woods, lakes, and animals. Later pictorial art moves toward the representation of the sublime rather than beauty alone, but when it is not what James Joyce called pornographic or didactic, often it too appeals to the glories of nature. Once again, it is far more difficult to find a painter without a love of nature than several with one.

What is represented as beautiful in nature will customarily correspond to those conditions that provided comfort and consolation in primordial human life: the trees, water, and fellow animals rather than the plains and the sands. The seascape painter Eugène Boudin's comments to the young Claude Monet on the content of beauty are not accidental: "The sea, the sky, the animals, the people and the trees are so beautiful, just as nature made them." Certainly, this conception of beauty is precisely what we find in Gainsborough and Constable, for example, and above all in Turner. It should not surprise us that the tree, and not sand or snow, is a sacred symbol of Christian and pagan traditions as well as those of Buddhism and Hinduism. Anton Chekhov wrote of the road from Batum to Taflis as "original and poetic," flanked with mountains, rivers, rocks, and waterfalls. After Taflis, it was "but a bald patch covered with sand ... not a single tree, not a blade of grass, everything horribly dreary." Not all of nature was worthy of our attraction, though, of course, sand, ice, and snow, bland in themselves, may become attractive in conjunction with other phenomena of nature. For the Taoist painters of the Sung dynasty (AD 960-1279) trees, mountains, and running water were the appropriate objects to be represented. Emperor Hui Tsung's collection of contemporary art included paintings of animals, birds, flowers, and fruit along with landscapes and portraits. The attraction is to nature, but especially the kind of nature we experienced in our human origin.

We sometimes fail to recognize this continuous orientation to nature in the Western tradition – and in other traditions too – because of the pervasive aesthetic relativism of Western philosophizing – a view notably absent from most of the representational artists themselves. To take but one example, in the *Norton History of the Environmental Sciences,* Peter J. Bowler argues for an aesthetic relativism and tells us that "mountains came to be seen as sublime expressions of Nature's power" in the eighteenth century "where once they had been feared as ugly and dangerous."[20] In *The Devils,* Dostoevsky essays to refute such relativist dogma with a simple question: "What is more beautiful, Shakespeare or boots, Raphael or petroleum?" Should we be more impressed by the fact that all cultures find similar expression and fulfilment in music, and by the significant similarities among instruments, forms, and harmonies, or by the readily recognized varieties of sound? Is it not a significant fact that a little listening and attention allow any open-minded individual from one culture enjoyment and appreciation of the music of another culture? While we may, and do, dispute the niceties of beauty, those disputes are about the dimensions, aspects, and experience of beauty rather than about beauty itself. Beauty, it may be suggested, is simple and consistent; the content of the beautiful complex, varied, and nuanced.

Just how accurate, indeed, is Bowler's relativist claim with regard to mountains? In fact, it ignores the paintings of not just the Orient, Giotto, and Joachim Patinir but of Quentin Metsys, Raphael, and François Clouet, among others, in the sixteenth century. In like vein, we can read in Thomas Burnet's *Sacred Theory of the Earth* (1681-9), "next to the great Concave of the Heavens ... there is nothing that I look upon with more pleasure than the wide Sea and the Mountains of the Earth. There is something august and stately in the Air of these things that inspires the mind with great thoughts and passions."[21] For John Ray in his *Wisdom of God in the Creation* (1691), not only do the smallest animalcules invoke our being "rapt into an Extasie of Astonishment and Admiration," but also the mountains "are very Ornamental to the Earth, affording pleasant and delightful prospects," no less than the "ravishing Prospect of the Sea."[22] Seventeenth-century depictions of the Alps included such phrases as "wild and multifarious confusion," "delightful Horrour," "a terrible joy," and "Mighty Atlas." Already in the fifteenth century, Leonardo reflected the awe felt for a mountainous vision. His famous drawing of 5 August 1473 – sometimes described as the first true landscape drawing in Western art – is dominated by rocks mixed with vegetation. A second of about the same period is of a rocky outcrop with a pool, a swan, and a duck. Leonardo's notebooks reflect an obsession with masses of rock, swift-flowing streams, and the roaring of the sea. Nonetheless, he indicates a "fear of the dark, threatening cave."

What misleads relativists is the failure to recognize that the "sublime" of which Bowler writes *is* dangerous, and will certainly be seen as fearful as well as awesome and wondrous. The concluding chapters of the fourth volume of John Ruskin's *Modern Painters* are entitled "The Mountain Gloom" and "The Mountain Glory." The mountains teach us the lesson, Ruskin writes, "that no good or lovely thing exists in this world without its correspondent darkness." The competing usages of "awful" as on the one hand "appalling" and on the other as "reverential" are not without relevance. And as Robertson Davies wrote in *World of Wonders,* "Wonder is marvellous but it is also cruel, cruel, cruel. It is undemocratic, discriminatory, and pitiless." The sublime may even be seen to be ugly, though it is more likely that any antipathy reflected the dangers the mountains held as the home of potential predators and even as the symbol of the unknown that is to be feared – as with Leonardo's cave. However, in looking at different *aspects* of the same focus beauty may be seen also to be present. It is certainly not difficult, and not unusual in the appropriate circumstances, to see a tiger or even a wolf as both. Indeed, in the traditional *Beauty and the Beast,* the beast is far more sublime than it is ugly. The reality is that the sublime adds a dimension to aesthetic arrest that takes us beyond beauty. In *Wild Frank's Return,* Walt Whitman describes a mare stampeded by a storm as "an image of beautiful terror." The terror heightens rather than hides the beauty. Too readily, because our sense of the beautiful and the sublime is complicated by competing factors, we misconstrue that complexity as an eye of the beholder relativism. Shakespeare's "Beauty is brought by judgement of the eye, / Not uttered by base sale of chapman's tongue" is far wiser than the customary subscription to aesthetic relativism. Stanley L. Jacki wrote perceptively of the absolute beneath the relative, acknowledging the latter while affirming the former. In *Kangaroo,* D.H. Lawrence reminds us that "even relativism is only relative. Relative to the absolute." Throughout his writings, but especially in *Ulysses,* James Joyce demonstrates that language controls thought more than thought language – that is, language often interferes with, though is indispensable to, objective understanding – but when he demonstrates that, he demonstrates an objective truth. Nor does such a relativist orientation to language hinder Joyce from accepting the objectivity of beauty. Epiphanies are real, conceived in the beautiful and experienced in the sublime.

Aquinas tells us there are three requirements for beauty: wholeness, harmony, and radiance (to borrow James Joyce's interpretative translation).[23] The aesthetic image must be seen as a whole, the parts must be in harmony, and the whole must be elevating, enlightening, fascinating. The aspect of harmony corresponds to the psychologically unifying conditions of the primordial life; the sacred place, tranquility, the home of the psyche at one with nature. It was Pythagoras's view that harmony exists in numerical proportion both in music and in the natural world. In the *Philebus,* Plato tells us that "measure and commensurability [that is, proportion and mathematical wholeness] are everywhere identifiable with beauty and excellence." It is those aspects of nature that conform to our ideas of the beautiful with which we customarily feel the greatest harmony.

However, there is not only proportion in nature. There is also the terror of the sublime in the water and the forests. They are dangerous as well as protective. They threaten us while they comfort us. The sublime arises readily from the beautiful. Leonardo was fascinated by water. He described it as the "vehicle of nature"; it was to the world, he opined, as blood to our bodies. Yet, although indispensable to humankind, animals, and plants, it is, he said, also the most terrible instrument of destruction that can be imagined. Any reader of George Eliot's *The Mill on the Floss* will recall both the river's allure and its destructiveness. The awe-inspiring quality of Michelangelo's art was termed *terribilità* by his contemporaries. The great composer to the wonders of nature, Ludwig van Beethoven, includes in his Pastoral Symphony the serene beauty of "Scene by the Brook" before he exhilarates us with the sublimity of the "Storm." Awe is the warning that within much that is beautiful lies the potential for harm, or is startlingly beyond our comprehension. That which may help us may also hurt us or astound us. There is a tension, a contradiction, in every human event – a "civil war within the soul," George Eliot calls it. The water can drown us as well as it can protect us from our predators; the forest can hide the sun from our sight, the dangerous snakes from our vigil. There is a biophobia as well as a biophilia. Our love of art involves the admiration of beauty and the arousal of the *terribilità*. One may go even further with Victor Hugo in the *Préface de Cromwell* (1827): "Ugliness is one detail of a great whole which escapes us and which harmonizes, not with man alone, but with all creation."

V

As we have noted, the Flemish Jesuit Cornelius a Lapide (1567-1637) found some creatures so distasteful he believed they could not have been created by God on the sixth day alongside the other animals. Instead, lice, fleas, maggots, and the like were said to be created by spontaneous generation, as lice from sweat. Lapide's influence was fast, pervasive, and exaggerated. By about 1606, Shakespeare was telling us in *Antony and Cleopatra* that "your serpent of Egypt is bred now of your mud by the operation of your sun; so is your crocodile." In his *Essays* (c. 1597), Francis Bacon praises the ant as "a *wise creature* for it self, [and] it is a shrewd thing in an Orchard or Garden." He has a less benevolent view of the fox and crocodile, which are self-interested deceivers. Self-interest is the *"Wisdom of the Fox,* that thrusts out the *Badger,* who digged and made room for him. It is the *Wisdom of Crocodiles,* that shed tears when they would devour."[24] Certainly, Bacon's view of the animal realm is not a uniform one. Nor is that of the hunter John Jorrocks in Robert Smith Surtees's *Handley Cross* of 1843, despite his avid protestations to the contrary. "It ain't that I loves the fox less," Jorrocks avows, "but that I loves the 'ound more." William Blake wrote songs with evident affection for robins, lambs, and horses but his tempera painting *The Ghost of a Flea* is filled with a conception of a malign presence, the reincarnate existence of excessively bloodthirsty humans, according to a message Blake claimed to receive from the ghost itself. Nor is it humans alone who make such distinctions. In general, young primates, for example, demonstrate an aversion to certain other species, including snakes and spiders, even in the absence of any threat. To be sure, one of the West's greatest errors has been to fail to recognize the vital importance of what are traditionally seen as "pests" to the maintenance of "the balance of nature," although Wordsworth requires us to respect "the weeds," a perception common among Romantics. But it is a failing of almost equal import in other cultures, to which the Kayapó misuse of ants (see page xxi) and the classification of bugs in the *Laws of Manu* (see page 204) would attest. It is in fact modern ecological research that is allowing us – albeit all too slowly – to overcome our traditional and dangerous ignorance.

While it is certainly appropriate to regard all species as valuable in terms of their role within the collectivity that is our global environment, it is equally important to recognize that traditionally we have viewed some animals as distinctly more valuable than others, as wholes and as ecologically contributory parts. Indeed, these conflicting conceptions are an important source of the fact that moral decision-making always involves balances, judgments, and sensibilities concerning the competing claims of legitimate claimants.

Generally speaking, there is a distaste felt toward rats and some other rodents as well as toward malaria-inducing mosquitoes and microbes as carriers of disease, as harmful creatures, though in *Too True to Be Good,* George Bernard Shaw does soliloquize on the rights of "a poor innocent microbe." It should not surprise us that the attitude toward harmful species is a less than entirely positive one. What should surprise us is that, in many instances, it is a not entirely negative one.

Such animals as lions, leopards, and tigers, polar bears and cheetahs, too, arouse our admiration even though they are potentially dangerous enemies when encountered in the wild. Even though we have – more realistically, had – good reason to fear the power of, say, the great cats, we also admire their grace, their beauty, their prowess, indeed their very awesome nobility – and, indeed, especially in more primitive times, we envied them their abilities and accomplishments. The sublime becomes infused with the beauty.

By contrast, we tend to have a negative estimation of the hyena (as indeed do lions) and, though perhaps less so, the shark. Perhaps in part this estimation is because the hyena is seen as a scavenger, although it is in fact also a formidable hunter, but largely because it lacks grace, proportion, and harmony. Its vocalizations are also less than sonorous. It lacks the rhythm we enjoy in sound (both in music and in poetry) and in sight (both in the pictorial arts and in nature itself). In short, it is "ugly." It corresponds to Shakespeare's misconceived image of the "toad, ugly and venomous" (*As*

You Like It, II, I) Hemingway detested the hyena. While he admired the courage of the lion, he described the hyena as an "hermaphroditic, self-eating devourer of the dead, trailer of calving cows, ham-stringer, potential biter-off of your face at night while you sleep." (And while he was wrong about the hermaphroditism, an ancient belief, the genders may only be distinguished by an expert.)

The shark is more ambivalent. It is seen as ferocious and yet sleek. It perhaps epitomizes the sublime – "Creature of terrible beauty," writes Bill Curtsinger of the grey reef shark.[25] The shark does not possess the lack of rhythm of the hyena. If other species are not our brothers but certainly our cousins (7), we must recognize that some are considered to live on the other side of the tracks. Moreover, there are family blood feuds with some of our potentially harmful relatives. We love them as our relatives but deplore them in their characters.

These are truths we have readily forgotten in the recent West, living in safety and security from predation. It is thus that we are inclined to treat animals generically in our philosophies. It was rarely so before this century, when philosophers would write, as did Henry Salt as late as 1892, that "it is not human life only that is lovable and sacred, but *all* innocent and beautiful life." Although modern animal liberationists have preferred to ignore it, Henry Salt meant the references to *innocent* and *beautiful* to be taken seriously. This qualification does not at all mean that the hyena and the shark and the lice do not have their rights. It means that a philosophy that ignores predation is utopian and one that applauds all nature equally lacks discrimination. Mindful of the poetry of William Blake, we should recognize that we have awe for the tyger and love for the lamb. They are rather different emotions.

The Vedic *Laws of Manu* encounter the problem faced by every self-reflexive society.[26] On the one hand, the scripture posits Nature as the good, mentions it as harmonious and worthy of protection by the political powers. On the other hand, it acknowledges the cruelties of a nature red in tooth and claw, which the laws must endeavour to control. It is the contradiction faced by John Locke in his discussion of the state of nature in his *Second Treatise of Civil Government* and from which he, and his readers, emerge no less confused than the readers of the *Laws of Manu*. It is raised equally, though ignored, by those who applaud nature indiscriminately but castigate humans for their sins, as though humans were somehow not an intrinsic element of the nature they applaud.

Nature is the norm, the criterion, the standard, by which we must live, and yet we witness it in both its glory and its shame. The naturalist has as much philosophical difficulty with the notion of a benevolent Nature as the religious devotee with the notion of a benevolent God. Both appear confounded by experience. Our choice is either to acquiesce and partake in the cruelties of nature, or to discover through reason or within our souls some criterion enabling us to discriminate between the valuable in nature (which we must applaud) and the valueless (in which we must necessarily acquiesce but in which we will not participate and which we will overcome to the extent we are able). The error of the West has not lain, as is sometimes claimed by those who criticize the West's "dualism," in its refusal to acknowledge the perfection of nature, but in its failure to recognize how much we are bound by its dictates. We are creatures whose potentialities are limited by nature, limitations the West has unfortunately learned to ignore. But the alternative is not to return to some even less fulfilling practical "state of nature" in which there is hunger, disease, predation, and no less alienation.

Following the Natural Law ideals of the Stoics, the medieval Christian tradition likewise posited Nature as the standard for the measurement of justice, but, recognizing the iniquities of contemporary nature, both human and general, they proclaimed the appropriate standard as Nature before the fall from grace. I doubt the zebra fleeing the lioness will have thought it much of a standard, but then in the medieval tradition many thought animals made in part for human use (and the zebra for the use of the lioness, one wonders). In fact, one encounters versions of this belief today with regard to the purpose of farm animals. But when we consider that primeval humans were far more prey than predators, we have to wonder at the very logic of the argument – unless it means that we should offer ourselves to the next leopard that comes along.

Again, *The Laws of Manu* are instructive. They are represented, in the anonymous manner of most religious texts, as the dictates of Manu – "the first man."[27] They are not *also* but *thus* the word of God. They are the authority of the *arche*. Truth, law, and perfection lie in the beginning. It may be our task, as Confucius saw in the *Analects,* and as medieval jurists saw their tasks in their *Commentaries,* to expound, to discover, the law, but not to determine or make it. The law was as sacrosanct in Mesopotamia, India, China, and medieval Europe as it still is for many Moslems, the Aboriginals of Australia, and, perhaps more precariously, the Aboriginals of North America.

In that state of nature, there is an acknowledgment of perfect peace, perfect justice, and perfect love. Rather than a description of nature, it may be seen as an improvement on nature, as a representation of an imaginary time, a dreamtime, "long ago, back when the animals could talk and people could understand them"[28] – a time when the conflicts and competition not of modernity but of nature itself were unknown: the "time" of unity, before natural conflict. It is an ideal-type conceptualization of nature – nature without the warts. It resembles the classical Greek sculpted statues that represent the unattainable human ideal rather than particular persons. With the Fall, competitive nature begins – "the survival of the fittest," according to Herbert Spencer. Thus, Milton writes in *Paradise Lost* after the perpetual accord of Eden: "Death introduc'd through fierce antipathy: / Beast now with beast gan war, and fowl with fowl, / And fish with fish." Humanity's fall cursed all of nature.

The Janus character of nature is embodied above all in the poetry of Matthew Arnold. While his writings embody it, they do not resolve the contradiction. On the one hand, Arnold excoriates those who would idealize nature:

> Nature is cruel; man is sick of blood:
> Nature is stubborn; man would fair adore:
> Nature is fickle; man hath need of rest:
> Nature forgives no debt, and fears no grave;
> Man would be mild, and with safe conscience blest.
> Man must begin, know this, where Nature ends;
> Nature and man can never be fast friends.
> Fool, if thou canst not pass her, rest her slave!

> – "To an Independent Preacher Who Preached
> that We Should Be 'In Harmony with Nature' "

On the other hand, Arnold wrote three elegies to animals and also asked of Nature:

> For oh, is it you, is it you,
> Moonlight, and shadow, and lake,
> And mountains that fill us with joy,
> Or the poet who sings you so well?

Unequivocally, for Arnold, the qualities lie in Nature rather than the poet:

> Loveliness, Magic, and Grace,
> They are here – they are set in the world –
> They abide – and the finest of souls
> Has not been thrill'd by them all,
> Nor the dullest been dead to them quite.
> they are the life of the world.

> – "The Youth of Nature"

If we are to find any consistency in Arnold, we must acknowledge three competing aspects of Nature: the Nature of beauty, the Nature of awe, and the nature of cruelty, wrath, and devastation. It is only the first two to which Arnold offers his obeisance.

Nor does Arnold stand alone. The Romantic clerical opponent of foxhunting, Charles Kingsley, wrote on the one hand of the beauties of nature, but on the other he invoked the myth of Andromeda in his poem of that name to argue that beauty and goodness were rescued from "the dark powers of nature," a phrase used also by Schopenhauer, by the exercise of Greek humanity. For both Arnold and Kingsley, Nature was not at one with nature. Nor for Shelley, Keats, and Shaw; and Victor Hugo's father wrote of the effects of Vesuvius in full spate as "one of nature's finest horrors," a vision reflected in more than one of his son's *Odes et Ballades*. We should not fail to recognize, however, that Arnold and Kingsley were writing against that growing Victorian feeling, exemplified in the sermon of the "Independent Preacher," that we should indeed live "In Harmony with Nature." Biruté Galdikas too (8) recognizes, against the increasingly dominant implicit strain of Western intellectualism, that nature provides no suitable standard for a healthy life. It was "nature" that failed to offer her beloved orangutans a safe haven. If only her esteemed Carl and Cara had possessed a nature-deviant culture, she suggests, they would have survived. She loves the beings of nature, but deprecates nature itself.

VI

Faced with the realities of competitive nature, our occasional biophobia will not surprise us. Our biophilia is quite astonishing. Whence does the natural compassion of our souls, of our primeval humanity, arise – even in some degree for the hyena, the shark, and the snake? While both Locke and Rousseau wrote of a state of nature in which we were at one with nature by common consensus, they did so rather confusedly. The concept is, in fact, captured most clearly not in philosophical discourse but in Alexander Pope's *Essay on Man*:

> God in the nature of each being founds
> Its proper bliss, and sets its proper bounds:
> But as he fram'd a Whole, the Whole to bless,
> On mutual Wants built mutual Happiness:
> So from the first, eternal ORDER ran,
> And creature link'd to creature, man to man.
>   …
> Nor think, in NATURE'S STATE, they blindly trod;
> The state of Nature was the reign of God:
> Self-love and Social at her birth began,
> Union the bond of all things, and of Man.
> Pride then was not; nor Arts, that Pride to aid;
> Man walk'd with beast, joint tenant of the shade;
> The same his table, and the same his bed;
> No murder cloth'd him, and no murder fed.
>   …
> See him from Nature rising slow to Art!
> To copy Instinct then was Reason's part;

Thus then to Man the voice of Nature spake –
"Go, from the Creatures thy instructions take:
Learn from the birds what food the thickets yield;
Learn from the beasts the physic of the field;

...

And hence let Reason, late, instruct Mankind[29]

In 1832, George Cornewall Lewis (political theorist, cabinet minister, and editor of the *Edinburgh Review*) offered us the definitive denunciation of state of nature arguments, which has retained its force, indeed enjoyed ready acceptance, until today:

The result of this account seems to be, that in the state of nature God ruled the world; that is, God alone ruled it, – there being no human rulers. Benevolence and self-love existed; but, notwithstanding the existence of self-love, all men lived in concord, and the feeling of pride was unknown. There were no arts or government: men lived with the beasts,[30] and subsisted exclusively on vegetable food. In the state of nature men killed neither beasts nor men. After some time, mankind learnt, by observing some of the lower animals, to imitate their ways; and having thus invented the arts of social life, upon the same model they formed societies under an established government.

Such is an outline of this puerile theory of the progress of society; untenable from its self-contradictions, even as a hypothesis, and distinctly refuted by facts: a theory which could only have arisen from the distempered imagination of some day-dreamer, and could only have been tolerated by a blind ignorance or wilful neglect of all history. Pictures of this description may delight the mind, when presented to it in an avowedly poetical and fabulous shape, as in the Greek legends of the golden age; but when introduced into a didactic poem, or a philosophical system of government, they shock the reason without amusing the fancy.[31]

Pope, Locke, and Rousseau must have shifted rather uncomfortably in their graves at such venomous and apparently justified ridicule.

Of course, Lewis is irrefutable in the detail of his argument but, in the success of the refutation, important and worthwhile grain is discarded along with the chaff. Certainly, as history it is predominantly (but not entirely) absurd. Yet the state of nature vision must be understood not as history but as an ideal, a standard by which to measure the failings of natural history. It is what Pope called in his *An Essay on Criticism* "Nature Methodiz'd." It is what Blake meant by "lost originals," what he implied by the "vision of the Eternal Now." For Blake, the nature we experience empirically is no more than the "Mundane Shell" or "Vegetative Universe" that is the vesture of Satan. Something we know in our heart of hearts lies beyond.

It is the thread of yoga – our experiences are of the broken images of a form; the ultimate reality, the harmony, lies beyond in a transcendence from the merely factual. It is what Baudelaire conceptualized as both the absence and the memory of paradise. It is the Platonic *Form,* the Jungian *archetype,* of Nature, not nature as she is wrought. We possess an *idea* of Nature that is contradicted by its contingent reality, which, according to Hugo, "is piti-less." And that "idea," that form, is best sought in poetry (or myth) for, as Aristotle tells us in the *Poetics,* "poetry tends to express the universal, his-tory the particular."

Even as history, the state of nature argument recognizes, even if it per-haps exaggerates, our quasi-vegetarian origins and the importance of our early psychology to our fundamental humanity. It also recognizes the human need to maintain its past as a part of its present. Of course, the "state of nature" is a myth but a myth more instructive than Lewis's reality. What Pope, Locke, and Rousseau are telling us inter alia is that an essential altruism and comforting psychological stasis in primeval human/ani-malkind has been diverted from human and other animal "thinghood" by the vicissitudes of history and should be employed as the utopian ideal of future human achievement to the degree consistent with the existence of our primordial self-interest. There is simply something primal in our souls that tells us that when we encounter self-love and altruism, it is altruism we admire more.

The golden-age state of nature arguments are present in some tribal myths, in Greek heroic legend, and in the Orient. It would be foolish to dis-miss them merely with scintillating logic as does Lewis. Beni Prasad describes the Hindu version of this legend in his *Theory of Government in Ancient India:*

> In a passage of poetic brilliance the Vånaparva records how in very ancient days men lived a pure godly life. They were, in fact, equal to gods. They could ascend to heaven and return to earth at will. The wishes of all were fulfilled. Sufferings were few and real trouble or fear was none. Perfect virtue and happiness reigned. The span of life extended over thousands of years. But all this was changed after a long while. The Santi-parva, too, has it that there was at first a sort of Golden Age wherein existed neither sover-eignty nor king, neither chastisement nor chastiser. All men used to protect one another righteously. But after a while their hearts were assailed by error. Their faculties of perception were clouded; their virtue declined; greed and avarice set in. The downward course continued.[32]

We are told also of a similar narrative of ancient human history in the *Buhaddharma Purana,* where, again, life was one of perfect virtue and happi-ness, free from all sorrow, sin, disease, and disputes.

The Chinese version of the Golden Age was described by Qwang-tse around the fifth century BC: "In the age of perfect virtue, men attached no value to wisdom ... They were upright and correct, without knowing that to be so was Righteousness: they loved one another, without knowing that to do so was Benevolence; they were honest and loyal-hearted, without knowing that it was Loyalty; they fulfilled their engagements without knowing that to do so was Good Faith."[33] In not dissimilar fashion the *Zend-Avesta,* the sacred scripture of the Persians, provides us with a description of a virtuous and benevolent paradise as the ancient but remembered homeland of the race. In Japanese, *natsukashii* refers to a recollection of revered earlier times and a yearning to return to the site of their occurrence. The Golden Age also has a place in modern Western literature. To take but one example, in Dostoevsky's *The Devils,* where Stavrogin's dream of "the Golden Age" is inspired by Claude Lorrain's painting *Acis and Galatea,* the vision is of a primeval earthly paradise of innocence and joy where harmony abounds – "A feeling of happiness hitherto unknown to me, pierced my heart till it ached."

The pervasiveness of the myth ought to tell us something about the importance of the message. Everywhere we can recognize the idea that, however much the reality of historical circumstance may interfere with its practice, there is a primal altruism, a primal identity with idealized Nature, present in the soul of the human race. We are primevally at one with Nature – or would be if we could transcend the cruel realities of nature. Moreover, and again the message is almost universal – though minimized in the contemporary *commercial* and *rationalist* West – as circumstance requires art and culture to deviate from nature, so they must deviate no more than required. Anything more must disturb the health of our psyche. Reason should copy instinct, not invent a culture, a human nature, or a public or private morality all of its own. In the *Reflections,* Burke referred disparagingly to those "so taken up with their theories about the rights of man, that they have totally forgot his nature." Confounded early by the failed promises of a life of reason, W.B. Yeats wrote, "All my moral endeavour for many years has been an attempt to recreate practical instinct in myself." Thomas Hardy believed that the human tragedy lay in the failure of the brain to understand the body's reality. Stéphane Mallarmé tells us that "to be truly human, that is to say Nature reflecting upon itself, you have to think with your entire body." In the Chinese *Book of Songs,* it is written, "The twittering yellow bird *rests* or alights on a little mound." Confucius commented, "When the bird *rests,* it knows where to *rest.* Should a human being be inferior to a bird in knowing where to *rest* (or in knowing what to *dwell in*)?"[34] To be sure, the writings of China's most influential philosopher display a greater concern with the fruits of ambition and the acquisition of wealth than with any respect for animated nature. Nonetheless, the implication for Confucius was that the human who imagines the capacity to transcend nature is less wise than the bird that knows its nature and abides by its limitations. This view does not proscribe any particular cultural mores. It proscribes an attitude to those mores. It requires an attachment to traditional practices except where evidence can demonstrate that circumstances have so changed that the traditional practices no longer fulfil their societal functions.

Echoing Pope and Confucius, the nineteenth-century psychologist William James wrote in *The Varieties of Religious Experience* that "instinct leads, intelligence does but follow." Yet while Pope and Confucius appear to offer a prescription, James appears to describe a psychological law. If so, James is emphatically wrong. In the nineteenth and twentieth centuries especially, humans have not only imagined themselves escaping the bonds of instinct, they have succeeded, at least intellectually, by devising an unnatural culture, but, as Pope and Confucius warned, at the expense of the solidarity of the community. In his essay "On the Duty of Civil Disobedience," Henry David Thoreau wrote, "If a plant cannot live according to its nature, it dies; and so a man."[35] We are unfortunately inclined to forget that we too have our natural limitations, that if not as constrained as a plant we are nonetheless animals and not free to alter our nature as though we were gods. In recent centuries, we have predominantly forgotten the need to relate our practices to our animal origins. One can take civilization out of the sophisticate but one cannot take the bonobo out of Homo sapiens. Our animal origins imply community before individuality, order before liberty, but we are only fulfilled as the creatures of culture that we have become if we balance individuality with community, liberty with order – when we progress with respect for, not in denial of, the road we have travelled. When we become creatures of choice and individuality alone, we lose the security and solidarity of our animal natures. John Steinbeck observed that "man is a double thing – a group animal and at the same time an individual. And it occurs to me that he cannot successfully be the second until he has fulfilled the first."

Yet, in warning, in effect, of the dangers of an individualism that threatens the imperatives of the primordial human (animal) psyche, Pope and those who think like him hint at the error later committed egregiously by Marx. He appears to make the unwarranted assumption that the solution to what is wrong must lie in its antithesis, in the collectivity alone. Thus we recall Pope's lines: "as he fram'd a Whole, the Whole to bless" and "Union the bond of all things, and of Man." One should be immediately mindful of Aristotle's criticism of Plato that his attempt to create a societal unity was at the expense of its natural diversity. The self-actualizing aspects of humanity are as essentially human and fulfilling as the altruism. Collectivism and individualism are not either/or concepts. A healthy society seeks an ever changing balance in which the individual and the society are each deemed ends in themselves – however incompatible those ends may be on occasion. Thus it is that neither history, nor politics, nor dispute, nor alienation will ever end. The right answer today must be the wrong answer tomorrow. Culture and the realities of nature have ensured it.

VII

In recent years, several thinkers have followed James Lovelock's early writings to suggest mother earth as an organism far grander and more complex than individual humans (though Lovelock's later writings back off from the simplicity of this initial suggestion). They follow Lucretius, who wrote of the earth as a living, breathing animal. And they have employed the name of Gaia for this super-organism, the name the Greeks used for the earth goddess.[36]

Whether the earth acts as an organism as Lovelock originally suggested is doubted by most scientists (and in later works by Lovelock himself, though he continues to find the concept a valuable one), but many environmentalists continue to employ the idea. What for our purposes is the relevant consideration is whether treating the earth as an organism, as an or perhaps *the* collective end in itself, is wise. Is it analogous to treating nature as an end in itself with all the difficulties we have witnessed pertaining to the idea of at oneness with nature? Certainly, historical experience warns us that when any entity is treated as the superordinate end in itself, whether state, church, cult, nation, ideology (or now Gaia), it has the potential to serve as an instrument of oppression, however noble the intent of its promoters. It is difficult to overestimate the importance of the troubadours who sang the medieval songs of individual bliss and self-directed destiny and aroused a new human awakening. Gottfried von Strassburg's *Tristan* of around the year 1200 stands as an important symbolic resurrection and advancement of the incipient Greek and later Stoic recognition of the importance of the individual as a self-directed end. It is difficult to overemphasize both the value and the significance of St. Thomas Aquinas's expression of the new thirteenth-century understanding that there is a "human good which does not consist in a community but pertains to each individual as a self."[37] Some of his contemporaries, on the other hand, came close to reducing citizens to what Michael Oakeshott called "mere role-performers in a *bonnum commune*."[38]

While it is undoubtedly true that the greatest failing at the turn of the millennium is the failure to recognize society or Gaia or nature as *an* end in itself, as the collectivity in which our individual ends are made complementary, it would be no less an error to lose sight of the importance of the individual as an end. Gertrude Stein declared, "A sentence is not emotional, a paragraph is." But she always sought the *mot juste*. Cézanne's paintings depend on the importance of each single stroke to create a striking composite. Stein, Fitzgerald, and Hemingway wanted to write as Cézanne painted. What we need is the language and reality of compassion, love, and mutual belonging to replace that of individual selfishness – but not to the detriment of an authentic self. Indeed, in a now almost entirely neglected work, once greatly admired by Hume, Herder, and Montesquieu – *Characteristics of Men, Manners, Opinions, Times* of 1711 – Anthony Ashley Cooper, third earl of Shaftesbury, argued wisely that in aesthetics, ethics, and politics alike, the right path lay always in a delicate equipoise, that in harmony, symmetry, and balance between the community and self lay the essence of sound judgment. That view also pervaded the nineteenth-century novels of George Eliot. She was self-consciously working on maintaining the *Gemeinschaft* values of Ferdinand Tönnies without their religious, gender, and racial prejudices, which, for Eliot, meant allowing for the fruition of individual self-fulfilment to the extent that it was compatible with societal solidarity. In the twentieth century, F. Scott Fitzgerald was convinced that "the test of a first-rate intelligence is the ability to hold two opposed ideas in the mind at the same time and still retain the ability to function."

The success of Nazism, which emphasized the worst aspects of *Gemeinschaft,* lay in its call to community, duty, and belongingness over what the fascists successfully portrayed as the selfish autonomous individualism of the protagonists of Weimar democracy. Unity was the message. In the poetry of Baldur von Schirach, the leader of the Hitler Youth, we read the appealing line, "We are a hundred thousand, yet only one soul." Eventually, the implication of von Schirach's message became clearer. "The more die for a movement," he wrote, "the more immortal it becomes."[39] The Nazis took the logic of collectivism to its natural end. The interests of the individual were entirely subordinate to the whole. But it is not only in extremist doctrine that the one-sidedness abounds. Thus the politically taciturn W.B. Yeats tells us that "every community is a solidarity, all depending upon each other, and each upon all." And so it is. But it is only fulfilling if the personhood of each is ennobled by the solidarity, the dependence, the belongingness. While humans achieve much of their humanity through sacrifice for the community of loved ones (many instances being just small examples of altruism), if it is to be a wholesome and healthy sacrifice it must also fulfil the individual as a self and not just as a member. Fusion *and* fission constitute human wholeness.

Naturally, none of the Gaia scientists would willingly countenance any fascistic conceptions. Nor, of course, did the scientists of the seventeenth century understand the implications of their theories for the excesses of individualism and materialism in the ensuing centuries. Whatever the scientists may imagine about their objective neutrality, the predominant theories promote an intellectual climate in which the sense of self and society corresponds to that of the dominant conceptual framework. The framework is the product of the dominant scientific and social theories rather than, as we are often told, that of the interests of the owners of the means of production. Marxism and its derivatives are more a reflection of the age of "bourgeois science" than a valid critique of it.

It is in fact unfortunate that James Lovelock chose Gaia as the name for the earth as organism because the notion of the earth as an end in itself counters the classical Greek awakening of the inherent dignity of the individual (although one had to await the Stoics for a clearer representation). Perhaps it would be appropriate to use the alternative form of *Gaea* as that which Greek thought increasingly implied: the primal goddess, the mother and nourisher of all things, the fount of compassion – the one who suffers alongside, as in other traditions with the Sanskrit concepts of *karuna* and *mudita*, the German *Mitleid*, or as the French *compassion*, which is intimated in *Larousse* as "bearing the punishments of another." She therefore represents not the earth as the end in itself but individual compassion to all in need of protection and nourishment. As earth goddess, she is the representative of our primal origins, the source of our altruism and above all the symbolic recipient of our love of nature, especially the waters and trees that protected us and the non-threatening animals to which we feel such a bond because they were our fellow travellers and fellow sufferers in the battle for survival. To treat Gaia or Nature as the primary end, that to which other interests must be subordinated, must, as with Nazism, ultimately lead to an oppression of nature's constituent elements – the other animals as much as human.

It is thus through *Gaea,* through a compassionate respect for nature's constituent parts, that we become harmonized with nature to the degree laudable. As Arthur Schopenhauer explained in his essay *The Basis of Morality* (1841), especially in times of psychological crisis, of heroic deeds or desperate needs, we become aware that we and the other are one, that we are two aspects of one life, while retaining our own individual life, and that our sense of a separate identity reflects only the specific conditions of our current place in time and space. In the words of Matthew Arnold: "My neighbour is merely an extension of myself ... deceiving my neighbour is the same as deceiving myself." To put it in more modern idiom, we share our identity with bearers of similar traditions, similar foci, especially with those whom we love, whether compatriot, friend, kinfolk, or spouse. Yet we become aware of sharing our identities in crisis situations, either personal as in a familial loss, or communal as in response to danger. It can, however, be brought to awareness most readily and completely in a love that fulfils both individuals while paradoxically obscuring their separateness. Indeed, the first passion of love is itself experienced as a psychological crisis, and it is not infrequently called a madness (by Walter Scott, Virginia Woolf, and Tennessee Williams, for example). It is but a small conceptual step to include animals in that community, thus both recognizing their worth in relation to ourselves, indeed as a part of our greater selves, and recognizing at the same time their rights as autonomous individual beings.

In the recognition of the beautiful and the sublime, we draw universal truths from individual instances. We love our individual places and times of tranquility and thus come to know and love tranquility itself. We love individual instances of justice and thus come to know and love justice itself. We love individual animals and thus come to know and love animality. We love our gardens and our parks and thus come to love nature. We move from the experience of the individual case to the awareness of the universal truth, and not vice versa. Having advanced this view in *The Mill on the Floss,* George Eliot asks cogently, "What novelty is worth that sweet monotony where everything is known, and *loved* because it is known?" Through experience, we engage in a dialogue with the intimations of the soul. To love peace or justice or animals or nature or Gaia in the philosophical abstract is not to love peace or justice or animals or nature or Gaia. Theoretical knowledge is only valuable if it corresponds to the requirements of practical experience. All too often, the utopian intelligentsia loves humanity but can't abide people in their naked reality. Those who espouse the rights of animals in the abstract receive their entitlement only through friendship with animals in the particular. As the German writer Richard Dehmel proclaimed, "A little kindness between individuals is better than love for all humanity" – and for nature, we might add.

VIII

In Madagascar, fourteen species of lemurs have been hunted to extinction by the native human population. The largest lemur species was once the size of a gorilla. Now the largest species is the size of a human infant. The human population of Madagascar has doubled in recent years to 11 million, and 80 percent of the island's vegetation has been destroyed. The forest has been slashed and burned, which produces acid rain and renders the soil useless after three years of cropping. New Zealand was settled by Maoris about AD 1200. Within 400 years, all eleven species of moa had been hunted to extinction. Nothing the West does could ever be any worse. If these actions constitute the oneness with nature of which the visitors to the Stockholm conference boasted, it is a unity we can well do without.

The West has undoubtedly a lot to feel guilty about in its indiscriminate slaughter of the North American bison from an estimate of about 13 million in 1870 to fewer than 1,000 by 1900. It was an appalling slaughter perpetrated in the main by those intent on feeding the masses of railway workers, by some inveterate and bloodthirsty "sportsmen" (now there's a euphemism!), and by those concerned to make a profit out of their hides. Yet one must also wonder at the equally destructive behaviour of those who reduced the buffalo count from an estimated 60 million in 1800 to some 13 million by 1870 – and certainly only a small fraction can be attributed either to climate or to white man's greed. And at least the West now recognizes and regrets its failings.

If the West is wise, it will listen well to what it is told by other cultures. Indeed, it will rejoice in the benefits to moral understanding advanced in the metaphors of other traditions. But it will assimilate what it learns through its own traditions, through the lessons of Pythagoras, Plutarch, and Porphyry, through Montaigne, Hume, Goethe, Schopenhauer, and Darwin, through Hugo's "Franciscan familiarity with the animal kingdom,"[40] or through the Laird of Abbotsford, Sir Walter Scott, who claimed to have "a fellowship ... with the sheep and lambs." The notion that "everything in nature is linked together" is not exclusively, not even primarily, an Aboriginal or Oriental conception. In *The King of the Golden River* (1841), John Ruskin excoriated those who failed to recognize the interdependence of all of nature – the blackbirds, the hedgehogs, the crickets, the cicadas, and humans, too. Nor did he stand alone, as we saw earlier with the examples of d'Alembert and Cézanne (see page 19). So too John Steinbeck in *The Log from the Sea of Cortez:* "Species are only commas in a sentence ... each species is at once the point and the base of a pyramid ... all life is related." He continued: "Most of the feeling we call religious, most of the mystical outcrying which is one of the most prized and used and desired reactions of our species, is really the understanding and the attempt to say that man is related to the whole thing, related inextricably to all reality, known as unknowable ... all things are one thing and that one thing is all things ... all bound together by the elastic string of time." The same theme is to be found in Victor Hugo's *Les Misérables*. The universe is a "machine made of spirit. A huge meshing of gears of which the first motive force is the gnat and the largest wheel the zodiac ... Every bird that flies carries a shred of the infinite in its claws." Moreover, through the scientific aspects of its mentality, the West is able to treat animals as autonomous ends in themselves; through the troubadours and the Renaissance, it can see and love them as individuals as well as respect them as species. We find the synthesis again in Victor Hugo's *Les Misérables*. After he has told us of the interconnectedness, he relates how Cosette "could watch the butterflies, although she never tried to catch them; tenderness and compassion are part of loving, and a girl cherishing something equally fragile in her heart is mindful of the wings of butterflies."

The secular West has a lot to learn about spirituality from other cultures – it has long diminished the spirituality it once possessed in abundance – but it should merge that spirituality into its own still recollected traditions. As the astute Southern Agrarian Stark Young wrote over six decades ago, "For no thing can there be any completeness that is outside its own nature, and no thing for which there is any advance save in its own kind."[41] The Navajo Emily Benedek writes with wisdom about her own Aboriginal experience: "When one doesn't know the traditions one has nothing to light one's way."[42] It is a profound truth. Indeed, it is a general truth. It applies every bit as much to the West as to the Navajo. It is a curious fact that much of the Western intelligentsia would applaud the profundity of the truth when applied to Aboriginals but would have little or no appreciation of its appropriateness for the West. The West has lost its way and needs to recover it in

light of the best of its own religious, cultural, moral, and intellectual traditions. As Goethe opined, one "must be thoroughly pervaded with the
national spirit, and through ... innate genius feel capable of sympathizing
with the past as well as the present" – a dictum valid for both Europeans and
the Navajo.

Carl Jung assesses the matter with his customary acumen: "When faced
with this problem of grasping the ideas of the East, the usual mistake of
Western man is like that of the student in *Faust*. Misled by the Devil, he con-
temptuously turns his back on science, and, carried away by Eastern
occultism, takes over yoga practices quite literally and becomes a pitiable
imitator ... And so he abandons the one safe foundation of the Western
mind and loses himself in a mist of words and ideas which never would have
originated in European brains, and which never can be profitably grafted
upon them."[43] Few Westerners have had more knowledge of, or sympathy
for, the Oriental mind than Jung, but he understood that each tradition
could approach the fulfilment of common archetypes only through an intricate web of time-honoured cultural norms. If we reject our own traditions,
we alienate ourselves from the potential for successful reform. We replace
wisdom with intelligence, imagination with fancy, and substance with sil-
houette. Aldous Huxley informs us wisely in *Island* that "every writer needs a
literature as his frame of reference; a set of models to conform to or depart
from." And every doer needs a culture as a frame of reference; a set of models
to conform to or depart from – a culture to provide the regularity from which
liberty proceeds. George Eliot demonstrates vividly in *Silas Marner* that an
outcast's "past becomes dreamy because its symbols have all vanished, and
the present too is dreamy because it is linked with no memories." And thus
utility rather than symbiosis becomes the purpose of life. Materialism supersedes community. Rationalism supersedes myth. We require a continually
recognized continuity with the past even though its myths require continuous adjustment in an ongoing engagement with the present.

In translating the *Upanishads*, Yeats wanted to effect a conciliation
between East and West, not to provide a model slavishly to follow. So does
Aldous Huxley in *Island*. Western action must evolve out of Western myth.
Yeats wanted to write his final poetry as quintessentially Irish as it had
always been, but he wanted to make his "last song, sweet & exuberant, a
sort of European *Geeta* or rather my *Geeta*, not doctrine but song." The universal human is found through cultural myth. "Man can embody truth,"
he wrote, "but he cannot know it." And he added, "You can refute Hegel
but not the Saint or the Song of Sixpence." For Yeats, truth was experienced
through the Irish fairy tales that were the literature of the peasantry. Truths
were universal, but the paths must be traditional and particular.

In *The Book of Songs*, edited by Confucius, we read: "The presence of the
Spirit: / It cannot be surmised, / How may it be ignored!"[44] It pervades us.
It is the universal spirit of Pythagoras, Percy Shelley, and Samuel Taylor

Coleridge, of the Inuit and the Tao that ultimately unites all, whether human or non-human animal, indeed all of nature. It is perhaps best expressed by John Dryden's versification of Ovid, again writing of the philosophy of Pythagoras:

> Then Death, so call'd, is but old Matter dress'd
> In some new Figure, and a vary'd Vest:
> Thus all Things are but alter'd, nothing dies;
> And here and there th'unbodied Spirit flies,
> By Time, or Force, or Sickness dispossest,
> And lodges, where it light, in Man or Beast;
> Or hunts without, till ready Limbs it finds
> And actuates these according to their kind;
> From Tenement to Tenement is toss'd;
> The Soul is still the same, the Figure only lost;
> And as the soften'd Wax new Seals receives,
> This face assumes, and that impression leaves;
> Now call'd by one, now by another Name;
> The Form is only chang'd, the Wax is still the same:
> So Death, so call'd, can but the Form deface,
> Th'immortal Soul flies out in empty space;
> To seek her Fortune in some other Place.[45]

While the universal spirit and primal memory may not be the most pervasive concepts of Western thought, they have a legitimate and honourable place in that tradition. The first great philosopher of becoming, Heraclitus, announced, "I have researched into myself."[46] For Heraclitus that meant going beyond the immediate and separate self into the universal soul. In the *Meno,* Plato acknowledged that practical reason may possess "right opinion" derived from a non-transmissible instinct. Pre-philosophical reasoning, for Plato, is but a very ancient memory, older than the person remembering. William Blake confounds Locke's conception of the mind at birth as a blank slate with his assertion that "Innate Ideas are in Every Man born with him. Man is Born like a Garden ready Planted & Sown."[47] The novelist Joseph Conrad claimed that "the mind of man is capable of anything – because everything is in it, all the past as well as all the future." Dudley Young argued, "We may have inherited from grandfather not only his blue eyes and a disposition to speak grammatically but also some remarkably old memories, perhaps of the days when we were hunted by snake or jungle cat, even pterodactyl."[48] Gary Kowalski avows, "In the substratum of the mind, animals and humans share memories of a time when the world was alive and magical, where the voices of departed ancestors mingle with the whispering leaves and blowing wind."[49] For Saul Bellow, the search for the essential self meant uncovering the original self deep within by deliberate introspection. The soul searches for its imprint in its origins. Answering the question "Who am I?" involves first asking "From what have I emerged?" Both Freud and Jung acknowledged a primordial state of mind among modern humans. For Jung, there is a collective unconscious, the seat of our instinctive patterns we recognize as perennial and universal human emotions and values. The primordial images that represent those emotions and values, which have their source in the unconscious, Jung calls archetypes – the common inheritance of all humankind.[50]

To be in harmony with Nature – if that is to mean something positive, something beyond nature as we experience it – requires that we acknowledge the dictates of the collective unconscious that, for Jung, indicated a common identity with the animal world. As Jakob Boehme proclaimed, "And Adam knew that he was within every creature, and he gave to each its appropriate name." That identity means that we are obligated to treat our animal relatives as kin. It is not enough to call an animal Brother. We must treat the animal with at least some of the respect we would accord a sibling – the respect and consideration the animal is entitled to as the being that it is. Perhaps that is the essence of the Shinto concept of *kami,* an awe-inspiring characteristic possessed not merely by animals, but by the trees, the mountains, and the seas as well. All natural objects possess their exclusive *kami* that reflects their distinctiveness and uniqueness. Each natural existence is unique and each merits our awe, but the distinctiveness of each *kami* requires a different obligation. Again with Boehme, "To each its appropriate name." All have merit but some deserve our attention more than others. If this concept has a modern Western equivalent, it is to be found in part in the archetypes of Jung and in part in the intimations of Thomas Hardy, who said he looked "upon all things in inanimate Nature as pensive mutes,"[51] and of E.M. Forster, who wrote "as though inanimate nature had purposes and volitions of its own."[52] Edgar Allan Poe was fascinated by *Androides,* inanimate entities, apparently imbued with spirits. Victor Hugo insisted that even stones have souls, although it was the "worst evil" that inhabited them. By contrast, William Wordsworth's "Excursion" expresses an animism that views the whole world as alive with intimations of the divine. In "Three Years She Grew," he writes of "a passive mergence" with "mute insensate things." His *Prelude* of 1799 is a hymn to the universal spirit – "I saw one life and felt that it was joy." The universal spirit is also present in the writings of Ralph Waldo Emerson (3) – specifically in the concept of "the oversoul" – of Joseph Conrad, James Joyce, and Saul Bellow, for whom the soul reflects the relationship to all of nature. And nowhere is it more fully or more mysteriously expressed than in Marcel Proust's *Jean Santeuil* and *Contre Sainte-Beuve* as well as *À la recherche du temps perdu,* where the idea of the oneness of nature recalls the lovers of Plato's *Symposium* who are intent on reuniting their separate selves into their original single wholeness. As well, for both John Ruskin and Albert Camus the unity of all natural and spiritual phenomena is reflected in the mystery of the universal soul. Stéphane Mallarmé insisted that he could only be understood as "an aptitude of the universal spirit." So too G.B.S.: "I believe in life everlasting; but not for the individual."

Pantheism – the doctrine that deity is manifest in nature and that all beings are essential elements of the universal whole, a common Aboriginal and Oriental perception and an aspect of the idea of the universal spirit – pervaded the minds of Spinoza, Blake, Goethe, Schiller, Cézanne, Wordsworth, and Carlyle among others. It is to be detected in the writings of Tennyson and Mallarmé. Even the Puritan John Milton is described by perhaps his most inspired biographer, Denis Saurat, as a man of "pantheistic ideas." The concepts we associate traditionally with Oriental and Aboriginal thought have a weighty place in the Western canon.

Walt Whitman advised us to get back in touch with nature and emulate the grace of animals. This path was the route to the realization of our souls. His credo began: "This is what you shall do: Love the earth and sun and the animals." On watching a "supinely happy and placid" calf "basking in the sun," Rabindranath Tagore exclaimed, "It made my heart ache with the desire to be at one with the great life that surrounds the earth." At their best, West and East are at one.

To be in harmony with the Nature of myth requires a conscious effort to treat appropriately our fellow animals with whom we identify in our personal unconscious as a part of the collective unconscious. Describing her lover D.H. Lawrence, Jessie Chambers claimed that "With wild things ... he was in primal sympathy – a living vibration passed between him and them." Only if those vibrations, those intimations of the soul, resulted in familially responsive behaviour can we acknowledge a being in harmony with nature. And in Lawrence's case, we have reason to question the validity of the claim. In Jeffrey Meyers's *D.H. Lawrence: A Biography,* we read: "When his little black snub-nosed French bull terrier, Pips, went into heat and became 'sex-alive,' she ignored Lawrence's commands and ran off with a big Airedale. Lawrence thought she had 'appropriated' his emotions, felt betrayed and was horrified by her indiscriminate love-making. He finally found the dog resting on Götzsche's lap, cursed her and screamed: 'So there you are you dirty, false little bitch,' struck her with all his might and knocked her to the floor ... he kicked her and hurled her to the ground."[53] And if we are willing to question claims made about D.H. Lawrence's "at oneness with nature" – he certainly failed to respect the bull terrier's nature, wild or not, and behaved in a deplorably cruel manner – we must be willing, if we are to be intellectually honest and consistent, to put others to the same behavioural test and not rely on pious yet unverified assertion. Lawrence's perverseness contradicted his philosophy. So does that of many another. In the cogent words of Laurence Sterne in *Tristram Shandy:* "Rhetorick and conduct were at perpetual handy-cuffs."

Even though Lawrence did not always treat animals with the respect to which they were entitled, he could, as Aldous Huxley said, "get inside the skin of an animal and could tell you in the most convincing detail how it felt and how, dimly, inhumanly, it thought."[54] To identify with the animal, as Lawrence did, was not necessarily to treat the animal well. The idea of being at one with nature, of identifying with other species, has many complex elements that require a complex understanding.

Ralph Waldo Emerson described Walt Whitman's *Leaves of Grass* as "a singular blend of the Bhagavad Gita and the New York *Tribune*," its voice "half song-thrush, half alligator." This is indeed synthetic wisdom. Starting from Western culture and listening to other relevant voices constitutes, for Whitman, a development of Western culture. It does not become something alien to itself but listens to powerful and persuasive voices that become a small but important part of its own voice. It does not forsake the historic self for a new self. It does not reject the verities of its own past but opens the present to a viable accommodation of the tried, the true, and the comfortable with new insights. This allows it to meet new circumstances with vigour and confidence rather than with self-doubt and alienation from its own identity.

Appropriately, Whitman's voice is "half song-thrush, half alligator," for that ambivalence, indeed downright contradictoriness, represents both the human condition and the condition of nature. The song-thrush and the alligator are ineradicable parts of both human nature and non-human nature. They are not subject to historical transcendence. They are the reality that only a capitalized Nature can transcend.

Philip Callow tells us that Whitman "was two: coarse and delicate, solitary and democratic, radical and conservative, buffalo and hermit thrush, man and woman."[55] We have already witnessed similar contradictions in Rousseau and Tagore. The opening words of Dutta and Robinson's *Rabindranath Tagore* tell us: "This is an ambivalent book. It has to be." It has to be because Tagore is ambivalent. But it is so not because Tagore differs in principle from others but because he epitomizes others. Tagore, Rousseau, and Whitman – and we might add Aristotle, Bacon, Shaftesbury, Burke, George Eliot, and Hawthorne, perhaps Hugo, Yeats, and Virginia Woolf – represent in their ambivalence the wisdom of those who would seek progress in humanity's journey not by offering rationalist solutions to complex problems but by trimming and tacking, seeking balance and equipoise, knowing what can be changed and what is best left alone, ultimately recognizing both humanity's worthy aspirations and inexorable limitations.

Ethical life for all in whatever culture involves seeking balances among competing principles and competing ends in themselves in order that we might develop our cultures in their own terms to produce an accommodation with our environment, whether human, other animal, vegetable, or mineral. In the final analysis, the goal, however ultimately unachievable, must be, in the words of one of the Concord sages, Margaret Fuller, to secure "that spontaneous love for every living thing, for man and beast and tree, which restores the golden age."[56] Writing over a century later, Jacquetta Hawkes (*A Land* [1951]) extended the vision. It was the task of humankind to rediscover its kinship with "earth, air, fire and water, past and future, lobsters, butterflies, meteors and man." And if the Golden Age is an unachievable myth, we may still respect the things of nature we cannot love, and love more dearly the things of nature we can.

To be "at one with nature" must involve an acquiescence, even a participation, in the harm and cruelties of nature. To experience jubilation in those parts of nature that are joyous and fulfilling is to reject a part of nature. This encounter with nature involves finding moral criteria to distinguish the better from the worse parts of nature, the healthy from the diseased, the beautiful from the plain, the necessary from the plastic, the just from the unjust – the discovery of a capitalized Nature. It is to be at one with justice allied with necessity, not to be at one with lower-case nature. With Goethe, who thought of each animal as end in itself, we must recognize that a standard for judging nature – Nature idealized – lies inside rather than outside every person.

"Nature" as a value in itself is a myth – whether in its Western, Oriental, or Aboriginal manifestations – but, as Lionel Trilling sagely wrote, "The value of any myth cannot depend on its demonstrability as a fact but only on the value of the attitudes it embodies, the further attitudes it engenders and the actions it motivates."[57] However much "Nature" is a myth, it is a myth we all require refracted through the lens of our respective cultures.

IX

In *The Brothers Karamazov* (1880), Dostoevsky tells us that "people sometimes speak about the 'animal' cruelty of man, but that is terribly unjust and offensive to animals, no animal could ever be so cruel as a man, so artfully, so artistically cruel."[58] For Dostoevsky, artful cruelty is a cultural characteristic of humanity, derived not from the instincts of the soul but from the myths we have developed and from individually deviant minds. It pervades all societies – Dostoevsky comments specifically on Russians, West Europeans (taking the Swiss as an example), Bulgarians, Turks, and Tartars. But it does not pervade all individuals. And not all societies in the same way or all of the time. There is also a goodness in humanity that permits us to overcome our baser selves. If we exert ourselves to find the grander spirit of our historical traditions, we may come to diminish the cruelty that lies within every individual – "a beast hidden in every man, a beast of rage, a beast of sensual inflammability."

With Dostoevsky's message in mind, I undertook the studies that led to the writing of this book. Initially, my respect for Dostoevsky's insights and my personal experiences rather than my research suggested that Western precepts and practices were no worse than, though somewhat different from, those of other cultures. The evidence arising from my investigations, which I have presented in this work, confirmed my original conceptions. But there should be a warning, too. We all tend to find the evidence that supports our hypotheses, that confirms our prejudgments. I have done my best to bear this in mind, to be scrupulously fair in testing my hypotheses against the available evidence, to be as faithful as possible to the evidence I have uncovered. I hope I have succeeded. But even if, despite my efforts, I have occasionally succumbed to the perennial intellectual temptation to be tendentiously selective, there should be little doubt there is far more of a healthy attitude to animated nature in the Western tradition than we are customarily led to believe. Much of the Western tradition has been unjustifiably dismissed in the existing literature employing cross-cultural comparisons. And, equally, there is much of the less salubrious aspects of the Aboriginal and Oriental worldviews that has been unjustifiably ignored.

Certainly, the more I researched, the more the evidence for a vital and respectful Western tradition became compelling – far more even than I had originally anticipated. Indeed, for reasons of space – and, as I have often been chastised in the preparation of this book, also to save the reader from being drowned in evidence – much that deserves attention has been omitted. The ideas of a number of the Presocratics – Xenophon on horses, for example – of Albrecht Dürer, Adam Smith, Lamartine, Harriet Beecher Stowe, Schiller, and Wagner were entitled to a prominent place but have gone largely unmentioned. Yet others from Blake and Voltaire through Darwin and Huxley to George Eliot, the Brontës – *Shirley* and *Agnes Grey*[59] are most instructive – Tolstoy, and Schweitzer deserved more emphasis than they received. There are also several more who seemed to have something of value to contribute but with whom my acquaintance was too slight to be confident of my reading of them on animal and nature issues – Louisa May Alcott, Edward Lear, Tennessee Williams, and James Joyce would have been admirable candidates for extensive consideration. There are impressive hints in Williams's *The Night of the Iguana*, and Bloom's animal sympathy in *Ulysses* would be a sound starting point for studying Joyce. *Ulysses* is also replete with the horrors of meat consumption, but Joyce has ribald points to make about vegetarians, too. Moreover, there must be many more who have written in similar vein but of whose work I am woefully ignorant – including the playwright Richard Brinsley Sheridan, who helped promote early animal welfare legislation in the British Parliament; Jack London, despite the unduly anthropomorphic nature of his animals; and the muse of Nature, Friedrich Klopstock.

What I think I have demonstrated is that the apparently pejorative language of the Western tradition has been largely misread, sometimes for ideological reasons, and that the commendatory usage has been largely ignored; that the distinction between human and non-human animals in the Western tradition is a complex one that has not always denigrated the animal realm and has often led to a readier appreciation; that the degree of Western rationalism has been overemphasized and that a number of the rationalists have still expressed a profound respect for animated nature; that the non-rationalist strain has had a commendable impact on Western thought, stimulating a healthy recognition of our due place in nature; that the scientific concept of objectivity has brought about a commendable recognition of the worthwhileness of the individuality of other species; and that, while other traditions have much to teach the West, so too has the West much of value to impart to others.

What I hope I have also provided is an image of Nature, especially animated nature, toward which we are irresistibly drawn and that will encourage us to treat fauna and flora with the respect that is their due.

Boys may kill frogs for fun,
But the frogs die in earnest

          – Plutarch, c. AD 100

Ymwrandawed dyn a'i gallon.
One should listen to the promptings of one's heart.

          – Morgan Llwyd, *Llyfr y Tri Aderyn* (*The Book of the Three Birds*), seventeenth century

The tree which moves some to tears of joy is in the Eyes of
others only a Green thing that stands in the way.

          – William Blake, letter to John Trussed, 1799

true wisdom's world will be
Within its own creation, or in thine,
Maternal Nature!

          – George Gordon, Lord Byron, *Childe Harold's Pilgrimage,* Canto 3, 46, 1817

Men can do nothing without the make-believe of a beginning.

          – George Eliot, *Daniel Deronda,* I, 1, 1876

Nature, with all her cruelty, comes nearer to us than do these crowds of [urban] men.

> – E.M. Forster, *Howard's End*, Chap. 13, 1910

Beauty is only the first touch of terror we can bear.

> – Rainer Maria Rilke, *Duino Elegies*, 1, 1912

We need another and a wiser and perhaps a more mystical concept of animals.

> – Henry Beston, *The Outermost House*, 1928

Man is a unit of the greater beasts, the phalanx. The phalanx has pains, desires, hungers and strivings as different from those of the unit man's as man's are different from [those of his] cells.

> – John Steinbeck, "Argument of Phalanx," unpublished ms., 1934

Notes

Preface

1 T.C. McLuhan, *The Way of the Earth: Encounters with Nature in Ancient and Contemporary Thought* (New York: Simon and Schuster, 1994).
2 In W. Jackson Bate, *Samuel Johnson* (San Diego: Harcourt Brace, 1979), 139. In like manner, Jean-Jacques Rousseau wrote: "Cast your eyes on all the nations of the world, go through all the histories. Among so many inhuman and bizarre cults, among this prodigious diversity of morals and characters you will find everywhere the same ideas of justice and decency, everywhere the same notions of good and bad" (*Emile,* ed. Allan Bloom [New York: Basic Books, 1994 (1762)], Bk. 4, 288). Rather more entertaining versions of the thesis are to be found in G.K. Chesterton's *The Napoleon of Notting Hill* (London: Penguin, 1991 [1904]), especially Bk. 1, Ch. 1, and Bk. 5, Ch. 3, and Voltaire's *Candide* (1759), passim, but especially Ch. 21. In *Resurrection* (1899, Pt. 1, Ch. 59) Leo Tolstoy offers a similar theme as does Victor Hugo in *Les Misérables* (1862, Pt. 4, Bk. 3, Ch. 3).

Introduction: The Denigration of the West

1 Roderick Frazier Nash, *The Rights of Nature: A History of Environmental Ethics* (Madison: University of Wisconsin Press, 1984), 117-9; Robert Isaak, *American Political Thinking: Readings from the Origins to the 21st Century* (New York: Harcourt, Brace, 1994), 251-4, contains a faithful representation of the original 1887 article in the Seattle *Sunday Star.*
2 Jim Mason, *An Unnatural Order: Uncovering the Roots of our Domination of Nature and Each Other* (New York: Simon and Schuster, 1993), 21ff.
3 Ibid., 30.
4 *Oxford Companion to Philosophy*, ed. Ted Honderich (Oxford: Oxford University Press, 1995).
5 Lynn White, Jr., "The Historical Roots of Our Ecologic Crisis," *Science* 155 (1967): 1203-7.
6 Nash, *The Rights of Nature,* 50-2.
7 Evans included the article in his *Evolutionary Ethics and Animal Psychology* (New York: W.D. Appleton, 1897), 82-104.
8 John Passmore, *Man's Responsibility for Nature: Ecological Problems and Western Traditions* (London: Duckworth, 1974), 6; Peter Singer, *Animal Liberation,* 2nd ed. (New York: New York Review of Books, 1990), 187.
9 John Brown, *The Self-Interpreting Bible* (Glasgow: Blackie, 1834 [1776]), 2; George Nicholson, *On the Primeval Diet of Man ... &c.* (Poughnill: Nicholson, 1801), 6; James Thomson, *Seasons,* "Spring," line 241; Joseph Ritson, *An Essay on Abstinence from Animal Food as a Moral Duty* (London: Richard Phillips, 1802), 164.
10 Hiroyuki Watanabe, "The Conception of Nature in Japanese Culture," *Science* 183 (1973): 280.
11 G. Naganathan, *Animal Welfare and Nature: Hindu Scriptural Perspectives* (Washington: Center for Respect of Life and Environment, 1989), 2, 1.
12 Timothy Severin, *Vanishing Primitive Man* (New York: American Heritage, 1973); Thomas Berry, *The Dream of the Earth* (San Francisco: Sierra Club, 1988), especially Ch. 14: "The Historical Role of the American Indian"; David Maybury-Lewis, *Millennium: Tribal Wisdom and the Modern World* (New York: Viking, 1992).
13 Peter Knudtson and David Suzuki, *Wisdom of the Elders* (Toronto: Stoddart, 1992), 51, 55.

14 Ibid., 35.
15 Ralph Helfer, *The Beauty of the Beasts* (Los Angeles: Tarcher, 1990).
16 Rod Preece and Lorna Chamberlain, *Animal Welfare and Human Values* (Waterloo: Wilfrid Laurier University Press, 1993 and 1995).
17 Knudtson and Suzuki, *Wisdom of the Elders*, 63, 65.
18 Idanna Pucci, *Bhima Swarga: The Balinese Journey of the Soul* (Boston: Little Brown, 1992), 68, 105, 98.
19 Ibid., 84, 55.
20 Richard Francis Burton, *Sindh, and the Races that Inhabit the Valley of the Indus*, quoted in Christopher Ondaatje, *Sindh Revisited: A Journey in the Footsteps of Captain Sir Richard Francis Burton; 1812-1849: The India Years* (Toronto: HarperCollins, 1996), 207.
21 *Young India,* 18 November 1926.
22 Ondaatje, *Sindh Revisited*, 205-7.
23 Rousseau, *Emile*, Bk. 1, 39.

Chapter 1: Advocacy Scholarship
1 Joachim Gasquet, *Cézanne* (London: Thames and Hudson, 1991 [1921]), 141.
2 Lone Thygesen Blecher and George Blecher, eds., *Swedish Folktales and Legends* (New York: Pantheon, 1993), xxi.
3 Ranchor Prine, *Hinduism and Ecology: Seeds of Truth* (London: Cassell, 1992), 5.
4 Quoted in P.N. Furbank, *E.M. Forster: A Life* (London: Abacus, 1993 [1977]), Vol. 1, 250.
5 Mohandas K. Gandhi, *An Autobiography: The Story of My Experiments with Truth* (Boston: Beacon Press, 1993 [1957]), 320.
6 Celia Haddon, *The Love of Cats* (London: Headline, 1992), 9.
7 See Simon J.M. Davis, *The Archaeology of Animals* (New Haven: Yale, 1987), especially 100-14.
8 M.W. Padmasiri de Silva, "Buddhist Ethics," in *A Companion to Ethics,* ed. Peter Singer (Oxford: Basil Blackwell, 1993), 65. Emphasis added.
9 Quoted in David Comfort, *The First Pet History of the World* (New York: Fireside, 1994), 123.
10 R.L. Stevenson, *Travels with a Donkey in the Cévennes* (London: Chatto and Windus, 1980 [1879]), 43, 45, 49, 126, 92.
11 *Works of William Wordsworth* (Ware: Wordsworth Editions, 1994), 23. Among the numerous poems one could mention that are similar in orientation, William Blake's "The Little Girl Found" is especially worthy of attention.
12 Laurence Sterne, *A Sentimental Journey through France and Italy* (London: Penguin, 1986 [1768]), 63. The information to the daughter is taken from A. Alvarez's introduction to the same edition, 11.
13 The quotation is to be found in the notes on Laurence Sterne in the 1882 edition of the *Dictionary of National Biography* (London: Oxford University Press, 1960).
14 See Keith Thomas, *Man and the Natural World* (London: Penguin, 1984), 136.
15 For examples, see *The Descent of Man and Selection in Relation to Sex* (New York: A.L. Burt, n.d. but reprint of second edition of 1874), 24, 25, 40, 61, 62, 73, 81, 87, 98, 105, 125, 133, 138, 153, and so on. To choose an instance at random: "The strong tendency in our nearest allies, the monkeys, in microcephalous idiots, and in the barbarous races of mankind, to imitate whatever they hear deserves our notice, as bearing on the subject of imitation" (98). Of course, Darwin was expressing no more than prevailing contemporary prejudices, but one might have expected more from such an exceptional scholar.
16 For example, see those of Gabriel Forigny, Denise Vairasse d'Alais, and the Baron de Lohantan. Even Kant poses the question of "whether we might not be happier living in a primitive condition where we would have none of our present culture" (quoted in Leo Tolstoy's *The Law of Love and the Law of Violence* [Ch. 16]). Parodoxically, Voltaire parodies "noble savage" ideas in *Candide* (Ch. 20).
17 See Basil Willey, *The Eighteenth Century Background: Studies on the Idea of Nature in the Thought of the Period* (London: Chatto and Windus, 1946 [1940]), 12.
18 For a discussion of the theme among Aboriginals, but not of these examples, see Mircea Eliade, "The Myth of the Noble Savage," in *Myths, Dreams and Mysteries* (New York: Harper, 1967), 39-56.
19 Hesiod, *Theogony* and *Works and Days* (Oxford: Oxford University Press, 1988), 42, 40.
20 A more complete list would include at least Aratus, Tibullus, pseudo-Seneca, Virgil, and Ovid.
21 Tacitus, *Annals* (Pennsylvania: Franklin, 1982 [c. AD 100]), 101.
22 J-narrative, 7, 5; see George Boas, *Primitivism and Related Ideas in the Middle Ages* (Baltimore: Johns Hopkins, 1997 [1948]), 187-8.
23 Boethius, *The Consolation of Philosophy* (Harmondsworth: Penguin, 1969), translated with an introduction by V.E. Watts, 68.

24 Quoted in Stelio Cro, *The Noble Savage: Allegory of Freedom* (Waterloo: Wilfrid Laurier University Press, 1990), 22 , 23-4.

25 And perhaps Oviedo, Pietro Bembo, and Francisco López de Gomara.

26 Michel de Montaigne, *Selected Essays* (New York: Oxford University Press, 1982 [1580]), 213, 214, 213.

27 Ibid., 215.

28 Ibid., 216.

29 Jean-Jacques Rousseau, *Emile,* ed. Allan Bloom (New York: Basic Books, 1994 [1762]), Bk. 1, 52.

30 Mary Wollstonecraft, "A Vindication of the Rights of Woman," in *Political Writings,* ed. Janet Todd (Oxford: Oxford University Press, 1994 [1792]), 83.

31 Cro, *The Noble Savage,* 88, 89.

32 Arthur O. Lovejoy, "The Supposed Primitivism of Rousseau's *Discourse on Inequality,*" *Modern Philology* 21 (1923): 165-86.

33 J.J. Rousseau, *Discourse on Inequality,* in *Rousseau's Political Writings,* ed. Alan Ritter and Julia Conway Bondanella (New York: W.W. Norton, 1988), 13.

34 Introduction to *Emile,* 7. The relevant passages are in Bk. 3, 184-8.

35 Daniel Defoe, *The Life and Adventures of Robinson Crusoe* (Harmondsworth: Penguin, 1985 [1710]), 201, 178.

36 Ibid., 130, 81, 82.

37 *Rambler* 33 (1750); *Adventurer* 67 (1753).

38 Lois Whitney, *Primitivism and the Idea of Progress in Popular English Literature of the Eighteenth Century* (New York: Octagon, 1973 [1934]), 1, 137.

39 They may also be discerned in the philosophy of David Hartley, Baron d'Holbach, Joseph Priestley, Mary Wollstonecraft, and Lord Monboddo.

40 See Willey's *The Eighteenth Century Background,* passim. Lord Monboddo's is an especially interesting case, although it is not discussed by Willey. See *Antient Metaphysics,* 6 vols. (Edinburgh: Caddell, 1774-99), Vol. 3, 41-2; Vol. 5, 235; Vol. 3, 103; Vol. 3, 201-2. For an elaboration of this topic, see below Ch. 8.

41 William Leiss, *The Domination of Nature* (New York: Braziller, 1972).

42 Rudolf Kaiser, "A Fifth Gospel, Almost: Chief Seattle's Speech(es): American Origins and European Reception," in *Indians and Europe: An Interdisciplinary Collection of Essays,* ed. Christian F. Feest (Aachen: Ed. Herodot, Rader-Verlag, 1987), 505-26.

43 *Black Elk Speaks* (New York: Pocket Books, 1975 [1959]).

44 A. Kehoe, *The Ghost Dance* (New York: Holt, Rinehart and Winston, 1989), 51-62.

45 *Animal Rights, Human Rights: Ecology, Economy and Ideology in the Canadian Arctic* (Toronto: University of Toronto Press, 1991), back cover. The view prevails throughout the book.

46 Alan D. McMillan, *Native Peoples and Cultures of Canada: An Anthropological Overview* (Vancouver: Douglas and McIntyre, 1988), 11.

47 See, for example, F. Wilman, *Land Filled with Flies: A Political Economy of the Kalahari* (Chicago: University of Chicago Press, 1989); E. Wilmsen and J.R. Denbow, "Paradigmatic History of San-Speaking Peoples and Current Attempts at Revision," *Current Anthropology* 31 (1990): 489-524; R.B. Lee, "Art, Science or Politics? The Crisis in Hunter-Gatherer Studies," *American Anthropologist* 94 (1992): 31-54; R.B. Lee and M. Guenther, "Problems in Kalahari Historical Ethnography and the Tolerance of Error," *History in Africa* 20 (1993): 185-235; J.R. Solway and R.B. Lee, "Foragers, Genuine or Spurious? Situating the Kalahari San in History," *Current Anthropology* 31 (1990): 109-46.

48 For an illuminating discussion of "The Great Syphilis Debate," see John W. Verano and Douglas H. Obelaker, "Health and Disease in the Pre-Columbian World," in *The Seeds of Change: Five Hundred Years since Columbus,* ed. Herman J. Viola and Carolyn Margolis (Washington: Smithsonian Institute, 1991), 209-21. It was once a commonplace to believe that syphilis was contracted by the Spaniards through sexual contact with New World sheep. That hypothesis is not discussed by Verano and Obelaker. Nor is the view of Francis Bacon that syphilis was to be attributed to feeding on human flesh.

49 See Daniel Boorstin, *The Discoverers: A History of Man's Search to Know His World and Himself* (New York: Vintage, 1985), 340.

50 For Maybury-Lewis, see *Millennium: Tribal Wisdom and the Modern World (New York: Viking, 1992),* 14, and for Ramenofsky, see Göran Burenhult, ed., *New World and Pacific Civilizations* (San Francisco: Harper, 1994), 216-7.

51 Ibid., 216-7. Emphasis added.

52 *I Ching,* trans. Thomas Cleary (Boston: Shambhala, 1992), 31. Some may read this as "self-possession." However, one will also read "adorned and luxuriant, you will be lucky if you are always

steadfast and true" (49), "Adornment succeeds" (48), and "The action of Nature is powerful; cultured people use it to strengthen themselves ceaselessly" (1-2).

53 Charles Darwin, *Descent of Man*, 135.
54 1845 preface to *Père Goriot* (London: Daily Telegraph, 1885 [1842]).

Chapter 2: Beastliness and Brutality

1 In one paragraph, we encounter a fish, a quail, a corncrake, linnets, a lamb, a lark, and cranes.
2 *The Ladybird, The Fox, The Plumed Serpent, Reflections on the Death of a Porcupine, The White Peacock, The Escaped Cock,* and *Kangaroo.*
3 In fact, in Western science, Linnaeus, the founder of binomial taxonomy, raised the status of the bat by numbering it among the primates. While nineteenth-century scientists rejected Linnaeus's conclusion, in 1988 Dr. John D. Pettigrew of the University of Queensland concluded that the flying fox, a bat, is indeed a primate.
4 John Austin Barker, foreword to Humphry Primatt, *The Duty of Mercy and the Sin of Cruelty to Brute Animals,* ed. Richard D. Ryder (Fontwell: Centaur, 1992), 10.
5 Mary Midgley, "The Origin of Ethics," in *A Companion to Ethics,* ed. Peter Singer (Oxford: Blackwell, 1993), 5.
6 Vail's *Marri's Vision,* in *Myths and Legends: Middle Ages,* ed. H.A. Guerber (London: Senate, 1994), 343.
7 Quoted in Erik Trinkaus and Pat Shipman, *The Neandertals* (New York: Knopf, 1992), 33.
8 C.G. Jung, *Memories, Dreams, Reflections* (New York: Vintage, 1985 [1963]), 58.
9 In the preface to *Mary Barton* (1848), Elizabeth Gaskell refers to the "dumb people" of the working classes not to suggest they are stupid but to indicate that, without education, they are inarticulate and unable to press their own case.
10 Not all approved of "pity," it should be noted. Stoics, Spinoza, and Nietzsche thought it a counter-productive emotion.
11 Quoted in Krishna Dutta and Andrew Robinson, *Rabindranath Tagore: The Myriad-Minded Man* (London: Bloomsbury, 1997 [1995]), 346.
12 From "Reflections on Death," in André Gide, ed., *The Living Thoughts of Montaigne* (London: Cassell, 1940), 26, 27. I have modernized the spelling used by Gide.
13 "Evolution of Bowerbirds' Bowers: Animal Origins of the Aesthetic Sense," *Nature* 297 (1982): 100.
14 "Bower Quality, Number of Decorations, and Mating Successes of Male Satin Bowerbirds (Ptilonorhynchus violaceus): An Experimental Analysis," *Animal Behaviour* 33 (1985): 266-71.
15 *De officiis,* ed. Thomas Cockman (Oxford: R. and R. Bliss, 1805), 37-8.
16 *Reflections of Eden: My Years with the Orangutans of Borneo* (Boston: Little, Brown, 1995), 356.
17 Reuben Halleck, *History of English Literature* (New York: American Book, 1900), 215.
18 For examples, see *Oxford English Dictionary,* compact edition (Glasgow: Oxford University Press, 1971), 1, 185, 737.
19 *Concise Oxford Dictionary of Current English* (Oxford: Clarendon Press, 1961), 101.
20 *Politics* 1.2.15-16, Barker edition (London: Oxford University Press, 1952), 7.
21 Thomas Hobbes, *Leviathan,* ed. Michael Oakeshott (New York: Collier, 1962), 100.
22 James Boyd Davies, *The Practical Naturalist's Guide containing instructions for collecting, preparing and preserving specimens in all departments of Zoology. Intended for the use of students, amateurs and travellers* (Edinburgh: Maclachlan and Stewart, 1858), 4.
23 Rod Preece and Lorna Chamberlain, *Animal Welfare and Human Values* (Waterloo: Wilfrid Laurier University Press, 1993 and 1995), 23-4.
24 Reflective of even sensitive eighteenth-century attitudes to other species, White wrote to Thomas Pennant in 1767:

> It gave me no small satisfaction to hear that the *falco* [in fact, a peregrine falcon] turned out an uncommon one. I must confess I should have been better pleased to have heard that I had sent you a bird that you had never seen before; but that, I find would be a difficult task.
> I have procured some of the mice mentioned in my former letters, a young one and a female with young, both of which I have preserved in brandy.

> —*The Natural History of Selborne* (London: Folio Society, 1962), 24

It was clearly thought that one could use other species at will, provided the purpose was educational.

25 Quoted in Frank McLynn, *Robert Louis Stevenson: A Biography* (London: Pimlico, 1994), 264.
26 Ibid., 284.

27 *Adversus Marcionem,* Vol. 1, 14, in George Boas, *Primitivism and Related Ideas in the Middle Ages* (Baltimore: Johns Hopkins, 1997 [1948]), 89.

28 Quoted in Michael Holroyd, *Bernard Shaw* (Harmondsworth: Penguin, 1990), Vol. 1, 87. A similar recognition of the conflict between the beauty and the "ravening" of nature is to be found in John Keats's verse epistle "To J.H. Reynolds, Esq." (25 March 1818). In *Isabella,* written in the same year, he castigated the capitalist class for its inhumanity: "for them in death / The seal on the cold ice with piteous bark / Lay full of darts." It was not the control of Nature he abhorred but its inhumane form, for he was a devotee of Owenite industrialism.

29 Quoted in Holroyd, *Bernard Shaw,* Vol. 1, 218. However, in *The Admirable Bashville,* in contrasting the supposed barbarities of boxing with the concealed cruelties of sport hunting, butchering, and animal experimentation ("Groping for cures in the tormented entrails / Of friendly dogs"), Shaw employs Nature as an implicit standard: "Oh, your ladies! / Seal skinned and eagret-feathered; all defiance / to Nature."

30 Martin Seymour-Smith, *Hardy* (London: Bloomsbury, 1995), 116-7.

31 The Earl of Beaconsfield, *Endymion,* 3 vols. (London: Longman's Green, 1880), Vol. 1, 231, 287.

32 Keith Thomas, *Man and the Natural World* (London: Penguin, 1984), 13.

33 *Orwell: The Authorized Biography* (London: Minerva, 1991), 49.

34 Ibid., 217.

Chapter 3: Animals All?

1 See Rod Preece and Lorna Chamberlain, *Animal Welfare and Human Values* (Waterloo: Wilfrid Laurier University Press, 1993 and 1995), 45.

2 "Are You an Animal?" in *Animal Experimentation: The Consensus Changes,* ed. Gill Langley (New York: Chapman and Hall, 1989), 17-8.

3 "Some Meanings of 'Nature,' " in *Primitivism and Related Ideas in Antiquity,* ed. Arthur O. Lovejoy and George Boas (Baltimore: Johns Hopkins, 1997 [1935]), 447-56.

4 Peter Singer, *Animal Liberation,* 2nd ed. (New York: New York Review of Books, 1990), 271.

5 Michael W. Fox, *Inhumane Society* (New York: St. Martin's, 1990), 98, 210, 230, 231, 100, 221, 228.

6 James Serpell, *In the Company of Animals* (Oxford: Basil Blackwell, 1986), 199 ff.

7 Carl Sagan and Ann Druyan, *Shadows of Forgotten Ancestors* (New York: Random House, 1992), 383.

8 Ibid., 374.

9 Today, the order Primate includes 11 families, 52 genera, and 181 species, ranging from dwarf and mouse lemurs and bush babies among the prosimians (lower primates) through the marmosets and tamarins to the Pongidae family (gorillas, common chimpanzees, pygmy chimpanzees or bonobos, and orangutans) and Homo sapiens. See *The Primates,* ed. David Macdonald (New York: Torstar, 1985), 10-1.

10 *The Origin of Species,* ed. J.W. Burrow (London: Penguin, 1985), 108.

11 *The Descent of Man and Selection in Relation to Sex* (New York: A.L. Burt, n.d. but reprint of second edition of 1874), 170.

12 A worthwhile account of their claims is to be found in David N. Livingstone, *Darwin's Forgotten Defenders: The Encounter between Evangelic Theology and Evolutionary Thought* (Edinburgh: Scottish Academic Press, 1987). See index and especially 59 ff. This is not the place to discuss creation science. Suffice it to say, then, that I feel justified in describing it as antiquated because the claims of its proponents have not been dismissed out-of-hand by the scientific community but met head on and refuted.

13 *The Neandertals* (New York: Alfred A. Knopf, 1992), 170. The quotation from G.G. Simpson is to be found here also.

14 *The Poetical Works of Robert Browning* (London: Smith, Elder, 1896), Vol. 1, 250-1, 408-12.

15 Quoted in Jan Marsh, *Christina Rossetti: A Literary Biography* (London: Pimlico, 1995), 541.

16 *Tales from King Arthur,* ed. Andrew Lang (Ware: Wordsworth, 1993), 83-4, 7.

17 *Silva Gadelica,* ed. Standish O'Grady (London: Williams and Norgate, 1892), Vol. 2, 1.

18 *Elephant Memories: Thirteen Years in the Life of an Elephant Family* (New York: Fawcett Columbine, 1988), 317.

19 Ibid., 303.

20 "Are You an Animal?" in *Animal Experimentation: The Consensus Changes,* ed. Gill Langley (New York: Chapman and Hall, 1989), 1-19.

21 *Through a Window: My Thirty Years with the Chimpanzees of Gombé* (Boston: Houghton Mifflin, 1990), 206, 207. Emphasis added.

22 It is apparently because they are social animals and compete for favours that Biruté Galdikas insists that "chimpanzees are political animals" (*Reflections of Eden: My Years with the Orangutans*

of Borneo [Boston: Little, Brown, 1995], 244). In Aristotle's terms, the chimpanzees would fail the test because they have not consciously constructed a state.

23 The D.G.M. Wood Gush Memorial Lecture, 1997.

24 Aristotle, *Politics* 1.2.10-12, Barker edition (London: Oxford University Press, 1952), 5-6.

25 *Discourse on the Origin and Foundation of Inequality among Men* in *The Social Contract and Discourses*, trans. G.D.H. Cole (London: Dent, 1968), 170.

26 *An Introduction to the Principles of Morals and Legislation*, ed. J.H. Burns and H.L.A. Hart (London: Methuen, 1982 [1789]), 17, 4, b, 282. For Rousseau, see *Emile*, ed. Allan Bloom (New York: Basic Books, 1994 [1762]), Book 2, 80, and Book 4, 251, for example.

27 Quoted in W.E.H. Lecky, *History of European Morals from Augustus to Charlemagne*, 2 vols. (New York: D. Appleton, 1875), Vol. 1, 47.

28 C.G. Jung, *Memories, Dreams, Reflections* (New York: Vintage, 1985 [1963]), 101.

29 "Intimations of Immortality from Recollections of Early Childhood" and "Lines Composed a Few Miles above Tintern Abbey," *Poetical Works of William Wordsworth* (Edinburgh: Nimmo, n.d.), 304, 179.

30 Louis Halle, *The Appreciation of Birds* (Baltimore: Johns Hopkins, 1989), 46.

31 Alan Watts, *Nature, Man and Woman* (New York: Vintage, 1970), 9.

32 Courtney Milne, *The Sacred Earth* (Toronto: Viking, 1992), 10.

33 A more complete list would have to include those numbered among the avowedly Christian animal advocates mentioned on page 32 together with Heraclides, Diogenes, Democritus, Dicaerchus, Aratus, Crates, Theophrastus, Zeno, Seneca, Lucretius, Cicero, Iamblichus, Plotinus, Celsus, Neckham, da Vinci, Erasmus, More, Gesner, Bruno, Hartley, Ray, Evelyn, Cavendish, Isaac Newton, John Newton, Leibnitz, Mandeville, Linnaeus, Cowper, Byron, Wakefield, Burke, Olmsted, Gleizes, von Humboldt, Lecky, Dodgson (that is, Lewis Carroll), Broome, Cobbe, Gompertz, Martin, Bergh, Angell, Henry Ward Beecher, Harriet Beecher Stowe, Williams, Salt, Swinburne, Yeats, Maitland, Kingford, Steiner, Vernadsky, Haeckel, Eliot, Lorenz, and Leopold; also, of course, those specifically commented on in the body of this book and countless more.

34 *Philosophy of Vegetarianism* (Amherst: University of Massachusetts Press, 1984), 62.

35 "The difference ... between Plato and Pythagoras is primarily one of style rather than doctrine" (Dominic J. O'Meara, *Pythagoras Revived: Mathematics and Philosophy in Late Antiquity* [Oxford: Clarendon, 1992], 13). Certainly, Porphyry, along with Iamblichus, our primary source for the ideas of Pythagoras, considered Plato to share Pythagoras's view (27-8).

36 *Essays* (London: R. Chiswell, 1706 [written c. 1600]), 31.

Chapter 4: Rationalism

1 Excerpted in *Early Greek Philosophy*, ed. and trans. Jonathan Barnes (London: Penguin, 1987), 294.

2 *Theogony* and *Works and Days,* trans. M.L. West (Oxford: Oxford University Press, 1988), 45, lines 276-80.

3 *Against the Mathematicians*, Ch. 9, 127-8, in *Early Greek Philosophy*, 200.

4 For example, Plato, Empedocles, and Pythagoras proclaimed the doctrine of metempsychosis, that is, reincarnation. Empedocles claimed, "I have already been in the past a boy and a girl, a shrub and a bird and a fish which lives in the sea." This doctrine is only encountered occasionally in later Western literature, notably in the writings of William Blake who told of the "books & pictures of old, which I wrote and painted in ages of Eternity before my mortal life" (quoted in James King, *William Blake: His Life* [London: Weidenfeld and Nicholson, 1991], 145). It is also *suggested* in the poetry of Baudelaire and the novels of Fielding. For Baudelaire, see "Former Life" in *Les Fleurs du mal* (New York: Dover, 1995), 8, and for Fielding *Joseph Andrews* (Oxford: Oxford University Press, 1980 [1742 and 1749]), Bk. 3, Ch. 1: "The Lawyer [that is, the author] is not only alive, but hath been so these 4000 Years [that is, since creation]." Perhaps more emphatically, if also more opaquely, it is to be found in Saul Bellow's "Cousins," where Ijah Brodsky (speaking for the author) exclaims, "We enter the world without prior notice, we are manifested before we can be aware of manifestation. An original self exists or, if you prefer, an original soul." It is innate. But, as the narrator says in Bellow's *The Bellarosa Connection* (New York: Penguin, 1989), "a tricky word, 'innate,' referring to the hidden sources of everything that really matters." A convincing case can be, indeed has been made, by the theosophists, for also including Robert Browning among the reincarnationists. And Oscar Wilde's iconoclastic mother, Lady Jane, claimed to have been an eagle in a previous existence, but her statement was probably made for rhetorical effect. The most obvious case is that of Madame (Helena Petrovna) Blavatsky and the Theosophist Society, which subscribed to an idiosyncratic version of the doctrine; however, theosophical popularity was limited to the closing decades of the nineteenth century. W.B. Yeats was a member for

a time (1887-90) and maintained a belief in reincarnation even afterward, to which *A Vision* (New York: Macmillan, 1938 [1926]) is witness. James Joyce makes frequent reference to metempsychosis in *Ulysses*, but I, for one, have difficulty discerning how seriously he intends the doctrine to be taken. For a discussion of Joyce's circular and typological view of history through metempsychosis, see Declan Kilberd's introduction to *Ulysses* (London: Penguin, 1992), xxvi-xxviii.

5 *Early Greek Philosophy*, 220. Emphasis added.
6 Quoted in Thomas Merton, *Zen and the Birds of Appetite* (Boston: Shambhala, 1993 [1968]), 198.
7 *Early Greek Philosophy*, 91.
8 Quoted in Joseph Frank, *Dostoevsky: The Stir of Liberation, 1860-1865* (Princeton: Princeton University Press, 1986), 210.
9 Juan Mascaró, ed. and trans., *Upanishads* (Harmondsworth: Penguin, 1965), 141.
10 Quoted from correspondence to Mascaró on the back cover of his *Upanishads*.
11 Alexander F. Skutch, *Origins of Nature's Beauty* (Austin: University of Texas Press, 1992), 245. Emphasis added. According to Elizabeth Marshall Thomas, wolves too sometimes sing for the joy of it (*The Hidden Life of Dogs* [New York: Pocket Star Books, 1993], 104).
12 Charles Hartsthorne, *Born to Sing* (Bloomington: Indiana University Press, 1973).
13 *The Early Days of Christianity* (London: Cassell, 1891), 6.
14 *Tibetan Book of the Dead* (Boston: Shambhala, 1992), xxi-xxii. An interesting comparison is to be found in James Joyce's *A Portrait of the Artist as a Young Man* (New York: Penguin, 1993 [1916]), in which he tells us that "art necessarily divides itself into three forms progressing from one to the next. These forms are: the lyrical form, the form wherein the artist presents his image in immediate relation to himself; the epical form, wherein he presents his image in immediate relation to himself and to others; the dramatic form wherein he presents his image in immediate relation to others" (231-2). He tells us further that the "lyrical form is in fact the simplest verbal vesture of an instant of emotion ... He who utters it is more conscious of the instant of emotion than of himself as feeling emotion" (232). Joyce develops the theme progressively until the "personality of the artists, at first a cry or a cadence or a mood and then a fluid and lambent narrative, finally refines itself out of existence, impersonalises itself, so to speak" (233).
15 "Utilitarianism," in *Utilitarianism, Liberty, Representative Government* (London: J.M. Dent, 1910 [1863]), 9. By way of contrast, Keats writes: "I would sooner be a wild deer than a Girl under the dominion of the [Scottish] kirk, and I would sooner be a wild hog than the occasion of a poor Creature['s] pennance before those execrable elders." Quoted in Andrew Motion, *Keats* (London: Faber and Faber, 1997), 279.
16 *Tibetan Book of the Dead*, 212, 223.
17 Incongruously though, in Book 10 of *The Republic*, Plato acknowledges that humans may choose to be reincarnated as other species for the qualities they possess, as well as vice versa.
18 The classical Greek Cyrenaios refuted such claims by valuing bodily pleasure above intellectual pleasure because it is more intense and powerful.
19 *Rogue Primate: An Exploration of Human Domestication* (Toronto: Key Porter, 1994), 52.
20 *Treatise of Human Nature*, ed. L.A. Selby-Bigge and H. Nidditch (Oxford: Oxford University Press, 1978 [1739-40]), Bk. 2, Pt. 2, Sec. 12, 398.
21 For an incisive and perceptive analysis of the "thou" perspective, with decidedly different conclusions from those I have reached, see M. Guenther, "Animals in Bushman Thought, Myth and Art," in *Hunters and Gatherers: Property, Power and Ideology*, ed. T. Ingold, D. Richess, and J. Woodburn (Oxford: Berg, 1988), 192-202.
22 See below, 216-7.
23 *Emile*, ed. Allan Bloom (New York: Basic Books, 1994 [1762]), Bk. 4, 223. Martin Buber's *I and Thou* (New York: Scribner, 1958) argues along the same lines, his concept of "thou" approximating my notion of the synthesis of "thou" and "you." Buber is, however, writing of human relationships and of the human relationship to God, not of the human-animal relationship.
24 One may be forgiven for failing to recognize Twain's substantial animal orientations. In the Pulitzer prize-winning biography of Twain (Justin Kaplan's *Mr. Clemens and Mark Twain* [New York: Touchstone, 1983 (1966)]), the only hints come in the first chapter in a terse, "he was sensitive about animals" (18), followed in the last chapter by an observation that Twain "wrote a sentimental story about cruelty to animals" (373). There is no elaboration and nothing in between.
25 Quoted in Dennis Brian, *Einstein: A Life* (New York: John Wiley, 1996), 389.

Chapter 5: Alienation from Nature

1 Quoted in Peter Singer, *Animal Liberation*, 2nd ed. (New York: New York Review of Books, 1990), 201.
2 *Treatise of Human Nature*, ed. L.A. Selby-Bigge and H. Nidditch (Oxford: Oxford University Press, 1978 [1739-40]), Bk. 3, Pt. 3, Sec. 4, 610.

3   *Popol Vuh,* ed. D. Goetz and S.G. Morley (Norman: University of Oklahoma Press, 1950), Vol. 3, 9, 188. The cantil was a form of monster.
4   *Treatise of Human Nature,* Bk. 2, Pt. 2, Sec. 12, 397.
5   As Voltaire indicated in a slightly earlier epoch, "God made man in his own image, but man has taken his revenge in kind."
6   *Two Treatises of Government,* ed. Peter Laslett (New York: New America Library, 1960 [1690]), 33, 329.
7   *Treatise of Human Nature,* Bk. 1, Pt. 3, Sec. 16, 179.
8   *Works* (Oxford: University Press, 1836 [1729]), Vol. 2, 24.
9   See page xxvii.
10 Juan Mascaró, Introduction, in *Bhagavad Gita* (Harmondsworth: Penguin, 1962), 10.
11 *Norton History of the Environmental Sciences* (New York: W.W. Norton, 1993), 298: "Although many aspects of Darwin's work reflect practical concerns, his overall vision is very much a product of the Romantic era, with its emphasis on the unity of Nature."
12 Excerpted in Mircea Eliade, *Essential Sacred Writings from Around the World* (San Francisco: Harper, 1992), 249.
13 Quoted in Daniel J. Boorstin, *The Creators* (New York: Vintage, 1993), 22.
14 David Freidel, Linda Schele, and Joy Parker, *Maya Cosmos: Three Thousand Years on the Shaman's Path* (New York: William Morrow, 1993), 43, 65, 60.
15 See Thomas Merton, *Zen and the Birds of Appetite* (Boston: Shambhala, 1993 [1968]), 69.
16 *Reflections on the Revolution in France* (London: Dodsley, 1790), 141, 143. The view is also expressed through the character of Mrs. Gould in Joseph Conrad's *Nostromo* (London: J.J. Dent, 1995 [1904]): "It had come into her mind that for life to be large and full, it must contain the care of the past and of the future in every passing moment of the present. Our daily work must be done to the glory of the dead, and for the good of those who come after" (Pt. 3, Ch. 11).
17 Alex Haley, *Roots* (New York: Bantam, 1977), 13.
18 *Literature and Revolution,* trans. Rose Strunsky (Ann Arbor: University of Michigan Press, 1960), 256.
19 Jacob Burkhardt, *Civilization of the Renaissance in Italy* (London: Phaidon, 1960 [1860]), 81.
20 *Currents of Mediaeval Thought with Special Reference to Germany,* Vol. 5 of Studies in Medieval History, ed. Geoffrey Barraclough (Oxford: Blackwell, 1960), 66.
21 *Blake* (London: Sinclair-Stevenson, 1995), 147.
22 See, for example, J. Woodburn "Egalitarian Societies," *Man* 17 (1982): 431-51; also, Gardner, "Foragers' Pursuits of Individual Autonomy," *Current Anthropology* 32 (1991): 543-72. See also the individualistic emphases in *Man the Hunter,* ed. R.B. Lee and I. Devore (Chicago: Nash Aldine, 1968), and Colin Turnbull, *The Mountain People* (New York: Simon and Schuster, 1972).

Chapter 6: From the Great Chain of Being to the Theory of Evolution

1   *The Great Chain of Being: A Study of the History of an Idea* (New York: Harper, 1960 [1936]), viii.
2   See, for example, "The Great Chain of Being – Scala Natura" [sic], in Richard Milner, *The Encyclopedia of Evolution: Humanity's Search for Its Origins* (New York: Henry Holt, 1990), 201. Keith Thomas, in his *Man and the Natural World* (London: Penguin, 1984), describes the idea as "ambiguous" but does not mention any of the more significant of its examples. For an amusing account of the chain applied to classes of humans, see Henry Fielding's *Joseph Andrews* (Oxford: Oxford University Press, 1980 [1742 and 1749]), Bk. 2, Ch. 13.
3   John Locke, *Essay Concerning Human Understanding,* 2 vols. (London: H. Hills, 1710 [1690]), Vol. 2, 49. Even Hobbes in *Leviathan* offers us the view that "there be beasts that, at a year old, observe more, and pursue that which is for their good more prudently, than a child can do at ten." Bentham repeats the theme in his *Principles of Morals and Legislation,* ed. J.H. Burns and H.L.A. Hart (London: Methuen, 1982 [1789]).
4   Aristotle, *Politics* 1.8.11-12 (London: Oxford University Press, 1952), 21. Perhaps surprisingly, Thoreau appears to subscribe to the proposition, too. See *Walking* (Harmondsworth: Penguin, 1995 [1862]), 20. In fact, Aristotle's dictum was still commonly subscribed to in the nineteenth century. Thus, for example, George Sand's 1842 Preface to her 1831 novel *Indiana* (Oxford: Oxford University Press, 1994), 8: "God who makes nothing without a use."
5   Thomas Aquinas, *Summa theologiae* (Turin: Carmello, 1952), II, II, 64, 1. The earliest instance of which I am aware in the later Western tradition of the claim that plants possess sentience rather than mere life is to be found in E.A. Poe's "The Fall of the House of Usher" (1839) in *Tales of Mystery and Imagination* (Ware: Wordsworth, 1993), 227-50. A case could be made for Shelley's "The Sensitive Plant" (1820), but, despite the title, that is probably not what Shelley meant.
6   Quoted in Lovejoy, *The Great Chain of Being,* 187.
7   Alfred W. Crosby, *Ecological Imperialism: The Biological Expansion of Europe 900-1900* (Cambridge:

Cambridge University Press, 1986); Richard D. Ryder, *Animal Revolution: Changing Attitudes toward Speciesism* (Oxford: Blackwell, 1989).

8   Quoted in Jeffrey M. Masson and Susan MacCarthy, *When Elephants Weep: The Emotional Lives of Animals* (New York: Delacorte, 1995), 235.

9   Lord Macaulay, *History of England*, 4 vols. (London: Longman, 1854), Vol. 1, 161.

10 See George Nicholson, *Primeval Diet of Man* (Poughnill: Nicholson, 1801), 183.

11 "Phaedo," in *The Trial and Death of Socrates* (New York: Dover, 1992), 81. This is such a prime early example of the *scala naturae* that I am surprised Lovejoy, who knew the works of Plato well, made no reference to it.

12 Pythagoras, Empedocles, and Plutarch, for example.

13 See Michael W. Fox, *St. Francis of Assisi, Animals, and Nature* (Washington, DC: Center for Respect of Life and Environment, 1989), 1-2.

14 See Sean Kelly and Rosemary Rogers, *Saints Preserve Us* (New York: Random House, 1993), 9, 15, 19, 39, 42, 85, 92, 117, 133, 140, 205, 244, 261. E.S. Turner in *All Heaven in a Rage* (Centaur: Fontwell, 1992 [1964]), 25, offers an impressive list entirely different from this one.

15 Peter Singer, *Animal Liberation*, 192.

16 St. Augustine, *Confessions* (London: Longman's Green, 1897), Bk. 4, Ch. 3, 72.

17 Ibid., Bk. 7, Ch. 12, 179; Ch. 13, 180.

18 See, for example, Singer, *Animal Liberation*, 195-6.

19 Quoted in Michael W. Fox, *St. Francis of Assisi, Animals, and Nature*, 3.

20 In her *Mary Barton*, Elizabeth Gaskell indicates that a belief in mermaids was still quite common in the mid nineteenth century.

21 Quoted in Louis Charbonneau-Lassay, *The Bestiary of Christ* (New York: Arkana, 1992), 288-9.

22 Translated from *Mandeville's Travels* in Middle English in *Fourteenth Century Verse and Prose*, ed. Kenneth Sisam (Clarendon: Oxford, 1985 [1921]), 103. Because I am not in any manner a Middle English scholar, I apologize for any inadequacies or infelicities in my translation. A host of similar stories may be gleaned from Willy Ley, *Exotic Zoology* (New York: Viking, 1959).

23 Seamus Deane's notes to James Joyce's *A Portrait of the Artist as a Young Man* (London: Penguin, 1993 [1916]), 324.

24 Quoted in Daniel J. Boorstin, *The Discoverers: A History of Man's Search to Know His World and Himself* (New York: Vintage, 1985), 330-1.

25 *Legends and Myths: Middle Ages* (London: Senate, 1994), 35.

26 John Cottingham, *A Descartes Dictionary* (Oxford: Blackwell, 1993), 16, 75; A. Kenny, *Descartes' Philosophical Letters* (Oxford: Clarendon, 1970), 207.

27 Quoted in Singer, *Animal Liberation*, 201-2.

28 Quoted from "A Free Enquiry into the Vulgarly Receiv'd Notion of Nature" (1686), in Peter J. Bowler, *Norton History of the Environmental Sciences* (New York: W.W. Norton, 1993), 89.

29 *Of the Laws of Ecclesiastical Polity* 1.10.12, in *The Works of Mr. Richard Hooker*, 2 vols. (Oxford: Clarendon, 1865 [1597]), Vol. 1, 194-5.

30 "Of Goodness, and Goodness of Nature," *Essays* (London: R. Chiswell, 1706 [1600]), 31.

31 *The Book of the Dead: The Hieroglyphic Transcript and English Translation of the Papyrus of Ani*, ed. E.A. Wallis Budge (New York: Gramercy, 1995 [1895]), 108, 110.

32 Quoted in Colin Spencer, *The Heretic's Feast: A History of Vegetarianism* (London: Fourth Estate, 1993), 204.

33 Quoted in Robert Sharpe, "Animal Experimentation – A Failed Technology," in *Animal Experimentation: The Consensus Changes*, ed. Gill Langley (New York: Chapman and Hall, 1989), 89.

34 In his *Second Treatise of Civil Government* (1690), John Locke had earlier insisted that the fewer laws passed by legislatures, the less the natural rights of citizens would be violated.

35 Reverend Thomas Jackson, *Our Dumb Companions: Or, Conversations about Dogs, Horses, Donkeys, and Cats* (London: S.W. Partridge, n.d., c. 1880s), iii-iv. The publishers also produced volumes on *Animal Sagacity*, *Our Four Footed Friends*, *Our Children's Pets*, *A Mother's Lessons on Kindness to Animals*, and so on.

36 Boston *Transcript*, March 1888.

37 Quoted in Spencer, *The Heretic's Feast*, 186.

38 *Enquiry Concerning the Principles of Morals*, Ch. 3.

39 Peter Singer, *Animal Liberation*, 202. Until the late nineteenth century, it was customary to employ "use" and "usage" to mean nothing more pernicious than "treatment" and the terms were used more of humans than of other species. Thus in *Hamlet*: "Use every man after his desert" (2.2); and in Henry Fielding's *Amelia*: "the cruel Usage of a Step-mother."

40 *A Philosophical Enquiry into the Origin of Our Ideas of the Sublime and the Beautiful* (London: Rivington, 1812 [1756]), 67.

41 Bk. 6, "Winter Talk at Noon," lines 560-4.
42 Quoted in H.G. Adams, *Beautiful Butterflies: The British Species* (London: Groombridge and Sons, 1854), 60. The same theme is to be found in Alexander Pope's *Essay on Man*.
43 Quoted in Priscilla Wakefield, *Instinct Displayed, in a Collection of Well-Authenticated Facts, Exemplifying the Extraordinary Sagacity of Various Species of the Animal Creation* (London: Harvey and Dalton, 1821, fourth edition), v. From *Paradise Lost*, Bk. 8, lines 369-74.
44 *The Practical Naturalist's Guide containing instructions for collecting, preparing and preserving specimens in all departments of Zoology. Intended for the use of students, amateurs and travellers* (Edinburgh: Machlachlan and Stewart, 1858), 4.
45 Epistle 3.2.
46 *The Works of Lord Byron*, 4 vols. (London: John Murray, [1828]), Vol. 3, 185. The inscription on the tomb, not included in the Murray edition, includes the words: "Near this spot Are deposited the Remains of one Who possessed Beauty without Vanity, Strength without Insolence, Courage without Ferocity, And all the Virtues of Man Without his Vices."
47 Jacob Bronowski, *The Ascent of Man* (London: Future, 1991 [1973]), 13.
48 The full title of Tyson's study was *Orang-Outang, sive homo sylvestris; or the anatomy of a Pygmie compared with that of a Monkey, an Ape, and a Man. Homo sylvestris* meant man of the woods (which is also the meaning of orangutan in Malay). The word "pygmie" was used confusingly to refer to pygmies proper, any of the great apes, or the chimpanzee explicitly – which was included within the "orang-outang." Today, the scientific term for the orangutan is *Pongo pygmaeus*.
49 *Instinct Displayed in a Collection of Well-Authenticated Facts, exemplifying the Extraordinary Sagacity of Various Species of the Animal Creation*, viii.
50 Oliver Goldsmith, *Oliver Goldsmith's History of the Natural World* (London: Studio, 1990 [1774]), 73; Darwin, *The Origin of Species* (London: Penguin, 1985 [1859]), 212.
51 Preface to *Père Goriot* (London: Daily Telegraph, 1885), Preface, v-vi.
52 "Each creature is only a modification of the other; the likeness in them is more than the difference, and their radical law is one and the same" (*Nature* [Harmondsworth: Penguin, 1995 (1836)], 31).
53 In a letter from Astapovo, 1 November 1910. Quoted in William L. Shirer, *Love and Hatred: The Stormy Marriage of Leo and Sofya Tolstoy* (New York: Simon and Schuster, 1994), 350-1. In *What Is Religion and of What Does Its Essence Consist?* (1902, Ch. 11), Tolstoy attempts to refute evolutionary theory by proclaiming the futility of its investigation. In *Religion and Morality* (1893), his refutation of the theory is an attack on its illegitimate offspring, social Darwinism.
54 Peter Levi, *Tennyson* (New York: Scribner's, 1993), 68.
55 Of course, Darwin did write on the descent of man, "descent" meaning provenance. But Twain is right that Darwin thought of humans as "higher."
56 *"Denn das allein / Unterscheidet ihn / Von allen Wesen / Die wir kennen."*
57 See Nicholas Boyle, *Goethe: The Poet and His Age* (Oxford: Oxford University Press, 1992), Vol. 1, 399.
58 Quoted in Edwin Haviland Miller, *Salem Is My Dwelling Place* (Iowa: University of Iowa Press, 1991), 216.

Chapter 7: Aboriginal and Oriental Harmony with Nature

1 Rachel Carson, *The Silent Spring* (New York: Fawcett Crest Books, 1962).
2 *Globe and Mail*, 9 February 1998.
3 "Species Reasoning," *Canadian Forum* 72 (1993): 45. For a similar argument at greater length, see Frederick E. Hoxie, "Traditional People of North America," in *Traditional Peoples Today*, ed. Göran Burenhult (San Francisco: Harper, 1994), 174.
4 Cited in Ann Doncaster, "Animals, Oranges and Lumps of Coal," in *Skinned*, ed. Anne Doncaster (North Falmouth, Mass.: International Wildlife Coalition, 1988), 37. I have been unable to locate Darwin's original statement or even "The Essay on Fur" from which it is said to come.
5 *Nature Power: In the Spirit of an Okanagan Storyteller* (Vancouver: Douglas and McIntyre, 1992), 224-31.
6 See Rod Preece and Lorna Chamberlain, *Animal Welfare and Human Values* (Waterloo: Wilfrid Laurier University Press, 1993 and 1995), 136.
7 James Serpell, *In the Company of Animals* (Oxford: Basil Blackwell, 1986), 5.
8 James George Frazer, *The Golden Bough* (London: Macmillan, 1987 [1922]), 518.
9 Back cover.
10 *America's Fascinating Indian Heritage*, ed. James A. Maxwell (Pleasantville, NY: Pegasus, 1978), 76. The coffee-table-type title of this book might give the cautious reader cause for concern about its reliability. However, its primary contributor, Stanley A. Freed, was curator of the Department of

Anthropology at the American Museum of Natural History. Of the thirteen special consultants, three were museum curators and ten were respected professors of anthropology at major American universities, and all were specialists in Amerindian culture.

11 "The Tehuelche of Patagonia," in *Traditional Peoples Today*, 197.
12 *America's Fascinating Indian Heritage*, 341, 381.
13 J.A. Burnet, C.T. Dauphiné, Jr., S.H. McCrindle, and T. Mosquin, *On the Brink: Endangered Species in Canada* (Saskatoon: Western Producer Prairie Books, 1989), 2, 16.
14 *Our Oriental Heritage* (New York: MJF Books, n.d. [1935]), 392 fn.
15 Carlin's tableau is reproduced on the front and back inside covers of Peter Matthiesson, *Wildlife in America* (New York: Viking Penguin, 1987).
16 Marion MacRae and Anthony Adamson, *Hallowed Walls: Church Architecture of Upper Canada* (Toronto: Clarke, Irwin, 1975), 3.
17 *America's Fascinating Indian Heritage*, 373.
18 John S. Brownlee, *Political Thought in Japanese Historical Writing* (Waterloo: Wilfrid Laurier University Press, 1991), 12.
19 *Rob Roy* (Edinburgh: Robert Cadell, 1891 [1829]), 58.
20 Introduction to Jack London, *The Call of the Wild, White Fang and Other Stories* (New York: Penguin, 1981), 7.
21 Quoted in John Nance, *The Gentle Tasaday* (New York: Harcourt, Brace, 1977), 217, 219. It has been suggested that the Tasaday are a fraud perpetrated on or by the Philippine government to discourage industrial development. I remain unconvinced of the totality of the hoax, although it is probable that the Tasaday's lack of a sophisticated mythology indicates they were torn away from their agricultural roots among the Monobo sometime in the last 100 years or so. For a balanced appraisal, see Thomas N. Headland, "The Tasaday: The Most Elaborate Hoax in Scientific History?" in *Traditional Peoples Today*, 74-5.
22 *Vanishing Primitive Man* (New York: McGraw Hill, 1973), 28.
23 *The Animal Contract* (London: Virgin, 1990), 84.
24 Reported in the *Globe and Mail*, 4 March 1995.
25 "Species Reasoning," 45.
26 "Traditional Peoples of Africa," in *Traditional Peoples Today*, 127.
27 Anthony Harding, "Bronze Age Chiefdoms and the End of Stone Age Europe," in *People of the Stone Age*, ed. Göran Burenhult (San Francisco: Harper, 1993), 109.
28 Joseph Campbell, *Historical Atlas of World Mythology*, Vol. 2, Pt. 3, "Mythologies of the Primitive Planters: The Middle and Southern Americas" (New York: Harper and Row, 1989), 334-5.
29 *America's Fascinating Indian Heritage*, 122, 161.
30 *Vanishing Primitive Man*, 93.
31 *Elephant Memories: Thirteen Years in the Life of an Elephant Family* (New York: Fawcett Columbine, 1988), 51, 53, 59, 46, 261, 222.
32 Ibid., 273.
33 Dale Peterson and Jane Goodall, *Visions of Caliban* (Boston: Houghton Mifflin, 1993), 58-9.
34 "Life and Death among the Toraja," in *Traditional Peoples Today*, 62.
35 *Millennium: Tribal Wisdom and the Modern World* (New York: Viking, 1992), 182.
36 *America's Fascinating Indian Heritage*, 362, 373, 379.
37 *Speaking for the Earth: Nature's Law and the Aboriginal Way* (Washington, DC: Center for Respect of Life and Environment, 1991), 27.
38 See, for example, Gaillard T. Lapsley, *Crown, Community and Parliament in the Later Middle Ages* (Oxford: Basic Blackwell, 1951), 192, 193, 221, 349.
39 *Natural Law and the Theory of Society* (Boston: Beacon Press, 1960 [1913]), 52.
40 See page 64.
41 See Joseph Campbell, "Mythologies of the Primitive Planter: The Middle and Southern Americas," 327.
42 *The Discoverers: A History of Man's Search to Know His World and Himself* (New York: Vintage, 1985), 102.
43 Catherine Caufield, *In the Rainforest* (London: Picador, 1986), 95.
44 *Reflections of Eden: My Years with the Orangutans of Borneo* (Boston: Little, Brown, 1995), 340.
45 It is certainly worthy of note that at least some modern science fiction (for example, *Star Trek* and Dan Simmons's Hyperion books) treat altruism as the ultimate aspect of human development.
46 Quoted in *America's Fascinating Indian Heritage*, 315.
47 It is sometimes argued that "black" slavery was less pernicious than "white" slavery because in the former case slaves were not formally "owned." Be that as it may, the control of the slaves' lives was practically indistinguishable from that in "white" slavery.

48   "The Carib," in *Handbook of South American Indians,* ed. J.H. Stewart (New York: Cooper Square Publishers, 1963), Vol. 4, 560, 558.
49   Simon J.M. Davis, *The Archaeology of Animals* (New Haven: Yale University Press, 1987), 110. Emphasis added.
50   Ibid., 102. On evidence of overhunting among the Pueblo Indians of New Mexico, see Katherine A. Spielmann, "Hunter-Farmer Relationships," in *New World and Pacific Civilizations,* ed. Göran Burenhult (San Francisco: Harper, 1993), 206-7.
51   *Self-Made Man: Human Evolution from Eden to Extinction?* (New York: John Wiley, 1993), 29.
52   *The Archaeology of Animals,* 113.
53   "The Lost Animals of Australia," in *The First Humans,* ed. Göran Burenhult (San Francisco: Harper, 1993), 169.
54   *Historical Atlas of World Mythology,* Vol. 1, Pt. 1, "Mythologies of the Primitive Hunters and Gatherers" (New York: Harper, 1988), 90.
55   *Reflections of Eden,* 4.
56   *Gorillas in the Mist* (Boston: Houghton Mifflin, 1983), 26, 28, 29.
57   *Animals, Nature & Albert Schweitzer,* ed. Ann Cottrell Free (Washington, DC: Flying Fox Press, 1988), 14. See also 11, 12.
58   See Joseph Campbell, *The Masks of God,* Vol. 2, *Oriental Mythology* (Harmondsworth: Penguin, 1970), 160-3.
59   Morris, *Animal Contract,* 42.
60   *Historical Atlas of World Mythology,* Vol. 2, Pt. 3, 287.
61   A.H. Blaikie and J.A. Henderson, *Nest and Eggs* (London: Nelson, n.d. but probably c. 1915), xii.
62   *Historical Atlas of World Mythology,* Vol. 2, 299.
63   *The Wisdom of Confucius,* ed. Lin Yutang (New York: Modern Library, 1966), 166. "Tse" and "Sze" are alternative spellings of the same name.
64   Foreword to Michael J. Caduto and Joseph Bruchac, *Keepers of the Animals* (Saskatoon: Fifth House Publishers, 1991), xii.
65   See Cicely Fox Smith, *Lancashire Hunting Songs and other Moorland Lays* (Manchester: J.E. Cornish, 1909), 29-30 for the full text; also passim for other examples.
66   Richard Jefferies, *The Open Air* (London: Chatto and Windus, 1908 [c. 1880]), 127.
67   "Characteristics and Attitudes of Hunters and Anti-Hunters," *Transactions of North American Wildlife and Natural Resources Conference* 43 (1978): 412-23.
68   Caduto and Bruchac, *Keepers of the Animals,* xvii, xviii.
69   "Hinduism," a reprint of a 1959 essay, Appendix A in Joseph Campbell, *Baksheesh and Brahman: Indian Journal 1954-1955,* ed. R. and S. Larsen and Antony Van Couvering (New York: HarperCollins, 1995), 271-2.
70   Ibid., 19.
71   Ibid., 46, 205, 210, 239.
72   "Species Reasoning," 45.
73   See Michael Holroyd, *Bernard Shaw* (Harmondsworth: Penguin, 1990), Vol. 3, 288-90.
74   G. Naganathan, *Animal Welfare and Nature: Hindu Scriptural Perspectives* (Washington: Center for Respect of Life and Environment, 1989), 15.
75   Idanna Pucci, *Bhima Swarga: The Balinese Journey of the Soul* (Boston: Little Brown, 1992), 49.
76   *Hinduism and Ecology: Seeds of Truth* (London: Cassell, 1992), 11. The words are those of Ranchor Prine, paraphrasing Salish Kumar.
77   Ibid. For a balanced view of the influence of the British of the Raj, see the interviews with Maharaja Raj Singh of Dungarpur, Ali Ahmed Brohi, and Zulfiqar Jamote in Christopher Ondaatje, *Sindh Revisited* (Toronto: HarperCollins, 1996), 72-4, 125-6, 184-7.
78   *The Laws of Manu* (Harmondsworth: Penguin, 1991), 12, 40; 12, 41, 12, 42; 12, 43; 12, 44; 282.
79   Ibid., 12, 56; 12, 55; 12, 57; 283-4.
80   Ibid., 10, 91; 246.
81   Introduction, in *The Lotus Sutra* (New York: Columbia, 1993), ix.
82   *The Lotus Sutra,* 74, 77.
83   Ibid., xiv.
84   Christopher Ondaatje, *The Man-Eater of Punanai* (Toronto: HarperCollins, 1992), 72.
85   Cited in Michael Shelden, *Orwell: The Authorized Biography* (London: Minserva, 1991), 117. Eric Blair (Orwell) was an imperial police official in Burma during the 1920s.
86   See Marvin Harris, *Cows, Pigs, Wars and Witches: The Riddles of Culture* (New York: Vintage, 1989 [1974]), 23, 76.
87   Quoted in ibid., 27.
88   "Auguries of Innocence," stanza 2.

89   26 January 1994, A1, A15.
90   Ralph D. Sawyer's introduction to *The Art of War* (New York: Barnes and Noble, 1994), 7.
91   For convenience, I have on occasion in this chapter written of the Orient as though it were monolithic. Of course, as I have mentioned before, but it deserves to be stressed, it is not. Indeed, no single major Oriental country is a monolith any more than is, say, the United States. Thus, in India, for example, for Zoroastrians (Parsees), "dogs are second to man," according to one of their priests; for Hindus, cows are sacred (after a fashion); and for Moslems, it is a serious sin to allow a dog in one's home.
92   Joseph Campbell, *The Power of Myth* (New York: Anchor, 1988), 53.
93   Miriam T. Gross, *The Animal Illustrated 1550-1900, From the Collection of the New York Public Library*, text by Joseph Kastner with commentaries by Miriam T. Gross (New York: Harry N. Abrams, 1991), 90.
94   F. Marion Crawford, *Mr. Isaacs: A Tale of Modern India* (London: Daily Telegraph, 1899 [1882]), 135.
95   Plato, *The Trial and Death of Socrates: Four Dialogues* (New York: Dover, 1992), 12.
96   *The Lotus Sutra*, 75.
97   Edward FitzGerald, trans. (London: Macmillan, 1905 [1859]), Vol. 58, 88. Edward FitzGerald's editor (W.A.W.) indicates there is a dispute as to whether there is any "original for the line about the snake" (111). However, Hakim Yama Khayyam, a descendant of Omar, published a revised translation (*Omar Khayyam Revisited* [Secaucus: Lyle Stuart, 1974]), in which the snake line is left as FitzGerald wrote it. Whatever the truth about the original, it is clear that Hakim found nothing in FitzGerald's line inconsistent with Omar's tenor.
98   See page 97.
99   See page 52.
100 Christopher Key Chapple, *Nonviolence to Animals, Earth and Self in Asian Traditions* (Albany: State University of New York Press, 1993).
101 1.1.2; 1.5.5. Quoted in Chapple, *Nonviolence to Animals*, 4.
102 See note 4 to Chapter 4.
103 See, for example, *Animal Rights, A Christian Assessment* (London: SCM Press, 1970); *Christianity and the Rights of Animals* (London: SPCK and New York: Crossroad, 1987).
104 36, 18. Quoted in Chapple, *Nonviolence to Animals*, 15.
105 XIII: 114: II. Quoted in ibid., 16.
106 1, 78.4. Quoted in ibid., 22.
107 See pages 157-8.
108 Quoted in Chapple, *Nonviolence to Animals*, 27.
109 See, for example, pages xviii-xxii, 5, 7 as well as the earlier instances in this chapter.
110 See pages 203-4, 85, 86-7, 209.
111 Chapple, *Nonviolence to Animals*, 42.
112 Ibid., 43.
113 Ibid., 7.
114 Quoted in Campbell, *The Masks of God*, Vol. 2, 422.
115 Quoted in Donald Prater, *Thomas Mann: A Life* (Oxford: Oxford University Press, 1995), 56. Obviously a popular phrase, it was repeated in a letter to his publisher (ibid., 76).
116 "Quietist and Social Attitudes in China," in *Interpretations of History: Confucius to Toynbee* (London: George Allen and Unwin, 1961), 20.
117 E. Pendleton Banks, "Traditional Peoples of the Asian Continents," in *Traditional Peoples Today*, 45.
118 James Boswell, *The Life of Samuel Johnson* (London: J.M. Dent, 1914 [1791]), Vol. 1, 268.
119 Introduction to *The Laws of Manu*, xiii.

Chapter 8: Gaea and the Universal Spirit
1   It is sometimes claimed that, once infancy was survived, life expectancy was customarily the statutory three score and ten. In the absence of reliable statistics, it seems more likely that the prevalence of death from smallpox, tuberculosis, typhoid, malnutrition, and the occasional plague, as well as childbirth, not to mention the frequent but less dramatic ailments, would have significantly reduced that figure.
2   *The Forest People* (New York: Simon and Schuster, 1962), 6, 5.
3   *Monstruosus* may mean "strange, singular, wonderful, [or] monstrous" (*Cassell's Latin Dictionary*). When Cicero wrote of *"monstruoissima bestia,"* he implied a beast that was worthy of our amazement rather than something obnoxious. It was "a most awesome beast." I suspect that Linnaeus held to a similar conception of *monstruosus*, containing elements of wonder mixed with a certain

repulsion. In discussing the excesses of Milan cathedral, Serge Bramly writes perceptively, "Personally, I have a soft spot for this neo-Gothic monstrosity. The monstrous can sometimes verge on the divine" (*Leonardo: The Artist and the Man* [London: Penguin, 1994], 205).

4　Quoted in Maybury-Lewis, *Millennium: Tribal Wisdom and the Modern World* (New York: Viking, 1992), 57.

5　*The Descent of Man and Selection in Relation to Sex* (New York: A.L. Burt, n.d., reprint of second edition of 1874), 193.

6　See Patrick Neal and David Paris, "Liberalism and the Communitarian Critique: A Guide for the Perplexed," *Canadian Journal of Political Science* 23 (1990): 426-7.

7　Maybury-Lewis, *Millennium*, 55.

8　"The Liberation of Nature?" *Inquiry* 20 (1972): 94.

9　See the discussion by R.G. Willis in his introduction to *Signifying Animals: Human Meaning in the Natural World*, ed. R.G. Willis (London: Unwin Hyman, 1990), 7 ff.; see also Tim Ingold's introduction to *What Is an Animal?* ed. Tim Ingold (London: Unwin Hyman, 1988), passim.

10　See C. Lévi-Strauss, *The Savage Mind* (Chicago: University of Chicago Press, 1966); see also his *Totemism* (London: Merlin, 1964). The argument is advanced in both books. See also page 28.

11　*Totemism*, 87.

12　See page 230.

13　*Totemism*, 89. "Good to think *with*" may sound more meaningful, but the translator wanted apparently to maintain the correlation of *"bon à manger"* and *"bon à penser."* My discussion of totemism here is a very restricted one. It should be pointed out that Lévi-Strauss's concern is not primarily with the human-animal relationship but with formal, logical, structural homologies.

14　See page 196.

15　See pages 166, 168.

16　Ovid, *Metamorphoses* (Harmondsworth: Penguin, 1955), 338.

17　*Childe Harold's Pilgrimage,* Canto 4.

18　Pt. 1, q. 5, art. 4, *"Pulchra enim dicuntur quae visa placent."*

19　*The Great Masters* (New York: Park Lane, 1986 [1550]). Vasari opens his "Life of Giotto" with the claim that the "very obligation which the craftsman of painting owes to nature, who serves continually as model to those who are ever wresting the good from her best and most beautiful features and striving to counterfeit and to imitate her, should be owed, in my belief to Giotto, painter of Florence" (27). Certainly, Vasari considered the beauties of nature to be that which the outstanding artist sought to imitate.

20　Peter J. Bowler, *Norton History of the Environmental Sciences* (New York: W.W. Norton, 1993), 104. See also page 8, where he claims, "A medieval European saw mountains as terrifying places of desolation – only with the coming of Romanticism did we begin to see them as beautiful." For a subtle yet lighthearted examination of aesthetic objectivity, see comedian/playwright Steve Martin's *Picasso at the Lapin Agile.*

21　Quoted in Basil Willey, *The Eighteenth Century Background: Studies on the Idea of Nature in the Thought of the Period* (London: Chatto and Windus, 1946 [1940]), 30.

22　Ibid., 36, 37.

23　*Summa theologiae* (Turin: Carmello, 1952), Pt. 1, q. 39, art. 9: *"ad pulchritudinem tria requiruntur, integritas, consonantia, claritas."* One should, however, not ignore Ezra Pound's remark that "Beauty is but a brief gap between one cliché and another." Perhaps banality is necessary for beauty to be recognized.

24　Francis Bacon, *Essays* (London: R. Chiswell, 1706 [c. 1597]), 62-3.

25　*National Geographic* 187 (1995): 66.

26　See Wendy Doniger, *The Laws of Manu* (Harmondsworth: Penguin, 1991), lvi-lvii.

27　Ibid., xxii.

28　Caduto and Bruchac, *Keepers of the Animals* (Saskatoon: Fifth House Publishers, 1991), 4.

29　*Alexander Pope: Selected Works*, ed. Louis Kronenberger (New York: Modern Library, 1951), 119-21 (3.3.1-6; 3.4.1-8; 3.4.23-8 and 34). These excerpts should not be considered an adequate substitute for a reading of the whole. For nature as the norm in Pope's works, see *An Essay on Criticism* (1711): "First follow Nature, and your Judgement frame / By her just Standard, which is still the same: / *Unerring Nature.*"

30　Lewis adds a footnote here: "This supposition implies a change in the nature of beasts, as well as of man: for beasts avoid man, and prey upon him, which have never been subject to his attacks."

31　*Remarks on the Use and Abuse of Some Political Terms*, ed. Charles Frederick Mullett (Columbia: University of Missouri Press, 1970 [1832]), 186-7.

32　*Theory of Government in Ancient India* (Allahabad: Beni Prasad, 1927), 219, 193.

33　Quoted in C. Northcote Parkinson, *The Evolution of Political Thought* (London: University of

London Press, 1958), 20. I am also indebted to Parkinson for the awareness of the Hindu legends described by Prasad.

34 *The Wisdom of Confucius* (New York: Modern Library, 1966), 141. This idea is strikingly similar to the ideas of Emanuel Swedenborg. See page 76. Also G.K. Chesterton in his 1929 short story "The Yellow Bird" expresses the same theme. "We are limited by our brains and bodies," Chesterton tells us, "and if we break out, we cease to be ourselves, and, perhaps, to be anything at all." James Joyce adopts the Swedenborgian stance explicitly in *A Portrait of the Artist as a Young Man* and Kenneth Grahame employs the "Great God Pan" in his writings for a similar purpose. The same theme may also be found in *The Brothers Karamazov,* Pt. 2, Bk. 4, Ch. 2(b).

35 *Walden, or Life in the Woods* and *On the Duty of Civil Disobedience* (New York: Signet, 1960), 234.

36 The argument was introduced by James Lovelock in 1971 and given its fullest treatment in his *Gaia: A New Look at Life on Earth* (London: Oxford University Press, 1979).

37 *Summa contra Gentiles* (Turin: Carmello, 1952), Vol. 3, 80.

38 *On Human Conduct* (London: Oxford University Press, 1975), 223.

39 *H.J. Marschiert: Das neue Hitler-Jugend-Buch,* ed. Wilhelm Fanderl (Berlin: Paul Franke, n.d. but 1933 or 1934), 8, 110. What von Schirach had in mind in the first line was perhaps some synthesis of von Schelling's "world soul" with the popular epigram of Franz von Münch-Bellinghausen: "Two souls with but a single thought, / Two hearts that beat as one." It was the error of such profound thinkers as Ezra Pound (who was an advocate of Social Credit as well as Mussolini) and Martin Heidegger to revel in fascist communitarianism without recognizing its destruction of individual personality. Heroism requires the glory of the individual subsumed within the belongingness of the community, not the subsumption alone.

40 Graham Robb, *Victor Hugo: A Biography* (New York: W.W. Norton, 1998), 361.

41 Quoted in Russell Kirk, *The Politics of Prudence* (Bryn Mawr: Intercollegiate Studies Institute, 1993), 109.

42 Emily Benedek, *Beyond the Four Corners of the World: A Navajo Woman's Journey* (New York: Knopf, 1995), 329.

43 "Commentary on 'The Secret of the Golden Flower' " (1929), in *Alchemical Studies* (Princeton: Princeton University Press, 1967). Robertson Davies expresses a similar view via Hugh McWearie in *Murther and Walking Spirits* (Toronto: McClelland and Stewart, 1991). In *Les Misérables* (Pt. 3, Bk. 3, Ch. 2), Hugo argues that one must show deference to all of our nation's noble past, however much its principles have been superseded; absolutism, revolution, restoration, democratization must all be viewed as a part of the history that constitutes ourselves.

44 *The Wisdom of Confucius,* 109.

45 Quoted in Robertson Davies, *The Cunning Man* (Toronto: McClelland and Stewart, 1994), 466-7. For the prose version, see Ovid, *Metamorphoses,* trans. Mary M. Innes (Harmondsworth: Penguin, 1995), Book 15, 339.

46 Quoted in Sir Ernest Barker, *Greek Political Theory: Plato and His Predecessor* (London: Methuen, 1957 [1918]), 90.

47 Quoted in Peter Ackroyd, *Blake* (London: Sinclair-Stevenson, 1995), 285.

48 Dudley Young, *Origins of the Sacred* (New York: St. Martin's Press, 1991), 40. The Conrad quotation is to be found on page 335. In reality, of course, humans and pterodactyls did not occupy the earth at the same time. The point must be symbolic.

49 *The Souls of Animals* (Walpole, NH: Stillpoint, 1991), 27.

50 For a succinct and illuminating explanation of "The Jungian View," see David Fontana, *The Secret Language of Symbols* (San Francisco: Chronicle Books, 1993), 11-9. Of course, for a full perspective, one must read Jung himself, although one may grasp the implications in literature by reading the later novels of Robertson Davies, beginning with *Fifth Business* and *The Manticore.*

51 30 May 1877. Quoted in Martin Seymour-Smith, *Hardy* (London: Bloomsbury, 1995), 240.

52 P.N. Furbank, *E.M. Forster: A Life* (London: Martin Secker and Warburg, 1978), Vol. 2, 216, n1.

53 Jeffrey Meyers, *D.H. Lawrence: A Biography* (New York: Vintage, 1992), 291-2.

54 Quoted by James Dickey in the introduction to Jack London, *The Call of the Wild, White Fang and Other Stories* (New York: Penguin, 1981), 12.

55 Philip Callow, *From Noon to Starry Night: A Life of Walt Whitman* (Chicago: Dee, 1996 [1992]), 208.

56 Quoted in Mason Wade, *Margaret Fuller: Whetstone of Genius* (New York: Viking, 1940), 4-5.

57 Lionel Trilling, *Matthew Arnold* (New York: Harcourt Brace Jovanovich, 1979 [1939]), 255.

58 *The Brothers Karamazov,* Pt. 2, Bk. 5, Ch. 3.

59 See in particular, for *Shirley,* Chs. 10, 12, 25, and 27; for *Agnes Grey,* Chs. 1, 2, 5, 11, 12, 18. Ch. 24 contains an inspired account of the delights of the sea and its environs.

Select Bibliography

Ackroyd, Peter. *Blake*. London: Sinclair-Stevenson, 1995.

Adams, H.G. *Beautiful Butterflies: The British Species*. London: Groombridge, 1854.

Adams, Richard. *Watership Down*. London: Penguin, 1974 (1972).

Adams, W.H. Davenport. *The Bird World*. London: Thomas Nelson, 1878.

Aesop. *Fables of Aesop*. London: Penguin, 1964.

Angermayer, Johanna. *My Father's Island: A Galapagos Quest*. London: Viking, 1989.

Anonymous. "New Morality." In *Poetry of the Anti-Jacobin*. London: J. Wright, 1799.

Aquinas, Thomas. *Summa contra Gentiles*. Garden City: Doubleday, 1955.

–. *Summa Theologiae*. Turin: Carmello, 1952.

Aristotle. *Ethics*. Ed. and trans. J.A.K. Thomson. London: Penguin, 1976 (1953).

–. *On Man in the Universe (Metaphysics, Parts of Animals, Ethics, Politics, Poetics)*. Ed. Louise Ropes Loomis. New York: Gramercy, 1971.

–. *Politics*. Ed. and trans. Ernest Barker. London: Oxford University Press, 1952.

–. *The Works of Aristotle*. 10 vols. Ed. W.D. Ross. Oxford: Clarendon Press, 1921.

Arnold, Matthew. *The Complete Works of Matthew Arnold*. 11 vols. London: Macmillan, 1903-4.

Augustine. *The City of God*. New York: Random House, 1950.

–. *Confessions*. London: Longman's Green, 1897.

Bacon, Francis. *Essays*. London: R Chiswell, 1706 (c.1597).

Balzac, Honoré de. *Père Goriot*. London: Daily Telegraph, 1885 (1842).

Barker, Ernest. *Greek Political Theory: Plato and His Predecessors*. London: Methuen, 1957 (1918).

Barnes, Jonathan, trans. and ed. *Early Greek Philosophy*. London: Penguin, 1987.

Bate, W. Jackson. *Samuel Johnson*. San Diego: Harcourt Brace, 1979.

Baudelaire, Charles. *Flowers of Evil*. New York: Dover, 1995 (1857).

–. *Oeuvres complètes*. 3 vols. Paris: Louis Conard, 1923-30.

Beaconsfield, Earl of (Benjamin Disraeli). *Endymion*. 3 vols. London: Longman's Green, 1880.

Bellow, Saul. *The Bellarosa Connection*. New York: Penguin, 1989.

–. *Mr. Sammler's Planet*. London: Penguin, 1995 (1970).

Benedek, Emily. *Beyond the Four Corners of the World: A Navajo Woman's Journey*. New York: Knopf, 1995.

Benson, Elizabeth, ed. *Dumbarton Oaks Conference on Chavin*. Washington, D.C.: Harvard, 1971.

Bentham, Jeremy. *Introduction to the Principles of Morals and Legislation*. Ed. J.H. Burns and H.L.A. Hart. London: Methuen, 1982 (1789).

Berkeley, George. *Philosophical Works, Including the Works on Vision*. Ed. Michael R. Ayers. London: J.M. Dent, 1996.

Berry, Thomas. *The Dream of the Earth*. San Francisco: Sierra Club Publications, 1988.

Beston, Henry. *The Outermost House: A Year of Life on the Great Beaches of Cape Cod*. New York: Rinehart, 1949 (1928).

Bingley, W. *Animal Biography*. London: R. Phillips, 1803.

Blaikie, A.H., and J.A. Henderson. *Nest and Eggs*. London: Nelson, n.d. (c. 1915).

Blake, William. *The Complete Works of William Blake*. Ed. Geoffrey Keynes. Oxford: Oxford University Press, 1966.

Blecher, Lone Thygesen, and George Blecher, eds. *Swedish Folktales and Legends*. New York: Pantheon, 1993.

Boas, George. *Primitivism and Related Ideas in the Middle Ages*. Baltimore: Johns Hopkins, 1997 (1948).

Boethius. *The Consolation of Philosophy*. Trans. V.E. Watts. Harmondsworth: Penguin, 1969.

Boorstin, Daniel. *The Creators: A History of Heroes of the Imagination*. New York: Vintage, 1993.

–. *The Discoverers: A History of Man's Search to Know His World and Himself*. New York: Vintage, 1985.

Borgia, G. "Bower Quality, Number of Decorations, and Mating Success of Male Satin Bowerbirds (Ptilonorhynchus violaceus): An Experimental Analysis." *Animal Behavior* 1985. 33: 266-71.

Boswell, James. *The Life of Samuel Johnson*. London: J.M. Dent, 1914 (1791).

Boyle, Nicholas. *Goethe: The Poet and His Age*. Vol. 1. Oxford: Oxford University Press, 1992.

Bramly, Serge. *Leonardo: The Artist and the Man*. London: Penguin, 1994.

Brian, Dennis. *Einstein: A Life*. New York: John Wiley, 1996.

Bronowski, Jacob. *The Ascent of Man*. London: Future, 1991 (1973).

Brontë, Anne. *Agnes Grey*. London: Penguin, 1988 (1847).

Brontë, Charlotte. *Shirley*. London: Penguin, 1985 (1849).

Brontë, Emily. *Wuthering Heights*. Franklin Center: Franklin, 1979 (1847).

Brown, John. *The Self-Interpreting Bible*. Glasgow: Blackie, 1834 (1776).

Browning, Robert. *The Poetical Works of Robert Browning*. 2 vols. London: Smith, Elder, 1890.

Brownlee, John S. *Political Thought in Japanese Historical Writing*. Waterloo: Wilfrid Laurier University Press, 1991.

Budge, E.A. Wallis, ed. *The Book of the Dead: The Hieroglyphic Transcript and the English Translation of the Papyrus of Ani*. New York: Gramercy, 1995 (1895).

Burenhult, Göran, ed. *The First Humans*. San Francisco: Harper, 1993.

–. *Old World Civilizations*. San Francisco: Harper, 1994.

–. *People of the Stone Ages*. San Francisco: Harper, 1993.

–. *Traditional Peoples Today*. San Francisco: Harper, 1994.

Burke, Edmund. *A Philosophical Enquiry into the Origin of Our Ideas of the Sublime and Beautiful*. London: Rivington, 1812 (1756).

–. *Reflections on the Revolution in France*. London: Dodsley, 1790.

Burkhardt, Jacob. *The Civilization of the Renaissance in Italy*. London: Phaidon Press, 1960 (1860).

Burnet, J.A., C.T. Dauphiné Jr., S.H. McCrindle, and T. Mosquin. *On the Brink: Endangered Species in Canada*. Saskatoon: Western Producer Prairie Books, 1989.

Burnett, Frances Hodgson. *The Secret Garden*. Ware: Wordsworth, 1993 (1911).

Burns, Robert. *Selected Poems*. Ed. Carol McGuirk. London: Penguin, 1993.

Burton, Richard Francis. *Falconry in the Valley of the Indus*. London: John Van Voorst, 1852.

–. *Wanderings in West Africa from Liverpool to Fernando Po*. London: Tinsley Brothers, 1863.

Butler, Joseph. *The Works of Joseph Butler*. 2 vols. Oxford: Oxford University Press, 1836 (1729).

Butler, Samuel. *Life and Habit*. London: A.C. Fifield, 1910.

Byron, Lord (George Gordon). *The Works of Lord Byron*. 4 vols. London: John Murray, 1828.

Callow, Philip. *From Noon to Starry Night: A Life of Walt Whitman*. Chicago: Dee, 1996 (1992).

Campbell, Joseph. *Baksheesh and Brahman: Indian Journal 1954-1955*. Ed. R. and S. Larsen and Anthony Van Couvering. New York: HarperCollins, 1995.

–. *Historical Atlas of World Mythology*. 2 vols. New York: Harper and Row, 1989.

–. *The Masks of God*. 4 vols. Harmondsworth: Penguin, 1970.

Carlyle, Thomas. *Latter-Day Pamphlets*. London: Chapman and Hall, 1898 (1850).

–. *Past and Present*. London: Chapman and Hall, 1899 (1843).

Carpenter, Edward. *Civilization: Its Cause and Cure*. London: George Allen and Unwin, 1919 (1889).

Carroll, Lewis. *Alice's Adventures in Wonderland* and *Through the Looking Glass*. New York: Signet, 1960 (1865 and 1869).

Carson, Rachel. *The Silent Spring*. Boston: Houghton Mifflin Company, 1994 (1962).

Caufield, Catherine. *In the Rainforest*. London: Picador, 1986.

Chadwick, Owen. *A History of Christianity*. New York: St. Martin's Press, 1995.

Chapple, Christopher Key. *Nonviolence to Animals, Earth and Self in Asian Traditions*. Albany: State University of New York Press, 1993.

Charbonneau-Lassay, Louis. *The Bestiary of Christ*. New York: Arkana, 1992 (1944).

Chaucer, Geoffrey. *The Complete Poetry and Prose of Geoffrey Chaucer*. New York: Holt, Rinehart and Winston, 1977.

Chekhov, Anton. *The Cherry Orchard*. Minneapolis: University of Minnesota Press, 1965.

Chesterton, G.K. *The Napoleon of Notting Hill*. London: Penguin, 1991 (1904).

Cicero. *De officiis*. Ed. and trans. Thomas Cockman. Oxford: R. and R. Bliss, 1805.

Cleary, Thomas, trans. and ed. *I Ching*. Boston: Shambhala, 1992.

Coleridge, Samuel Taylor. *The Poetical Works of Samuel Taylor Coleridge*. Ed. Ernest Hartley Coleridge. London: Henry Frowde, 1912.

Collins, Wilkie. *Heart and Science: A Story of the Present Time*. Peterborough: Broadview, 1996 (1883).

Comfort, David. *The First Pet History of the World*. New York: Fireside, 1994.

Confucius. *The Analects of Confucius*. Ed. W.E. Soothill. New York: Paragon Book Reprint Corporation, 1968.

Conrad, Joseph. *Lord Jim*. New York: Oxford University Press, 1984 (1900).

–. *Nostromo*. London: J.M. Dent, 1995 (1904).

Cooper, James Fenimore. *The Deerslayer*. Oxford: Oxford University Press, 1993 (1841).

Copleston, Frederick, S.J. *A History of Philosophy. Vol. 1: Greece and Rome*. New York: Doubleday, 1993 (1944).

Cottingham, John. *A Descartes Dictionary*. Oxford: Blackwell, 1993.

Cowley, Abraham. *The Poetry and Prose of Abraham Cowley*. Oxford: Clarendon, 1949.

Cowper, William. *The Poetical Works of William Cowper*. London: Oxford University Press, 1934.

Crawford, F. Marion. *Mr. Isaacs: A Tale of Modern India*. London: Daily Telegraph, 1899 [1882].

Cremony, John C. *Life among the Apaches*. New York: Indian Head Books, 1991 (1868).

Cro, Stelio. *The Noble Savage: Allegory of Freedom*. Waterloo: Wilfrid Laurier University Press, 1990.

Crosby, Alfred W. *Ecological Imperialism: The Biological Expansion of Europe*. Cambridge: Cambridge University Press, 1986.

Curtsinger, Bill. "The Grey Reef Shark." *National Geographic* 187 (1995): 1.

Darwin, Charles. *The Descent of Man and Selection in Relation to Sex*. New York: A.L. Burt, n.d.

–. *The Origin of Species*. London: Penguin, 1985 (1859).

Davies, James Boyd. *The Practical Naturalist's Guide*. Edinburgh: Maclachlan and Stewart, 1858.

Davies, Robertson. *The Cunning Man*. Toronto: McClelland and Stewart, 1994.

–. *The Deptford Trilogy*. London: Penguin 1983 (1970-5).

–. *Murther and Walking Spirits*. Toronto: McClelland and Stewart, 1991.

Davis, Simon J.M. *The Archaeology of Animals*. New Haven: Yale University Press, 1987.

Defoe, Daniel. *The Adventures of Robinson Crusoe*. London: Penguin, 1965 (1710).

Diamond, J. "Evolution of Bowerbirds' Bowers: Animal Origins of the Aesthetic Sense." *Nature* 297 (1982): 99-102.

Dickens, Charles. *The Charles Dickens Library*. London: Educational Book, 1910.

Dombrowski, David. *Philosophy of Vegetarianism*. Amherst: University of Massachusetts Press, 1974.

Doncaster, Anne, ed. *Skinned*. North Falmouth, Mass.: International Wildlife Coalition, 1988.

Doniger, Wendy, ed. *The Laws of Manu*. Harmondsworth: Penguin, 1991.

Donne, John. *The Poetical Works of John Donne*. London: Oxford University Press, 1968.

Dostoevsky, Fyodor. *The Brothers Karamazov*. New York: Alfred A. Knopf, 1992 (1880).

–. *Crime and Punishment*. Franklin Center: Franklin Library, 1982 (1866).

–. *The Devils*. London: Penguin, 1971 (1871).

–. *The Diary of a Writer*. New York: George Braziller, 1954 (1873-81).

–. *Memoirs from the House of the Dead*. New York: Oxford University Press, 1983 (1861-2).

–. *Notes from Underground* and *The Grand Inquisitor*. New York: E. P. Dutton, 1960 (1864).

–. *Stories*. Moscow: Progress Publishers, 1971.

Doyle, Arthur Conan. *Memories and Adventures*. Oxford: Oxford University Press, 1989 (1924).

Dryden, John. *Dryden: Poetry, Prose and Plays*. London: Rupert Hart-Davis, 1952.

Durant, Will. *Our Oriental Heritage*. New York: MJF Books, n.d. (1935).

Dutta, Krishna, and Andrew Robinson. *Rabindranath Tagore: The Myriad Minded Man*. London: Bloomsbury, 1997 (1995).

Eadie, John. *The Classified Bible*. London: Griffen, Bohannd Co., 1856.

Edmonds, Margot, and Ella E. Clark. *Voices of the Winds: Native American Legends*. New York: Facts on File, 1989.

Eliade, Mircea. *Essential Sacred Writings from around the World*. San Francisco: Harper, 1992.

–. *Myths, Dreams and Mysteries*. New York: Harper, 1967.

Eliot, George. *Adam Bede*. London: Penguin, 1980 (1859).

–. *The Lifted Veil*. New York: Penguin, 1995 (1859).

–. *The Mill on the Floss*. Franklin Center: Franklin Library, 1981 (1860).

–. *Silas Marner*. London: Penguin, 1996 (1861).

–. *The Spanish Gipsy*. Boston: Ticknor and Fields, 1918 (1868).

Eliot, T.S. *Four Quartets*. London: Faber and Faber, 1989 (1944).

–. *Notes towards the Definition of Culture*. New York: Harcourt Brace Jovanovich, 1948.

–. *The Waste Land and Other Poems*. London: Faber and Faber, 1990 (1940).

Emerson, Ralph Waldo. *Nature*. Harmondsworth: Penguin, 1995 (1836).

Eschenbach, Wofram von. *Parzival*. New York: Vintage Books, 1961.

Evans, Edward Payson. *Evolutional Ethics and Animal Psychology*. New York: D. Appleton, 1897.

Fanderl, Wilhelm, ed. *H.J. Marschiert: Das neue Hitler-Jugend Buch*. Berlin: Paul Franke, n.d. (1933 or 1934).

Farrar, F.W. *The Early Days of Christianity*. London: Cassell, 1891.

Fénelon, François de. *Oeuvres*. Paris: Gallimard, 1994.

Feuerbach, Ludwig. *The Essence of Christianity*. London: Chapman, 1854 (1841).

Fielding, Henry. *Champion* 56 (1740).

–. *Covent-Garden Journal*, 22 February 1751-2.

–. *The Craftsman*, 28 June 1735.

–. *Joseph Andrews* and *Shamela*. Oxford: Oxford University Press, 1980 (1742 and 1749).

–. *Miscellanies*. Vol. 1. London: Fielding, 1743.

Filmer, Robert. *Patriarcha and Other Political Works*. Ed. Peter Laslett. Oxford: Blackwell, 1949.

FitzGerald, Edward, ed. and trans. *The Rubaiyat of Omar Khayyam*. London: Macmillan, 1905 (1859).

Flaubert, Gustave. *Madame Bovary*. New York: Oxford University Press, 1985 (1857).

Fontana, David. *The Secret Language of Symbols*. San Francisco: Chronicle Books, 1993.

Fossey, Dian. *Gorillas in the Mist*. Boston: Hougton Mifflin, 1983.

Fourier, Charles. *Utopian Vision of Charles Fourier; Texts on Works, Love and Passionate Attraction*. Boston: Beacon Press, 1971.

Fox, Michael. *Inhumane Society*. New York: St. Martin's Press, 1990.

–. *St. Francis of Assisi, Animals and Nature*. Washington, DC: Center for Respect of Life and Environment, 1989.

Frank, Joseph. *Dostoevsky: The Stir of Liberation, 1880-65*. Princeton: Princeton University Press, 1986.

Fraser, David. D.G.M. Wood Gush Memorial Lecture, 1997.

Frazer, James. *The Golden Bough*. London: Macmillan, 1987 (1922).

Free, Ann Cottrell, ed. *Animals, Nature and Albert Schweitzer*. Washington, DC: Flying Fox Press, 1988.

Freidel, David, Linda Schele, and Joy Parker. *Maya Cosmos: Three Thousand Years on the Shaman's Path*. New York: William Morrow, 1993.

Furbank, P.N. *E.M. Forster: A Life*. London: Abacus, 1993 (1977).

Galdikas, Biruté M.F. *Reflections of Eden: My Years with the Orangutans of Borneo*. Boston, Little Brown, 1995.

Gandhi, Mohandas K. *An Autobiography: The Story of My Experiments with Truth*. Boston: Beacon Press, 1993 (1957).

–. *The Essential Gandhi: An Anthology*. Ed. Louis Fischer. New York: Random House, 1962.

–. *Young India*. 18 November 1926.

Gantz, Jeffrey, trans. and ed. *The Mabinogion*. New York: Barnes and Noble, 1996.

Gardner, F. "Foragers' Pursuits of Individual Autonomy." *Current Anthropology* 32 (1991): 543-72.

Gaskell, Elizabeth. *Mary Barton*. London: Penguin, 1996 (1848).

Gasquet, Joachim. *Cézanne*. London: Thames and Hudson, 1991 (1921).

Gide, André, ed. *The Living Thoughts of Montaigne*. London: Cassell, 1940.

Gierke, Otto. *Natural Law and the Theory of Society 1500–1800*. Boston: Beacon Press, 1960 (1913).

Gilbert, W.S. *The Mikado* [1885]. In *The Savoy Operas*. Ware: Wordsworth, 1994.

Goethe, Johann Wolfgang von. *Werke*. 14 vols. Hamburg: Christian Wegner Verlag, 1949-60.

Goetz, Delia, and Sylvanus G. Morley, eds. *Popul Vuh: The Sacred Book of the Ancient Quiché Maya*. Norman: University of Oklahoma Press, 1950.

Gogol, Nikolai. *Dead Souls*. Trans. David Magarschack. London: Penguin, 1961 (1842).

Goldsmith, Oliver. *A History of Earth and Animated Nature*. 2 vols. London: Blackie, 1866 (1774).

–. *Oliver Goldsmith's History of the Natural World*. London: Studio, 1990 (1774).

–. *The Vicar of Wakefield*. London: Penguin, 1986 (1766).

Gompertz, Louis. *Moral Inquiries on the Situation of Man and Brutes*. London: J. Johnson, 1824.

Goodall, Jane. *Through a Window: My Thirty Years with the Chimpanzees of Gombé*. Boston: Houghton Mifflin, 1990.

Gordon, Mary. *The Company of Women*. New York: Random House, 1980.

Gross, Miriam T. *The Animal Illustrated. From the Collection of the New York Library*. New York: Harry N. Abrams, 1991.

Guerber, H.A. *Myths and Legends: Middle Ages*. London: Senate, 1994.

Haddon, Celia. *The Love of Cats*. London: Headline, 1992.

Haley, Alex. *Roots*. New York: Bantam, 1977.

Halle, Louis J. *The Appreciation of Birds*. Baltimore: Johns Hopkins, 1989.

Halleck, Reuben. *History of English Literature*. New York: American Book, 1900.

Hardy, Thomas. *Selected Poems*. Mineola, NY: Dover, 1995.

–. *Tess of the d'Urbervilles*. New York: Oxford University Press, 1982 (1891).

–. *Two on a Tower*. London: Macmillan, 1882.

Harris, Marvin. *Cows, Pigs, Wars and Witches: The Riddles of Culture*. New York: Vintage, 1989 (1974).

Hartsthorne, Charles. *Born to Sing*. Bloomington: Indiana University Press, 1973.

Hawkes, Jaquetta. *A Land*. Newton Abbott: David and Charles, 1987 (1951).

Hawthorne, Nathaniel. *The House of the Seven Gables*. New York: Signet, 1961 (1851).

–. *Selected Tales and Sketches*. London: Penguin, 1987 (1830-50).

Helfer, Ralph. *The Beauty of the Beasts*. Los Angeles: Tarcher, 1980.

Hemingway, Ernest. *Death in the Afternoon*. New York: Charles Scribner's, 1932.

–. *A Farewell to Arms*. New York: Charles Scribner's, 1929.

–. *The Old Man and the Sea*. New York: Charles Scribner's, 1952.

Hesiod. *Theogony* and *Works and Days*. Ed. and trans. M.L. West. Oxford: Oxford University Press, 1988.

Hobbes, Thomas. *Behemoth, or the Long Parliament*. Ed. Ferdinand Tönnies. New York: Vintage, 1989 (1974).

Holroyd, Michael. *Bernard Shaw*. 4 vols. London: Penguin, 1988-94.

Homer. *The Odyssey*. Trans. T.E. Lawrence. Ware: Wordsworth, 1992.

Honderich, Ted, ed. *The Oxford Companion to Philosophy*. Oxford: Oxford University Press, 1995.

Hooker, Richard. *The Works of Mr. Richard Hooker*. 2 vols. Oxford: Clarendon Press, 1865.

Hopkins, Gerard Manley. *The Poems of Gerard Manley Hopkins*. Ed. W.H. Gardner and H.H. Mackenzie. London: Oxford University Press, 1967.

Hugo, Victor. *Cromwell*. Paris: Flammaron, 1968 (1827).

–. *Les Misérables*. Trans. Norman Denney. London: Penguin 1976 (1862).

–. *Notre-Dame of Paris*. Trans. John Sturrock. London: Penguin, 1978 (1831).

–. *Selected Poems of Victor Hugo*. London: Methuen, 1929.

Hume, David. *Enquiries Concerning Human Understanding and Concerning Morals*. Ed. L.A. Selby Bigge and P.H. Nidditch. Oxford: Clarendon, 1975 (1748 and 1751).

–. *A Treatise of Human Nature*. Ed. L.A. Selby Bigge and P.H. Nidditch. Oxford: Clarendon, 1992 (1739-40).

Huxley, Aldous. *Island*. London: Penguin, 1994 (1962).

Huxley, T.H. *Man's Place in Nature*. New York: Humboldt, n.d. (1863).

Ibsen, Henrik. *Peer Gynt: A Dramatic Poem*. Philadelphia: Lippincot, 1936 (1867).

Ingold, T., D. Richess, and J. Woodburn, eds. *Hunters and Gatherers: Property, Power and Ideology*. Oxford: Berg, 1988.

Ingold, T., ed. *What Is an Animal?* London: Unwin Hyman, 1988.

Isaak, Robert. *American Political Thinking: Readings from the Origins to the 21st Century*. New York: Harcourt Brace, 1994.

Jackson, Thomas. *Our Dumb Companions*. London: S.W. Partridge, n.d. (c. 1880s).

–. *Our Dumb Neighbours*. London: S.W. Partridge, n.d. (c. 1880s).

Jaki, Stanley L. *The Absolute beneath the Relative and Other Essays*. Lanham: University Press of America, 1988.

James, William. *The Varieties of Religious Experience: A Study in Human Nature*. New York: Signet, 1958 (1902).

Jefferies, Richard. *The Open Air*. London: Chatto and Windus, 1908 (c. 1880).

Johnson, Samuel. *Yale Edition of the Works of Samuel Johnson*. New Haven: Yale, 1958-75.

Joyce, James. *A Portrait of the Artist as a Young Man*. London: Penguin, 1993 (1916).

–. *Ulysses*. London: Penguin, 1992 (1922).

Jung, C.G. *Alchemical Studies*. Princeton: Princeton University Press, 1967.

–. *Memories, Dreams, Reflections*. New York: Vintage, 1985 (1963).

Kaiser, Rudolf. "A Fifth Gospel, Almost: Chief Seattle's Speech(es): American Origins and European Reception." In *Indians and Europe: An Interdisciplinary Collection of Essays*. Ed. Christian F. Feest. Aachen: Ed. Herodot, Rader Verlag, 1987.

Kaplan, Justin. *Mr. Clemens and Mark Twain*. New York: Touchstone, 1983 (1966).

Kehoe, A. *The Ghost Dance*. New York: Holt, Rinehart and Winston, 1989.

Kellert, S.R. "Characteristics and Attitudes of Hunters and Anti-Hunters." *Transactions of North American Wildlife and Natural Resources Conference* 43 (1978): 412-23.

Kelly, Sean, and Rosemary Rogers. *Saints Preserve Us*. New York: Random House, 1993.

Kenny, A. *Descartes' Philosophical Letters*. Oxford: Clarendon, 1970.

Khayyam, Hakim Yama. *Omar Khayyam Revisited*. Secaucus: Lyle Suart, 1974.

King, James. *William Blake: His Life*. London: Weidenfeld and Nicholson, 1991.

Kingdon, Jonathan. *Self-Made Man: Human Evolution from Eden to Extinction*. New York: John Wiley, 1993.

Kingsley, Charles. *Yeast: A Problem*. London: Macmillan, 1890 (1849).

Kipling, Rudyard. *The Day's Work*. London: Penguin, 1988 (1898).

–. *The Jungle Book*. London: Macmillan, 1965 (1894).

–. *Just So Stories*. Ware: Wordsworth, 1993 (1902).

Kirk, Russell. *The Politics of Prudence*. Bryn Mawr: Intercollegiate Studies Institute, 1996.

Knudtson, Peter, and David Suzuki. *Wisdom of the Elders*. Toronto: Stoddart, 1992.

Kowalski, Garry. *The Souls of Animals*. Walpole, NH: Stillpoint, 1991.

Lamarck, J.B.P.A. de Monet de. *Histoire naturelle des animaux sans vertèbres*. Paris: Verdière, 1815-22 (1801).

–. *Philosophie zöologique*. Paris: Dentu, 1809.

Lang, Andrew. *Tales from King Arthur*. Ware: Wordsworth, 1993.

Langley, Gill, ed. *Animal Experimentation: The Consensus Changes*. New York: Chapman and Hall, 1989.

Lapsley, Gaillard T. *Crown, Community and Parliament in the Latter Middle Ages*. Oxford: Blackwell, 1951.

Lawrence, D.H. *Kangaroo*. London: Penguin, 1997 (1923).

–. *Lady Chatterley's Lover*. London: Heinemann, 1961.

Lecky, W.E.H. *History of European Morals from Augustus to Charlemagne*. New York: D. Appleton, 1875.

Lee, R.B. "Art, Science or Politics? The Crisis in Hunter-Gatherer Studies" *American Anthropologist* 94 (1992): 31-54.

Lee, R.B., and M. Guenther. "Problems in Kalahri Historical Ethnography and the Tolerance of Error." *History in Africa* 20 (1993): 185-235.

Leiss, William. *The Domination of Nature*. New York: Braziller, 1972.

Levi, Peter. *Tennyson*. New York: Scribner's, 1993.

Lévi-Strauss, Claude. *The Savage Mind*. Chicago: University of Chicago Press, 1966.

–. *Totemism*. London: Merlin, 1964.

Lewis, C.S. *The Screwtape Letters*. Westwood, NJ: Barbour, n.d. (1942).

–. *That Hideous Strength*. London: The Bodley Head, 1945.

Lewis, George Cornewall. *Remarks on the Use and Abuse of Some Political Terms*. Ed. Charles Frederick Mullett. Columbia: University of Missouri Press, 1970 (1832).

Ley, William. *Exotic Zoology*. New York: Viking, 1959.

Linnaeus, Carolus. *Systema naturae*. London: British Museum, 1956 (1735).

Linzey, Andrew. *Christianity and the Rights of Animals*. London: SPCK, 1987.

Livingston, John. *Rogue Primate: An Exploration of Human Domestication*. Toronto: Key Porter, 1994.

Livingstone, David N. *Darwin's Forgotten Defenders: The Encounter between Evangelical Theology and Evolutionary Thought*. Edinburgh: Scottish Academic Press, 1987.

Locke, John. *Essay Concerning Human Understanding*. London: Hills, 1710 (1690).

–. *Two Treatises of Government*. Ed. Peter Laslett. New York: New American Library, 1960 (1690).

London, Jack. *The Call of the Wild, White Fang and Other Stories*. London: Penguin, 1981 (1903-7).

Lorenz, Konrad. *King Solomon's Ring: New Light on Animal Ways*. New York: Cromwell, 1952.

Lovejoy, Arthur O. *The Great Chain of Being: A Study of the History of an Idea*. New York: Harper, 1960 (1936).

–. "The Supposed Primitivism of Rousseau's *Discourse on Inequality*." *Modern Philology* 21 (1923): 165-86.

Lovejoy, Arthur O., and George Boas. *Primitivism and Related Ideas in Antiquity*. Baltimore: Johns Hopkins, 1997 (1935).

Lovelock, James. *Gaia: A New Look at Life on Earth*. London: Oxford University Press, 1979.

Lubbock, John. *The Beauties of Nature*. London: Macmillan, 1898 (1892).

Lucretius. *On the Nature of the Universe (de rerum natura)*. London: Penguin, 1994.

Macaulay, Lord (Thomas Babbington). *History of England*. 4 vols. London: Longman, 1854.

Macdonald, David, ed. *The Primates*. New York: Torstar, 1995.

Machiavelli, Nicolo. *The Prince* and *The Discourses*. Ed. Max Lerner. New York: Random House, 1950 (1513 and 1519).

–. *Il principe*. Torino: Einaudi, 1961 (1513).

Mackintosh, James. *Vindiciae Gallicae: Defence of the French Revolution and Its English Admirers, against the Accusations of the Right Hon. Edmund Burke*. 3rd ed. London: G.G. and J. Robinson, 1791.

MacLean, Hope. "Species Reasoning." *Canadian Forum* 82 (1993): 824.

MacRae, Marion, and Anthony Adamson. *Hallowed Walls: Church Architecture of Upper Canada*. Toronto: Clarke, Irwin, 1975.

Marsh, Jan. *Christina Rossetti: A Literary Biography*. London: Pimlico, 1995.

Marx, Karl. *Karl Marx: Selected Writings*. Ed. David McLellan. Oxford: Oxford University Press, 1977.

Mascaró, Juan, ed. and trans. *Bhagavad Gita*. London: Penguin, 1962.

–. *Dhammapada*. London: Penguin, 1973.

–. *Upanishads*. London: Penguin, 1965.

Mason, Jim. *An Unnatural Order: Uncovering the Roots of Our Dominion of Nature and Each Other*. New York: Simon and Schuster, 1993.

Masson, Jeffrey M., and Susan MacCarthy. *When Elephants Weep: The Emotional Lives of Animals*. New York: Delacorte, 1995.

Mathiesson, Peter. *Wildlife in America*. New York: Viking Penguin, 1987.

Maurier, Daphne du. *Jamaica Inn*. New York: Sun Dial Press, 1937.

Maxwell, James A., ed. *America's Fascinating Indian Heritage*. Pleasantville, NY: Pegasus 1978.

Maybury-Lewis, David. *Tribal Wisdom and the Modern World*. New York: Viking, 1992.

McLuhan, T.C. *The Way of the Earth: Encounters with Nature in Ancient and Contemporary Thought*. New York: Simon and Schuster, 1994.

McLynn, Frank. *Robert Louis Stevenson: A Biography*. London: Pimlico, 1994.

McMillan, Alan D. *Native Peoples and Cultures of Canada: An Anthropological Overview*. Vancouver: Douglas and McIntyre, 1988.

Melville, Herman. *Moby Dick, or the Whale*. London: Penguin, 1992 (1851).

Merlet, Gustave. *Anthologie classique des poètes du XIXème siècle*. Paris: Alphonse Lemerre, 1890.

Merton, Thomas. *Zen and the Birds of Appetite*. Boston: Shambhala, 1993 (1968).

Mill, John Stuart. *The Principles of Political Economy*. Fairfield, NJ: A.M. Kelley, 1987 (1848).

–. *Utilitarianism, Liberty and Representative Government*. London: J.M. Dent, 1910.

Miller, Edwin Haviland. *Salem Is My Dwelling Place*. Iowa: University of Iowa Press, 1991.

Milne, Courtney. *The Sacred Earth*. Toronto: Viking, 1992.

Milner, Richard. *The Encyclopedia of Evolution: Humanity's Search for Its Origins*. New York: Henry Holt, 1990.

Milton, John. *Poetical Works*. London: T. Nelson, 1855.

Molière. *Comedies*. New York: Oxford University Press, 1985.

Monboddo, Lord (James Burnet). *Antient Metaphysics*. 6 vols. Edinburgh: Caddell, 1774-99.

–. *Of the Origin and Progress of Language*. New York: Garland, 1970 (1770).

Montaigne, Michel de. *Selected Essays*. New York: Oxford University Press, 1982 (1580).

Montesquieu, Charles Secondat de la Brède, Baron de. *Lettres persanes*. Paris: Flammarion, n.d. (1721).

More, Thomas. *Utopia*. London: J.M. Dent, 1994 (1516).

Morris, Desmond. *The Animal Contract*. London: Virgin, 1990.

Moss, Cynthia. *Elephant Memories: Thirteen Years in the Life of an Elephant Family*. New York: Fawcett Columbine, 1988.

Motion, Andrew. *Keats*. London: Faber and Faber, 1997.

Myers, Jeffrey. *D.H. Lawrence: A Biography*. New York: Vintage, 1992.

Naganathan, G. *Animal Welfare and Nature: Hindu Scriptural Perspectives*. Washington, DC: Center for Respect of Life and Environment, 1989.

Nance, John. *The Gentle Tasaday*. New York: Harcourt Brace, 1977.

Nash, Roderick Frazier. *The Rights of Nature: A History of Environmental Ethics*. Madison: University of Wisconsin Press, 1984.

Neidjie, Bill. *Speaking for the Earth: Nature's Law and the Aboriginal Way*. Washington, DC: Center for Respect of Life and Environment, 1991.

Neihardt, John. *Black Elk Speaks*. New York: Pocket Books, 1975 (1959).

Newton, John Frank. *Return to Nature; or a defence of the vegetarian regimen*. London: T. Cadell and W. Davies, 1811.

Nicholson, George. *The Primeval Diet of Man*. Poughnill: Nicholson, 1801.

O'Grady, Standish, ed. *Silva Gadelica*. London: Williams and Northgate, 1992.
O'Meara, Dominic J.O. *Pythagoras Revived: Mathematics and Philosophy in Late Antiquity*. Oxford: Clarendon, 1992.
Oakeshott, Michael. *On Human Conduct*. London: Oxford University Press, 1975.
Ondaatje, Christopher. *The Man-Eater of Punanai*. Toronto: HarperCollins, 1992.
–. *Sind Revisited: A Journey in the Footsteps of Captain Sir Richard Francis Burton; 1812-1849: The India Years*. Toronto: HarperCollins, 1996.
Orwell, George. *Animal Farm: A Fairy Story*. London: Penguin, 1983 (1945).
Oswald, John. *The Cry of Nature; or, an Appeal to Mercy and Justice, on Behalf of Persecuted Animals*. London: J. Johnson, 1791.
Ovid. *Metamorphoses*. Trans. Mary M. Innes. Harmondsworth: Penguin, 1995.
Paley, William. *Natural Theology*. New York: American Tract Society, n.d. (1802).
Parkinson, Northcote. *The Evolution of Political Thought*. London: University of London Press, 1958.
Pascal, Blaise. *Pensées*. Paris: Librairie Garnier Frères, n.d. (1670).
Passmore, John. *Man's Responsibility for Nature: Ecological Problems and Western Traditions*. London: Duckworth, 1974.
Peterson, Dale, and Jane Goodall. *Visions of Caliban*. Boston: Houghton Mifflin, 1993.
Plato. *Laws*. Baltimore: Penguin, 1951.
–. *Republic*. Trans. H. Spens. Glasgow: Foulis, 1763.
–. *Symposium* and *Phaedrus*. New York: Dover 1993.
–. *The Trial and Death of Socrates: Four Dialogues (Euthyphro, Apology, Crito, Phaedo)*. New York: Dover, 1992.
Pliny the Elder. *Natural History: A Selection*. London: Penguin, 1991.
Plutarch. *Essays*. Trans. Robin Waterfield. London: Penguin, 1992.
–. *Moralia*. 13 vols. London: Heinemann, 1927-36.
Poe, E.A. *Tales of Mystery and Imagination*. Ware: Wordsworth, 1993.
Pope, Alexander. *Alexander Pope: Selected Works*. Ed. Louis Kronenburger. New York: Modern Library, 1951.
–. *Prose Works of Alexander Pope*. Ed. Norman Ault. Oxford: Blackwell, 1936.
–. *The Works of Alexander Pope*. Ware: Wordsworth, 1995.
Prasad, Beni. *Theory of Government in Ancient India*. Allahabad: Beni Prasad, 1927.
Prater, Donald. *Thomas Mann: A Life*. Oxford: Oxford University Press, 1995.
Preece, Rod, and Lorna Chamberlain. *Animal Welfare and Human Values*. Waterloo: Wilfrid Laurier University Press, 1993.
Primatt, Humphry. *The Duty of Mercy and the Sin of Cruelty to Brute Animals*. Ed. Richard D. Ryder. Fontwell: Centaur, 1992 (1776).
Prine, Ranchor. *Hinduism and Ecology: Seeds of Truth*. London: Cassell, 1992.
Pucci, Idanna, ed. *Bhima Swarga: The Balinese Journey of the Soul*. Boston: Little, Brown, 1992.
Pushkin, Alexander. *The Queen of Spades and Other Stories*. London: Penguin, 1962.
Radcliffe, Anne. *The Romance of the Forest*. Oxford: Oxford University Press, 1986 (1791).
Ray, John. *Wisdom of God Manifested in the Works of Creation*. New York: Garland, 1979 (1691).
Richardson, Samuel. *Pamela*. New York: W.W. Norton, 1993 (1741).
Rinpoche, Guru. *Tibetan Book of the Dead*. Boston: Shambhala, 1992.
Ritson, Joseph. *An Essay on Abstinence from Animal Food as a Moral Duty*. London: Richard Phillips, 1802.
Robb, Graham. *Victor Hugo: A Biography*. New York: W.W. Norton, 1998.
Robinson, Harry. *Nature Power: In the Spirit of an Okanagan Storyteller*. Vancouver: Douglas and McIntyre, 1992.
Rollin, Bernard. *Animal Rights and Human Morality*. Buffalo NY: Prometheus Books, 1981.
–. "Animal Welfare, Science, and Value." *Journal of Agricultural and Environmental Ethics* 6 (2) 1993: 44-50.
Rousseau, Jean-Jacques. *Émile, or on Education*. Trans. and ed. Allan Bloom. New York: Basic Books, 1979 (1768).
–. *Rousseau's Political Writings*. Ed. Alan Ritter and Julia Conway Bonadella. New York: W.W. Norton, 1988.
–. *The Social Contract* and *Discourses*. Trans. G.D.H. Cole. London: Dent, 1968 (1762, 1749, 1754).
Ruskin, John. *Modern Painters*. New York: Knopf, 1987 (1843-60).
–. *Unto This Last and Other Writings*. London: Penguin, 1965 (1862).
Sagan, Carl, and Anne Druyan. *Shadows of Forgotten Ancestors: A Search for Who We Are*. New York: Random House, 1992.
Saint-Pierre, Bernardin de. *Paul et Virginie*. Paris: Garnier, 1964 (1788).

Salt, Henry S. *A Plea for Vegetarianism.* Manchester: Vegetarian Society, 1886.
–. *Seventy Years among Savages.* London: G. Allen and Unwin, 1921.
Sandars, N.K., ed. *The Epic of Gilgamesh.* London: Penguin, 1972.
Saul, John Ralston. *The Doubter's Companion: A Dictionary of Aggressive Common Sense.* Toronto: Viking, 1994.
Schopenhauer, Arthur. *On the Basis of Morality.* Indianapolis: Bobbs Merrill, 1965 (1841).
–. *Parerga and Paralipomena.* Oxford: Oxford University Press, 1974 (1851).
–. *The World as Will and Representation.* 2 vols. Cambridge: Harvard University Press, 1958 (1818).
Scott, Walter. *Rob Roy.* Edinburgh: Caddell, 1891 (1829).
Seidlmayer, Michael. *Currents of Medieval Thought with Special Reference to Germany.* Oxford: Blackwell, 1960.
Seneca. *Moral Essays.* Cambridge: Harvard University Press, 1967.
Serpell, James. *In the Company of Animals.* Oxford: Blackwell, 1986.
Seton, Ernest Thompson. *Wild Animals I Have Known.* New York: Penguin, 1987 (1898).
Severin, Timothy. *Vanishing Primitive Man.* New York: American Heritage, 1973.
Sewell, Anna. *Black Beauty.* New York: Macmillan, 1962 (1877).
Seymour-Smith, Martin. *Hardy.* London: Bloomsbury, 1994.
Shaftesbury, Anthony Ashley Cooper, 3rd Earl. *Characteristics of Men, Manners, Opinions, Times.* London: J. Darby, 1723 (1711).
Shakespeare, William. *The Complete Works of William Shakespeare.* London: Ramboro, 1993.
Shaw, George Bernard. *The Complete Plays of Bernard Shaw.* London: Hamlyn, 1965.
Shelden, Michael. *Orwell: The Authorized Biography.* London: Minerva, 1991.
Shelley, Percy Bysshe. *Shelley's Poetry and Prose.* Ed. Donald H. Reiman and Sharon B. Powers. New York: W.W. Norton, 1977.
Shirer, William L. *Love and Hatred: The Stormy Marriage of Leo and Sofya Tolstoy.* New York: Simon and Schuster, 1994.
Singer, Peter. *Animal Liberation.* 2nd ed. New York: New York Review of Books, 1990.
–, ed. *A Companion to Ethics.* Oxford: Blackwell, 1993.
Sisam, Kenneth, ed. *Fourteenth Century Prose and Verse.* Oxford: Clarendon, 1985 (1921).
Skutch, Alexander F. *Origins of Nature's Beauty.* Austin: University of Texas Press, 1992.
Smart, Christopher. *Collected Poems of Christopher Smart.* London: Routledge and Kegan Paul, 1949.
Smith, Cicely Fox. *Lancashire Hunting Songs and Other Moorland Lays.* Manchester: J.E. Cornish, 1909.
Smollett, Tobias. *The Expedition of Humphry Clinker.* London: Penguin, 1985 (1771).
Solway, J.R., and R.B. Lee. "Foragers, Genuine or Spurious? Situating the Kalahari San in History." *Current Anthropology* 31 (1990): 109-46.
Steele, Flora Annie. *On the Face of the Waters.* London: William Heinemann, 1899.
Steinbeck, John. *The Log from the Sea of Cortez.* London: Penguin, 1995 (1941).
–. *Sweet Thursday.* New York: Viking, 1954.
–. *To a God Unknown.* Leicester: Ulverscroft, 1974 (1933).
Sterne, Laurence. *A Sentimental Journey through France and Italy.* London: Penguin, 1986 (1768).
–. *Tristram Shandy.* New York: Alfred A. Knopf, 1991 (1759-65).
Stevenson, Robert Louis. *The Amateur Emigrant – Across the Plain – The Silverado Squatters.* New York: Scribner, 1892.
–. *The Strange Case of Dr. Jekyll and Mr. Hyde.* New York: Dodd, Mead, 1961 (1886).
–. *Travels with a Donkey in the Cévennes.* London: Chatto and Windus, 1980 (1879).
Stewart, J.H., ed. *Handbook of South American Indians.* New York: Cooper Square, 1963.
Strassburg, Gottfried von. *Tristan.* London: Penguin, 1967.
Sun-tzu. *The Art of War.* Trans. Ralph D. Sawyer. New York: Barnes and Noble, 1994.
Surtees, Robert Smith. *Handley Cross.* London: Methuen, 1910 (1843).
Swedenborg, Emanuel. *Divine Love and Wisdom.* London: Dent, 1921.
Swift, Jonathan. *Gulliver's Travels.* London: Penguin, 1967 (1726).
–. *A Modest Proposal.* Columbus, OH: C.E. Merrill, 1969 (1729).
Tacitus. *Annals.* Franklin Center: Franklin, 1982.
Tagore, Rabindranath. *Collected Poems and Plays of Rabindranath Tagore.* New York: Macmillan, n.d.
–. *Later Poems of Rabindranath Tagore.* New York: Funk and Wagnall, 1974.
Tennyson, Alfred. *The Works of Alfred Lord Tennyson.* 2 vols. London: Macmillan, 1892.
Thomas, Elizabeth Marshall. *The Hidden Life of Dogs.* New York: Pocket Star Books, 1993.
Thomas, James. *The Seasons* and *The Castle of Indolence.* Oxford: Clarendon Press, 1991.

Thomas, Keith. *Man and the Natural World: Changing Attitudes in England 1500-1800*. London: Penguin, 1984.

Thoreau, Henry David. *Walden, or Life in the Woods* and *On the Duty of Civil Disobedience*. New York: Signet, 1960 (1854 and 1847).

–. *Walking*. Harmondsworth: Penguin, 1995 (1862).

Tolstoy, Leo. *A Confession and Other Religious Writings*. Trans. Jane Kentish. London: Penguin, 1987 (1893-1908).

–. *How Much Land Does a Man Need? and Other Stories*. Trans. Ronald Wiles. London: Penguin, 1993 (1853-86).

–. *Resurrection*. Trans. Rosemary Edmonds. London: Penguin, 1966 (1901).

Trilling, Lionel. *Matthew Arnold*. New York: Harcourt Brace Jovanovich, 1979.

Trinkaus, Eric, and Pat Shipman. *The Neandertals*. New York: Alfred A. Knopf, 1992.

Trollope, Anthony. *The Eustace Diamonds*. London: Oxford University Press, 1930 (1873).

Trotsky, Leon. *Literature and Revolution*. Trans. Rose Strunsky. Ann Arbor: University of Michigan Press, 1960.

Troyes, Chrétien de. *Oeuvres complètes*. Paris: Gallimard, 1994.

Turnbull, Colin. *The Forest People*. New York: Simon and Schuster, 1968 (1961).

Turner, E.S. *All Heaven in a Rage*. Centaur: Fontwell, 1992 (1964).

Twain, Mark. *Short Stories*. London: Penguin, 1993 (1865-1909).

Vasari, Giorgio. *The Great Masters*. New York: Park Lane, 1960 (1550).

Vatsayana. *The Kamasutra of Vatsayana*. London: Crown, 1992.

Viola, Herman J., and Carolyn Margolis, eds. *The Seeds of Change: Five Hundred Years since Columbus*. Washington, DC: Smithsonian Institute, 1991.

Voltaire. *Candide and Other Stories*. Trans. Roger Pearson. Oxford: Oxford University Press, 1990 (1739-74).

Wade, Mason. *Margaret Fuller: Whetstone of Genius*. New York: Viking, 1940.

Wakefield, Priscilla. *Instinct Displayed in a Collection of Well-Authenticated Facts, Exemplifying the Extraordinary Sagacity of Various Species of the Animal Creation*. 4th ed. London: Harvey and Dalton, 1821 (c. 1790).

Watanabe, Hiroyuki. "The Conception of Nature in Japanese Culture." *Science* 183 (1973): 280.

Watson, Burton, trans. and ed. *The Lotus Sutra*. New York: Columbia University Press, 1993.

Watts, Alan. *Nature, Man and Woman*. New York: Vintage, 1970.

Waugh, Evelyn. *Black Mischief*. London: Penguin, 1965 (1932).

Wenzel, George. *Human Rights, Animal Rights: Ecology, Economy and Ideology in the Canadian Arctic*. Toronto: University of Toronto Press, 1991.

White, Gilbert. *The Natural History of Selborne*. London: Folio Society, 1962 (1788).

White, Lynn, Jr., "The Historical Roots of Our Ecologic Crisis." *Science* 155 (1967): 1203-7.

Whitman, Walt. *Leaves of Grass: All the Poems Written by Walt Whitman*. New York: Modern Library, 1950.

–. *The Works of Walt Whitman, as Prepared by him for the Deathbed*. 2 vols. New York: Funk and Wagnall, 1968.

Whitney, Lois. *Primitivism and the Idea of Progress in Popular English Literature of the Eighteenth Century*. New York: Octagon, 1973 (1934).

Widgery, Alban G. *Interpretations of History: Confucius to Toynbee*. London: George Allen Unwin, 1961.

Wilde, Oscar. *De Profundis*. London: Methuen, 1911.

Willey, Basil. *The Eighteenth Century Background: Studies in the Thought of the Period*. London: Chatto and Windus, 1946 (1940).

Williams, Tennessee. *Sweet Bird of Youth, The Rose Tattoo*, and *The Night of the Iguana*. New York: Signet, 1976 (1959, 1950, and 1961).

Willis, R.G., ed. *Signifying Animals: Human Meaning in the Natural World*. London: Unwin Hyman, 1990.

Willman, E. *Land Filled with Flies: A Political Economy of the Kalahari*. Chicago: University of Chicago Press, 1989.

Wilmsen, E., and J.R. Denbow. "Paradigmatic History of San-Speaking Peoples and Current Attempts at Revision." *Current Anthropology* 31 (1990): 489-524.

Winokur, John. *The Portable Curmudgeon Redux*. New York: Dutton, 1992.

Wollstonecraft, Mary. *Political Writings of Mary Wollstonecraft*. Ed. Janet Todd. Oxford: Oxford University Press, 1994.

Woodburn, J. "Egalitarian Societies." *Man* 17 (1982): 431-51.

Woolf, Leonard. *After the Deluge*. London: Hogarth Press, 1955 (1931).

–. *The Wise Virgins*. New York: Harcourt Brace Jovanovich, 1968.

Woolf, Virginia. *Collected Essays*. 4 vols. London: Hogarth Press, 1966-7.

–. *Flush*. London: Hogarth Press, 1963 (1933).

Wordsworth, William. *The Prelude: A Parallel Text*. Ed. J.C. Maxwell. London: Penguin, 1988.

–. *The Works of William Wordsworth*. Wordsworth: Ware, 1994.

Wright, Richard. "Pagan Spain." In *Richard Wright Reader*. Ed. Ellen Wright and Michael Fabre. New York: Harper and Row, 1978.

Yeats, W.B. *A Vision*. New York: Macmillan, 1938 (1926).

Young, Dudley. *Origins of the Sacred*. New York: St. Martin's Press, 1991.

Young, Edward. *The Complaint; Or, Night Thoughts on Life*. London: F.C. and J. Rivington et al., 1813.

Young, Thomas. *An Essay on Humanity to Animals*. London: T. Cadell, Jun. and W. Davies, 1798.

Yutang, Lin, ed. *The Wisdom of Confucius*. New York: The Modern Library, 1996.

Zaehner, R.C., trans. and ed. *Hindu Scriptures*. London: J.M. Dent, 1996.

Zimmer, Heinrich. *Philosophies of India*. Princeton: Princeton University Press, 1969.

Zola, Émile. *La Bête Humaine*. Trans. Leonard Tancock. London: Penguin, 1977 (1889-90).

Index

Set in Stone by Val Speidel

Printed and bound in Canada by Friesens

Copy editor: Maureen Nicholson

Proofreader: Mary Williams